The Tyler Genealogy

The descendants of Job Tyler, of Andover

Massachusetts, 1619-1700

(Volume I)

Willard I. Tyler Brigham

Alpha Editions

This edition published in 2019

ISBN : 9789353809973

Design and Setting By
Alpha Editions
email - alphaedis@gmail.com

THE TYLER GENEALOGY

VOLUME I

THE
TYLER GENEALOGY

THE DESCENDANTS OF
JOB TYLER, OF ANDOVER,
MASSACHUSETTS, 1619-1700

BY

WILLARD I. TYLER BRIGHAM

VOLUME I

PUBLISHED BY
CORNELIUS B. TYLER, of Plainfield, N. J.
AND
ROLLIN U. TYLER, of Tylerville, Conn.
MCMXII

A 457190

CONTENTS

INTRODUCTION

A SHORT ACCOUNT OF THE VARIOUS TYLER IMMIGRANTS TO AMERICA.

This representative family has its roots deep in the colonial soil of New England, Virginia, New Jersey and Maryland, and all the numerous branches are supposed to have an English origin.

Representatives of the Tyler family were in nearly every one of the original thirteen States at the time of the formation of the Union. In the early wars, in the War of the Revolution and in the War of 1812 they were conspicuous, and in the Civil War some of their achievements were brilliant. Socially, the Tylers have reached " from the White House to the poor-house." Were their deeds stricken from the annals of our country the loss would be appreciable.

There were several immigrant ancestors of the Tylers and therefore a number of independent lines. In detail, this history treats only of the New England lines, but a brief outline follows herewith of the numerous branches in America.

Chronologically, the first record we have seen of Tylers in America, occurs in Camden Hotten's excellent book (based upon English Admiralty reports), which contains lists of emigrants to America between 1600 and 1700. It appears therefrom, that William Tyler, and his wife Elizabeth, set sail from England for Virginia, in 1620, on the ship *Francis Bonaventure*. He was a person of property; for, in 1622, he brought over, on the ships *Providence* and *Hopewell*, the following six servants: " Robart More," aged 50; " Wm. Broune," aged 26; " Robert Hodd," aged 20; " Anthonie Burt," aged 18; " Samiell Bennett," aged 40, and " Joane Bennett." In another entry in the said volume (in a list of " Living in Va., 16 Feb., 1623 "), we find the said William and Elizabeth Tyler are at " Hogg Island." (This island is a little down the James River from Jamestown, the first English-American settlement, 1607.) It would seem that these parties intended permanent residence; yet, strange to say, not a jot of evidence has been found to show that they ever had descendants. Regretfully as we admit it, it seems impossible to learn anything further of this pair; who were, probably, the very first bearing the name Tyler, that had courage to seek remote and perilous shores of a literally " New World."

From the number of Tylers early found settled on the Chesapeake, we are inclined to an hypothesis; that they (at least some of them) had a common cis-Atlantic ancestor (presumably, the above William Tyler). Conclusive evidence of such genealogic links, however, is (and probably will always remain) wanting.

Existing records point to three **VIRGINIA TYLER BRANCHES:**

(1). YORK COUNTY BRANCH; founded by Henry Tyler, born in England in 1604, came to Virginia by 1645; where, in 1652, he had a grant of 254 acres at " Middle Plantation." This is the line of John Tyler, President of the United States.

(2). WESTMORELAND COUNTY BRANCH; founded by Charles Tyler, about 1690; who died about 1723, leaving four sons.

(3). ESSEX COUNTY BRANCH; founded by Richard Tyler, about 1690; who was licensed, in 1723, to keep an " ordinary ". and died in 1734, leaving three sons and two daughters.

IN BEAUFORT COUNTY, NORTH CAROLINA, are found early Tyler records; possibly of a line migrated from Virginia.

IN MARYLAND we find several early Tylers domiciled; between whom appears no record of relationship:

(1). Edward Tyler was brought over in 1657 by John Waghop; but no land grant or settlement of his estate is found.

(2). Robert Tyler was brought over in 1649 by Henry Catlin; and will was probated in Calvert Co., in 1674; he left an only son, who resided at " Brough," Prince George Co., on Patuxent River.

(3). John Tyler settled on Smith's Island, Somerset Co., before 1700; who, by two marriages, left five sons. Will probated 1733.

(4). William Tyler, of Pomonkey, Charles Co., leaves a will in 1755; which mentions a son and two daughters.

(5). The will of Edmund Tyler of " Bohemia Manor," Cecil County, 1738, mentions three sons.

Near SALEM, N. J., on Alloway's Creek, about 1688, William Tyler, Quaker, from Greinton, Somerset County, England, settled. Descendants known as " THE SALEM, N. J. LINE."

In CONNECTICUT we find several early clansmen who may have been closely related.

(1). Roger Tyler (previously in Massachusetts), leaves an inventory of an estate in New Haven in 1673. It has been thought by some that he was the progenitor of the " Branford " Tylers, but proof is lacking.

(2). In BRANFORD, CONN., four brothers, George, Peter, Francis and Charles appear on the records about 1667 and their descendants are called " THE BRANFORD LINE."

(3). William Tyler took the " Oath of Fidellitie " in New Haven in 1657, and his descendants are known as " THE WALLINGFORD LINE."

In RHODE ISLAND John Tyler was in Portsmouth as early as 1655. The branch is known as " THE RHODE ISLAND LINE."

In PROVIDENCE, R. I., " Widow Joan Tiler " appears as early as 1638, where she shared in Roger Williams' tract.

The MASSACHUSETTS BAY COLONY furnished a surprisingly large number of original immigrants of the Tyler name, some of whom have left descendants who have been traced.

In and about Boston we find the following:

(1). John Tyler, shopkeeper in Charlestown by 1696. He had a son John, born in 1696. The father died in Carolina. If there are latter-day descendants they are thus far untraced.

(2). Thomas Tyler was of Boston before 1685. His descendants are known as " THE THOMAS TYLER BOSTON LINE."

(3). William Tyler, a ropemaker, was in Boston in 1784.

His descendants are known as "THE WILLIAM TYLER BOSTON LINE."

(4). Mrs. Ann Tyler, widow of John Tyler, died in Boston, April 30, 1694, aged 40 years and was buried in the Granary burying-ground on Tremont street, where her stone may still be seen. It is probably the oldest American Tyler grave-stone.

In ESSEX COUNTY, MASS., we find the following:

(1). Job Tyler, in Andover, about 1640. His descendants, comprising by far the larger part of this History, are known as "THE JOB TYLER LINE."

(2). Abraham Tyler, in Haverhill, by 1640. Left no descendants, but his record, will and inventory are given herein.

(3). Nathaniel Tyler, of Lynn. Mass., by 1640. No record of descendants.

(4). John Tyler, of Gloucester. Descendants known as "THE GLOUCESTER LINE."

(5). Roger Tyler, of Lynn. The same man who is mentioned under "Connecticut."

In MAINE a man named Thomas Taylor settled in Bowdoinham and changed his name to Tyler. He has living descendants known as "THE BOWDOINHAM LINE."

In CANADA Captain Isaac Bartholomew Tyler was found by 1790, and later settled in Lewiston, Niagara County, N. Y.

Abraham, Nathaniel and Job are all heard of, among the first settlers of their respective neighborhoods, about the year 1640. This fact suggests possible relationships. The only corroborative evidence (if we may thus dignify so remote facts) lies in the recollection that Moses, son of Job, had sons "Joseph" and "Nathaniel" (both of whom died s. p.). The immigrant, Nathaniel. had an only "son Joseph"—and Moses had also a son "James." whose son "Abraham" brought in some later generations by that name. We do not lean heavily upon such hypothesis; having learned, after strenuous labors, much to distrust general record-suggestions, as well as vague traditions. So, having raised the question (unanswerable), we pass on the well-trodden path.

Though two of the above first settlers touched but briefly
our colonial history, we give the records found.

ABRAHAM TYLER, was in Haverhill, Mass., in 1640; died
May 6, 1673; married, December 26, 1650, Hannah Freeman.

Chase's *History of Haverhill* says: " The first company of
settlers in the wild woods of Pentucket [Haverhill] were from
Ipswich and Newbury, and were twelve in number." He places
the year at 1640; Cotton Mather says, 1641; Winthrop says,
about 1643 (Andover being settled at this same period). Whatever the date, Abraham Tyler, with three others, from Ipswich,
and eight from Newbury, came " in June " to remain. In
1645 Abraham was one of the thirty-two landholders there.
In 1648, his valuation is put at £60. June 7, 1652, the Second
Division of plough-land was laid out, in the proportion of four
acres to one acre of house-lot; of the forty-one sharers, Abraham (No. 5) had four acres. [Thomas Whittier, probably an
ancestor of the poet, had 7½ acres.] September 7th of the same
year, the town voted, that Abraham should blow his horn to
call the people to meeting, and receive one peck of corn from
every family for the year ensuing. (Early historians adver-
tised the stipend as " a pound of pork." But careful Mirick
says, a " close " inspection of the records reads, beyond doubt,
a " peck of corn.") At the May, 1653, session of the General
Court, we find Abraham's name on a petition, praying for a
revocation of previous sentence, passed upon one Pike of Salisbury, who had been heavily fined and disfranchised for openly
declaring, " such persons as did act in making that law [*i. e.*,
prohibiting certain persons from exhorting the people on the
Sabbath, in the absence of a minister] did break their oath to
the country, for it is against the liberty of the country, both
civil and ecclesiastical." [Following the hubbub raised thereby,
the Haverhill signers " acknowledged their offence ": Pike paid
the fine, and was relieved of the disability.] In July, 1667,
" accommodation " land was laid out to " Goodman [Abraham]
Tiler," to the amount of " 4 acres." (" Haverhill " then included, not only most of Methuen, Mass., but also Salem,
Hempstead, Plaistow and Atkinson, New Hampshire.) Children:

Abraham[2], born H., June 4, 1652; died aged two years.

Hannah, born H., Dec. 16, 1655; died aged six years.
Abraham, born H., May 21, 1659; died aged nine years.

Five years after he had seen his hope of a posterity fade from sight, May 5, 1673, he executed his will, by " marke." He died before " ye 14th: 8th. mo: 1673," on which date, the " relict " takes order from the Court at Hampton; and April 14, 1674, witnesses the probate duly made, at Salisbury. (*Norfolk Co. Recs.*, " lib. 2d, pa. 321," and *Salem files* No. 28, 426.) April 14, 1674, came " Inventorie " for £105; which is extremely interesting, both as a study in phonetic orthography and as showing the personal effects of a Puritan pioneer. Surely our clan will read, not without a certain interest, of the well-intended efforts of this fated line; and join in wishing their undiscoverable grave, *Requiescat in pace!*

I, Abraham Tyler, of Haverhill, being sicke & weak of body but of good and pfect memory doe make this my last will & Testament as followeth: I give to Robert Clement ye sone of Robert Clements y^t twenty acres of forth Division of upland wch goodman Sharwood did give mee.

My house & house lott & all ye land about my house & ye remainder of ye land I bought of Steven Kent I give to my loveing wyfe to bee fully & soley at her Disposeing. I doe likewise make my wife my full & sole Executrix & to receive all such Debts as are due to me & to pay such debts as I owe & to take care for my buriall.

In witness hereunto I have hereunto sett my hand & seal this 5th of May, 1673.

Witness hereunto   ABRAHAM TYLER, his marke
JOHN WARD.
HENRY PALMER.   & Seale to it=A

Hannah Tyler, y^e Relict of Abraham Tyler deceased, p^{e}senting this will of Abraham Tylers her late husbands to y^e Country Court held at Hampton y^e 14th=8th=$^{o/m}$=1673, the witnesses being absent, the Court doth order y^t y^e witness make oath thereto before Capt. Saltonstall & y^t y^e will & Inventory bee p^{e}sented to y^e next County Court to bee held att Salisbury. THO BRADBURY rec^s.

Mr. John Ward & Henry Palmer according to order or direction of y^e Court Appeared & made oath y^t this was y^e act of Abraham Tyler & declared by him to bee his will & y^t they know of no other==, taken, Aprill y^e 10th 1674 before mee.

NATH^{LL} SALTONSTALL, Comsr.

This will was returned & delivered into y^e Court at Salisbury Aprill y^e 14th 1674 according to y^e order of y^e Court made in that case== as atests.

THO== BRADBURY, rec S.

Entered y^e 23 Aprill 1674.

An Inventorie of Abraham Tylers land & estate being deceased of y^e month of May *1673*.

		£	S	D
It	a house & house lott and land about it adjoyning to it wee prize at fifty pounds..	50	00	00
It	another pcell of land lying by it about six acres	10	00	00
It	two bedds & bedding belonging to it	10	00	00
It	two potts, a posmitt, a frying pan	01	00	00
It	a brass pan & a warming pan & some small pewter	01	00	00
It	a slice, tonges, Tratnell & pot hookes, other iron	01	00	00
It	a table & other wooden implem^{ts}, chests, boxes	01	10	00
It	a pcell of flaxen yarne	01	00	00
It	a pecll of cotton wooll, sheeps wooll cards....	01	00	00
It	a Sadell bridell pillion linning twine	01	00	00
It	in barrels & chayers tobbs & bottles	01	00	00
It	a muskitt bandeleers a sword	01	00	00
It	his cutting tools & home	01	00	00
It	his wareing Aparrell	04	00	00
It	2 cows, 2 calves, one mare, 7 swine	20	00	00
	Total sum £105		0	0

Johannah Tyler testified upon oath as a Administratrix to Abraham Tyler: This Inventory here p^{t}sented is a true Inventorie of y^e estate, of w^t y^e Sd Tyler died seized off & if more appeare She is to add it to the estate as attests.

THO== BRADBURY, rec^s.

Salisbury Court Aprill y⁰ 14th-1674. Ent= yᵗ 23d day of Aprill 1674.

NATHANIEL TYLER, according to the *History of Lynn*, was a resident of that place in 1640.

He does not seem satisfied by prospects, however, for by deed, October 1, 1652 (*Essex Co. Registry*, Vol. I, p. 20), he and wife, Jane, sell unto " Philip Kirtland, shoemaker," all their " lands and houses, with their appurtenances, in Lynn." On the 16th of October, of the same year (1652), we find his " will " on record at Boston (*Suffolk Deeds*, Vol. I, p. 248), wherefrom it is evident: that he is setting out on a sea voyage; that he takes aboard £80, to be paid " by bill of exchange " in London or Shrewsbury, England, leaving £24 to be sent on within a month; that, if he dies before reaching his journey's end, his son Joseph Tyler, of Shrewsbury, shall have £50, and his wife Jane, the remainder; but, if she die on the voyage, Joseph is to have all and pay 40/ to testator's sister Jane, wife of Edward Sanford of London.

No further record of him has been found in this country.

THE DESCENDANTS OF JOB TYLER

Descendants of Job Tyler, The Immigrant

FIRST GENERATION

JOB[1] TYLER was born about 1619, as in a deposition of 1659, his age is stated as "about 40 yeares." The author of this history (who died before its publication) left a note stating that he had never been able to "find a scintilla of evidence upon which to base" the tradition that Job Tyler was a native of Shropshire, England. Job's death is nowhere recorded. It is conjectured that he died in Mendon and was there buried, but no proof is at hand to confirm the supposition. He married Mary ———. It has been thought by one of the descendants of Job engaged in research that she may have been a widow Horton, but the proof of this statement has not been forthcoming. She was dismissed to the church in "Mendham" from the church in Roxbury on the 28th day of the third month (May), 1665. Her birth and death are unrecorded so far as present research has gone.

The first known of Job Tyler in this country may be found in the *Rhode Island Collections*, p. 92, as follows: "Inhabitants admitted at the Towne of Nieu-Port since the 20th of the 3rd 1638 . . . Job Tyler." No other person of this name is known except the Job Tyler who appeared soon after in the Massachusetts Bay Colony. From the same authority (p. 24), we learn that a "Widow Tyler" in the same year, 1638, was one of the 54 who received lots out of Roger Williams' tract in Providence. In 1640 (p. 31, *Ibid.*), she was still a widow but was more fully described as "Joan" and signed the "Compact." The author was inclined to think she was a relict of a brother of Job Tyler, though Savage says she was "possibly his mother." There was an early John Tyler who died in Portsmouth, R. I., in 1700, whom the author took to be a near relative of Job. He founded a line of his own which has a place in this history, known as "The Rhode Island Line."

Job Tyler is said to have been found in Andover, Mass., by the first colonists there, a solitary squatter, about 1639-40; the earliest dates of the settlement of Andover are conjectural, as the town records before 1650 are lost, and the records of the church which have been preserved date from 1708. A few years later he was in Roxbury, Mass., as witness the following from the old records: "11 month, 1 day, 1646, Lambert Genry hath liberty to sell his Land beyond the mill Creeke to —— Tyler of Roxberye." (*Dedham Town Records.*) "1646, Month 1, day 28. A lit infant also a twinn of Job Tilers dyed." (*Roxbury Church Records.*) He soon returned to Andover, for March 5, 1650, "Jobe Tyler of Andover" mortgaged property there to John Godfrey, the beginning of trouble for Job and others.

1650—Job's Mortgage, mentioned in *Boxford History.* Also *Andover Rec.,* Book iv, p. 8.

Witnes these presents. that Jobe Tiler of Andover in ye county of Essex, doth acknowledge himselfe to be owing & indebted unto John Godfry of Newbury in the Said covnty, the full & just some of Sixteene pounds to be paid to him the said John Godfry. the one halfe, viz: the eight pounds in good merchantable wheat at fowerer Shillings p. bushell & ye other halfe in like good & merchantable rye at three Shillings & Six pence p. bushell, the payment to be made on the first of March come two yeare next after this date, to the which payment well & truly to be made. the said Jobe Tyler doth binde himselfe, his heires, executors, administrators & assignees firmly by these presents, and hereunto hath sett to his hand, this fift day of March, 1650. The said Jobe Tyler doth bind over his house & land & three cowes, in further assurance for his performance of this bill; wch house and land & three cowes, Scituate in Andevour aforesd, the said Jobe Tyler shall not anyway dispose of, from ye Said John Godfry, directly or indirectly, by letting or selling, according to ye tenor purport and true intent of these presents.

　　witness　　　　　　　　　　　　　　JOBE TYLER.
Richard Barker.
Joana Barker.

Also from *Andover Rec.*, Bk. II, p. 1, the following:

Know all men by these presents, that I Job Tiler of Andover, in the covntye of Essex. have given, granted, Sovld and Sett over vnto John Godfry of the Same Towne and covntye. my dwelling house in which I now dwell, with a barne and land about it. Contenining twenty five acres, be it more or less, both broke up and unbroke up, as it is fenct in with a logg fence and rayle fence. also two parcells of meddow one of them lyeing about halfe a mile from the said plow land by a pine swamp, the other parcel of meddow lying about a mile off; both of the sayd parcells of meddow being granted and layd out for nyne acres, the latter parcell lying by the meddow of John Rvss, together with the fences & appvrtenances belonging to it. To have and to hovld all that my said house, barne land fences and appurtenances, and the two parcells of meddow unto him the Said John Godfry, his heirs and assigns forever. In witness whereof I the sd Job Tiler have herevnto sett my hand and Seale, the 18th of Aprill, 1662. The condition of this bargaine and Sale is Svch, that whereas the Said Job Tiler hath Signed and delivered three Several bonds vnto John Godfry aforesaid which bonds were written by Anthony Svmerby at one tyme, but payable at three Severall tymes: if the Said Job Tiler shal well and truly Sattisfie and pay or cause to be Sattisfied and payd, the said three bonds vnto the sayd John Godfry his heirs, execvtors, or assignees. according to the tymes of payment as they shall become dew, according to the true intent & meaning thereof, that then this above Said bargaine and sale to be voide and of none effect, or elce to remaine and abide in full force. Strength and virtve.

JOB TILER.

Signed, Sealed & d.d.   (An autograph signature)
in the presence of us.   [With a seale.]
    Robert Lord.
    Mary Lord.

Job Tiler acknowledged this his act & deed before me.
DANIEL DENISON.
April 18: 1662.

Job had much legal trouble in Andover.
We find in 1658 that a charge was brought against John

Godfrey of witchcraft and the accuser and principal sufferer from his " wiles " was Mary, wife of Job Tyler. This accusation was brought in connection with a law-suit against Godfrey and the accusation was not established. One annalist calls Godfrey " this hard-bitted money lender " and hints that there may have been some cause for the bitterness shown by the Tylers toward him. This was a day of superstition, and although the delusion of witchcraft had not attacked the community as a whole, a little deposition in which Job's family joined against Godfrey shows the temper of the time. The " deposicion " although sworn to in 1659 was brought forward in 1665 again, and reads as follows:

" The Deposicion of Job Tylar aged about 40 yeares, Mary his wife, Moses Tylar his son aged between 17 and 18 yeares and Mary Tylar about 15 yeares old. These deponents witnesse, that they saw a thing like a bird to come in at the door of their house, with John Godfrey, in the night, about the bigness of a blackbird, or rather bigger, to wit, as big as a pigeon and did fly about, John Godfrey laboring to catch it and the bird vanished as they conceived through the chinck of a joynted bord. . . . This was as they remember about 5 or 6 yeares since. Taken upon oath of the above four mentioned ptie this 27, 4, '59, before me, Simon Bradstreet.

" Owned in Court 7 March, 1665 by Job Tyler & Moses Tyler, E. R. Sec.

" Owned in Court 13 March '65 by Mary Tyler on her former oath. E. R. Sec."

Drake, in his *Annals* says: " It is very reasonable to suppose that the evidence against Godfrey was of too ridiculous a character to be seriously considered and that he was discharged."

Other legal trouble arose in connection with Thomas Chandler of Andover, to whom Job had apprenticed his son, Hopestill, and which bargain, for some reason, Job desired to dissolve. He went to the house of Nathan Parker, where the signed instrument was kept, and took it from the house in the absence of Mr. Parker, thus giving rise to much hard criticism. The matter was a cause of long controversy for over ten years and was carried from court to court. Finally Job lost the suit and the decision or " award " was that as Job was poor he should not be fined above six pounds, but the following penalty was imposed:

" We do order that Job Tyler shall nayle up or fasten upon the posts of Andover & Roxbury meeting-houses in a plain legible hand, the acknowledgement to remain so fastened for the space of 14 days, it to be fastened within the 14 days at Andover and to-morrow being the 27th of January, 1665 at Roxbury. . . ."

This confession and acknowledgment was as follows:

" Whereas it doth appear by sufficient testimony that I, Job Tiler, have shamefully reproached Thomas Chandler of Andover by saying he is a base, lying cozening, cheating knave, that he hath got his estate by cozening in a base reviling manner & that he was recorded for a liar & that he was a cheating, lying whoreing knave fit for all manner of bawdery, wishing that the devill had him, Therefore I Job Tiler doe acknowledge that I have in these expressions most wickedly slandered the said Thomas Chandler & that without any just ground, being noe way able to make good these or any of these my slanderous accusations of him & therefore can doe noe lesse but expresse myselfe to be sorry for them & for my cursing of him desiring God & the said Thomas to forgive me, & that noe person would think the worse of the said Thomas Chandler for any of these my sinfull expressions, and engaging myself for the future to be more carefull of my expressions both concerning him & other·wise and desiring the Lord to help me soe to doe."

Job has a parting blow from Godfrey in 1661-62, in a suit regarding wheat for which Job owed him, and the £5 demanded included going to Salisbury to fetch the writings out of the court.

In 1662, three years before the above penalty was given by the court, Job had paid his last minister's rate, 10 shillings, and had shaken the soil of Andover from off his feet. Not only had he not been popular with some of his neighbors, but something had occurred to cause him to give up his holdings in Andover, and in one case, that of Godfrey, no consideration is named in the instrument.

1662. 9mo. 21. (*Salem Rec.*, Bk. II, p. 58.)

Know all men by these pr'sents, yt wee Job Tyler of Andevor,

in ye County of Essex, husbandman, & Mary Tyler wife of ye
sd. Job Tyler for & in consideration of ye svme of ten povnds,
tenn shillings alredy paid unto us in hand in a horse; have sold
& doe by these pr'sents bargaine & sell unto Thomas Abbott of
the same towne & covntie, all that twelve acres of land of mine,
being in Andever aforesd, & bounded on ye northwest with the
high waie going to Little Hope, one ye southwest with ye lott
of Steven Osgood, on ye southeast with the high waye to
Bilreky; to have & hould ye said land unto the said Thomas
his heires & his assignes forever, together with one acre & halfe
of pr'vilidg in ye comon, that is not yeat granted. he ye sd
Thomas paying unto the minister six shillings by ye yeare. so
long as this waye of rating remayne, & we ye sd Job & Mary
Tyler due hearby covenant & pr'mise, to & with ye sd Thomas
Abbott his heires & assignes. yt he ye sd Thomas, his heires,
executors, administrators & assignes, shall & may qvietly &
peaceably in joye the sd land, with out any lett, trouble or
molestation, by us or either of us, our heires, executors, administrators or assignes, or by any other p'son or p'sons whatsoever, lawfully clayming by or under us, or them or any of
them. In witnes whereof, wee the sd Job & Mary Tyler, have
sett our hands & Seales, this tenth day of June in ye yeare of
our Lord, one thousand, six hundred Sixty & two, & in ye
fowerteen yeare of ye raigne of our Soveraigne Lord, King
Charles ye second, King of England, Scotland, France & Ireland.

JOB TYLER & his seale.

Sealed & dd   the mark — of MARY TYLER & seale.
in the pr'sence of
    Edward Faulkner.
    George Abbott Junr.
    Job Tyler acknowledged this his act & deed & Mary his wife
did fully resigne her thirds in the lands herein conveyed before
me.   DANIELL DENISON June 11: 62.

    1662. 9 mo. 21. (*Rec.*, Bk. I, p. 58.)
    Know all men by these pr'sents yt wee Job Tyler of Andever,
in ye covnty of Essex, husbandman & Mary Tyler wife of ye
said Job Tyler, for & in consideration of ye sume of twenty nine
pounds fifteen shillings alredy pd unto us in hand by George
Abbott, tayler of ye same towne & countie, have sold & by these

pr'sents doe bargaine & sell. unto ye sd George Abbott, his heires & assignes, one house lott, containing by estimation fower acres, be it more or less, lying & scittuat in ye towne of Andever aforesaid, & bovnded on ye north with ye lott of Richd Sutton, on the south with ye lott of John Aslett on ye east with ye common, on ye west ye high waye; and alsoe a p'cell of land more, containing by estimation two acres, be it more or less, being & scittuate in Andover aforesd, & bounded on ye east with ye high waye, on ye west with ye land of John Fry Senr, on ye south with ye land of John Aslett, both which said house lott & p'cell of land, wee ye sd Job & Mary Tyler due hearby acknowledg to have sold, unto ye sd George Abbott, together with my dwelling house thereupon, & oarchard & all ye fences belonging thereunto, reserving & keeping unto myselfe all pr'vilidges, rites, titles & interest in all lands & meadows alredy granted, only I ye sd Job & Mary Tyler due herby acknowledg to have sold unto ye sd George Abbot, together with ye sd land, one acre pr'vilidg in ye common not yet gravnted or laid out, all which sd lott, land, house, oarchard, fences & pr'vilidg, wee ye sd Job & Mary due acknowledg to have sold unto ye sd Georg to have & to hold to him, his heirs & assignes forever, and wee ye sd Job & Mary Tyler due hereby covenant & p'mise to & with ye sd George Abbott his heires & assignes yt he ye sd George his heires, executors, administrators & assignes shall & may quietly & peaceably enjoye ye sd lott, land, house, orchard, fences, & pr'vilidges, without any lett, trouble or molestation by us or either of us, our heires, executors, administrators or assignes, or by any other p'son or p'sons whatsoever lawfully claymeng by or under us, or them or any of them, in witness whereof wee ye sd Job & Mary Tyler have sett our hands & Seales, this tenth day of June, in ye yeare of our Lord, one thousand, six hundred Sixty & two. & in the fowerteene yeare of ye raign of our Soveraigne Lord, King Charles ye second, King of England, Scotland, France & Ireland, alsoe ye sd George is to pay unto ye minister fower shillings by ye yeare, soe long as this waie of rating remayne.

JOB TYLER & his seale.

ye mark of

MARY X TYLER.

Sealed & delivered
in ye pr'sence of
  Edward Faulkner.
  Thomas Abott.

Job Tiler acknowledged this his act & deed & Mary his wife
resigned her third in ye lands herein conveyed, before me
June 11: 1662.   DANIELL DENISON.

1662: 12 mo. 14.

Know all men by these pr'sents, that I Job Tyler of Andevor,
in ye Covnty of Essex, husbandman, have & by these pr'sents
due alienate enfeofe & confirme, unto John Godfrey, all my
lands, meadow & upland together with ye oarchard & all ye
buildings and edifices, & all other privilidges with yt appurtenances therevnto belonging, sett, & being in ye towne of Andover aforesd, together with all other lands & accomodations
that at any time heareafter. Shall or may be allotted unto ye
said Joab Tyler, or any other p'son or p'sons, for. by. or under
him, all ye said land & meddow aforementioned, alredy in ye
possession of ye said Job Tyler, is bovnded & limitted in manner & forme following, that is to say, on ye east side joyning
to ye Common land, and soe likewise are the other three sides,
all wch said land & meddow, contayning by estimation forty
acres more or less. To have & to hould all ye premises, with
ye apurtenances unto ye sd John Godfery, his heires & assignes
forever, to ye only use & behoofe of ye sd John, his heires and
assignes forevermore. And ye sd Job Tyler doth by these
pr'sents p'mise & gravnt, to & with ye said John Godfery, that
he ye sd John, shall & may freely & willingly occupy, possess
& injoy ye aforesaid lands & pr'mises, with all & every ye appurtenances thereunto belonging, without any lett, disturbance,
ejection, eviction or contradiction, of him ye said Joab, or any
other p'son or p'sons, for, by or under him, claiming any right,
title or interest, clayme or demand thereunto.

In witness whereof, I have hereunto sett my hand & Seale,
the eight & twenty day of Avgust. Anno. Dom. 1662.

JOB TYLER
& his seale.

Sealed & delivered
in ye pr'sence of
   William White.
   George Abbott seniyr.
Job Tyler acknowledged this writing to be his act and deed
before me Aug: 29: 1662.

DANYELL DENISON.

Mary Tyler did surrender up her thirds or interest of dowry, in ye houses & lands hearby conveyed before me
November 12: 1662

DANIELL DENISON.

Doubtless Job never intended to return to Andover, when he set his face toward Roxbury once more and probably the horse, for which he had bargained his 12 Andover acres, accompanied him.

The year 1665 was to prove an eventful and unpleasant year for Job. In January the court decided against him in his suit against Godfrey and, as shown in the foregoing deposition he had to take back, in a public manner, his accusations against Chandler's character. To get even with his Andover foe, Godfrey, he and his family again take oath in court to the old deposition of 1659 in March 1665.

In Roxbury, or rather in or near the present town of Natick, Job again gets into trouble, as the following document will show:

"Sept. 11, 1665. Owannamang Indian Chiefe, neere Marlborough complained of Job Tyler of Roxbury for cutting and carrying off hay from his meadows. Fined 2 shillings and six pence, and cost 10 shillings. Attested by me, Daniel Gookin," September 22, 1665, John Eliot (the Apostle to the Indians) certified that Job Tyler had paid.

At some period after his migration from Andover to Roxbury in 1662, Job went to Mendon, and he is among those who drew lots in June, 1671, "for dubling of their houselots." But previous to this he had some controversy, in 1669, with both town and church authorities in Mendon. Therefore we find that:

"July 14, 1669 the Selectmen mett and ordered to send to the Constable to Summon before us Job Tyler the next fryday at one of the clock, at Gregory Cook's house, to answer his contempt of our orders, and alsoe why he refuses to worke aboute the Selor [cellar] at the Minister's house, at yt tyme ye Constable Retourne his answer to us. . . . July 16. The Selectmen met accordingly and the said Constable made his Retourne that he had warned in Job Tyler before us. his answer was he could not nor would come, but if the Selectmen had more to say to him than he to them they might come to him. Upon this answer of Job Tyler's the Townesmen Resolved to make their complaint to the Magistrates of his contempt of several of the Selectmen's orders and of his Miscarriages of the Lord's Day & at Publique assemblies if he doe not Submytt, wch he did not." (Job was a true descendant of that primal irrepressible family rebel, Wat Tyler, "Kentish man," of England.)

Job must, however, have possessed some of the graces of human nature, for his shortcomings were readily condoned. On the following "December 1st," he is "on the list," helping to confirm (in his humble way) Rev. Joseph Emerson, the first settled minister of Mendon. Later comes entry (in as formally dignified tones as the accusation):—"Whereas there has been complaint against Job Tiler heretofore recorded, he has given satisfaction for that ofence."

After this date we hear no more of Job's controversies.

In 1676 the birth of one of his grandchildren was recorded in Roxbury, and he may have returned there on account of King Philip's war, as Mendon was burned and the inhabitants fled.

"When the outbreak of King Philip's war came, everybody buried the pewter plates and the brass kettles in the swamps, loaded the   . . .   horses with the precious feather beds and children and   . . .   simply ' skedaddled ' to safety . . . Neither red nor white brother let Job rest. . . . In 1680 he is living in Rowley Village with all the other good kickers against Rowley taxes, and Moses and old Goodman Tyler are duly inspected to see if they go to church." (Miss Charlotte Abbott's *Annals of Andover.*)

In 1680 Job was in Rowley Village and he may have been in Andover in 1681, but in 1688, 1689, 1691 and 1695 he was paying minister's rates in Mendon. The last item credited to Job is of a deed to his son Moses of land in Mendon. This is dated 1700 and is recorded in the *Boston Registry of Deeds*, Book XX, p. 127.

Job Tyler to Moses Tyler.

To all Christian People to whom these presents shall come Job Tyler of Mendon in ye County of Suffolk in the Province of ye Massachusetts Bay in New England sendeth Greeting.

Know ye that I the above sd Job Tyler for & in Consideration
of the Sum of Sixty Pounds of Current money of New England
to me in hand paid by Moses Tyler of Andover in the county of
Essex in ye Province aforesd the receipt whereof I the said
Job Tyler doth acknowledge & myself herewith fully satisfyed
contented & paid and thereof & of every part & parcel thereof
Do exonerate acquit & discharge the said Moses Tyler his heirs
Exectrs admtrs & assigns & every of them forever by these
presents. Have given granted bargained and sold, enfeoffed &
confirmed, and by these presents do fully clearly & absolutely
give grant bargain sell aliene enfeoffe & confirm unto the said
Moses Tyler his heirs and assigns forever One house lott Containing fifteen acres of Land be it more or less, scituate lying
& being in ye Township of Mendon aforesd which said Lott
with five acres of ye doubling lot or 2nd Division of Land belonging to said Lott, being Twenty acres more or less is
Bounded Southerly upon the land of Saml Tyler of Mendon
deced, northerly upon the Land of Ebenezr Reed, easterly upon
a brook commonly known by the name of Muddy Brook. &
Westerly upon the house lott of Jno Moore Deceased now in
the Possession of Samuel Moore. Together with all the buildings, roods, trees, lying standing or growing upon the said
Lands, with all other allotments of lands & Meadows thereunto
belonging wch are already granted or yt shall be hereafter
granted or thereunto accrue or grow, due by dividend or otherwise, with all rights, libertyes priviledges commons or commonage thereunto belong—or appertain—wth all & singular
the appurtces unto the said premises or any part of them belonging or any ways appertaining, and also all ye Estate right
title interest use possession property claim & Demand whatsoever I the said Job Tyler have of or into the premises with their
appurtces. To have and to Hold the said house-lott containing fifteen acres beit more or less lying & being in the township
of Mendon as it is bounded with all other Divisions of Lands
Divided or undivided in whose hands or possession soever unto
the said Moses Tyler his heirs & assignes forever and to yearly
proper use & behoof of him the said Moses Tyler his heirs &
assigns forever. And the said Job Tyler doth hereby Covenant promise grant & agree to & with the said Moses Tyler,
that he the said Job Tyler was the true & proper owner of the
said bargained premises with their appurtces at ye time of the

sale & alienation thereof & had full power good right & lawful authority to grant & Convey all & Singular the bargained premises with their appurtces unto ye said Moses Tyler his heirs & assignes forever in manner & form aforesd and yt the said premises are free & clear & freely & clearly acquitted exhonoreated and discharged of & from all manner of former grants bargains sales gifts titles leases mortgages suits attachments actions judgmts & of & from all other titles troubles charges incumbrances whatsoever From the beginning of the world to the time of the bargain & sale hereof. And yt the said Moses Tyler his heirs & assigns & every part & parcel thereof shall quietly have, hold use occupy possess to his & their proper use & behoof forever, and if I will well & truly defend ye premises from any manner of person or persons from by or under me claiming any interest in them or any part or parcel of them forever, whereby the said Moses Tyler his heirs or assigns shall or may be molested in or evicted out of the possession of the same. And I the above sd Job Tyler doth for myself my heirs, Extrs & assigns Covenant & promise to & with the said Moses Tyler his heirs & assigns that upon lawful demand I or they will or shall do & perform what may be further in law necessary to be done for the sure making the title tenour of the premises according to the true intent & meaning of these presents. In Witness Whereof I the said Job Tyler have hereunto set my hand & fixed my seal this 27th day of November in ye year of Our Lord 1700 & in ye Twelvth year of our Sovereign Lord William of England, Scotland, France & Ireland King.

JOB TYLER *S* his mark & a Seal.

Signed Seald & delvd ye day & year above in ye presence of us Saml Reed Senr Benjamin Wheelock, John Lovet.

Job Tyler personally appeared before me the subscriber one of His Majtys Justices for ye County of Suffolk & owned this instrument to be his Act & Deed. Decembr 14° 1700

TYMO DWIGHT.

Recd to be recorded Janry 10th 1700-01 & accordingly entered & examined

per Ad'ton Davenport Reg.

The land was granted by Moses Tyler to John Farnum of Andover (Hopestill's son-in-law who was afterwards of Men-

don), for £61, 8 July, 1701, signed by Moses Tyler. Witnesses
Thomas Barnard and Benjamin Barker. Acknowledged be-
fore Dudley Bradstreet, 2 May, 1706, Addington Davenport,
Registrar.

In these old records we thus have a word-picture of this
ancestor of a long line of Tylers, such as hardly has been found
of any other American immigrant. Professor Henry M. Tyler
has said of him: " He was a rude, self-asserting, striking
personality. Not to be left out of account in the forces which
were to possess the land." There are but few high-lights in
the picture; the shadows are all there. He did not, as Professor Tyler said, " learn prudence very fast, but he was himself. . . . He had a good deal of individuality and he
gave utterance to it at times with more vigor than grace. He
did not shape his words to suit sensitive ears. He resented
dictation and found it hard to restrain himself from what he
wanted to do through any prudential policy." Yet, when you
shall read hereafter what manner of men his sons and grandsons
were and what they stood for in all the places where they lived;
as you come down through the years, generation by generation,
and see what thousands of his descendants have stood for in
their homes and before the public, in peace and in war, as
pioneers and as dwellers in the cities, you will realize that there
must have been good stock in the old man; and he trained a
family to be useful and honored in the communities where they
dwelt. Superstitious, wilful, hot-tempered, independent and
self-reliant Job Tyler lives and breathes in this record nearly
three centuries after his time. He did not have saints to live
with; were all the truth known, it would be seen that he was
on a par with a large proportion of his neighbors. The Puritan iron rule, which made no allowances for any man, met a
sturdy opposition in this possible descendant of Wat Tyler of
England, and it is now too late to determine whether or not he
was always justified. From this old canvas there gazes steadily
out, not an ideal but a very real personage, an out and out
Yankee type.

It had been suggested that the progenitor of so many thousand men and women, covering the greater part of three centuries which have passed since the early voyager set his foot
(the first permanent one) upon Andover soil, should be honored
by some fitting monument, since none was in existence. Ac-

cordingly, in response to written appeal, numbers of the clan joined their "mites," to thus honor their forebear, and the memorial was dedicated at the sixth Tyler Reunion, September 4, 1901. The spot selected was beside the grave of the immigrant's eldest son, Moses, whose ancient slate slab, with its legend of "1727," has survived with wonderful completeness. Here, under a giant evergreen, upon a cubic yard of cement and cobble stones which was brought just to the surface of the ground, was placed a large hard-grained boulder, brought from the old Tyler farm (now known as the Woods place), four miles distant in West Boxford; a homestead which has known Tyler blood and heirship uninterruptedly from the first generation, when it was acquired from the Indians, to the present day.

Upon the boulder was securely riveted a bronze tablet, cast in Boston, which bears the following legend:—

IN MEMORIAM
JOB TYLER
IMMIGRANT FIRST SETTLER
ANDOVER ABOUT MDCXXXIX
BORN MDCXIX   DIED MDCC.

Dedicated by his whole clan, Sept. 4, 1901.

The dedicatory address was delivered by Prof. Henry M. Tyler, of Smith College.

The eldest child was born in Roxbury or Andover as was probably the third; the fifth and sixth in Roxbury; the others are uncertain. They were:

2+   Moses Tyler, born in 1641 or 1642.
3+   Mary Tyler, born about 1644.
4+   Hopestill Tyler, born about 1645 or 1646.
5   Child, who died in infancy, "1646, month 1, day 28."
6+   Hannah Tyler.
7   John Tyler, born about 1650; died in Andover, Sept. 28, 1652.
8+   John Tyler, born April 16, 1653.
9+   Samuel Tyler, born May 24, 1655.

SECOND GENERATION

2 QUARTERMASTER MOSES[2] TYLER (JOB[1]), born in Andover or Roxbury, Mass., 1641 or 1642; died in Andover, October 2, 1727; married (1), July 6, 1666, Prudence Blake, born April 15, 1647; died March 9, 1689; daughter of George and Dorothy Blake, of Gloucester, Mass. (who early moved to Boxford) ; married (2), about 169+, Sarah (Hasey) Sprague, born about 1647; died 1718; widow of Phineas Sprague, of Malden, he having died in 1690; she had several daughters by her first marriage; married (3), July or August, 1718, Mrs. Martha Fisk, born about 1649; died February 13, 1735.

From the " deposicion," before Gov. Bradstreet, of Job Tyler, wherein the son joined, " 27, 4, 1659," we know, that Moses Tyler was then "between seventeen & eighteen yeares."

In " Rowley Village," on the old homestead, which has long been called (from one of Moses' sons), " The Captain John Tyler place," Moses began to clear a farm, rear a family, and became a locally conspicuous citizen. As Job, the immigrant, was undoubtedly here for a time with his son (in 1680), and the place still remains in a direct Tyler descent, it is, historically speaking, the most interesting of any of our various Tyler homesteads, in that it has been in the family two and a third centuries, and sheltered members of every generation from the first (something which cannot be said of any other spot). (See No. 11.)

The Tyler homestead came within that part of ancient Rowley, known as " Rowley Village," Moses Tyler being on the committee to fix the bounds between the parent and offspring towns. The main settlement of Rowley Village was in the present village of old Boxford; while Moses' homestead was within the portion incorporated, June 28, 1735, into the new, West Boxford. (There were continuously male Tylers here, from Moses' arrival, 1666, to the time of death of the late Phineas Tyler, 1885; while the blood, through intermarriage, is yet abundant.) Moses Tyler was prominent from the outset in Boxford town

17

matters; but, while most of his townsfolk went over to Topsfield "to meeting," Moses found it nearer and more convenient, to continue his church affiliation at Andover.

He repeatedly served his town as selectman, committee-man, surveyor, constable, etc., so often that we can plainly read, he was a very prominent town citizen. In 1685 he was on a committee to lay out several highways; in October, 1690, he became a "freeman"; in 1691, '94, '95, '98 and 1712, he was a selectman; May 11, 1699, was on committee to settle bounds between Boxford and Salem, Topsfield, Andover and Bradford, or any townships formerly granted out of the confines of old Rowley.

January 8, 1689, the town selectmen made a rate of £8, to lay in its first stock of ammunition; Moses Tyler (with three others) being ordered to gather it and expend for " Poudr & bullets and flents." Additions thereto were made from time to time, especially during Indian hostilities; and August 14, 1696, Moses became the custodian of "ten pound of powder, sixty pound of bullets and fifty flintes," and " hee is to keep this part of the Town Stock teall the Select men See Caues to lodg it in Sum other place. For such services, he acquired the title of " Quartermaster," which was usually applied to him; though on his gravestone we see, he, or somebody, preferred the plain " Mr.," which was a title of dignity in those days.

For many years after incorporation, Boxford had no church; most of its citizens attended at Topsfield, where Boxford, till 1702, paid " minister's rates." In 1691 Boxford appointed a committee of five, to fix upon a central site for a local church edifice; Moses being one of the five. The construction of this church (probably for lack of means) dragged along for a period of ten years, during which, January 29, 1695, Moses is appointed on the committee to carry on the building. In 1701 it was done, and, January 9, presented to the town; being in the present " East Parish." *

* As this church is so historic of our early generations, a list of Tyler communicants is set out. As Job paid " ministers' rates " here, it is reasonable to think both he and his wife, Mary, were early attendants, though at a period of which records were lost. His sons Hopestill, John and wife were communicants, until their removal to Mendon; also Moses, eldest son of Job and wife Prudence, died while members. Jacob (Moses' only son to live at Andover) took up his pew with his wife, in 1721, and his 2nd wife was admitted in 1729; Jacob, Jr., and his wife, in 1750, and his 2nd wife in 1752; also, in 1756; his brother Moses and wife, and sister Abigail, became members. These brothers removing (the one to Haver-

Moses, while actively interested over Boxford church building, affiliated with Andover congregation, whose records are missing up to 1708. However, from a "List of communicants in 1686," we see that Moses, as well as his wife, was a member at that date. From the preserved records we learn how prominent a member Moses really was. When the subject, dividing Andover into two parishes, came up, it caused much feeling. October 2, 1710, he is placed on the committee of five, " To warn Precinct meetings, and are empowered to warn a meeting when they shall see cause." On the 23d of the same month, Moses is one of a committee of four " To proportion the work on the precinct, in providing timber for the new meeting house according to previous vote." March 19, 1711, he is on the committee of three, " Chosen to discourse the South precinct in any matter in controversy, referring to petition lately offered to General Court." December 24, same year, he is on committee of seven, " To take account of the work ye men have done about the new meeting house, & set valuation on it," etc. June 30, 1712, he is on committee, " To tak an account of cost that the committee was at that may manage the precint's affairs at the General Court, or otherwise, in order to the recovering of the 300 families back again to us." October 31, 1715, " Quartermaster M. Tyler was chosen Treasurer, till another is chosen in his room in ye office for said precinct." And he was re-elected for the consecutive terms, 1717, '18, '19, '20. Before this, while a resident of Rowley Village in 1681 (with some other distant members) it had been allowed " to set a house for their convenience for families and horse, on Sabbath days."

We find Moses' rate of 1692 on record, but are unable to give a fairly complete account, until his later years, as follows:

1712, Moses Tyler's rate and proportion for minister's salary, 18s., 6d.; 1715, 17s., 3d.; 1716, 19s., 10d.; 1718, £1, 9s., 11d.; 1719, £1, 11s., 7d.; 1720, £1, 12s., 7d.; 1724, £1, 6s., 9d.; 1726, £1, 2s., 6d.

The foregoing exhibits a high-rate payer; therefore, a man of means.

From Salem deeds, we know he was a large landed proprietor; frequently acquiring, seldom parting with, real estate. The

hill, the other to Woburn), the family ceased to be represented in the community, for the time being. Since those times, later branches have been affiliated with this organization, from which the blood, by intermarriage, has never at any point of its history been entirely lacking.

old homestead, as later taxed, shows how much had hung together, though much had meantime been granted to others of the kin, or alienated to strangers. From Boxford town rate, 1687 (under Gov. Andros), we see: " Moses Tyler, 3 heads; 1 house; 20 acres; 4 oxen, 3 horses; 5 cows, 5 young cattle; 20 sheep; 3 swine; tax, 11/ 6d." (Only two stood higher.) In 1699, Nov. 25, he bought of Nathan Stevens of Andover, 5 acres, meadow and upland, and thus became owner of a saw-mill; in 1698, Moses (wife " Sara " joining) for £15, sells Philip Atwood of Bradford, ½ of some " salt marsh at Plum Island in Rowley." In 1700, Nov. 27, he, for £60, has of his father, Job, a house lot in Mendon, 15 acres, with 5 acres added from 2nd division; which he sold the following year at £1 profit, to John Farnum of Andover, son-in-law of Moses' brother Hope-still. 1708, May 20, Moses (with consent of Sara), *gives* to John Tyler (his 2nd son), of Boxford, 107 acres in Boxford. (Probably part of the old homestead.) " 1 line running to a tree in Andover line, about 50 rods from the Great Hill end, then to run Easterly upon said line till it meets with Ephraim Foster's line, which is part of the 400 acres laid out by Rowley town to John Commins, Thomas Dorman & Robt. Stiles." In 1712 (with consent of " Sara "), Moses, for " love of his son Jonathan, carpenter, of Boxford," gives Boxford land, 80 acres north of Ipswich road, near brother Ebenezer's land, also near brother James' land, " some sponges of meadow," with " Shaven Crown to Clay Pit Swamp," a boundary line (which localities are still so known). In 1718, Moses (then a widower) deeds to his son Jacob, youngest born, ½ of his arable land, meadow, orchard, west end of dwelling house, cellar, stock and husbandry tools in Andover. Again, in 1718, he deeds to son-in-law, Eben-ezer Stevens (husband of his step-daughter, Sara Sprague), " shoe meadow," a valuable tract of old Tyler Boxford home-stead. Moses' second wife, by her Sprague marriage, had had several daughters, who thus came to live with their stepfather; which was the occasion of general authority, Savage, and the local authority, Perley (*Hist. of Boxford*), making the mistake of recording them as Moses' own daughters. In extenuation of which error, however, we find the girls named in Moses' will in such terms as to admit of the supposition, and further, at least, one of them was later called by the name " Tyler," as evidenced by witchcraft proceedings, wherein one is designated as " Martha Tyler, alias Sprague." Indeed, the custom became so established that, according to Andover records, when " Martha " married (June 5, 1701, Richard Friend, seaman, of Salem), she married as a " Tyler." (See *Charlestown Genealogies* by Wyman, also *Witchcraft Papers*, p. 61, in Mass. State House.)

Moses Tyler's wife Sarah died in 1718; whereupon, without long widowerhood, he married the widow, Martha Fisk. The town records say the ceremony took place July 25, 1718; but the church annals put the solemnization August 13, 1718. They appear to have lived congenially together for almost a decade, when Moses, from Andover, whither he removed from Boxford about 1697, passed off the scene.

WILL OF MOSES TYLER

Probated at Salem, Mass., October 13, 1727, case 28452. No Inventory.

" I, Moses Tyler of Andover, in the County of Essex and Province of Massachusetts Bay in New England, husbandman, being at present of sound mind and memory, but considering my mortality, have thought meet to make this my last will and testament.

" And first of all, I commit my soul into the hands of God, who gave it, and my body I commit to the earth in hope of a blessed resurrection at the last day, through the merits of my Lord and Savior, Jesus Christ ;—and, as for my wordly estate, which God has given me, I give and dispose of the same in manner following.

" As for my sons, Moses, John, Ebenezer, Job, Jonathan, James and Joshua, I have formally given them their full portions out of my estate according to my ability. Also, I give to my six sons, first mentioned, ten pounds apiece, and to my son Joshua the last mentioned, twenty pounds, all which sums are to be paid by my executor in the space of eight years after my decease, and he shall be obliged to pay but ten pounds a year, and shall pay the younger before the elder.

" I give to my son Jacob all my homestead in Andover and my dwelling house, with all my other buildings, that are upon said homestead, and all my meadows, in Andover, and all my stock of cattle and sheep and swine and household goods, and other moveables. Excepting so much of my household goods, which my second wife brought to me, as shall be left at my decease, which shall be equally divided between my son Jacob and his three sisters, Martha, Katherine and Sarah, and the children of his sisters, Joanna and Abagail, deceased; the children of each sister to have one share, and my son Jacob shall have the choice of the beds and furniture thereof that was his mothers; and if my son Jacob shall die without issue lawfully begotten, then the lands, which I have given him in this my will, shall be equally divided among my other sons. And I do hereby constitute, make and ordain my son Jacob the sole executor of this my last will and testament, and if there is any part of my real or personal estate, that I have not disposed [of] in this my last will and testament, I give it to my said executor, and I do hereby revoke and disannul all and every other will and testament by me made.

"Rectifying and confirming this and no other to be my last will and testament.

"In witness whereof, I have hereunto set my hand and seal this ninth day of April, Anno Domini, 1725, and in the eleventh year of the reign of our Sovereign Lord, George of England, Scotland, France and Ireland, King, &c.

(Signed)   MOSES TYLER.   (Seal.)

" Signed, sealed and delivered by the said Moses Tyler to be his last will and testament in presence of us the subscribers.

(Signed)   JOHN BARNARD.
DANIEL COLBE.
SARAH BARNARD."

CHILDREN, by first marriage:

10+   Moses Tyler, born Feb. 16, 1667.
11+   John Tyler, born Sept. 14, 1669.
12   Joseph Tyler, born Sept. 18, 1671; died in Salem, Mass., or the West Indies in 1699, intestate (See Admn., Case No. 28,443, Salem Probate); married Martha ———, who died Feb. 11, 1745, aged 74.

His widow, " Martha," with brother-in-law, Job Tyler, of Andover, execute a bond, £300, with father-in-law, Moses Tyler, and Daniel Grant, " chaundler," of Salem, sureties. Several interesting accounts appear. A note of intestate, dated Oct. 11, 1699. for 30/. received from Samuel Wakefield, of Salem, is presented, which " I do promise to Lay out for sd Wakefield

in Barbadoes (God Sending me Safe there), in whatt I shall
think most for said Wakefield's best advantage." A bill of
lading appears, from John Higginson, of Salem, dated Oct. 8,
1699,—" Shiped on bourd the Ship Lyon," &c., " for my proper
Accott & Risque & does Consigned to Mr. Joseph Tyler, for
Sales & Returns,—

1 large Bay mare.................	6
6 new Barrls	18
2 tt hay 10/......................	10
12 bushell of Oates...............	18
Rum, halter, bucket, boatage, &c.....	10

£8 16 "

Lastly, is thrown a side-light upon collateral relations.
The deceased, had had from " Phineas Sprague, Jr., of Malden " (brother of Joseph Tyler's half-sisters, and who also
went to Barbadoes), Oct. 7, 1698, " one Brown horse on bord
the Ship Lion," &c., " Bound for Barbadoes," there to be sold,
" should he live, and " I to lay out the neett produse in Barbados
goods—that goods I shall think Best." It may have been,
that Joseph died in the West Indies. In 1692, he had been
among the " confessed " witches; led into it (with two cousins,
Martha and Joanna Tyler) " by Abigail Faulkner."

13+ Ebenezer Tyler, born Sept. 18, 1673.
14+ Job Tyler, born Dec. 16, 1675.
15   Samuel Tyler, born May 2, 1678; died young.
16   Nathaniel Tyler, born Aug. 14, 1680; probably died
        young. (Savage says that two children died young.)
17+ Jonathan Tyler, born March 8, 1683.
18+ James Tyler, born May 7, 1685.
19+ Joshua Tyler, born in Boxford, July 4, 1688.

CHILD, by second marriage:
20+ Jacob Tyler, born Jan. 9, 169—.

3 MARY[2] TYLER (JOB[1]), born about 1644; married
(1), November 18, 1662, Richard Post, of Woburn, Mass.,
born about 1627; killed in Mendon, Mass., July 14, 1675, by

the Indians (he married (1), February 27, 1649-1650, Susanna Sutton, who probably died s. p.) ; married (2), March 1, 1677-1678, John Bridges, a widower of Andover, a blacksmith and constable there in 1678 ; son of Edmund Bridges, the immgirant. He had a son and daughter by first wife. Mary was accused of witchcraft. Children, by first marriage:

21   Mary Post, born Sept. 29, 1664.

She was accused of witchcraft, and tried at Salem, in January, 1692-3, as vouched by the following papers in the case:

" Mary Post, of Rowley, in the County of Essex, single woman, being indicted by the jurors for our Sovereign Lord & Lady, the King & Queen, upon their oathes, by two several indictments, that is to say: 1st., For that she, the said Mary Post, of Rowley in the Co. of Essex, single woman, about three years ago, in the town of Rowley aforesaid, wickedly, malitiously and feloniously, a covenant with the Devil did make and signed the Devil's book, and was baptized by the Devil, & renounced her former Christian baptism, by which diabolical covenant, with the Devil made, she, the said Mary Post, is become a detestable witch, contrary to the peace of our Sovereign Lord & Lady, the King & Queen, their crown and dignity, & the laws in that case made and provided. 2d. For that she, the said Mary Post of Rowley, single woman, sometime in the month of July last, in the year 1692 aforesaid, & divers other days and times, as well before as after, certain detestable arts, called witchcrafts and sorceries, wickedly, malitiously and feloniously hath used practiced and exercised at and in the town of Andover, in the Co. of Essex aforesaid, upon and against one Timothy Swan, of Andover aforesaid, by which said wicked arts, the said Timothy Swan the day and year aforesaid and divers other days and times as well before as after was and is tortured, afflicted, tormented, consumed, pined & wasted, against the peace of our Sovereign Lord & Lady, the King & Queen, their crown and dignity & against the laws in that case made and provided." " Upon the aforesaid indictment and each of them, the said Mary Post was then & there before the Jurors of our Lord & Lady, the King & Queen aforesaid, arraigned and upon her arraignment did then and there, the day and year aforesaid, plead to them & each of them not guilty, & put herself upon trial by God and her country."

" A Jury being called, Benayah Titcomb, Foreman, John Witt, Joseph Little, John Pickard, Edmund Gale, John Emerson, John Ordway, John Abby, Seth Story, John Hall, Nathaniel Emerson & Eleazer Gyles, and accordingly sworn, no exception being made by the prisoner, the said indictments and each of them being read, together with evidences and examinations and the prisoner's defence being heard, the Jury went out to agree on their verdict, which returning did then and there in open court deliver their verdict, that the said Mary Post was guilty of covenanting with the Devil, for which she stood indicted in the second indictment. The Court ordered the keeper of the Goale to take care of the prisoner according to law." Soon after, she was sentenced to death: but was finally reprieved."

N. B.—The Clerk of Court's records of Salem, of this period, verifies that many of the accused and their friends claimed, and received, " damages," for false accusations; their receipts being on file. We illustrate as follows:—" By His Excellency, the Governor. Whereas ye General Assembly in their last session accepted ye report of their comitte appointed to consider of ye Damages Sustained by Sundry persons prosecuted for Witchcraft in ye year 1692 Vizt. . . . Mary Post, £8. 14."

22 Joanna Post, born Sept. 13, 1666; she was an accuser in a witchcraft trial, and herself, at another time, was accused, but acquitted.

23 John Post, born April 14, 1669.

CHILDREN, by second marriage:

24 Mary Bridges, born Jan. 27, 1679-1680; accused of witchcraft at the age of 12.

25 Samuel Bridges, born July 19, 1681.

26 Elizabeth Bridges, born June 5, 1683.

27 Mehitable Bridges, born April 29, 1688.

4 HOPESTILL[2] TYLER (JOB[1]), born about 1646, probably in Roxbury or Andover, Mass.; died in Preston, Conn., January 20, 1734, " in ye 89th year of his age " according to the rather rude stone which marks his grave in the old burying ground in Preston; married in Mendon, January 20, 1668, Mary Lovett, born in Mendon, March 7, 1652-53; said to have

died in 1732; daughter of Daniel Lovett, of Braintree and Mendon. Hopestill went to Andover with his father, who apprenticed him in 1658 to a blacksmith of Andover, Thomas Chandler; the boy was to be taught the blacksmith trade "so far as he was capable to learn" for a period of 9½ years; was to be taught to read the Bible and write so as to keep a book for his trade, and to be allowed "convenient meat and drinke, washing, lodging and clothes." Something occurred to sicken the father of this bargain and he took arbitrary steps to get possession of his son, which lead to a long legal battle, rather disastrous and humiliating to Job. When the family moved to Roxbury, Hopestill went also, and later went to Mendon. In 1671 he shared in the land division of Mendon; the next year he drew "Lot 30" in a swamp land division; in 1673 he was "surveyor of highways." In 1675 when the inhabitants fled from the Indian raid he went to his old home in Roxbury, for his child Martha ("Mathew" in records and will) was baptized there, and the next year his son John was born there. By 1681 he is at Andover, as children are recorded there. His name is on the church list there of 1686. He was the first Tyler citizen in the newly settled part of Andover, in the south part of the town, and in 1687, by permission, he "set up a shop in ye streete near his house." This was on the Boston road near the inn of Joseph Parker, who buys of Hopestill in 1710. He also owned the "Devil's Den," as well as the great frog-ponds. He was again made freeman in 1691; also chosen tythingman. In 1692 the terrible scourge of witchcraft touched his home; his wife was accused and imprisoned, but was finally released.

STORY OF MARY TYLER'S CONFESSION

The following is a digest of the "recantation" obtained from Hopestill Tyler's wife by the Rev. Increase Mather, the same being followed by *Bailey's Sketches of Andover*, pp. 222 and 223.

"Goodwife Tyler did say, that when she was first apprehended, she had no fears upon her, & did think, that nothing could have made her confess against herself. But, since, she has found to her great grief, that she had wronged the truth & falsely accused herself." When she was being taken from

her home in Andover to prison in Salem, her brother-in-law
Bridges rode beside her; and, during the memorable ride, told
her that she *must* be a "witch," because *the afflicted were
raised* out of their fits "by her touch." She stoutly denied the
accusation, and begged him not to urge her to confess. But,
arrived at Salem (shall we not rather say, temporary "Pande-
monium"?), she had to combat, not only a stubbornly mis-
guided brother on one side, but also on her other side, "John
Emerson"; which latter stoutly took up the cudgel of accusation, on calling her a witch, declaring he could *see the Devil before her eyes*, whereupon, with his hands, he proceeded to beat
him off. In short, her persecutors so harassed her for confession,
that she would have "preferred a *dungeon*," to their presence.
Finally, they threatened to leave her; declaring that, in such
event, *she would be undone body and soul forever.* To their
reiterations, that she "could *not lie* by confessing," she retorted,
"I *shall* lie, *if* I confess; and then, *who shall answer unto God*
for my lie?" Their final resort always was, "You will'be
hanged, if you do not confess!" In short, they so protracted
their unmerciful treatment, that the poor woman began to
doubt her very life and reason: whereupon they proceed to have
her "agree to say" what they should "suggest." But, in
her *real* "confession" to Rev. Mather, she insisted, "she
wronged her conscience in so doing, was guilty of a great sin
in belying herself & desired to mourn for it so long as she
lived." And the said Mather adds, "Her affliction, sor-
row, relenting, grief and mourning, exceeds any pen to describe
and express the same."

VERDICT ON MARY TYLER

MARY TYLER wife of Hopestill Tyler of Andover, Black-
smith, being Indicted by the Jurors for oᵣ Soveraigne Lord and
Lady the King and Queen upon these Oaths. try these Severall
Indictments. That is to say; 1st—For that shee the said Mary
Tyler wife of Hopestill Tyler of Andover in the County of
Essex, Blacksmith, about seaven Years since in the Town of
Andover aforesaid wickedly Malitiously and ffeloniously a
covenant with the Devill did make and signed the Devills Book,
and promised to serve the Devill as long as she lived &c. &c. The
Jury went out to agree on their verdict, who returning did then

and there in open Court deliver their Verdict. That the said
Mary Tyler was Not Guilty of the ffellony by witchcraft for
which shee stood Indicted in & by the said Indictments, and
each of them. The Court ordered Mary Tyler aforesaid to be
discharged paying her ffees.

His daughters Hannah, Martha and Joanna were likewise
accused, and their father and their uncle, John Bridges, gave
a bond for surety in the sum of £100 for the appearance of
Martha and Joanna. In Nevin's " *Witchcraft in 1692*," in
Appendix A appears the name of " Hope Tyler " in the list of
the accused, but the author found no details of any proceedings
in such cause. In all there were eleven of the Tyler name and
blood who were accused and taken out of their homes. They
were all acquitted. Whether the witchcraft episodes had anything to do with it or not, there is nothing to show, but after
a few years Hopestill moved to Preston, Conn. In 1697 he
sold his land and house at Andover, and in Connecticut, for
generations, his descendants grew rapidly in numbers and pres-
tige. He is one of twelve men who organized the first church in
Preston, November 16, 1698. It is believed that he went to
Preston the preceding summer. He built his house in the forest,
about a mile from the hamlet, and the primitive stone-fireplace
was standing a few years ago, strong and massive, where an
8-foot log could be rolled in. The old well exists, and the same
old rocks, doubtless, for it is a rocky region, and Hopestill must
have gained his competence more by blacksmith work than by
farming. The old andirons, which were probably his handi-
work, more than two hundred years ago, are heavy, with a ring
in the top, fashioned wholly of iron, burned and rusty; this
hearth, preserved so long, is the earliest one that can be indubi-
tably proved to be connected with the descendants of Job Tyler
of Andover. The fireplace is boarded up and never used. The
house, for the most part, is said to have been burned a great
many years ago. The chimney bears a date, 1768, and it is
said to be nearly a reproduction of its protoype. The deed
of this farm of one hundred and ten acres was given by Robert
Gear to Hopestill under date of June 28, 1715. He was something of a landlord; became a purchaser of " Common lands "
and he continued to own lands in Massachusetts for some years.
While yet in Andover, he had granted to his brother Samuel

(then of " Rowley Village "), for £30, a 15-acre house lot in
Mendon, five of which had come from his " father Tyler."
And it also seems, that he had early made purchase in Preston;
for we find deed to " Hope " from Samuel Mason, January 10,
1689.   In 1703, he deeded land in Groton, Conn., to his son
Daniel, whereupon is situated a place long known as " Tyler
Hill."   In 1706, he deeds a piece to his son James; and in
1713, another to son Hopestill, Jr.   He seems to have retained
interests in Massachusetts, after his departure; for we find, at
Salem, two deeds from him in the years 1710 and 1713.   June
20, 1704, he had a deed in Connecticut from Thomas Averill;
June 28, 1715, another from his son-in-law, Robert Geer.
The inventory of his estate amounted to over £842.   He possessed a " Close-bodied coat," which with " beaver hat " and
" muff " must have made him both comfortable and stylish for
his day.   He also had an " orange cloak."   His life, in an
unusual degree, seems to have been removed from the realm of
the commonplace, he having, for various reasons, lived in four
towns, and having passed through the horrors of Indian raids
and the terrors of the witchcraft delusion, which attacked those
nearest and dearest to him.   His will, dated May 15, 1728, was
recorded in New London, Conn., August 9, 1734 (See *Wills*,
Book VI, Folios 155-156).   Of the children whose birthplaces
are known, the second and those after the fifth were born in
Andover.

WILL OF HOPESTILL TYLER, SR.

In the name of God, Amen, May the fifteenth, 1728.   I
Hopestill Tyler, of Preston, being aged and of parfet mind and
memory, thanks be given to god for the same, caling unto mind
the mortality of my body and knowing that It Is appointed
for all men once to dye do make and ordain this my last will and
testament.   That is to say principally and first of all I give
and recommend my Soul Into the hands of God that gave It
and my body i recommend to the earth to be buried In decent
Christian burial at the discretion of my executtors, nothing
doubting but at the general resurrection i shall reseaive the
same again by the mighty power of god and as touching Such
wordly estate wharewith It hath pleased god to bless me In

this Life I give Demise and Dispose of the same in the following manner and form.

Imprimis:—I give and bequeath to my Loving wife mary [she had *died* meanwhile, 1732] of my estate as the Law dierets.

" Then to my dafter mary furnnum I give fifty shillings besides what she has allready had. Then I give to my dafter hanna busel her children teen pound besides what she has already had. I give unto my dafter mathew teen pound besides what shee has allready had. I give unto my dafter abigel three score pound besides what she allready has had. I give unto my Son Daniel teen pound besides what he allready has had. I give unto my Son James five pound besides what he allready has had. I give unto my granson moses tiler In Boston fifty Shillings besides what hee allreadye has had. Then I give unto my Son Hopstill all my Land In the township of preston with all my housing and Shope tols. I allsoe constitut make and ordain my Sole exsexaters my Son James and my Son Hopestill and my dafter Abigel my will Is that my dafter abigel shall have a room In the hous to live in as long as she lives unmarried.

his
HOPESTILL X TYLER.
mark

Witnesses:
    Thomas Stanton,
    Jabez Fitch,
    Anna Stanton."

Recorded in the 6th book of wills for New London district, Folio 155-156 Aug. 9th, 1734.

RICH. CHRISTOPHER Clerk.

Preston Jan. 30, 1733-4 then the within named Thomas Stanton, Jabez Fitch and Anna Stanton did all parsonally appear and made oath that thay did se ye within named Hopestill Tyler sign and seal ye within written instrument and that thay herd him then publish and declare ye same to be his Will and Testament and that he was then in his perfect mind and memory and that thay did then all thereunto sign as witnesses in ye presence of ye sd Hopestill Tyler dec'd—before me John Cooke. Justice of Peace.

INVENTORY

Wearing apparel ....
The building & part of the homestead
    mentioned in the will............ £600. 0. 0.
A fifty acre loot of land lying in the
    Northeast Corner of Preston..... £50.
The black smith Shoop & tools, &c.......
I yoke of oxen.................... £18. 0. 0.
1 3 year old heifer.................
1 4 year old heifer.................
1 3 year old steer.................
1 yearling heifer....................
1 calfe ....
1 horse five years old...............
1 maire nine years old..............
1 maire seven years old.............
1 maire two years old.............
14 sheep ....
17 goats ....
Money in Daniel tiler's hands........
Money in Jacob Parkes' hands.........
Money in Hopestill Tiler's hands......
Money in Moses Tiler's hands........
Money in Job Tiler's hands..........
        &c....................

Total....................... £842. 7. 3.

CHILDREN:

28+ Mary Tyler, born in Mendon, Mass., Jan. 31, 1669.
29+ Martha (Mathew) Tyler, born April 9, 1676.
30+ John Tyler, born in Roxbury, Mass., Feb. 19, 1677.
31+ Daniel Tyler.
32+ Hannah Tyler.
33 Joanna Tyler, born Nov. 21, 1681; died s. p. before
    1728; was accused of witchcraft.
34+ James Tyler, born Dec. 28, 1683.
35+ Hopestill Tyler, born Oct. 16 (or 26), 1685.
36 Mehitable Tyler, born June 4 (or Jan.), 1687; died
    young.

37   Abigail Tyler, twin to Mehitable; died March 13, 1771;
     married Daniel Fitch. Her father names her in his
     will: " My dafter abigel three score pound besides what
     she allready has had." She joined the Preston church
     Sept. 3, 1721, when she was unmarried. The old
     grave-stone in the Preston burying ground is " In mem-
     ory of Mrs. Abigail ye wife of Mr. Daniel Fitch &
     daughter of Mr. Hopestill Tyler."

     6 HANNAH² TYLER (JOB¹), married, January 20,
1668. Lieut. James Lovett, born July 8, 1648, son of Daniel
Lovett.

CHILDREN:

38   Hannah Lovett, born Oct. 2, 1669.
39   John Lovett.
40   Mary Lovett, married ―― Morse.
41   Martha Lovett, married ―― Perry.
42   Joanna Lovett, married ―― Perry.
43   Daniel Lovett, born Sept. 6, 1860; married Abigail
     Sprague, daughter of Phineas Sprague of Woburn.
44   Sarah Lovett, born Jan. 13, 1682; died young.
45   Abigail Lovett, born April 25, 1685; married Ebenezer
     Sumner.
46   Sarah Lovett, born Jan. 11, 1688; married Ebenezer
     Sumner, her sister's widower.
47   James Lovett, born May 13, 1693.

     8 DEACON JOHN² TYLER (JOB¹), born in Andover,
Mass., April 16, 1653; baptized in Roxbury, Mass., June 4,
1665, in John Eliot's church; died May 4, 1742, in Mendon,
Mass.; buried there with stone still standing; married, September 14, 1682, Hannah Parker, born in Andover May 14, 1659;
daughter of Nathan Parker and his second wife, Mary; her
father was early in Newbury, and in Andover by 1645. He
doubtless spent some years of his youth in Mendon with his
father, with whom he must have fled at the outbreak of King
Philip's War to Rowley Village, and later went to Andover.
He and his wife became members of the first church of Andover, where they appear upon the list of 1686, though the
exact year of their first communion is not recorded. With his
elder brother Hopestill, and his brother-in-law, John Bridges,

he became a " freeman," April 18, 1691. Between the births of his two children, Bethia and Mary, he moved to Mendon, and in 1693 he and his wife joining, made a conveyance to John Marston.

In 1695, he first appears at Mendon upon the minister's rate, " £00.10.7, county pay, and £00.02.10, money." March 7, 1698, the town voted " to grant a Streame for the Incoradgment of a Corn Mill within the bounds of the town," and John Tiler was on the committee " to view the streams and pich upon a place for that purpose, and make Return of ye same." In 1699, he shares in a division of proprietor's land, and pays on minister's rate, " £01.00.06 and 6 ft. of wood." March 3, 1701, he was on the committee to give the selectmen instructions. March 17, 1701, a schedule of claims presented, and John Tyler on committee, " to goe about the town and Take a valuation and bring it to the selectmen In order to ther making of the towne Rate." In 1702, he was elected selectman. In 1704, his rate on payment of town debts was " £00.04.10," and he received for his charge against town, £00.05.08." In 1708, he was one of three trustees, to take town valuation. In 1709, he was again a selectman; and " Jan. 8 " of that year, when the town voted to put up their first school-house, he was upon the building committee. In 1712, he put in a bill to the town, " for 4 days about ye Ministry and Scool lots, . . . £00.10.00." In 1711, there had been a committee of nine chosen, to see about seating the meetings; but as their labors did not seem to give satisfaction, in 1713, we see that Deacon (John) Tyler (with two other deacons) are made a committee, to see if better arrangements cannot be made for seating the meeting house. In the same year, " November 23," he is authorized to take from the town treasury money to pay the preacher for the past two weeks, " and, If sd. money comes In by Contrybution, within one month, then to Return the same to the Treasurer, otherwise to be made up by the towne." March 28, 1715, Deacon Tyler was on a committee, " to take care to provide a Minister [to succeed Rev. Rawson], for the Town, from time to time, until they shall provide a man, so far to the Town's acceptance, as to give a call to settlement." February 24, 1716, he is on the committee, to agree with Rev. Joseph Dorr to be the minister in Mendon. In the " Seventh division " of land, in 1719, his lot drawn is No. 110.

From this time, as he was getting to be an old man, we do not hear so much of him through the records; his sons John, Jr. and Nathan, come in; especially the latter, who was probably the most ubiquitous of any Tyler who ever lived in the town. In March, 1729, old Deacon Tyler (and the town clerk), with characteristic independence (though nearly four score), " protests against irregularities in the choice of town officers "; and the same year, in December, enters protest against the committee " for stating the place for the Meeting House." The very last we hear of him, is the following season, from which time he appears to have retired to private life, not, however, without a word of warning to such as shall follow after: for we see " February 15, 1730," when it was decided to build a new meeting-house, at the request of John Tyler and others, it was put to vote, " whether the town should repair the old Meeting-House, or the town be divided," it being decided in the negative. Whereupon, Deacon John, and his sons, John, Jr., Nathan, Robert and Joseph Tyler, entered a protest.

It is recorded at Mendon that Deacon John Tyler " died of Jandows, 4 May, 1742, aged 90 years," and the place of his interment is yet to be seen, marked by a fine slate slab. We find no probate of his estate; probably, like his father, he settled his earthly possessions while living. For we find (*Boston Deeds*, Bk. 45, p. 148), December 15, 1712, his deed to his son Nathan Tyler (acknowledged, September 18, 1713, and recorded March 4, 1730), conveying the " contents of a two acre right," with a two acre right in all future divisions and town commonage. Also, " 13 Jan. 1723/24 " (*Boston Deeds*, Bk. 38, p. 103), John Tyler, So., of Mendon, grants " the one full & equal second part (the whole into two parts to be divided) of my Homestead whereupon I now dwell, with the one half of the edifices & buildings thereon erected . . . bounded as Mendon records will fully demonstrate," &c., to his " well beloved " son, Joseph Tyler.

The four elder children were born in Andover; the others in Mendon.

CHILDREN:

48   John Tyler, born Aug. 16, 1684; died apparently unmarried, 1753. He lived in Mendon, where he shared in the " 7th Division Lots," being No. 23 in 1719; was constable in 1728; was chosen in 1744 with one other

to care for the "Preservation of ye Deer"; the inventory of his estate was dated May 28, 1753, showing real estate, £144.13.4, and the property was divided among his brothers and sisters and heir of
Bethia.   Nathan was administrator.

49+   Nathan Tyler, born Feb. 17, 1687.

50+   Robert Tyler, born July 19, 1689.

51+   Bethia Tyler, born Feb. 17, 1692.

52+   Mary Tyler, born May 24, 1694.

53+   David Tyler, born June 15, 1696.

54+   Joseph Tyler, born Oct. 21, 1701.

55   Mercy Tyler, born March 26, 1704; was dead in 1753
      when her interest in her brother John's estate was
      awarded her "only heir"; married, Oct. 13, 1732,
      Daniel Hazeltine, of Mendon.

9   SAMUEL[2] TYLER (Job[1]), ("husbandman"), born
in Andover, Mass., May 24, 1655; baptized in John Eliot's
church in Roxbury, Mass., June 4, 1665; died December 17,
1695, in Mendon, Mass.; buried there; married Hannah ——.
"Samuel Tiler's" name is found on the list of those "impressed" at Rowley, November 29, 1675 (at the age of 20.)
He appears to have been assigned to Major Appleton's command, which, under the commander-in-chief, Governor Winslow,
of Plymouth, the following month set out from Dedham, on
the Narragansett Expedition.   A detailed account of the ensuing conflict may be found in many histories.   *Two* of the
reported slain, bore the name of "Samuel *Taylor*," one being
credited to Ipswich, the other to *Rowley*.   It is an undoubted
fact (as suggested by Mr. Bodge in his excellent *Soldiers in
King Philip's War*), that this "Samuel Taylor of Rowley,"
reported "slayne," was in *reality* Samuel *Tiler* of Rowley.   And
it is also quite clear, that Samuel Tiler must have been wounded
in that bitter fight, and left behind; and so, later, reported
dead.   This is further made probable from his subsequent early
death at forty years, while his three brothers all lived to be
over eighty years old, as did his father.   His descendants had
a marked military tendency:—one son of two was a captain;
of his grandsons, one was a lieutenant, one a captain and one
a major-general; among the greatgrandsons, were one captain, one major and one colonel; besides several, meanwhile, in

the humbler "private" ranks. Few families, in proportion to numbers, make as honorable showing.

Bodge (p. 155), further enlightens us, that " Samuel Tiler " was " credited, March 24, 1675/6 . . . £03.07.08." In accordance with the Governor's proclamation, made prior to the fight, that, " if they took the fort and drove out the Indians from Narragansett," the soldiers should have " *a gratuity of land*," as well as wages; we find, in 1728, under " *Narraganset Township No. 3, Souhegan West,* now Amherst, New Hampshire," that " Samuel Tyler," of Andover, through his " son, Ebenezer," plants a successful " claim ": though the land is " drawn " by James Parker (presumably, the legally qualified grantee.)*

Samuel, in all probability, had been with his father at Mendon, when its settlers were driven away, at the very outbreak of Philip's War; and the fact, that *so soon after* he is " impressed from *Rowley,*" lends strong coloring to the supposition, that *Job* Tyler repaired thither, rather than to Roxbury: especially, is this tentative supposition, when we notice the very next recorded item of Job, comes in *1680* at *Rowley.* The fact that Samuel, in his land drawing, is credited with service from " Andover," may lend some basis for assuming that he was living there some time after returning from Philip's War; but in 1682, he was still of " Rowley Village," when, for £30 and a swine, his brother Hope deeded him his fifteen-acre house lot at Mendon, his future home; where, February 9, 1691, for £10, he has from Angel Torry of Mendon, twenty more local acres, upon " Muddie Brooke." In 1685 he paid his first minister's rate there, 16s. 01d.; and not far from this date, undoubtedly took up his homestead, located about a mile south of the present Mendon Center Village. From that time down to about 1830 (the approximate departure of Deacon Nathan Tyler, last of the line in the place), the family " Were all prominent in church and town affairs." Samuel Tyler was chosen surveyor of highways, " 3 Jan. 1686," constable, " 2 Jan. 1687," and again, " 24 Jan. 1689." On Rev. Mr. Rawson's salary

---

* Massachusetts (from first to last) found it necessary to make no less than seven Narragansett "Township Grants," whose names are here given, in order:—Buxton, Me., Westminster, Mass., Amherst, N. H., Greenwich, Mass., Bedford, N. H., Templeton, Mass., and Gorham, Me. Connecticut likewise granted her heroes a single township, which took the name (I suppose, for obvious reason) " Voluntown."

rate, October, 1688/89, we find "No. 33 Job & Sam Tiler . . . £01.s.14.d.04." On a similar rate for 1691, we see "No. 24 Job Tiler & Samuel . . . £01.s.18.d.00." In 1693, Samuel was "tything-man" (the first year the town seems to have elected one.) In 1695, the town, as usual, made two semi-annual rates for the minister; Samuel Tiler's proportion was "county pay" (*i. e.*, in produce), "£00.13.03 . . . Money, £00.03.08." That year, "17 Dec. 1695," came his untimely end. His sincerely sorrowing fellow-citizens bore their young fellow-townsman, shrouded in his plain board coffin, upon their brawny shoulders to the old "Center burying-ground."

A mortgage, in which he was interested, is recorded at East Cambridge, Mass., in Vol. 11, p. 148, bearing date, September 29, 1692, in the sum of £60, payable twelve years afterwards, with interest at £3.10 annually, given by Joseph Wilson and wife, Dorcas, of Malden, being secured upon eight acres of land, house and orchard. It was "discharged" by Samuel's widow, Hannah, September 27, 1704. Two other deeds at Taunton.

Perhaps, like many other Tylers, he died suddenly, for he left no will; "Letters" in his estate being granted the widow, April 9, 1696, upon which date was filed inventory of his property, "£243.10," *Boston, Mass., Probate Book II*, pp. 149, 150.

His widow, Hannah, then of "Rehoboth," October 9, 1704, had a mortgage, in the sum of £12.6.8, from Joseph Tree, of Attleboro; which her son Ebenezer, June 19, 1710, "discharged." (*Taunton Deeds*, Bk. 5, p. 149.)

Boston Prob., Bk. 11, pp. 149, 150. Est. *Saml. Tyler* of Mendon:

Letters of Administration granted unto *Hannah* Tyler, widow of late husb. Saml T. "Husbandman," decsd. 9 Apr. 1696.

An Inventory of the Estate of Samuel Tyler late of Mendon, Dece[d] taken and apprized by us the subscribers, Feb[ry] 25th 1695/6:

	£	s.
His wearing apparrell with a piece of cloth to make up.	3	00
In the inner Room 1 feather bed wth all furniture to it.	5	00

	£	s.
1 bedstead and cord 5/ 1 chest and 2 wheeles 10/..	0	15
In the outer Room, 1 feather bed with all furntiure thereto belonging	5	10
1 small Trundle bed, bedstead and furniture	2	00
A small box with some Linnen in it and a Bible	0	6
Iron Ware: a musket 16/ 3 Iron pots and a box Iron.	1	10
Brass Ware: 2 old kettles and a warming pan	0	12
Pewter: 1 platter & 2 basons and a pot	0	7
In yᵉ chamber: of corne Twenty-five bushells	0	00
In yᵉ Cellar: of provision Beefe and Porke	1	00
Lumber in the cellar & about the house with chaires..	1	2
Wooden Ware: Vizt. Dishes, Trayes and pails with a pʳ of Cards	0	6
Without doors: 9 small swine 2℔ Iron chains, a logg chain & chaines for a horse 1℔. 3 hoes and an ax 6/	3	6
Cart Irons, that is, hoopes and boxes and a ring and staple	1	5
Wheat unthreast in the Barne 2 bushells	0	00
Cattle: 2 oxen and 4 cows and 1 yearling and calfe..	16	00
Six sheep 1℔ 1 horse 10s. Flax undrest the quantity unknowne	1	10
Due to the Estate from Benjamin Wheaton	1	00
Due from Isaac Lenarson	1	00
Linnen Yarne, a small quantity	0	00
Sheeps wool about five pounds	0	00
2 Cow Bells and a cart rope	0	5
Housing & Lands & orchards that is to say a fifteen acre Lot on which the House and Barne stands wᵗʰ all priviledges and Divisions thereto belonging	60	00
A fifteen acre Lot bought of his Broʳ Hope Tyler wᵗʰ all rights & priviledges	30	00
Twenty acres of Land bought of Angel Torrey	10	00
A parcell of Meadow and Upland bought of John Darling, the Upland already sold, but no Deeds given	12	00
A parcell of Meadow bought of Edward Pratt	5	00
Money out at use, for which a House and Land at Maulden is mortgaged, the Mortgage not being out in seven or eight year yet to come	60	00

£   s.

Money in the hands of John Darling not recoverable
yet this seven yeares...................... 20   00

£243   10

Joseph White.
John Mansfield.
Josiah Torrey.

By the Honble William Stoughton, Esqr, Judge of Probate
&c., Hannah Tyler admin^{trx} presented the within written and
made oath that it containes a just and true Inventory of the
Estate of her late Husband Samuel Tyler Dece^d so far as
hath come to her Knowledge. And that if more hereafter
appeares she will cause it to be added.

Jurat Cor. WM. STOUGHTON.

Boston, April 9th 1696.
Exam^d Pr. Is^a Addington Reg^{trius.}

The children were born in Mendon.

CHILDREN:

56+   Ebenezer Tyler, born April 28, 1685.
57+   Mary Tyler, born Feb. 21, 1689.
58   Elizabeth Tyler, born March 17, 1691; married Samuel
        Field(?).
59+   Hannah Tyler, born Feb. 12, 1692.
60+   Samuel Tyler, Jr., born Feb. 26, 1695.

THIRD GENERATION

10 MOSES[3] TYLER (Moses[2]), born Rowley Village (now West Boxford), February 16, 1667; died October 11, 1732; married, January 3, 1694, Ruth Perley, of Ipswich; born 1676; died in Andover, May 10, 1738, but was buried with her husband in Rowley. It is stated in the *History of Boxford* that he moved just within the bounds of Andover about 1698, but in 1703 he is constable in Rowley. His name is on the 1711 Rowley tax list; in 1714 his "Province tax" was "£1.9.3"; he is on the preacher's rate of 1720; in 1722 his "Province tax" is "£0.18.8" and "Minister's rate, £0.15.7.", while in 1726, it is, respectively, "£3.8.11" and "£1.4.5." In 1728 he is selectman there. In 1723, with his brother Jacob, he deeds (recorded 1725, *Salem*, Bk. 45, p. 98), from "Andover," John Johnson, Jr., for £15, 1/4 of a saw-mill, on a river, "*alias* brook, called Cachechorrick"—1/4 part of the iron-work—1/4 part wooden work—1/4 part utensils—1/4 part stream—1/4 part woodyard—1/4 part upper dam—1/4 part ditch from dam to mill for course of water. In 1736, upon the first incorporation of the second church in (West) Boxford, his widow and eldest daughter, Sarah (Porter), were among the "admitted," having requested "dismission" from the First church.

CHILDREN:
61+ Sarah Tyler, born in 1696.
62+ Lydia Tyler, baptized Jan. 7, 1702.
63+ Mary Tyler, baptized Oct. 30, 1709.
64+ Mehitable Tyler, baptized in 1712.

11 CAPTAIN JOHN[3] TYLER (Moses[2]), born in Rowley Village, Mass., September 14, 1669; died June 17, 1756; married, November 14, 1695, Annie Messenger, of Boston; born about 1676; died February 11, 1745. He enlisted and served for five months in King William's War, in 1688, and he was the second of Job's descendants to bear arms, but he is believed

to have acquired his title of Captain as Master Mariner on a merchant ship, and is said to have spent twenty years on the ocean. He lived for a time after his marriage in Charlestown, where the birth of his eldest child is recorded. Not long after, however, he returned to his native place; for we find a deed, of date March 1, 1702/3, from Ephraim Foster, of Andover, blacksmith, in consideration of £70 in silver, paid by " Mr. John Tiler, living in Boxford, Mariner," conveying a house and land in Boxford, upland and swamp ground, and further " one third part of the great swamp * * pond meadow * * little meadow & * * great meadow," being 1/3 of the right therein of Robert Eams, Sr., purchased of Jacob Eams, who had it from his father's estate.

We also find deed to John Tyler, from his father, Moses, dated May 20, 1708 (acknowledged, June 7, 1712; rec. March 1, 1726), conveying 107 acres of Boxford land, "one line running to a Tree in Andover line, about 50 rods from the great Hill End, then to Run Easterly upon sd. line till it meets with Ephraim Fosters Land or line, which is part of the 400 acres of land which was laid out by the Town of Rowley to John Commins, Thomas Dorman & Robert Stiles." His home, now known as the " Captain John Tyler place," in Boxford, is the most ancient family seat of the Tylers thus far identified in Essex County, (Mass.), the old home of immigrant Job, 1640. Job's house must have been among the first built in North Andover (he mortgaged his "house and barn " in " 1650," and land " fenced and unfenced,") but has not been located, and may never be.

The eldest son of Job, " Quartermaster " Moses, settled upon the " Captain John " place (where father Job *probably* passed some later years of *his* life), and was thus one of the first settlers of West Boxford (contiguous to northerly North Andover.) The house at present standing (that is, the *rear part*) was built by Moses' son, Captain John Tyler, *probably* about the time of Moses' death, 1727. Some " bricks " have recently been found buried in the present driveway, which would appear to locate the old fireplace of Moses at a few rods to the east of the present dwelling: and it is not at all unlikely, that when the first house was abandoned for purposes of living, it continued to be used as a storehouse, until it finally passed off the scene in decay. It must have been a very simple structure, judging from reports of the typical first settler's cabin.

Of the many Tylers who have lived in this dear old home, none has left a memory more quaintly attractive than " Aunt Prue," who was herein born, where she passed away at the remarkable age of 100. She was to have been wed in younger days, and the visitor is shown a Bible, the gift of her betrothed; though she did not marry him, nor did she pine away, one may easily see how dear he was in memory—very unusual memory of a love affair that could survive through more than the divinely allotted " three score and ten." Captain John's will provided a room for her " on the lower floor " of his house; she had kept house for him, after his wife died in 1745, until he himself left eleven years later. Gideon, who succeeded Captain John, also died four years before " Aunt Prue." She is buried near by, in the old West Boxford cemetery. Let all Tylers who pass this mound think kindly benediction towards a faithful kinswoman, who longer than any other was familiar to these beloved accustomed paths and haunts.

The present imposing country house is due to the kindly efforts of Gideon Tyler, son of Captain John, who succeeded to the premises upon his father's death. The presence of *three* chimneys (very unusual in so old a dwelling) is accounted for by this interesting bit of history: Gideon had two daughters, Mehitable and Anna (commonly called " Hitty " and " Nanny "), who died aged spinsters, both in September, 1833, at eighty-four and eighty, respectively. Gideon (with a paternal kindness worthy of later day imitation), built for these the west ell, with a single room upstairs and down, where for long years, in well-ordered privacy, they lived comfortably and happily. Upon their deaths, the rooms were closed, and have ever since remained unoccupied.

Captain John's " rear rooms " are very well preserved and quaint, being quite low-posted, with heavy beams exposed to view, and the poem of a cozy fire-place, identical line for line with " The days of auld lang syne." In the front room, too, is a time-honored hearthstone, wherefrom rises the flames of domestic joys upon inclement days.

When in 1800 Gideon died, his eldest son, John, fell heir to the old place; upon whose demise, in 1823, his daughters, Mehitable and Mercy, succeeded to possession. Mercy lived to so recently as 1880, " singly " to her eighty-seventh year. Mehitable survived until 1891, aged ninety-three. Her husband was Captain Enoch Wood (descendant of an ancient Essex County family), who left (among others) a daughter, Rebecca Tyler Wood, and a son, John Tyler Wood, born in 1830 and 1831 respectively, who carry on the premises in the old God-fearing way. Having no living descendants, who shall inherit the old landmark when they shall have gone to their long rest? (Written in 1896).

Captain John appears on the Boxford tax list of 1711; and in 1714 was Selectman, as well as " Constable to gather the Province Tax," wherein his portion was £1.4.6. By 1722 his " Province Tax " had risen to £9.15.10, and his minister's rate the same year was £1.4.6. Evidently he was prospering! In 1726 his town tax was £2.2.11, and minister's rate, £1.3.4. In 1735, upon the formation of the Second parish, he was elected its first treasurer; and May 1, 1737, on dismission from the First church, became, with his wife, a member of the Second church. In September, 1745, with others, he was suspended from " ye special privileges of Sacred fellowship & Communion," for " receiving into their houses Itinerant Preachers & holding meetings in opposition to ye repeated entreaties of their Brethren," &c.; but, April 9, 1747, he made " Confession & acknowledgment," and was reinstated. He appears, like his father, to have been a member of the North Andover church, from records of his " rates " there in 1745, 1747 and 1749.

His will was probated in Salem, Mass., July 12, 1756, Case 28438.

The second (as well as the eldest child) was probably born in Charlestown; the others in Boxford, on the old home-place.

CHILDREN:

65+   John Tyler, born Nov. 6, 1696.
66+   Moses Tyler, born July 14, 1700.
67+   Anna Tyler, born Jan. 1, 1702.
68+   Martha Tyler, born Feb. 5, 1704.
69 ·   Prudence Tyler, born Jan. 15, 1706; died July 23, 1804, unmarried; her headstone says " aet. 100."
70+   Abner Tyler, born Feb. 1, 1708.
71   Joshua, born March 2, 1711; died Feb. 8, 1715.
72+   Gideon, born Dec. 8, 1712.
73   Sarah, born April 1, 1713(?); died in infancy.

74   Hannah, born June 13, 1714; probably died in infancy;
        not mentioned in father's will.
75+   Abigail, born Aug. 2, 1715.
76+   Ruth.

13   EBENEZER[3] TYLER (Moses[2]), born in Rowley
Village, Mass., September 18, 1673; died December 1, 1743;
married Elizabeth Walker, born about 1668; died April 9,
1745; daughter of Richard Walker. He resided in Boxford,
Mass. His name is on the tax list of 1711 in Boxford; also in
1714; in 1721 he deeds thirty-seven acres to his son Samuel.
    May 23, 1744, appears a Q. C. deed (*Rec. Salem*, VI. 94,
p. 104), to which all his surviving children seem to be parties;
wherein Samuel, Nathaniel and David Tyler, husbandmen, of
Boxford, with Elizabeth and husband, Philip Chaplin, of Boston, Susanna Larrabee, of Boston, widow and spinster, " all
children of Ebenezer Tyler, deceased, late of Boxford," quit
claim right in father's land, then possessed by brother Richard,
the former deed thereto not having been properly acknowledged.
There is no probate of his estate.

CHILDREN:
77+   Samuel Tyler, born May 9, 1694.
78   Joseph Tyler, born Sept. 6, 1695; probably died young.
79   Prudence Tyler, born Nov. 4, 1697; probably died young,
        unmarried.
80+   Richard Tyler, born Feb. 14, 1699.
81+   Nathaniel Tyler, born April 4, 1702.
82   Ebenezer Tyler, born Feb. 17, 1703; probably died
        young, unmarried.
83   Elizabeth Tyler, born Dec. 4, 1708; married, May 29,
        1738, Philip Chaplin, of Boston, probably son of
        William and Martha Chaplin; they had no children
        in Boston.
84+   David Tyler, born June 5, 1710.
85   Sarah Tyler, born June 5, 1712; probably died young,
        unmarried.
86   Susanna Tyler, born in 1713; died s. p. in Boxford, June,
        1750; married, June 16, 1737, Jonathan Larrabee, of
        Boston; born in Boston, Oct. 7, 1713; son of William
        and Lydia Larrabee; in 1744 she is recorded as
        " widow and spinster of Boston."

14 JOB[3] TYLER (Moses[2]), born in Rowley Village,
Mass., December 16, 1675; died in Rowley, Mass., in 1754;
married (1), Margaret Bradstreet, born in Andover, Mass.,
February 19, 1674; died before 1736; daughter of Colonel
Dudley Bradstreet and his wife Ann (Wood) Price Bradstreet,
(the widow of Theodore Price); grand-daughter of Governor
Simon Bradstreet of Massachusetts Bay colony and his wife,
Anne (Dudley) Bradstreet; married (2), June 1, 1736, Priscilla Peabody, of Boxford, Mass.; she then eighteen years of
age and he sixty-one; she died s. p.; married (3), September 11,
1747, Mrs. Mary Brockelbank, who died in 1755. All his
children were by the first marriage, and it is fitting to speak of
the grandmother of Mrs. Margaret Bradstreet Tyler, the
gifted Anne Dudley Bradstreet. Reared amid the refinement
and elegances of an English castle (her father, Governor
Thomas Dudley had been steward to the Earl of Lincoln), at
the age of eighteen, she came with her husband, Simon Bradstreet, to seek a home in the wilderness of North America.
She is reputed to be the first American poetess. In Andover,
in the Bradstreet House, built about 1667 by Governor Bradstreet, were born her last three of eight children. This house
has a massive frame of heavy timbers, its walls lined with
brick; its enormous chimney, running up through the center,
shows in the garret like a fortification, and might, with care,
last another half century. Among her descendants may be
named William Ellery Channing, Oliver Wendell Holmes, Wendell Phillips and Richard Henry Dana. Here was born about
the year 1648, her son Colonel Dudley Bradstreet, who lived
to the great age of ninety-four. He was the first person to
breast and mark a turning point to the dreadful delusion of
witchcraft. His only living descendants *are those tracing
through the children of his daughter Margaret and her husband Job Tyler.* This history will show how pertinaciously
the names Bradstreet and Dudley have clung as " given "
names to the descendants of " Margaret and Job." Among
the descendants of their son, William Tyler, is the author of
this volume. Job Tyler was administrator of the goods not
previously acted upon by former administrators of his father-
in-law, Colonel Dudley Bradstreet. (See *Salem Probate Records,* Case No. 3068.) He gave bonds in the sum of £400.
In 1708 Job Tyler had given a receipt to the previous adminis-

trator for £800, being "in part of what is due to me the Subscriber from said estate." In 1709 he gave a receipt for £26, "pr order from Madom bradstreet Relick widdow of the said Collonll Dudley bradstreet in part of what was allowed to her by the Judge of probate in the settlement of Said Estate." In 1706 he was constable of the recently erected municipality of Boxford; selectman in 1716 and in 1744, and served on town and church committees. April 25, 1732, he became one of a committee "to renew the bounds between Boxford & Andover"; and, in 1735, was on the committee of three to oversee and manage the building of the Second (i. e. original West Boxford) church. His will was dated April 26, 1754 and probated December 16, 1754. He lived in Rowley, now Georgetown, and he made numerous land grants.

CHILDREN, by first marriage:
87+   Dudley Tyler, born in 1700.
88+   William Tyler, born July 4, 1701.
89+   Margaret Tyler, born March 24, 1703.
90+   Job Tyler, born Feb. 28, 1705.
91+   Asa Tyler, born April 25, 1708.
92+   Hannah Tyler, born June 5, 1710.

17 JONATHAN³ TYLER (Moses²), born in Rowley Village, Mass., March 8, 1683; married, June 14, 1708, Phoebe Chandler, of Andover. He is on the Boxford tax-list of 1711; in 1714, his "Province tax" was £0.16.10; 1720, on minister's rate; 1722 was Constable to collect Province tax, his share being £0.13.12, with minister's rate, £00.11.11; 1726, his town tax was £1.15.11, minister's rate, £0.12.4. In 1725, he rose to the dignity of selectman. 1712 shows a deed from his father, "for love of my son Jonathan, carpenter, of Boxford," of eighty acres on north of Ipswich road, near Ebenezer Tyler's land, and that of his brother James, "Shaven Crown to Clay Pit Swamp," being one of its boundaries. The last record found (Mass. Archives, Vol. CV, p. 124), exhibits him as one of two petitioners for the town of Boxford, February, 1727. It had been a custom to cut lumber in New Hampshire on the Merrimac, and float it down the river to coast, where it was used for ship-timber; as it was often swept to sea, it involved great losses; wherefore this petition to General Court, to

erect a boom across, just above Haverhill, between Gage's and Griffin's ferries. This being done, we are inclined to think, Jonathan moved to Haverhill, and was a ship-"carpenter." No record of death or will, of self or wife, are found. Like his brother James, he might have gone into Maine, where the record loss by Portland fire,* leaves many a genealogical gap unspanned. His son Jonathan, as will be seen, went to Maine to settle.

CHILDREN:

93+ Jonathan Tyler, baptized in 1715.

94 Phebe Tyler, married, June 3, 1736, Joseph Milliken; lived in Boxford, s. p.

95+ Joseph Tyler, baptized in 1720.

18 JAMES³ TYLER (Moses²), born in Rowley Village, Mass., May 7, 1685; died in June, 1749; married (1), January 19, 1708, Mary (Green) Kimball, who died before 1724; widow of Abraham Kimball and probably daughter of Isaac Green of Salisbury; married (2), before 1724, Phoebe Royall, daughter of John Royall, of North Yarmouth, Me., who was a son of William and Phoebe (Green) Royall, of Salem, Boston, and Dorchester, Mass.

James Tyler was living in "Bradford," January 11, 1716, when he sells land in Cape Porpoise, (Me.), to Jabez Dorman; also, December 14, 1716, when he has land of Nicholas Mooney; also, February 14, 1717, when he has land of Ezra Rolfe. As no wife joins in 1716, she may have died; as she certainly had before 1724, when we find his second wife, "Phebe," joining in conveyances.

By his Rolfe deed of 1716, he acquired land, meadow and marsh, between the Black Poynt River and Saco River, and about this time went to Maine.† Bradbury's *History of Ken-*

---

* The great fire of Portland, Me., *burned all the Probates* from 1760 to 1866. As it was early the county seat of a vast tract, much knowledge thus irreclaimably perished.

†The immigrant Royall had early grants in Maine; "Royall's Side," or "Royall's Neck," were named after him; also, "Royall's River," North Yarmouth. The above John Royall had a brother Joseph, whose daughter, Sarah, in 1710, married William, son of Thomas Tyler of Boston. Thus we find "Royall" used as a Christian name in both the Boston and Andover Tyler lines. Ridlon's *"Saco Valley"* makes the mistake, of placing our James Tyler in the Boston Tyler line of descent. Bradbury's *Hist. Kennebunkport,* because of James' son Abraham, infers, that he came of the (extinct) line of Abraham Tyler of Haverhill.

nebunkport dates his arrival there at about 1715, where he lived at " The Cape," just over the modern short causeway, on the right hand side, on ground in the present hands of the Grant family. The cellar of his removed house has been filled up in recent years; it stood upon a little knoll, which ran down in the rear to water at high tide. Thereafter, for the sake of a mill-site, he removed to a rough wooded piece, near tidewater, some two miles distant, where he built a mill upon " Tyler's Brook " site. Not many rods distant, he built his log house; nothing of which now remains, but some portions of a garden wall: the high rock to the rear of his home, which it sheltered from north winds, is still called " Tyler's Back."

The Collections of the Maine Historical Soc., Vol. III, p. 225, says, " James Tyler came from Cape Porpoise (Arundel) and settled on Blue Point in 1718." *The Hist. of Kennebunkport* says (p. 281), he " changed his place of residence several times after 1720; but finally settled at Scarboro." (He certainly was an active man, and not unlikely was at times forced to be so by the Indians: these broils made the entry and keeping of complete records impossible.) At the first legal meeting (after resettlement), held " Att Arondell, Ela Cape Porpus, on the 31 day of March 1719, being warned by order of a warrant from John Wheelwright, Esq., one of his Maj. Justus of the peac to meet and make choyce of town officers," . . . " James Tyler and Allison Brown " (the latter soon to become a Tyler-intermarriage family), were chosen " haywards or field-drivers." At this meeting, was located " a highway of four rods wide from the western end of the persell of land " lately bought of " James Tyler " *et al.*, " for to build a fort upon, which highway runeth down upon the back of the creek," &c., " near where the pound now standeth, and so," &c., " passes near to montagues neck so called." The third warrant for town meeting (being the first on record) is, " Arondell November, the 5th, 1719. The inhabitants of this town are to take notice that there is to be a town meeting on Wensday the eighteenth day Instant at ten of the clock in the morning at the house of Mr. James Tyler, to Rectifye and Reform some things that have been acted in said town," &c. At the " Nov. 18, 1719 " meeting, is made a " grant unto James Tyler 50 acres of Land anywhere that may be convenient on the Town Common (to be laid no way infringing on any former Grant)."

On town records, in 1719, 1720, are numerous entries of land
laid out by " James Tyler, lot Layer for Arundell "; March
12, 1720, he had a further forty acre grant; May 17, 1720, he
appears as Land-surveyor; and, on 30th, same month, his
name is one of the thirteen made " free Commoners." In 1728,
he alienated to Samuel Preble, " for and in consideration of
one Negro man " certain lands in Kennebunkport.* (This
gives one much such a shock, as felt on viewing the " shelf "
whereupon the old slave used to sleep in Wayside Inn, Sudbury, Mass.) His name appears on a muster roll in *Mass.
Archives,* under Captain Johnson Harmon, from February 28—
November 20, thirty-eight weeks, as " Centinel," (no residence
given; being, probably, in 1721-22.)

The date of his burial, June 8, 1749, is recorded at the
Second (Dunston) church of Scarboro, where he was undoubtedly buried; but patient search fails to find his (or any
other Tyler) stone in the contiguous ground. His will, dated
January 17, 1748, was probated July 3, 1749. (See " *York
Wills*," p. 599.) Inventory, September 15, following, £1920,-
0.3. It has long ceased to be a Tyler center, and the records
are both meager and conflicting. The two elder children were
born in Bradford, Mass., the others probably in Scarboro.

CHILDREN, by first marriage:
96+ Dorothy Tyler, born Dec. 19, 1709.
97+ Abraham Tyler, born March 17, 1712.
98+ Abigail Tyler.

CHILD, by second marriage:
99+ Royall Tyler.

19 JOSHUA³ TYLER (Moses², Job¹), born July 4,
1688; died before May 14, 1735; married, November 13, 1712,
Margaret Lombard, or Lambert, died before July 4, 1775, at
which date her will was probated (*Salem, Wills*, Case 28,448.)
He was a mariner. From Salem Deeds office, we learn, through
Deposition of George Jackson, November 2, 1719, that " one
Joshua Tyler came to my house in Marblehead," and upon en-

---

* Do not confuse with " Kennebunk " (which in later years has been
taken off old Wells), from whose railway station it is about 2½ miles to
Kennebunkport, commonly called " The Cape " (i. e. Porpoise).

quiry what boat it was that "road dangerously out in the harbor," Tyler replied that the Master was sick, and had gone to Salem, and that he (Tyler) had brought her in and taken care of her. Upon being advised to go aboard, Tyler said, " she is safe enough." Upon proceedings in the case in 1724, " Sam Walton, of full age," testifies that " 2 Nov., 1719, he was on board the schooner called the *Restoration,* William Dove, Master, he being a passenger bound for Boston, but the boat being pushed into Marblehead by contrary winds, he heard the Captain order 'mate' Joshua Tyler, as he was getting over the side, to go ashore, being very sick, to take care of the vessel, and, when the wind freshened, to ' veer out more cable' and carry the other anchor. Mate replied, he would take all the care he could. It seems they were bound from North Carolina to Boston." From *The American Weekly Mercury,* May 5, 1720. From *New Jersey Archives,* First Ser. Vol. XI, newspaper extracts, page 49, we get another glimpse of the wanderer: " Custom House, Salem [N. J.] Apr. 23. Entered Inwards [by this time, he seems to have become a Captain], Joshua Tyler, sloop *Dragon* from Virginia."

No record appears of the time and manner of death, which seems to have come at the age of forty-six; his estate being administered at Salem, May 14, 1735, Case No. 28,446. The children were born in Salem.

CHILDREN:

100   Joshua Tyler, born Jan. 1, 1713.

101   Benjamin Tyler, born March 3, 1715; married, Oct. 19, 1740, Martha Liscomb, of Salem, where he seems to have died for Martha Tyler married Thomas Downing in 1744.

102   Joseph Tyler, born June 23, 1719.

103   Margaret Tyler, born June 18, 1723; married, April 24, 1764, Aaron Crumb, of Salem.

104   Mary Tyler, baptized Jan. 21, 1727; married (1), July 2, 1745, Jacob Manning, of Salem; married (2), June 7, 1750, Stephen Webb, born Feb. 13, 1722; died Mar. 24, 1796. By her second marriage, according to her mother's will, Mary had ten children.

20   JACOB[3] TYLER (Moses[2]), born in Boxford, Mass., January 9, 169–; died in Woburn, Mass., March 24, 1778;

married (1), February 12, 1719, Abigail Kimball; born April 12, 1699; died of small-pox March 25, 1722, daughter of Thomas and Deborah Kimball of Bradford; a little slate slab in the old cemetery marks her grave and that of her infant, and is the earliest stone extant in Job's line; he married (2), July 13, 1727, Abigail Foster, born November 22, 1697; died in Woburn, Mass., December 20, 1758; daughter of Jonathan and Abigail Foster; she was in the fourth generation from Reginald Foster of Ipswich. In 1718 his father deeded him one-half of his arable land, meadow, orchard, west end of dwelling, one-half of cellar, one-half of stock and husbandry tools. The death of his wife and child may have upset his plans, for the following year, 1723, he, with his brother Moses disposed of his interest (one-fourth), in a mill and appurtenances upon " Cachechorrick " brook. In 1725, from June 24 to July 7 we find him a " trooper " on Captain Richard Kimball's muster roll (*Mass. Archives.*) In 1727, shortly after his second marriage, his father died, of whose estate he became executor. He inherited in 1727 from his father the remainder of the Andover homestead, where he continued to live until he removed to Woburn. In 1729 he deeded land to one Skales and in 1731 made a grant to Samuel Farnum. Sometime after 1738, he removed to Woburn. His will, dated June 25, 1759, was probated June 2, 1778 (*East Cambridge Records*, case 16,502.) Jacob, having had his portion, gets but £10. Abigail and Mary have each £36 in three annual installments, all the household goods and the privilege of the " east chamber " while they remain single, but if their brother Moses wishes to sell they are to relinquish it on receipt of £2 each. Moses has all the buildings and lands in Woburn, lands in Andover, with rights and interest in common and undivided lands there; also the stock, utensils, monies, etc.; to act as executor and to pay the debts. The inventory was £1,851,4. Jacob and his son, Jacob, Jr., were members of the Andover church, where their children were baptized and in whose old burial ground rest their wives and some of their children.

CHILD, by first marriage:

105   Elizabeth Tyler, born 1719; died April 26, 1722; she and her mother died of the small-pox.

CHILDREN, by second marriage:

106+   Jacob Tyler, born April 16, 1728.

107+   Moses Tyler, born March 5, 1731.
108+   Jeremiah Tyler, born 1733; died Oct. 2, 1755, in camp
       at Lake George; was in Colonel Titcomb's regiment
       in the expedition against Crown Point.
109   Abigail Tyler, born in 1735; a member of the An-
       dover church in 1756.
110+   Mary Tyler, born in 1738.

28   MARY³ TYLER (Hopestill², Job¹), born in Mendon, Mass., January 31, 1669; died before 1733; married, June
30, 1693, John Farnum,* of Andover, Mass., born April 13,
1672; died September 9, 1749, son of John Farnum (Ralph¹);
he married (2), November, 1733, Abigail Marsh, of Bellingham, Mass. He moved to Mendon in 1700/1701. The Far-
nums lived upon the original Tyler homestead in Mendon.
This, as we have already seen, Job deeded, for £60, to his son
Moses, in 1700; which, the following year, Moses to Farnum,
for £1 increase, then of Andover, but soon of Mendon; where
in 1709, Ebenezer Tyler (son of Samuel, Job), for £40, deeds
Farnum most of the "20 acre Smith's lot," quit-claiming at the
same time his interest in "The Fifteen Acre Right, which he,
the said John Farnum is now settled upon, formerly belonging
to his Grand Father Job Tyler, late of said Mendon deceased,
* * * with the housing Barns and Fences thereon Erected
Orchards thereon planted Enclosures Arrable or Pasture or
Meadow Lands therein contained with all the Divisions," etc.
The children were born in Andover, except the youngest.

CHILDREN:

111   Mary Farnum, born in 1694; married, Dec. 5, 1716,

* The year previous to marriage, John Farnum appears to have been
mixed up in the "witchcraft" proceedings; for "*Woodward's Copies of
Court Papers,* Vol. II, p. 152, has the following:—"The deposition of
Abigell marten of Andovr Aged about sixteen years, this deponant tes-
tifyeth and sayeth that some time last winter Samuel wordwall being at
my fathers hows with John ffarnom; J heard said John farnom ask said
wordwall his forteen, which he did and told him that he was in love with
a gurl but should be crost and should goe to the Sutherd which said
farnom oned to be his thought said wordwall further told he had like
to be shot with a gon, and should haue a foall of from his horse or should
haue, which said farnom after oned that he told right. J heard him tell
Jeams bridges his forten that he loued a gurll at fourteen years old
which said bridges oned to be the truth but cold not imagin how said
wordwell knew; for he neuer spake of it; John bridges, father of said
ieams bridges sayeth he heard Jeam say J wonder how wordwall cold teell
so true. *Jurat in Curia,* by both."

Deacon Nathan Penniman, of Mendon, Mass.; born
in Braintree, Mass., 1689; had seven children.

112 Ann Farnum, born in 1696; died April 20, 1696.

113 John Farnum, born Dec. 26, 1697; married, Nov. 8,
1722, Mary Wood, of Mendon, Mass.

114 Ann Farnum, born in 1701; married Joseph Penniman,
born in Braintree, May 29, 1692; had 7 children.

115 Moses Farnum, born in Mendon, Sept. 8, 1705; died in
Uxbridge, Mass., Sept. 8, 1770; married, Nov. 10,
1726, Abigail Sanford, who died Oct. 2, 1773.

29 MARTHA[3] TYLER (Hopestill[2]), baptized at Roxbury, April 9, 1676; died in Groton, Conn., September 18,
1741; married, April 3, 1700, Robert Geer; born January 2,
1676, died November 20, 1742. She was both an accuser and
accused during the witchcraft delusion. They lived in North
Groton (Ledyard). They first attended Preston church, where
their three eldest children were recorded; the wife was admitted
to privileges of baptism there, July 2, 1701, and joined,
March 5, 1704. The parents are buried in Ledyard, in the
ground surrounding the first church; to whose memory, a
modern monument has been erected by their descendants.

" Memorand[m] in m[r] George Burroughs Tryall besides y[e] written Evidences y[t] was Sworn Sev[ll] who gave y[rs] by word of mouth
Majo[r] Browne holding out a heavy Gun wth one hand.

Thomas Ruck of his sudden coming in after y[m] & y[t] he could
tell his thoughts.

Thomas Evans y[t] he carried out Barr[lls] Molofses & meat &c
out of a Canoo whilst his mate went to y[e] fort for hands to help
out wth y[m].

Sarah Wilson Confes[t] y[t] y[e] night before m[r] Burroughs was
Executed y[t] y[r] was a great meeting of y[e] witches Nigh Sarg[t]
Chandlers y[t] m[r] Bur. was y[r] & yy had y[e] Sac[t] & after yy had
done he tooke leaue & bid y[m] Stand to y[r] faith & not own anything.

MARTHA TYLER saith y[e] same wth Sarah Wilson & Severall
others."

" dorritye fforkner and Abigale fforkner children to Abigall
fforknor of Andover now in prison confarsed befor the hon-
oured majastrats upon theire examination heare in Salam the

16 day of this enstant subtember 1692 that thire mother apared
and mayd them witches and also MARTHY TYLER JOHANAH
TYLER and Sarih Willson and Joseph draper all acknowlidge
that thay ware lead into that dradfull sin of witchcraft by her
meanse the fores^d Abigale forknor. The above named persons
each & every one of them did affirm before ye Grand inquest that
the above written evidences are truth 17 sep^t 1692."

CHILDREN:

116   Mary Geer, born in Groton, Conn., May 14, 1701;
       married, Oct. 22, 1720, John Spicer, of Groton, born
       Jan. 1, 1698; died Aug. 28, 1753; son of Edward and
       Katherine (Stone) Spicer, descended from Peter Spicer,
       who probably came from Virginia to Groton, and mar-
       ried Mary Busecott, of Warwick, R. I. John's son
       Edward,—born April 14, 1721, and died Dec., 1797,—
       married for his first wife, Hannah Bill, by whom he had
       seven children. Their daughter, *Mary*, married Ros-
       well Button, and became the ancestor of *Gilbert But-
       ton*, who married Lydia Witter, daughter of Lydia
       Tyler, No. 525.
117   Martha Geer, born March 18, 1704.
118   Robert Geer, born April 5, 1707; his son Amos was
       graduated from Yale College in 1760.
119   Ebenezer Geer, born April 1, 1709; his son Robert was
       graduated from Yale College in 1763.
120   James Geer, born Dec. 7, 1711; died 1755; married
       Sarah ——.

30   JOHN³ TYLER (Hopestill², Job¹), born in Roxbury, Mass., February 19, 1677; died in Boston, May 19, 1705;
married by Cotton Mather, November 2, 1699, Deborah Leatherland, born October 2, 1678; died, his widow, January 1,
1721; daughter of Zebulon² Leatherland (William¹, in Winthrop's fleet, 1630; at Anne Hutchinson's controversy; moved
from Boston to Newport, R. I., where was town clerk). John
was probably buried in King's Chapel burying-ground, with
two infant sons. His wife's stone in that place still exists.
She was administratrix, September 11, 1706. The children
were born in Boston. Children:
121   John Tyler, born Aug. 15, 1700; died Oct. 2, 1702.

122+   Moses Tyler, born July 23, 1702.
123   John Tyler, born Oct. 4, 1704; probably the " ch. Mr. Tiler's bur. 8 Mch., 1705 " mentioned in " Old Sexton's Bill." This child is not mentioned in Hopestill's will.

31   DANIEL³ TYLER (Hopestill², Job¹), born in Roxbury or Andover, Mass., between 1676 and 1681; died, in Groton, Conn., ——; married, May 28, 1700, Anna Geer, born January 6, 1679, daughter of George * and Sarah (Allen) Geer, of New London, Conn. Daniel had land in Groton (where he removed), from his father, including " Tyler Hill."† The children were born in Groton. Children:
124+   Daniel Tyler, born Feb. 22, 1700-01.
125   Sarah Tyler, born Aug. 16, 1702; baptized, Sept. 17, 1704.
126+   John Tyler, born March 24, 1705.
127+   Job Tyler, born Feb. 14, 1710.
128   Zebedee Tyler.

32   HANNAH³ TYLER (Hopestill²), married, December 9, 1697, Robert Buswell, born February 8, 1666-1667; son of Samuel Buswell (Isaac¹ " weaver " of Salisbury, Mass., 1640.) She was accused of witchcraft; they moved to Preston, Conn., where the children were born and baptized and Hannah received into the church, July 22, 1705.

INDICTMENT

Province of the Massachusetts
Bay in New England, Essex.
Anno R. R. & Regina Guillelmii & Maria Anglia &c. Quarto Annoq, Dom. 1692.

* George Geer, born England about 1621 (traditionally son Jonathan of Havitree, Devon), with brother Thomas, left orphan; an uncle deprived them of schooling, and procured a captain to abduct them to Boston, Mass., 1635; whence George was New London settler, 1651. By wife, Sarah Allen (daughter Robert), had 11 children. The 2d, Jonathan's daughter, Dorithy married William Tyler (son Job, Moses, Job), of Willington: the 8th, Robert, married Martha Tyler: the 9th, Anne, married Daniel Tyler *supra.* The old (Ledyard) Geer homestead is still in family.

†(*Groton Deed* Bk. I, p. 41.) This is probably the site of the Daniel Tyler homestead.

The Jurors for our Sov. Lord & Lady the King & Queen Present. That HANNAH TYLER of Andover in the County of Essex aforesaid—SINGLE WOMAN—on or about the Seaventh Day of September and in the year of our Lord 1692 aforesaid and sundry other days & times as well before as after certain detestable arts called witchcraft & sorcery. wickedly Mallitiously & folloniously hath [?] practised & exercifed at and in the town of Andover aforesaid upon & against one Rose ffoster of Andover aforesaid by which said wicked Art the said Rose ffoster the Day & Year aforesaid & divers other Days & times as well before as after was & is afflicted Tortured confounded Wasted & tormented. Against the peace of our Sov. Lord & Lady the King & Queen. Their Crowne & dignity And the Laws in that case made & provided.

INDICTMENT

vs.

HANNAH TYLER, for
bewitching ROFE FFOSTER.

PETITION

To the Honored Generall Court now sitting in Boston this 12 of October, 1692.

Right honored Gentlemen and fathers. We your honored petitioners whose names are under written petition as followeth, viz: We would not trouble your honours with a [————?] but brieffly spread open our distrefsed condition and by Your honore favour and pitty in affording what Relief may be thought convenient as for the Matter of our trouble, it is the distrefsed Condition of our wifes & Relations in prison at Salem. who are a company of poor distrefsed creatures, as full of inward grievances & trouble as they are able to bear up in life withall. and besides that agravation of outward troubles and hardships they undergo: want of food convenient: and the coldness of the winter Season yt is coming may soon dispatch such out of the way that have not been used to such hardships: and besides that the exceeding great Charges & expenses that we are at, Your Mony accounts which will be two tedious to give a particular account of which will fall heavy upon us. especially, in a time of so great charge & expense upon a General account in the country which is expected of us to bear a part as well as others which is put all together upon families and greatly will be brought to Ruin, if it cannot in time be prevented, having spread open our condition; we humbly make our addrefs to Your honors to Grant to our wifes & Relations, being of such that have been approved as penitent Confefsions—might be Returned home to us from that bond Your honors shall agree too, and we do not petition to take them out of the hands of persons but to Remain as prifoners under bond in their own family where they may be more tenderly cared for. and may be ready to appear to Answer charges when the honored Court shall call for them.   We humbly crave your honors favour and Justice for us and our hearin, having left known our troubled grievances before you we humbly pray for Your honors.

Petitioners: John osgood in behalf of Friendship.

John ——— in behalf of his wife.

John Maston in behalf of his wife Mary Maston.

Christopher ofgood in behalf of his daughter Mary Maston.

Jofeph Willson in behalf of his wife.

JOHN BRIDGES *in behalf of his wife & children.*

HOPE TILER *in behalf of his wife & daughter.*

Ebenezer Barker for his wife.

Nathaniel Dane for his wife.

VERDICT

HANNAH TYLER

Records of the Superior Court of Judication, Vol. 1: 1692-1695.

HANNAH TYLER of Andover in the County of of Efsex. SINGLE WOMAN, being Indicted by the Jurors for our Soveraigne Lord and Lady the King and Queen upon their Oaths by Two Severall Indictments. That is to say—1st. That shee the said Hannah Tyler of Andover in the County of Efsex, single woman, sometime in the month of Aprill laft, in the Year of our Lord one thousand six hundred ninety two in the Towne of Andover aforesd Wickedly, Mallitiously and ffeloneously a covenant with the Devill did make whereby she gave both her soule and body to the Devill and signed his booke and promised to hon^r and serve him forever. And unto the Devill did renounce her Christian Baptisme and God and Christ By which *Diababallical* & wicked Covenanting with the Devill as aforesaid the said Hannah Tyler is becom a detestable Witch, contrary to the peace of our Soveraigne Lord and Lady the King and Queen their Crowne and Dignity and the Law in that Case made and provided.

2ly. For that she (the said Hannah Tyler) on or about the seventh day of September last in the year of our Lord one thousand six hundred ninety two aforesaid and on other dayes and times as well before as detestable arts called Witchcraft, and [——]ickedly Mallitiously and feloneously ha[—] used practised & Exercised in the Towne of Andover aforesd upon and against one Rose ffoster of Andover aforesd By which said wicked Arts the said Rose ffoster the day and Year aforesaid & divers other dayes and times as well before as after was and is afflicted Tortured Consumed pined Wasted and Tormented against the peace of our soveraigne Lord and Lady, the King & Queen, and Their Crowne and dignity and the Lawes in the case made & provided.

Upon the aforesd Indictments and each of them, the said Hannah Tyler was then and there before our Justices of our Lord & Lady, the King & Queen aforesd Arraigned & upon her arraignment the sd. Hannah did then and there the said day & Year aforesd plead to them & each of them not—Guilty, & put herselfe upon Tryall by God & her Country. A Jury being called, Nathaniel Howard fforeman, & accordingly sworn, no Exception made by the prisoner, the said Indictments being read together with Evidence & Examinations and the Prisoners defence being heard, the Jury went out to agree on their verdict, who Returning did then and there in open Court deliver their Verdict, That the said Hannah Tyler was not Guilty of the ffelony by Witchcraft for wch shee stood Indicted in & by the said Indictm^{ts} & each of them. The Court ordered Hannah Tyler aforesaid be discharged paying her ffees.

CHILDREN:

129   Moses Buswell, born May 17, 1701; died Aug. 24, 1704.
130   Hannah Buswell, born May 24, 1705; baptized July 15, 1705.
131   Moses Buswell, baptized Sept. 11, 1709.

34 CAPTAIN JAMES³ TYLER (Hopestill²), born in Andover, Mass., December 28, 1683; died in Griswold, Conn., November 2, 1754; married (1), October 8, 1705, Hannah Safford, who died November 24, 1728, in her forty-seventh year; daughter of Joseph and Mary (Baker) Safford, of Ipswich, who owned land in Norwich, Conn.; married (2), September 2, 17— ("Sary Juet"), Sarah Jewett. Nothing is known of the origin of his title, but he is called "Captain" on his tombstone, and in the town records. He lived in the northern part of Preston, Conn., now known as Griswold, where the children were born. His will was dated October 3, 1753, and probated February 25, 1755, in Norwich.*

CHILDREN:

132+ Moses Tyler, born Feb. 19, 1707.
133+ James Tyler, born Dec. 22, 1708.
134+ Hannah Tyler, born Oct. 11, 1711.
135+ Mary Tyler, born Sept. 13, 1714; mentioned in father's will in 1753.
136+ Mehitable Tyler, twin to Mary.
137+ Joseph Tyler, born Nov. 8, 1717.
138 Samuel Tyler, born Feb. 20, 1719; died Dec. 16, 1722.
139+ John Tyler, born Dec. 29, 1721.

35 HOPESTILL³ TYLER (Hopestill²), born in Andover, Mass., October 16, 1685; died October 7, 1762; married, January 25, 1709-10, Anna Gates, born about 1685; died March 27, 1766. He lived in Preston, Conn., where his children were born and with his wife was buried there. "All my Land In the township of preston, with all my housing and shope tols" went to him by his father's will, of which he was a co-executor. Though he had the tools, he did not seem to take to the "smithing" trade of his senior; contented in working his farm, at least a portion of its surface being sufficiently rocky and stony to need more than ordinary attention.

CHILDREN:

140+ Joseph Tyler, born Aug. 4, 1711.
141+ Elizabeth Tyler, born Nov. 4, 1714.
142 Anna Tyler, born Dec. 27, 1716; baptized Feb. 17, 1717.

* He had several grants from his father, one being located on "Pachaug" River.

143   Martha Tyler, born April 9, 1719; baptized May 17,
          1719; married, September 21, 1737, Stephen Downer.
144   Ruth Tyler, baptized July 30, 1721; not mentioned in
          father's will of 1754.
145   Timothy Tyler, born Oct. 12, 1723; probably died
          young.
146+   Abigail Tyler, twin to Timothy.
147+   Caleb Tyler, born May 13, 1726.

49 CAPTAIN NATHAN³ TYLER (John²), born in
Andover, Mass., February 17, 1687; died December 28, 1782;
married (1), March 2, 1715, Mary Read, born August 11,
1694; died August 6, 1742; daughter of Samuel Read,* of
Mendon; married (2), December, 1743, Abigail Maynard, born
1700; died March 15, 1778; daughter of John Maynard of
Marlboro. Her will, probated in Worcester, Mass., April 1,
1778, bequeaths legacies to Thankful Corbett, brother James
Maynard of Westboro, children of brother Daniel of Marlboro,
deceased, and of brother Reuben of Westboro, deceased; brother
Hezekiah, executor. In 1710, March 6, the local records give
his entrance into a long and prominent public service, by mak
ing him one of a committee of thirteen, appointed to see that
swine were " yoked and wringed as the law directs." February
16, 1716, he is mentioned as " Deacon," in connection with a
committee to raise funds for ordination of Rev. Mr. Dorr.
February 16, 1719, he shared in the " Seventh Devision " lots,
as No. 143. May 17, 1721, he protested against the receiving
of " Bills of Credit," which were, when redeemed, " to be burnt
to ashes "; but in 1728, he appeared on Mendon Board of
Trustees, to manage its share (£270) of said Bills. In 1727,
he presented a bill of 4s. against the town. In 1729, '33, '34,
'38, '48, '50, he served as Selectman. In 1730, he was on
committee, to treat with Uxbridge concerning the ministry and
school laws; and the same year, together with his father and
brother Joseph, protested against building the meeting-house

* By her father's (Samuel Read of Mendon), will, she had, in addition
to former gifts, " all that my Land on both Sides of the great River up
Stream of Woodland Thompson, lying in two parcels, with a five acre
right in the Commons of Mendon from and after the Seventh Division,
she paying the Sum of one hundred and fifty pounds to my Executors, in
one year after my decease."

nearer the burying-ground than within twenty rods of the old meeting-house. In 1731, he, and others, were allowed 3/ each, for treating with Uxbridge committee about school lands. In 1732, on committee " to finish that affair with Uxbridge about the school money, according to the former vote "; and later on, made charge of 4/ for the same. The same year, on committee to see the new meeting-house finished. In 1734, under the title of " Ensign " Nathan Tyler, was on a committee, one of whom was to assist the representative in the General Court, in the matter of the Hazelton petition for a new town: which, the following year, was formed, and called Upton, within whose bounds fell the farm of Nathan (which, nevertheless, remained a part of Mendon.)

In 1738, Mendon voted £40, to let fish up Pawtucket Falls, and Captain Tyler was to look after the matter: the same year, he was a grand-juryman. In 1740, on committee for preservation of deer, pursuant to Chap. III, Sec. 4, *Acts of 1739*. In 1741, his name is on petition to make Mill River a " precinct " of Mendon. In 1749 and 1751 he was on important committees. In 1752, '53, '54, '55, he was representative to the General Court. In 1755, August 8 to November 5, was " Ensign " on Crown Point expedition, though at advanced age.

From the foregoing, it is evident that we are treating of a very prominent citizen of early Mendon: his line, in truth, is the most prominent there of all the clan, and for a century and a half furnished descendants conspicuous in that municipality in civil, religious and military annals. He also was largely interested in lands. His will was dated August 25, 1780, and probated May 27, 1783. (See *Boston Deeds*, Book xxxlx, p. 315.)

CHILDREN:

148 Elijah Tyler, born Feb. 25, 1716; died July 6, 1720.
149 Deborah Tyler, born Sept. 19, 1719; died Dec. 20, 1719.
150 Abigail Tyler, born July 30, 1722; died Nov. 30, 1722.
151 Comfort Tyler, born April 26, 1724; died May 22, 1743; married, Nov. 26, 1739, Samuel White, born in Mendon, Sept. 21, 1700; son of Captain Joseph White.
152 Mary Tyler, born April 17, 1727; died April 4, 1728.

153+   Nathan Tyler, born Oct. 31, 1729.
154+   John Tyler, born Sept. 27, 1731.

50   ROBERT³ TYLER (John²), born in Andover, Mass., July 19, 1689; married, December 13, 1721, Hannah Sampson, of Duxbury, Mass., daughter of Stephen Sampson, and grand-daughter of Henry Sampson, who came over in the *Mayflower*. He lived at Mendon, Mass., until the incoropration of Upton in 1735, when he appears to have become a citizen of that town. Doubtless his farm was in that portion of Mendon set off to Upton, as was Nathan Tyler's, but whose farm was allowed to "remain forever in the town of Mendon as heretofore." Robert was a selectman of Upton in 1740. The children were all born in the town of Mendon.

CHILDREN:

155+   Dorcas Tyler, born Sept. 23, 1722.
156+   Zilpha Tyler, born March 22, 1724.
157+   Elijah Tyler, born Nov. 8, 1727.
158+   Hannah Tyler, born Nov. 8, 1729.
159   Robert Tyler, Jr., born June 4, 1735; died Feb. 27, 1736.

51   BETHIA³ TYLER (John²), born in Mendon, Mass., February 17, 1692; married, May 18, 1716, George Woodward, of Mendon. The children were born there. Children:
160   Ebenezer Woodward, born Oct. 10, 1718; died before 1754, s. p.
161   George Woodward, born Oct. 5, 1720; died before 1754, s. p.
162   Bethia Woodward, born June 21, 1722; living in 1753, unmarried, when inheriting land from her uncle John's estate.

52   MARY³ TYLER (John²), born in Mendon, Mass., May 24, 1694; married, June 9, 1720, Samuel Torry; born in Mendon, June 7, 1692; died in Milford, 1753; son of Angel Torry of Braintree. The children were born in Mendon. They had more than are here recorded. Children:
163   Hannah Torry, born April 4, 1721.

164 Samuel Torry, died Oct. 19, 1769; married Sarah
Thwing.
165 Joseph Torry, married Deborah Holbrook.

53 DAVID³ TYLER (John²), born in Mendon, Mass.,
June 15, 1696; married (1), December 7, 1722, Elizabeth
Averill, of Preston, Conn.; married (2), May 26, 1746, Rachel
Brabrook, of Concord, Mass. Records of him are fragmentary.
July 6, 1717 (then 21 years old), he exchanged land with
brother Nathan, 21 acres, etc. (which he likely had of his
father's estate), for 33 acres and 53 rods of land. February
16, 1719, he is No. 33 as sharer in the "Seventh Devision"
of land in Mendon; and the same year, October 9 (*Boston
Deeds*, Bk. XXXIV, p. 121) for £25, has from his kinsman
Samuel Bridges, of Mendon, 30 acres in Mendon. June 3,
1720, for £15, he conveys to brother Nathan 18 acres and 128
rods of land in Mendon, between North Hill and West River.
It is possible that he removed from Mendon to Connecticut, as
his first wife was of that colony, and in 1721 he had a deed to
one hundred acres in Ashford, Conn. At the time of his
second marriage he was probably living in Upton, Mass. He
may have been the sergeant David Tyler, recorded in the *Mass.
Archives*, as having served under Captain Jeremiah Moulton,
January 18 to May 11, 1725.

CHILDREN:

166 Hannah Tyler, born March 4, 1724; married, Jan. 10,
1744, William Green, of Upton, Mass.
167 Elizabeth Tyler, born May 15, 1725.
168 Mary Tyler, born April 10, 1728.
169 Bethia Tyler, born April 13, 1730; married, March
22, 1753, Elias Parmenter, of Upton, Mass.

54 JOSEPH³ TYLER (John²), born in Mendon, Mass.,
October 21, 1701; died in Uxbridge, Mass., December 18,
1779; married (1), Mehitable Hazeltine, of Mendon; died in
Uxbridge about 1754; married (2), September 23, 1756, Mary
Draper, of Roxbury. Not long after attaining majority, January 13, 1723/4 (*Boston Deeds*, Bk. XXXVIII, p. 103), had
grant from his father of one-half of the homestead. In 1730,
together with father and brothers, protested against building

of meeting-house upon site selected, and without money on hand. From about 1733 to 1742 he seems to have been a resident of Sutton, Mass., where several of his children were born. About 1743 he removed to Uxbridge. His estate at Uxbridge consisted, in part, of a five-acre tan-yard and buildings at the Center village, bought of William Adams in 1733, eighteen acres, then called "Egremony Swamp," now Capron's Pond, bought of John Farnum, Sr., 1745—and a farm of about 150 acres, known in recent years as the Benjamin Tucker place. March 25, 1757, he is recorded in the *Mass. Archives* as a member of the train band and alarm list of Captain John Taft's "Second Foot Company." His will was dated December 3, 1778, probated March 2, 1780. The eldest child was born in Mendon, the next three in Sutton and the others in Uxbridge.

CHILDREN, by first marriage:

170   Abner Tyler, born Feb. 15, 1731; was killed in the French War and probably died unmarried.
171   Timothy Tyler, born June 2, 1735; died young.
172+   Joseph Tyler, born May 21, 1738.
173+   Timothy Tyler, born May 21, 1742.
174+   Mehitable Tyler, born Dec., 1744.
175   Ruth Tyler, born Feb. 7, 1751; an invalid and cripple, died unmarried, in 1797; resided in Uxbridge with her brother Solomon.

CHILDREN, by second marriage:

176+   Solomon Tyler, born Sept. 23, 1757.
177   Benjamin Tyler, born July 28, 1759; died young.

56 EBENEZER[3] TYLER (Samuel[2]), born in Mendon, Mass., April 28, 1685; died in Attleboro, Mass., June 28, 1736; married about 1712, Catherine Bragg, born about 1690; died in Attleboro, November 9, 1763. He lost his father at ten, and went with his mother to live in Rehoboth, Mass., where he acts as her agent, in the discharge of a mortgage, in 1710. He deeds, January 13, 1709, to his cousin John Farnum, of Mendon, for £40 (*Boston Deeds*, Book 26, pages 2, 3), about 20 acres in Mendon, they quit-claiming also the "Fifteen Acre Right, which he, the said John Farnum, is now settled upon, formerly belonging to his grandfather, Job Tyler, late of said

Mendon, deceased," claimed by the heirs of Samuel, deceased, son of said Job. The same year, he had a grant of many hundreds of acres in Rehoboth, for £100, from Boston parties. (*Boston Deeds*, Book 6, p. 108, 109, 110). In 1713, he is No. 66 on a division of Cedar Swamp land in Mendon, and in 1735 acquired 349 acres in Ashford, Conn. His gravestone is standing in the rear of the present First church edifice in Attleboro (showing much wear from the elements), which some kind descendant, in recent years, has put upon a substantial base together with those of his wife, his son John and wife and John's daughter Phoebe. The Tylers of this line were prominent in this church, now known as the Oldtown Congregational church of Attleboro, for over a century, and Ebenezer and his wife were undoubtedly members though its records prior to 1740 have disappeared. The old Tyler homestead stood on present Locust street, about one and one-half miles south of Attleboro village; it was burned. The date of his removal to Attleboro is unknown, but it was after 1711. His will was dated May 29, and probated August 9, 1736. He owned considerable land in Attleboro and at least, 650 acres in Ashford.

ATTLEBORO CEMETERY

Right in the center of the modern-built village lies the old burying-ground of ancient Attleboro, which, after the English custom, immediately environs the place of worship. Originally the meeting-house stood on what is called the common, between which and the graveyard runs the railway. A miniature facsimile of the original Lord's house, a few feet in dimensions, stands by the side of the present edifice. The present burying plot is nearly triangular in shape, wherein lie the remains of many scions of the earliest settlers. Most of the stones are of comparatively recent date. Deacon Peter Thacher, one of the early church magnates, and his son Peter, Jr., with their wives and some of their descendants are here entombed.

Ebenezer Tyler, son of Samuel, son of Job, the immigrant, with his wife, Katherine, their son Captain John, his wife, and maiden daughter Phebe, are side by side, with old stones raised onto a common base and their inset in modern renaissance. The older stone showing considerable wear.

CHILDREN:

178+ Ebenezer Tyler, born March 31, 1714.
179   Elizabeth Tyler, born June 15, 1715; died s. p., May 4,
      1777; married (1), Ebenezer White; her father leaves
      Elizabeth White 7½ acres of land and calls her
      daughter; married (2), Joseph Enos, Union, Conn.
180+ Phebe Tyler, born July 2, 1718.
181+ Catherine Tyler, born May 19, 1721.
182   Hannah Tyler, born April 10, 1723; died Oct. 2, 1723.
183+ John Tyler, born Sept. 19, 1724.
184+ Job Tyler, born June 18, 1727.
185+ Hannah Tyler, born Dec. 15, 1728.
186+ William Tyler, born Feb. 22, 1732.

57 MARY³ TYLER (Samuel²), born in Mendon, Mass.,
February 21, 1689; died February 2, 1772; married October
3, 1717, William Balcom, born in Rehoboth, September 3,
1692; died March 30, 1774, son of Alexander Balcom, of
Providence. The children were born in Attleboro, Mass.
Children:

187   Mary Balcom, born Aug. 11, 1718; married John
      Fisher, of Norton.
188   Sarah Balcom, born Aug. 11, twin with Mary, died
      Oct. 9, 1718.
189   William Balcom, born June 21, 1723; died Feb. 21,
      1724.
190   William Balcom, born May 4, 1726; died June 9, 1726.

59 HANNAH³ TYLER (Samuel²), born in Mendon,
Mass., February 12, 1692; died in Rehoboth, Mass., December
1, 1781; married, October 4, 1708, John Wilmarth, born in
Rehoboth, December 11, 1685; died there, July 24, 1774, son
of John Wilmarth. Children:

191   John Wilmarth, born July 5, 1714.
192   Timothy Wilmarth, born May 15, 1717.
193   Rebecca Wilmarth, born Jan. 24, 1719.
194   Thaddeus Wilmarth, born Nov. 23, 1721.
195   Joseph Wilmarth, born Nov. 17, 1723.
196   Ephraim Wilmarth, born June 7, 1726; died 1766,
      had a son Ephraim, who died in infancy.
197   Hannah Wilmarth, born Jan. 13, 1728; died May 31,
      1755.

198   Sarah Wilmarth, born Jan. 11, 1730.
199   Priscilla Wilmarth, born May 26, 1733.
200   Abel Wilmarth, born Oct. 2, 1737.

60   CAPTAIN SAMUEL³ TYLER (Samuel²), born in Mendon, Mass., February 26, 1695; died May 17, 1759; married, December 19, 1719, Mary Capron, born 1696; died January 26, 1780; daughter of Banfield Capron. April 9, 1757, he was Captain of the First company (" South Town ") of the Attleboro train band (*Mass. Archives*). He was selectman of Attleboro, 1724, 1728, 1732, 1737, 1738, 1739, 1747, 1748, 1749, 1750, 1751, 1753, and representative to the General Court, 1737, 1745, 1747, 1748, 1749. His will was dated May 16, 1759, and probated June 11, 1759. He was far the most important early Tyler of the locality. In 1707 (aged but 12), he is on record as sharing, No. 9, in fifth division of Mendon lands; probably, however, it is the *estate* of his father (also named " Samuel "). June 13, 1715, for £100, he acquired land of Matthew Short. His line is distinguished for its military vigor: all his three sons becoming Revolutionary veterans, one being a lieutenant, and another major-general of militia; five of his grandsons also served in the Revolution, thus making eight all told, from this immediate family, of the ten Tylers furnished by the town to that cause.

CHILDREN:

201   Mary Tyler, born Jan. 29, 1719; died June 28, 1724.
202   Samuel Tyler, born May 20, 1720; died April 27, 1724.
203+   Moses Tyler, born May 4, 1722.
204   Samuel Tyler, born Aug. 12, 1724; died Oct. 15, 1748.
205   Benjamin Tyler, born Aug. 11, 1726; died Sept., 1726.
206   Mary Tyler, born March 6, 1728; married David Dexter.
207+   Nathan Tyler, born June 24, 1730.
208+   Huldah Tyler, born Nov. 14, 1733.
209   Habijah Tyler, born May 7, 1735; probably died young, unmarried, not mentioned in father's will of 1759.
210   Elizabeth Tyler, twin to Habijah; married, Dec. 8, 1764, Timothy Read.
211+   Ebenezer Tyler, born May 25, 1740.

FOURTH GENERATION

61 SARAH[4] TYLER (Moses[3]), born in Boxford, Mass., February 16, 1696; married, January 30, 1716, Benjamin Porter, born in Wenham, Mass., 1691-92, died in Boxford, June 30, 1778; son of John Porter. The children were born in Boxford. Children:

212   Moses Porter, born Nov. 18, 1719; died Nov., 1811; married (1), Dec. 3, 1741, Mary Chadwick; later he married two other wives. He had eight children by the first marriage.

213   Mary Porter, born in 1720; married, June 12, 1738, Thomas Chadwick, of Boxford. They had four children.

214   Benjamin Porter, Jr., born Oct. 21, 1721; married Ruth Foster, of Andover. A son (Tyler) sold his grandfather Porter's farm in Boxford, which he inherited and moved to Sebago, Me.; he had a son (Tyler), who was living in Weston, N. Y., in 1853.

215   Sally Porter, born March, 1726.

216   Lucy Porter.

62 LYDIA[4] TYLER (Moses[3]), baptized in Boxford, Mass., January 7, 1702; died in Wenham, Mass., November 2, 1785; married, intention published August 30, 1724, Jonathan Porter, of Wenham; son of John Porter. He was representative to the General Court, 1745, 1746, 1747. Children born in Wenham. Children:

217   Benjamin Porter, born March 12, 1726; married, Mar. 27, 1755, Sarah Rea, sister of Dr. Caleb Rea. A son was Gen. Moses Porter.

218   Mary Porter, born June 29, 1728; married Joseph Low, of Newbury.

219   Ruth Porter, born Jan. 5, 1731; married, 1751, Dr. Caleb Rea, of Danvers, born in 1727.

220   Jonathan Porter, born June 20, 1733; married, in 1760, Mehitable Rea, sister of Dr. Caleb Rea.

221 (Dr.) Tyler Porter, born Nov. 23, 1735; probably died in 1811; published, Sept. 7, 1760, to Dorcas Emerson, of Topsfield, Mass. They had three sons and one daughter.

222 William ("Billy") Porter, born Aug. 23, 1739. He was a Major.

223 Lydia Porter, born Feb. 9, 1741; married Joseph Emerson, of Topsfield.

63 MARY[4] TYLER (Moses[3]), baptized at Boxford, October 30, 1709; died October 29, 1788; married, October 1, 1728, Caleb Cogswell, of Ipswich; son of Adam[3] Cogswell. They removed to Littleton, Mass. Children:

224 Jeremiah Cogswell, born 1732; died April 17, 1820; married, (1), Elizabeth Hall; married (2), Sarah Fletcher.

225 Adam Cogswell, born April 20, 1733; died Christmas Day, 1781; married Sarah Burnham.

226 Ruth Cogswell, married Nathaniel Tuttle.

227 Mehitable Cogswell, married Samuel Hall.

228 Benjamin Cogswell, born Jan. 4, ——.

64 MEHITABLE[4] TYLER (Moses[3]), baptized in Boxford, Mass., 1712; died December 30, 1742; married, April 1, 1730, Isaac Dodge; born in Wenham, Mass., June 7, 1708: son of William Dodge. After Mehitable's death he married (2), Abigail Tyler, No. 75. Children:

229 Samuel Dodge, born in Topsfield; baptized Aug. 20, 1732.

230 Mehitable Dodge, born June 10, 1732; married Amos Milliken. They lived at Sutton, Oxford, Lansingburg and Townsend, Mass.

231 Nancy Dodge, born Dec. 18, 1736; married, Dec. 15, 1757, Stephen Marsh.

232 Moses Tyler Dodge, born June 29, 1739; married, Feb. 11, 1762, Lydia Gibbs; lived in Sutton, Mass.; removed to Charlton, Mass., 1790; seven sons and two daughters.

233 Ruth Dodge, born May 8, 1742; married Caleb Marsh.

65 DEACON JOHN[4] TYLER (John[3]), born in

Charlestown, Mass., November 6, 1696; died in Western (now Warren), Mass.; estate probated in 1790; married Sarah Barron, of Canterbury, Conn., (?), born September 29, 1695, daughter of Isaac Barron, of Chelmsford, Mass. (son of Moses, Ellis, of Watertown, 1641). He was selectman in Tolland, 1746-1751, where he settled. He then went to Western (now Warren), Mass. He was administrator of his father-in-law's estate in 1739. His will was dated August 19, 1784, and son Abner was made executor. The records of his descendants were largely kept by Dr. John Tyler, Bloomfield, Conn. The seven elder children were born in Tolland.

CHILDREN:

234+ Mary Tyler, born Jan. 25, 1722.
235+ Sarah Tyler, born Feb. 18, 1724.
236+ Annah Tyler, born March 12, 1727.
237+ Moses Tyler, born Feb. 25, 1730.
238+ Ruth Tyler, born Feb. 28, 1732.
239+ Prudence Tyler, born Nov. 26, 1735.
240+ Abner Tyler, born 1738.
241+ John Tyler, born ——.
242   Isaac Tyler, born ——; died (will filed Feb. 25, 1810); married widow Margaret (Rockwell) Blodgett, of Stafford, Conn.; settled in Warren, Mass.; had no children; may have married twice, as in his will, dated May 14, 1799, he mentions wife "Lucy," who is executor. He was a farmer, and owned "Pew No. 13 on the floor of the Meeting-house," and "Pew No. 3 in the gallery."

66 MOSES[4] TYLER (John[3]), born in Charlestown, Mass., July 14, 1700; died ——; married, September 25, 1734, Miriam Bailey, of Bradford, born about 1705; died in West Boxford, Mass., September 17, 1781. He was a member of the second company of militia of Boxford in 1757, and belonged to the train band; he was a private soldier. He resided in Chester, N. H., where his five elder children were born, and also in Suncook, Hopkinton and Pembroke, N. H.

244   Hannah, born in 1737 (or 1739).
245+ Adonijah, born in 1739.
246+ Jepthah, born in 1741.
247+ Abigail, born in 1743.
248+ Joshua, born in Hopkinton, N. H.
249   Hespiah. { Possibly were children of Moses, though
250   Nancy.   { nothing further is known of them.
251+ Lucretia, born in Pembroke in 1748.

67   ANNA⁴ TYLER (John³), born in Boxford, Mass.,
January 1, 1702; married, April 3, 1728, John Harris, of Boston, Mass., who died December 18, 1770, aged 68. He is
buried in Copps' Hill burying-ground. Their children were
born in Boston.

Children:

252   Nathaniel Harris, born March 9, 1729.
253   Anna Harris, born Aug. 24, 1731.
254   John Harris, born Jan. 4, 1734.
255   Mary Harris, born Sept. 9, 1736.
256   Abigail Harris, born Oct. 20, 1739.
257   Prudence Harris, born March 2, 1740-1.
258   Job Harris, born March 20, 1741-2.
259   Elizabeth Harris, twin to Job.
260   Rachel Harris, born Oct. 17, 1743.

68   MARTHA⁴ TYLER (John³), born in Boxford,
Mass., February 5, 1704; married in Boston, by Rev. Thomas
Foxcraft, August 18, 1725, Samuel Reade, son of Samuel
Reade, descendant of Richard Read, of Whittlesey, County
Kent, England, who came to America with Governor Winthrop
in 1630; his sons settled in Marblehead, Mass. Mr. Reade
was a landowner, including " Reed Hill " in Marblehead.

Child:

261+ Benjamin Tyler Reade.

70   ABNER⁴ TYLER (John³), born in Boxford, Mass.,
February 15, 1708; died in Brookfield, Mass., December 8,
1777; buried in North Brookfield; married, February 1, 1742,
Hannah Stevens, born in 1719, died November 17, 1789, daugh-

ter of Captain Benjamin Stevens, of Andover, Mass. Abner
went to Brookfield in April, 1747. He was a farmer. He
was paralyzed in 1762, but worked for years afterwards. In
his will, dated September 29, 1773, and probated January 8,
1778, he mentions the "mansion house in which I now live"
and appoints his son John executor and made him residuary
legatee. His two elder children were born in Boxford and the
others in Brookfield.

CHILDREN:

262   Nathan Tyler, born Nov. 14, 1743; died in Warren,
       Mass., in 1759, of small-pox, on his way home from
       the French and Indian War.

263+   John Tyler, born March 13, 1745.

264+   Gideon Tyler, born July 1, 1747.

265   Hannah Tyler, born Feb. 15, 1749; married (pub-
       lished Feb. 27, 1769) Thomas Tufts; moved to New
       York.

266+   Molly Tyler, born Sept. 1, 1753.

267+   Moses Tyler, born March 16, 1756.

268+   Joshua Tyler, born Aug. 12, 1758.

269   Patty (Martha) Tyler, born Jan. 13, 1763; married
       (published May 13, 1781) Dr. John Hibbard, of
       Leicester, Mass.

270+   Nabby (Abigail) Tyler, born Dec. 15, 1765; married
       (published Sept. 7, 1783) Jesse Ayres, of Brookfield;
       they moved to Leverett, Mass., and their descendants
       probably went to Vermont. They had two daugh-
       ters.

72   GIDEON[4] TYLER (John[3]), born in West Boxford, Mass., December 8, 1712; died there, October 7, 1800;
married in 1748, Mehitable Kimball, who died July 4, 1777,
aged 52. He resided on the old Tyler farm in West Boxford.
He was in the second Boxford company of militia, probably
belonged to the train band. In 1776 he was ensign of a
company and was in the Continental Army, and in that year
he was also one of a committee to hire soldiers for "future
public Service." His will, dated September 13, 1792, gives
land to his two daughters, Mehitable and Anna, also, "convenient room in my dwelling house and in the cellar under the
same so long as they live a single life, they not admitting any

family to live with them." They were also to have all household goods and furniture save " 1 bed and my silver tankard."
They and their sister Sarah received £40 each. His son John
had land in Boxford, and his son Jonathan also had land.
John had the buildings, stock, utensils, crops, 1 bed and the
silver tankard, and was to act as executor. John, Jonathan
and Stephen had 6 acres of salt marsh in Rowley. Stephen
had previously received £400. Dean, the third son, received
£5. The estate was valued at $12,076.58, and included 280
acres of land in Boxford and Andover.

CHILDREN:

271   Mehitable Tyler, born Dec. 21, 1743; died Sept. 26,
        1833, unmarried.

272+ John Tyler, born April 1, 1751.

273+ Jonathan Tyler, twin to John.

274   Anna Tyler, born Feb. 16, 1753; died Sept. 23, 1833,
        unmarried. In her will, dated Sept. 11, 1833, she
        distributed land equally among the children of her
        brother, Stephen Tyler, deceased. Sally Tyler,
        daughter of her brother Jonathan Tyler, and John
        E. Gage, his grandson, were also given a piece of
        land. The inventory of the real estate was $665, and
        the personal $460.83.

275   Dean Tyler, born June 3, 1755; died in Marietta, Ohio,
        Oct., 1802. He was a graduate of Harvard Col-
        lege in 1776. He had a brilliant mind, an agreeable
        person and refined manners. He was crossed in love
        and went to Europe, and finding his sweetheart dead
        on his return, he fell violently ill. He went to Ohio
        with the " Ohio Company," who founded Waterford
        in 1789, his lot being 100 acres. The garrison was
        called " Fort Tyler." He was brave and active in
        the community, where he taught school, acted as
        chaplain and was very zealous in repulsing the
        Indians. He died a bachelor.

276   Sarah Tyler, born Feb. 8, 1758; married John Robinson,
        of Andover, Mass., April 3, 1781.

277+ Stephen Tyler, born June 9, 1760.

278   William Tyler, born January, 1764; died aged ten
        months.

75 ABIGAIL[4] TYLER (John[3]), born in Boxford, Mass., August 2, 1715; married, April 12, 1744, Isaac Dodge, widower, who married (1), her cousin, Mehitable Tyler, No. 64. She was dismissed to the First church in Sutton, Mass., October 15, 1749. The three elder children were born in Boxford. Children:

279 Molly Dodge, born March 20, 1745; married, March, 1763, Nathan Stockwell.
280 Isaac Dodge, born April 15, 1746; married Abigail Morse.
281 Prudence Dodge, born Feb. 19, 1747; married Solomon Parsons, Gloucester, Mass.
282 Sarah Dodge, born in Sutton, March 1, 1750; married, Feb. 25, 1771, John Kidder.

76 RUTH[4] TYLER (John[3]), born in Boxford, Mass., married, March 3, 1742, Daniel Hovey, of Sutton, Mass. (*History of Sutton*). The children were born in Sutton. Children:

283 Moses Hovey, born Oct. 28, 1748; died Oct. 29, 1813; married, Aug. 14, 1777, Phebe Tenney, and had ten children.
284 Mary Hovey, born Sept. 16, 1755; married, July 15, 1779, Stephen Humes.
285 Benjamin Hovey, born March 12, 1758.

77 SAMUEL[4] TYLER (Ebenezer[3]), born in Boxford, Mass., May 9, 1694; married, January 12, 1720, Sarah Tenney, of Bradford, Mass., who died in Ashburnham, Mass., in 1778. He was dismissed to the church in Littleton, Mass., January 10, 1747, and is on the poll tax for that town in 1772. Children:

286 Elizabeth Tyler, born May 17, 1722; died Sept. 19, 1736.
287+ Sarah Tyler, born April 9, 1724.
288 Hannah Tyler, born Feb. 25, 1727; died Sept. 13, 1736.
289 Richard Tyler, baptized Oct., 1736.

80 RICHARD[4] TYLER (Ebenezer[3]), born in Boxford, Mass., February 14, 1699; died February 14, 1781; married, February 14, 1726, Elizabeth Lull, of Rowley, Mass. His

name occurs on a list of men belonging to the second company of militia in Boxford, dated April 19, 1757. He probably belonged to the train band. He was a charcoal burner. Children:

290+   Abigail Tyler, baptized April 21, 1728.

291   Elizabeth Tyler, baptized March, 1729; published to Thomas Bodkin, of Marblehead, Mass.

292   Joseph Tyler, baptized Sept. 24, 1732, in East Boxford.

81   NATHANIEL⁴ TYLER (Ebenezer³), born in Boxford, Mass., April 14, 1702; married, May 14, 1741, Sarah Wood, of Rowley, Mass. His name appears on a muster roll, dated Boston, 1755. He was a "Centinel" and the service was from February 9, 1755, to March 31, 1755. In March, 1765, he was dismissed to the church at Dracut, Mass. He was a chairmaker. Children:

293   Jesse Tyler, born April 4, 1742; died Oct. 7, 1748.

294   Eunice Tyler, born Feb., 1743; married, Feb. 9, 1769, Nathaniel Pettingill, 3d.

295+   Betty Tyler, born Sept. 1, 1745.

296+   Nathaniel Tyler, born Oct. 4, 1747.

297   Sarah Tyler, born Oct. 29, 1749; married, March 5, 1772, Joseph Cross.

298+   Jesse Tyler, born March 8, 1752.

299+   Simeon Tyler, baptized Jan. 27, 1754.

300+   Daniel Tyler, born in Dracut, Sept., 1756.

301+   Polly Tyler, born in Methuen, in 1770.

84   DAVID⁴ TYLER (Ebenezer³), born in Boxford, Mass., June 5, 1710; died in Piermont, N. H., aged about 95; married in 1735 Martha Howard, of Lynn, Mass., who also died in Piermont, aged about 95. He was dismissed from the Boxford church, April 14, 1751, to Hebron, Conn., but settled in Lebanon, Conn., in 1751. In the spring of 1768, Daniel Tyler, his son, went to Piermont, N. H., and in the autumn David Tyler, his wife and son Jonathan, came from Lebanon, Conn. In 1781, Jonathan related that the "Northern Army," as he called the famous pest of worms which extended from Northfield, Mass., to Lancaster, N. H., left Piermont so destitute of provisions that, had it not been for an

extraordinary crop of pumpkins and a great quantity of pigeons, they would have had to desert the town. David drew hay on a hand sled on the ice from Newbury to keep the cow, the next winter. The three Tylers, David, Daniel and Jonathan began taking pigeons on the meadow west of Haverhill Corner; in ten days they had taken more than four hundred dozen. At Piermont they had a "bee" for picking them. Those invited had the meat of all they picked, and the Tylers the feathers. In this way they had four beds of those feathers. The six elder children were born in Boxford, and the three younger in Lebanon, Conn.

CHILDREN:

302   Child, born ——; died Nov. 8, 1737.
303   Joseph Tyler, baptized Oct. 29, 1739; died the same day.
304   Lydia Tyler, baptized June 28, 1741.
305   Joseph Tyler, baptized Aug. 28, 1743; died Nov. 18, 1756.
306+   Daniel Tyler, baptized Aug. 11, 1745.
307+   Ebenezer Tyler, born Aug. 8, 1747.
308+   David Tyler, born Nov. 4, 1749.
309+   Jonathan Tyler, born Jan. 1, 1752.
310   Eleanor Tyler, born Feb. 20, 1754.
311   Resign Tyler, born March 14, 1757.

87   LIEUTENANT DUDLEY[4] TYLER (Job[3]), born in Rowley, Mass., about 1700; died in Haverhill, Mass. (will probated June 28, 1790); married (1), November 23, 1738, Phebe Coleman, of Newbury, Mass.; married (2), March 3, 1769, Mary Willson, of Haverhill, whose will was probated April 7, 1794, Job Tyler, her son-in-law, being named as executor. She divided her estate among the children of Job Tyler, her stepson, Joseph Tyler being residuary legatee. Also, her will provided: "In case Cæsar, the negro man who lives with me, should live to be past his labour, then if what my former husband left for him is not enough to support him, that he have his support out of what I give to the said Joseph Tyler." In 1757, Dudley had the rank of clerk in the company commanded by Captain Richard Thurston, was in the train band and on the alarm list. In 1765, he was lieutenant

in the 2d Rowley company in the 3d regiment of militia in
Essex County. He was executor of his father's will. He kept
the Tyler Tavern in Georgetown, Mass., and moved to Haverhill in 1769, where he was a slave-owner as late as 1776, which
is the last date in which negroes are entered in the town valuation lists. In 1780, he donated six shirts to assist in clothing
the army. He was hogreeve in 1773 and 1774; he was surveyor of highways from 1775-1782. In 1776 he was paid for
timber, plank and work on the Mill bridge, £4 10s, and in
1782 he was paid for plank and timber on the same bridge, £1
5s 4d. All his children were by his first marriage. His will
was dated March 5, 1788, and probated June 28, 1790.

CHILDREN:

312+ Dudley Tyler, baptized Dec. 2, 1739.
313+ Thomas Tyler, baptized Feb. 22, 1741.
314 Anna Tyler, baptized Nov. 28, 1742; died in 1754.
315 Phebe Tyler, baptized July 27, 1746; died before 1788;
married —— Pike; father's will showed she had four
children.
316+ Job Tyler, baptized Aug. 28, 1748.
317 Mary Tyler, baptized Feb. 18, 1753; married (1), William Huston, of Haverhill, who was in the Revolution; married (2), —— Pike.
318 John Tyler, baptized Nov. 23, 1755; was a fifer in the
Revolution; seems to have been named as belonging
to the company of Captain Moses McFarland, in
1776, with his brothers, Dudley Tyler as 2d Lieutenant, and Theodore and Thomas Tyler. Also, enlisted April, 1779, served in Captain Benjamin Pike's
Company. Reported as sergeant; enlisted for the
war. In his father's will he is spoken of, in 1788,
" if still alive."
319+ Theodore Tyler, baptized Jan. 22, 1758.

88 WILLIAM⁴ TYLER (Job³), born in Boxford,
Mass., July 4, 1701; died ——; married Dorothy Geer, who
was baptized in Preston, Conn., July 8, 1705; youngest child
of Jonathan Geer, who was descended from the emigrant,
George Geer, whose old homestead is still in the family and who
lived to be 105 years old; Jonathan was a petitioner for the

grant of Preston, Conn., where he lived.   From his will William
received £41, 2s, 6d.   William lived in Willington, Conn., where
the children were born.   (See *Geer Genealogy* for interesting
traditions of the Geer immigrants.)   Children:

320+   Bradstreet Tyler, born June 11, 1725.
321   Mehitable Tyler, born July 15, 1727.
322+   William Tyler, born June 22, 1730.
323   Margaret Tyler, born June 5, 1732.
324   Hannah Tyler, born Dec. 24, 1736.
325   Lucy Tyler, born Jan. 26, 1740.
326+   Jonathan Tyler, born April 12, 1744.

89   MARGARET[4] TYLER (Job[3]), born in Rowley,
Mass., March 24, 1703; died in 1784; married, January 30,
1723, Zebediah Foster, born in Boxford, September 28, 1702;
died in 1772; admitted to the church, January 28, 1728.   Children:

327   Margaret Foster, born July 13, 1724.
328   Lydia Foster, born Feb. 24, 1725.
329   Anne Foster, born May 13, 1728; died April 9, 1748.
330   Zebediah Foster, born Dec. 14, 1730; died Nov. 8, 1734.
331   Abner Foster, born April 23, 1733.
332   Zebediah Foster, born Aug. 25, 1735.
333   Dudley Foster, born Feb. 21, 1737; married, in 1767,
       Rachel Steele, of Andover, and had four daughters.
334   Abigail Foster, born June 25, 1740; married Nathan
       Kimball, Junior, of Boxford.
335   Lucy Foster, born March 25, 1747.

90   JOB[4] TYLER (Job[3]), born in Boxford, Mass., February 28, 1705; died June 1, 1777; married, July 17, 1730,
Elizabeth Parker, of Bradford, who died in Rindge, N. H.,
October 22, 1789, aged 74.   He removed to Rindge in May,
1777.   He was in the second company of Boxford militia in
1757 and on a muster roll dated March 1, 1759, of Captain
Chandler's company of Andover, which marched to the relief
of Fort William Henry.   He was a cordwainer.   All but the
eldest of the children were born in Boxford.   Children:

336   Asa Tyler, born in Bradford, Mass., Feb. 15, 1732;
       died young.
337+   Abraham Tyler, born June 9, 1735.

338+   Phineas Tyler, born Nov. 22, 1736.
339+   Moses Tyler, born Sept. 18, 1738.
340+   Elizabeth Tyler, born Feb. 27, 1740.
341+   Hannah Tyler, born Oct. 4, 1741.
342+   Asa Tyler, born Oct. 23, 1743.
343+   Bradstreet Tyler, born Aug. 27, 1745.
344+   Joshua Tyler, born Jan. 27, 1747.
345   Rachel Tyler, born March 30, 1749; married ——
        Holmes, and lived in Sterling, Mass.
346+   Parker Tyler, born Jan. 31, 1752.
347+   Frances Tyler, born in 1754.
348   Zebediah Tyler, born March, 1761; died March 17,
        1763.

    91   ASA⁴ TYLER (Job³), born in Boxford, Mass., April
25, 1708; "tradition says killed at Lexington and Concord,
1775" (Gage's *History of Rowley*); married, in 1734, Hannah Peabody, born in Boxford April 22, 1714, daughter of
Deacon Nathan and Hannah (Putnam) Peabody. He is on
a list of men of the company commanded by Captain Richard
Thurston, dated June 15, 1757; he is reported as belonging to
the alarm list, and also that he had a tumor in his throat.
Gage's *History of Rowley* says, "Asa Tyler was soldier in the
Revolutionary War." He lived in Rowley. Children:
349+   Margaret Tyler, born June 1, 1735.
350   Nathan Tyler, born Feb. 3, 1738.
351+   Lucy Tyler, born Oct. 1, 1739.
352   Hannah Tyler, born Sept. 3, 1741; married, Aug. 3,
        1763, Moses Tyler, No. 339.
353   Elizabeth Tyler, born April 22, 1746; married, June
        23, 1768, Asa Tyler, No. 342.
354+   Asa Tyler, born Dec. 21, 1748.
355   Priscilla Tyler, born in 1752; died in 1754.

    92   HANNAH⁴ TYLER (Job³), born in Boxford,
Mass., June 5, 1710; married, October, 1728, Captain John
Spofford, of Rowley, born March 19, 1704; son of Captain
John and Dorcas (Hopkinton) Spofford (John², John¹); he
was the fourth John in direct descent. In 1727, he built a
house on "The Hill" in Georgetown, Mass.; thence, in 1737,
to No. 4 (Charlestown), N. H., where he erected the first saw

and grist mill in the town in 1744. The town was burned by
the Indians in 1746, and he was taken prisoner and carried to
Canada. He returned in 1747, and by petitioning to the State
(Massachusetts) he rebuilt the mill in 1757, to which settlers
resorted as far as Lancaster, 124 miles. He was twice elected
selectman. He was one of ten to form the church under Rev.
Mr. Olcutt.

CHILDREN:

356   Eunice Spofford, born Sept. 15, 1729, in " Boxford, in
       the Bay Province."
357   Bradstreet Spofford, born in Rowley, Sept. 2, 1731;
       married, Oct. 16, 1752, Mary Page, of Lunenburg,
       Mass.
358   Phebe Spofford, born in Rowley, July 1, 1733; married,
       in 1750, John Grout, of Lunenburg.
359   Peggy Spofford, born in Rowley, June 30, 1735; mar-
       ried Benjamin Allen.
360   Asa Spofford, born in Rowley, Jan. 30, 1737; was cap-
       tured by the Indians and taken to Canada in 1757;
       exchanged and while in Quebec, on the way home, died
       with the small-pox.
361   Mary Spofford, born in Rowley, Sept. 20, 1739.
362   Abigail Spofford, born March 26, 1741.
363   Relief Spofford, born June 30, 1744; died in 1758.
364   Harriet Spofford, born in Leominster, Mass., Jan. 30,
       1747.
365   Job Tyler Spofford, born March 14, 1749; died June
       15, 1750.
366   Tyler Spofford, born April 28, 1752; died in Lennox-
       ville, Canada, in 1844, aged 90; married Experience
       Crosby. Went through the War of the Revolution,
       and settled at Windsor and Fairfax, Vt., and thence
       in 1799 to Lennoxville, Canada.

93 JONATHAN[4] TYLER (Jonathan[3]), baptized in
Boxford, Mass., October, 1715; died ——; married Rebecca,
whose surname was probably Morse. He was at Haverhill,
Mass., May 25, 1743. Was at the first proprietors' meeting
in New Gloucester, Maine, November 22, 1763; signed a petition there, January 14, 1762; was elected one of a committee
of three to manage the prudential affairs of the town; also

January 16, 1765, was on a committee of three to provide for the ordination of the first minister; January 10, 1764, at "Block House" proprietors' meeting, was elected moderator; also on committee to make sale of saw and grist mill on Royal River; in 1767, he and his wife Rebecca, granted land in New Gloucester to son Jonathan. In the Portland, Maine, Real Estate Records is the following: " Jonathan Millwright and Samuel Tyler, Yeoman, of New Gloucester, April 16, 1773, interested in grant of lands in North Yarmouth, Maine." Descendants of Jonathan say that in 1777 he went from New Gloucester to Buckfield, Maine, with his son-in-law, Abijah Buck. Rev. Paul Coffin, of Buxton, Maine, a missionary to the earliest settlements, records in his journal that Jonathan Tyler built 200 mills; that he lost part of one of his hands and that he was a man of note. Mrs. Tyler was living at Buckfield as late as 1800; she was born at Haverhill, Mass., and had known Hannah Dustin. Children probably born in Haverhill.

CHILDREN:

367+ Phebe Tyler, born about 1740.
368+ Jonathan Tyler, Jr., born July 6, 1742.
369+ Nathaniel Tyler.

95 JOSEPH[4] TYLER (Jonathan[3]), baptized in October, 1720, and probably born in Andover; died in 1778; married, in 1748, Phebe Wood, of Boxford, Mass. He was one of the petitioners, under date of May 25, 1743, to have the easterly part of Haverhill set off into a separate parish. This was the second petition and was successful. Jonathan[3] Tyler and Jonathan[4] Tyler were also signers to this petition. Another petition dated March 28, 1748, concerning the alleged illegal actions of the town meeting of March 1, 1748, was also signed by Joseph. He lived in Haverhill for a time and later moved to Chelmsford, Mass., where he had a house near the head of Pawtucket Falls, but as late as 1749-1750, he was hogreeve in Haverhill. He marched on the Lexington Alarm from Chelmsford, as a private in Captain Oliver Barrow's company, and served ten days. He was in Captain John Ford's volunteer company of Colonel Jonathan Reed's regiment of Massachusetts Militia, in 1777, and served 23 days, and in 1781, he enlisted as a private for three years in Captain Noah

Allen's company of Colonel Joseph Vose's First Massachusetts Bay regiment. The five elder children were born in Haverhill, the youngest in Chelmsford.

CHILDREN:

370+   Joseph Tyler, born April 8, 1749.

371+   Phebe Tyler, born March 23, 1750.

372+   Mary Tyler, born Nov. 17, 1754.

373   Jonathan Tyler, born in 1756; killed in a sawmill, in 1772, aged 16, at Pawtucket Falls.

374+   Nathan Tyler, born in 1757.

375+   Moses Tyler, born in Rowley, Mass., in 1758.

376   Sarah Tyler, born 176— (place unknown); died aged 5 of scarlet fever.

377   Jonas Tyler, born 176— (place unknown); died young, unmarried.

378   Silas Tyler, born 176— (place unknown); died at sea, unmarried, aged about 25.

379+   Sarah Tyler, born in Chelmsford, Oct., 1768.

96 DOROTHY[4] TYLER (James[3]), born in Bradford, Mass., December 19, 1709; died before date of father's will, January 17, 1748, wherein his sons and daughters are mentioned; married —— Lovet. "Abraham Leavitt," of Scarboro, was doubtless her husband. James Tyler has it "Lovet" in his will; therefore it may be the Andover and Mendon line, with previous Tyler intermarriages. It has changed (permanently) in Maine to "Leavitt," where the records are sadly lacking. Child:

380   Sarah Leavitt, born ——, in Scarboro, Black Point, Sept. 25, 1763; she acknowledged the covenant of the Second Congregational church.

97 CAPTAIN ABRAHAM[4] TYLER (James[3]), born in Bradford, Mass., March 17, 1712; died in Frankfort, Maine, February 3, 1807; at the home of his son Dominicus; he was published July 5, 1735, to Esther Sayward, of York, Maine, but no marriage is recorded; married (1), August 11, 1743, Elizabeth Brown, daughter of Allison Brown, of the old Biddeford family of Browns; she was received into the Second Congregational church in Scarboro, June 9, 1745; married (2),

Martha ——, probably of Gorham, Maine; married (3), widow
Sarah Jordan; her maiden name was Grundy (she married [1]
—— Libby; married [2], Captain Jordan); married (4), January 13, 1788, Mary Cumstock, who died in Saco, Maine, November 7, 1839, aged 80. Captain Abraham and his wife
Martha acknowledged the covenant at the Second church in
Scarboro, September 25, 1763. On the 20th of January, 1802,
he made the following deposition: " I, Abraham Tyler, ninety-
three or ninety-four years, testify and do say that I came to
live in Scarboro about seventy years ago." This statement
would make his birth 1708 or 1709 instead of 1712, and the
date of his first going to Scarboro, 1732. Southgate states
that he went there in 1743; it has, however, usually been considered that he lived in Andover, Mass., at the time of his
father's death, in 1749, who speaks of him in his will as a " very
undutiful son." At 19 he went with General Wolfe and
fought on the Plains of Abraham. He received a bullet in
the thigh which was cut out many years after. He was in
the militia in Scarboro. When the news of the Battle of
Lexington reached Falmouth Neck, Maine, before daylight,
April 21, 1775, Abraham Tyler's company marched toward
Boston, but at Welles, Maine, they were advised to remain and
protect the towns on the seacoast, around Falmouth. He
entered the service April 24, 1775, in Colonel Phinney's regiment; the council recommended that he be commissioned by
General Washington in 1775. He was at the Battle of Bunker
Hill and at the siege of Boston. He was in the army for three
years with rank as captain. His journal gives an account of
his movements in the war after the three years of his enlistment
was out. He spent a long and useful life at Scarboro; was
deputy-sheriff of York County; part owner of the old mill at
Saco, and the last person in charge of the ferry at Blue Point.
On the Portland, Maine, records from 1760 to 1870 (110
years), are 22 pages of index to Tyler grants, amounting to
877 entries. Of these, about 80 are under the head of Abraham senior, and Abraham junior. His name is on the Limington petition to build a road, March 21, 1795. His children
were born in Scarboro; they were baptized in the First and
Second churches in that place, except the eldest. His journal
contains an account of his war experiences as follows:

"A JOURNAL OF A. TYLER IN THE REVOLUTIONARY WAR.

"I joined the army at Boston, and was in the whole siege.
"When the eighth month was out, I enlisted for one year.
Then marched for Canida. My time was out the last day of
December, 1776. Then I enlisted for three years under Capt.
Silas Burbank in the Twelfth Massachusetts Regiment, Commanded by Col. Samuel Bauer (Bruer).

"Left the Army—Colo. Sprouts took command, all my
officers are dead—both General and Field, Captains and
Sebolton Officers—except Captain Mains, he was a Lieutenant
—the year 1779. Promoted to a Capt in Sprouts Regiment
and continued during the war. I received an honorable discharge some time in March 1780. Then in order to make up
my losses, I thought I would try the sea. I shipped on Board
of a 20 gun ship Capt Jeremiah O'Brien commander. This
ship was named the *Horrable*—Built in Newburyport—out
about thirty days, and was captured by two of the enemys'
Frigates and then carried in to New York and put on board of
the old ship *Jersey* and remained there three months—suffered
everything but Death. I made my escape by swimming the
second day of December, got on the Island betwixt the two
channels at Hellgate, there we lie in Bushes all the next day.
When it came night we began to walk around the Island to see
what we could find. We found a field of corn where this had
been planted, and we hunted for the gleanings of the field and
found some short nubins—and this we ate raw, and a sweet
morsel it was to us—2 of us only. Then we were at a stand
how to make our escape. The enemy all around us—we hunted
around the Island—found a rail fence and took them and made
a small raft—got each of us a small paddle, which I made
with my knife—then we shipped on board our raft and went
through the whole British fleat that lay oposite the City of N.
York, and got ashore after great effort on the Jersey side. I
was in the siege of Boston. Then went to Canida in '76. Was
in the defeat at Ticonderoga. In the Battle of Hubbardston—
in both Battles taken Burgoine and at the storming of Stoney
Points under Gen. Wayne. Then in the Battle of Monmouth.
All this service I did naked and without pay."

CHILDREN:

381   Hannah Tyler, born June 10, 1744; baptized in Biddeford, June 17, 1744; owned the covenant in Second
Congregational church in Scarboro, Dec. 29, 1771.

382   Allison Brown Tyler, born Oct. 27, 1745; probably died
young.

383+   James Tyler, born June 21, 1747.

384   Abraham Tyler, born Feb. 26, 1749; died Feb. 27,
1749.

385   Elizabeth Tyler, born Aug. 30, 1752; married, Sept.
11, 1777, Allison Brown, son of Andrew Brown, of
Arundel, Maine. They had a daughter who died in
1795.

386   Abraham Tyler, born May 12, 1754; buried July 6,
1756.

387   Humphrey Tyler, born Nov. 2, 1755; estate administered in Alfred, Maine, April 21, 1794, by wife Sarah,
bond £20. Was in the Revolution in his father's
company, during portions of 1775 and 1776.

388+   Andrew Tyler, baptized June 18, 1758.

389   Mary Tyler, baptized Aug. 24, 1760.

390   Abraham Tyler, baptized Aug. 6, 1762; died young.

CHILDREN, by second and third marriages:

391   Anna Tyler, baptized Sept. 25, 1763.

392   John Stephens Tyler, twin to Anna.

393   Sarah Tyler, baptized June 24, 1764; died young.

394   Mary Tyler, born Aug., 1765; married, March 8,
1782, Benjamin Weymouth.

395   Martha Tyler, born in 1766.

396+   Dominicus Tyler, baptized Feb. 15, 1767.

397+   Sarah Tyler, born April 3, 1768.

398   Abigail Tyler, born Sept. 24, 1769.

399+   Abraham Tyler, born Oct. 28, 1770.

400+   John Smith Tyler, born Oct. 2, 1772.

401+   David Tyler, baptized July 20, 1774.

402   Dean Tyler, born March 3, 1776; married, Sept. 16,
1797, Hannah Dyer. He moved to Litchfield, Maine,
about 1800; thence to Bowdoinham, Maine, where he
had deeded him 150 acres Dec. 18, 1802, for $280,
his brother, David Tyler, witnessing the document.

Dean and his wife Hannah quit claim lands at Cape Elizabeth, Maine, Feb. 10, 1804, to Christopher Dyer, mariner, possibly his wife's father. There are no children recorded.

403   Eleanor Tyler, baptized May 31, 1778; died young, unmarried.

404+ Daniel Tyler, born May 28, 1780.

405+ Samuel Tyler, born in 1781.

98   ABIGAIL[4] TYLER (James[3]), born in Scarboro, Maine, probably about 1714; died ——; married, in Scarboro, March 22, 1738, Samuel Walker, of Scarboro. One or both of them were living in 1748. Child:

406   Nathaniel Walker, baptized in Scarboro July 3, 1743.

99   ROYALL[4] TYLER (James[3]), born probably in Scarboro, Maine; he lived and died at Blue Point, Scarboro; married Phebe Berthia ——. He " owned the covenant " of the Second Congregational Church in Scarboro, November 29, 1747, where the baptisms of his children are recorded. In 1763 he came into the possession of " one half of a certain saw mill in partnership with Abraham Leavitt, his brother-in-law, situated on Little River, Scarboro." In a deed to Benjamin Parker, merchant, Portsmouth, N. H., dated January 24, 1770, he is spoken of as " husbandman and mariner," and for £300 grants his interest in lands at Scarboro bought of Sir William Pepperell, and also grants rights under the will of his father. Also, July 20, 1770, one Richard King, of Scarboro, secures judgment against Royal in the amount of £37, 19s, 6d, and " levied upon and sold land, house and barn at Blue Point, left him by his father." He belonged to a company of militia, in Scarboro, in 1757, and was reported on the training band. His children were all born in Scarboro. (The records are taken from the *Portland, Maine, Registry of Deeds.*)

CHILDREN:

407   Phebe Tyler, baptized Nov. 29, 1747; buried May 15, 1749.

408   Berthia Tyler, baptized Dec. 17, 1749.

409+ Joseph Tyler, baptized March 29, 1752.

410   Betty Tyler, baptized Nov. 4, 1758.

411 Phebe Tyler, baptized Aug. 24, 1760.

412+ Samuel Tyler, baptized June 13, 1762.

413 Elizabeth Tyler, baptized April 22, 1764; married, Oct.
     25, 1781, John Sawyer (or Sayre).

414+ James Tyler, baptized Oct. 13, 1782.

415 Eleanor Tyler, twin to James; married Aug. 20, 1801,
     Captain Isaac Thomas, of Saco, Maine, and had a
     large family.

106 CAPTAIN JACOB[4] TYLER (Jacob, Moses, Job),
born in Boxford, Mass., April 16, 1728; died in Chelmsford,
Mass., October 4, 1795; married (1), November 23, 1749, Abigail Bridges, of Andover, Mass., who died June 7, 1752, aged
26; married (2), August, 1754, Lydia Varnum, of Dracut,
Mass. He lived in Haverhill and in Chelmsford. His will
was dated September 11, 1795; probated March 8, 1796. He
was captain of an Andover company in Colonel Bridge's 27th
Regiment of Massachusetts militia, which was, in part, represented at the Battle of Bunker Hill. It is probable that he
was one who marched on the Lexington Alarm, April 19, 1775.

CHILDREN, by first marriage:

416 Abigail Tyler, born November, 1750; not mentioned in
     her father's will in 1795; probably died before, s. p.;
     married, Aug. 3, 1769, John Pearson, Junior.

417+ Jacob Tyler, born May 27, 1752.

CHILDREN, by second wife:

418 John Tyler, born in 1755; died Aug. 16, 1784; probably
     single; buried in the old North Andover cemetery.
     He may have been in the Revolution, though no
     certain record is found.

419+ Lydia Tyler, born in 1756.

420+ Sarah Tyler, born Sept., 1758.

421 Phebe Tyler, born April, 1760; died Nov. 13, 1762.

422 Jeremiah Tyler, born in 1762; died in Chelmsford,
     Mass., in 1796; no child or wife mentioned in the
     probate records. He was a blacksmith. He deeded
     150 acres of land in East Andover, Maine, to Stephen
     Webster, of Methuen, Mass., in 1795. He was execu-
     tor of his father's will, and was to pay the debts, and

receive what was left of the estate, also father's blacksmith tools.

423 Phebe Tyler, born Oct., 1765; she and her sister Sarah were to have what was left of mother's share of the estate, at her death.

424 James Tyler, born Sept., 1768; living in 1795; he received his portion of his father's estate before 1795; he was left one-third of his father's wearing apparel.

107 MOSES[4] TYLER (Jacob[3]), born in Boxford, Mass., March 5, 1731; probably died in Woburn, to which place he removed; married (1), April 17, 1755, Elinor Bridges, of Andover, Mass.; who died January 31, 1766; married (2), June 28, 1770, Anna Munroe, of Woburn, who died March 18, 1781; she was probably a widow, and the daughter of Nathaniel Kendall. (*East Cambridge Probate Records*, Case 9261), who left her 18 acres of land in Woburn, and a share in the residue of his estate. Moses was lieutenant of the first Andover company in 1757, and belonged to the train band. He was in the Revolutionary army three years. The children were born in Woburn.

CHILDREN, by first marriage:

425+ Jeremiah Tyler, born Nov. 20, 1755.

426+ Moses Tyler, born Sept. 12, 1757.

427+ Jonathan Tyler, born June 14, 1760.

428 Sarah Tyler, born Aug. 3, 1762; married —— Pierce; mentioned in brother Moses' will.

429+ Eleanor Tyler, born Aug. 7, 1764.

430 Hannah Tyler, born Jan. 18, 1766; married, Nov. 26. 1797, Caleb Wright, of Boston; family now extinct; mentioned in brother Moses' will.

CHILDREN, by second marriage:

431 Benjamin Tyler, born May 1, 1771; died Sept. 24, 1782.

432+ Jonas Tyler, born May 31, 1773.

433 John Tyler, born April 4, 1775; probably died in infancy in Woburn.

434 John Tyler, born April 4, 1777; died April 29, 1782, in Woburn.

110 MARY⁴ TYLER (Jacob³), born in Andover, Mass., in 1738; died, probably in Woburn, Mass., June 24, 1814; married, October 9, 1760, Samuel Converse, of Woburn, Mass.; born November 23, 1735; died December 2, 1775; son of Josiah and Sarah Converse, (Josiah and Hannah [Sawyer], James, James), an old Woburn family. The children were born in Woburn. Children:

435   Mary Converse, born April 2, 1761.
436   Samuel Converse, born Sept. 2, 1763.
437   Jeremiah Converse, born Aug. 12, 1765.
438   Abijah Converse, born Aug. 23, 1767.
439   Joseph Converse, born Aug. 1, 1769.
440   Lydia Converse, born March 8, 1773.
441   Jacob Converse, born Aug. 30, 1775.

122 MOSES⁴ TYLER (John³), born in Boston, Mass., July 23, 1702; the inventory of his estate was made, in Boston, May 28, 1782; married (1), by Rev. Cotton Mather, July 31, 1723, Margaret Hutchins, who died November 24, 1724, aged 21 years and 8 months; buried in Copp's Hill burying-ground; married (2), February 18, 1730, Hannah Luther. He was probably brought up by his mother's people, the Leatherlands; he was co-administrator of William Leatherland's estate, March 17, 1746. In 1743 he bought an estate of Moses Williams in the north end of Boston on " Fleet and Moon streets." Was admitted to the New North Church in Boston, December 1, 1771. He was a shipwright. In Hopestill's will (of Preston, Conn.), he mentions " My grandson Moses of Boston." The inventory of Moses' estate amounted to £709, 15s, 4d., and includes a dwelling house and land on Ship street in the north end, Boston, £550. The children were born in Boston.

CHILDREN, by second marriage:

442   John Tyler, born Nov. 29, 1731; must have died young.
443   John Tyler, born Nov. 12, 1732; died in Boston, June 9, 1768; married, Sept. 18, 1764, Sarah Compton. His will was dated Jan. 6, 1767, and he was buried in King's Chapel burying-ground. He appears to have left no children.
444+ Moses Tyler, born Nov. 26, 1734.

445   Edward Tyler, born about 1736; his will was probated
        Jan. 27, 1812, mentions no children; married Abigail
        ———. He was probably a naval captain in the Revo-
        lution. He administered upon his father's estate by
        letter of attorney, March 12, 1782. He appears to
        be the spokesman for the family. In his will he
        leaves his wife $15,000.00, the plate and a pew in
        Rev. Mr. Buckminster's " Meeting."
446+   Sarah Tyler, born April 12, 1738.
447   Deborah Tyler, born July 23, 1739; must have died
        young.
448+   Hannah Tyler, born June 24, 1742.
449+   Elisha Tyler, born April 16, 1744.
450+   Ellis Tyler, born Sept. 16, 1745.
451   Deborah Tyler, born Nov. 15, 1747; not living Aug.
        20, 1795; probably died s. p., as no children are men-
        tioned in her brother Edward Tyler's will; married,
        Sept. 26, 1765, Benjamin White.

    124 DANIEL⁴ TYLER (Daniel³), born in Groton,
Conn., February 22, 1700-1701; died in Brooklyn, Conn.,
February 20, 1802, aged 100 years, 11 months, 15 days; married (1), in Canterbury, Conn., December 31, 1722, Jane Cady,
born in Groton, Conn., April 1, 1706; died in Brooklyn (then
Canterbury), Conn., May 1, 1741; daughter of Daniel Cady;
her family came from Groton, Conn., to Canterbury, Conn.;
she is interred with Daniel and his other wives in the Brooklyn
cemetery; married (2), in Canterbury, September 16, 1742,
Mehitable Shurtleff, born in Plympton, Mass., August 30,
1716; died in Brooklyn (then Canterbury), May 17, 1769;
daughter of Thomas and Phebe (Shaw) Shurtleff, of Plympton; married (3), Mary Herrick, of Prescott, Conn. Daniel,
throughout his long life was an active and useful member of
society, closely identified with the growth of the church and
the town of Brooklyn, where he lived. The church edifice of
1733 as well as that of 1770-1771, was constructed under his
oversight. The second church, built at his expense and that of
several others, was pronounced " a very genteel meeting-house,"
and he was soon after on a committee " to pew the church."
In 1750, on condition that they should mend the glass in the
first meeting-house, he and Israel Putnam (" Old Put ") were

permitted " to replace the hindmost slats below with pews for their private use, if they spile not above two seats on a side." His will was dated October 14, 1797, and his son Daniel was executor; his son Asa was to have his wearing apparel. By his three wives he had 21 children, and at the time of his death 6 children were living and he had upwards of 50 grandchildren and 120 great-grandchildren. These facts are mentioned on his gravestone, and the following lines given:

> " Altho one hundred years I've seen,
> My life was short, t'was all a dream."

CHILDREN, by first marriage:

452+ Mabel Tyler, born June 30, 1724.
453   Elijah Tyler, born April 19, 1729; not mentioned in father's will with the other heirs and had probably died young.
454+ Asa Tyler, born March 5, 1731.
455+ Amy Tyler, born Dec. 10, 1733.
456+ Lucy Tyler, born Nov. 13, 1735.
457   Job Tyler, baptized July 8, 1739.
458   Elisha Tyler, baptized Sept. 21, 1740.

CHILDREN, by second marriage:

459+ James Tyler, born July 25, 1743.
460+ Elizabeth Tyler, born Dec. 15, 1744.
461   William Tyler, born Aug. 6, 1748; died Sept. 13, 1754.
462+ Daniel Tyler, born May 21, 1750.
463   Leah Tyler, born June 30, 1752.
464+ Zilpha Tyler, born June 28, 1758.

Of the 21 children born to Daniel[4] Tyler the names and dates of birth of eight are unrecorded, nor is it known to which of his wives these unrecorded children belong. They doubtless died in infancy.

126   JOHN[4] TYLER (Daniel[3]), born in Groton, Conn., March 24, 1705; baptized April 28, 1706; died ——; will dated April 15, 1791; presented for probate July 5, 1791; married Elizabeth ——. He settled in Canterbury, Conn., where his children were all probably born. Oliver was executor

of the will, and Zebulon appears to have appealed. He was
an Ensign in the Colonial Wars, and lieutenant of the train
band of Groton. The inventory of estate amounted to £395,
9s, 4d. Children:

465   Zebulon Tyler, born March 11, 1736; living in 1791,
        when he appealed from his father's will; married,
        April 17, 1766, Betty Adams. In 1770 he was one
        of three Tylers " adjacent to Brooklyn " who recom-
        mended the building of a church.
466+   Phineas Tyler, born May 17, 1738.
467   Oliver Tyler, born March 2, 1740; died June 4, 1750.
468   Prudence Tyler, born Feb. 16, 1742.
469   Betty Tyler, born April 11, 1745; married Simon New-
        ton.
470   John Tyler, born April 30, 1748; died Jan. 20, 1770.
471+   Oliver Tyler, born Jan. 2, 1754.

127   JOB[4] TYLER (Daniel[3]), born in Groton, Conn.,
February 14, 1710; died ——; married, August 25, 1732,
Bial Williams. He lived in Groton. He was commissioned as
Ensign of the fourth company or train band, October, 1744.
In October, 1777, he was Lieutenant of the 10th company of
the 5th regiment and on the alarm list. Children:

472   Solomon Tyler, born Jan. 25, 1754.
473   Anna Tyler, born Oct. 6, 1739.
474   Amy Tyler, born March 5, 1742.
475   Molly Tyler, born March 29, 1744.
476   Job Tyler, born April 18, 1746.
477   Bial Tyler, born July 28, 1748.

132   CAPTAIN MOSES[4] TYLER (James[3]), born in
Preston, Conn. (now known as Griswold), February 19, 1707;
died in Preston, January 22, 1787; married (1), November
20, 1729, Mary Belcher, who died April 19, 1742, in her 31st
year; married (2), November 11, 1742, Joanna Denison,
daughter of Samuel Denison, of Stonington, Conn. (George[2],
George[1]), born December 13, 1715; died February 6, 1786.
He resided in Preston. He was a man of force of character
and considerable worldly success, and owned several farms, on
one of which he built a " mansion house," in 1755, which remained in the family until 1835, and is still standing. He was

deputy from Preston in 1760, 1761 and 1769. His son-in-law, Benjamin Coit, writing to Nathaniel Cove, in 1786, says of the kinsfolk in Preston: "Our friends are generally well, except Father Tyler, and he is much better than he has been. The poor old man appears to be as anxious about the world and the things thereof as ever he was, and as careful about giving and squandering his estate." The inventory of his estate was made March 30, 1787, and amounted to £2916, 10s, 9d. The first part of his will was made in 1779. A codicil was dated July 18, 1785, and further reference to it was made on June 16, 1786. (See *Norwich Probate*, Book 8, page 12.)

CHILDREN, by first marriage:

478+   Mary Tyler, born Sept. 12, 1730.
479   Moses Tyler, born July 10, 1732; died Sept. 28, 1751.
480+   Elisha Tyler, born Aug. 5, 1734.
481   Hannah Tyler, born March 25, 1736; married John Smith, of Stonington, Conn.
482+   Sarah Tyler, born Sept. 30, 1738.
483+   Esther Tyler, born Dec. 9, 1740.

CHILDREN, by second marriage:

484   Elijah Tyler, born Dec. 2, 1743; died Sept. 17, 1746.
485   Thankful Tyler, born Sept. 27, 1745; died Oct. 6, 1746.
486   Elijah Tyler, born Sept. 19, 1746; died young.
487   Daniel Tyler, born Sept. 24, 1747; died April 16, 1752.
488   Lucretia Tyler, born Sept. 19, 1749; died April 19, 1752.
489   James Tyler, born Sept. 28, 1751; died Nov. 4, 1754.

133   CAPTAIN JAMES[4] TYLER (James[3]), born in Preston, Conn. (present town of Griswold), December 22, 1708; died in Preston, March 10, 1736; married, October 7, 1731, Hester Bishop, of Lisbon, Conn. Children:

490   Hester Tyler, born Sept. 9, 1732; probably died young; not mentioned in her grandfather James' will, in 1753.
491+   Samuel Tyler, born Aug. 21, 1734.

134   HANNAH[4] TYLER (James[3]), born in Preston, Conn., October 11, 1711; died in 1797; married, January 30,

1738, William Denison, born in 1705; died in North Stonington, Conn., where he lived, January 29, 1760; son of William Denison (John[2], George[1]). The inventory of his estate was £2268, 17s, 8d. (He married (1), Hannah Burrows, who died January 5, 1737.) Children, by second marriage:

492   Nathan Denison, born Feb. 24, 1739; died May 28, 1742.

493   Daniel Denison, born July 20, 1740; married Martha Geer.

494   Amy Denison, born March 27, 1742; married Thomas Swan.

495   Ann Denison, born Sept. 12, 1744; married George Palmer.

496   Esther Denison, born April 23, 1746; married John James.

497   Sarah Denison, born Feb. 7, 1748; married John W. Geer.

498   John Denison, born Nov. 5, 1749; married Abigail Minot.

499   Elijah Denison, born Nov. 6, 1751; married Mary Geer.

136   MEHITABLE[4] TYLER (James[3]), born in Preston, Conn. (now Griswold), September 13, 1714; died before the date of her father's will, October 3, 1753; married, November 22, 1732, Joseph Freeman. Her children are all mentioned in their grandfather's will. Children:

500   Daniel Freeman.

501   Mary Freeman, born Aug. 10, 1735; married Samuel Leonard, and had children.

502   Mehitable Freeman.

503   Anna Freeman.

504   Hannah Freeman.

505   Elizabeth Freeman.

137   DEACON JOSEPH[4] TYLER (James[3]), born in Preston, Conn. (now Griswold), November 8, 1717; died in Preston, October 13, 1807; married, September 24, 1741, Anna Stephens, of Plainfield, Conn.; born in 1719; died January 22, 1805. He lived in Preston. He may have been the " Ensign " of the Preston company " to be sent against his

Majesty's enemies at Cape Breton," in February, 1745; in which case, he was probably Ensign in 1752, also. Children:

506   Anna Tyler, born 1742.

507   Anna Tyler, born in 1743; died Aug. 31, 1746.

508   Joanna Tyler, born in 1745; died April 24, 1752.

509+   Joseph Tyler, born April 11, 1748.

510   Amy Tyler, born June 27, 1750.

511   Anna Tyler, born Oct. 27, 1752; married, Feb. 14, 1711, Ebenezer Freeman.

512   Joanna Tyler, born Oct. 1, 1754; married, Oct. 15, 1775, Thomas Cheeseborough, of Stonington, Conn.

513+   James Tyler, born May 18, 1757.

514+   Zuriah Tyler, born Aug. 25, 1759.

515   Stevens Tyler, born in 1762; died Feb. 3, 1781.

139 GENERAL JOHN[4] TYLER (James[3]), born in Preston, Conn. (now Griswold), December 29, 1721; died there July 29, 1804; married, December 14, 1742, Mary (Spalding or Spaulding) Coit, born in Plainfield, Conn., July 7, 1716; died November 11, 1801; daughter of Thomas and Mercy (or Mary) (Welch) Spalding (or Spaulding), and great-granddaughter of Edward Spalding (or Spaulding), of Chelmsford, Mass., the first settler of the name in New England; widow of Joseph Coit, who died July 21, 1741; son of Rev. Joseph and Experience (Wheeler) Coit, of Plainfield; by this marriage she had two daughters, Elizabeth and Mary. General Tyler's services in the Colonial and Revolutionary wars were varied. He was appointed lieutenant of the 3rd company or train band of the town of Preston, his commission being signed October 30, 1752, by Governor Roger Wolcott. In the campaigns of 1756, 1759, 1760 and 1764 he was successively appointed lieutenant, captain-lieutenant, and captain in various companies and regiments which were raised to defend the country against the French and Indians. His commissions were signed by Governor Fitch. In the last campaign he was under Lieutenant-Colonel Israel Putnam. When the Revolutionary War broke out he was commissioned, May 1, 1775, as lieutenant-colonel of the 6th regiment, his commission being signed by Governor Jonathan Trumbull; he was also captain of the 2nd company, recruited from New London, Hartford and Middlesex counties. He remained on duty in New Lon-

don until June 17, 1775, when the troops were ordered to the Boston camp. In 1776, he was appointed colonel of the 10th regiment of the Continental army. After the siege of Boston, at which he was present in General Spencer's brigade, he went to New York with his regiment. He succeeded Gurdon Saltonstall as brigadier-general of the 3rd brigade of militia, June 5, 1777, and served in that capacity in Rhode Island on state alarms under General Sullivan and engaged in the attempt to dislodge the British from Newport, in 1778, and was at the battle of Long Island, August 29, 1778. During the New Haven alarm in 1779, he commanded the militia along the east coast of New Haven, and during a part of that year was at New London and Groton. When the Revolutionary army was disbanded the soldiers could not get their pay, nor had they for a long time received any; there is a tradition that General Tyler used his own money and paid off his soldiers. At the close of the war he returned to his old home in Preston (now Griswold), where his old house is still standing, in 1907. He lived for 21 years after the war. He began a career in the General Assembly of Connecticut at the age of 35, and served as follows: 1756, 1758, 1759, 1763, 1767, 1770, 1773, 1774, 1775, 1783, 1787. He was also justice for five consecutive years following 1773, in and for the county of New London. General Tyler's tomb is in the old cemetery at Griswold, he having bought a right in the Wheeler and Coit tomb. The inventory of his estate was $20,220.81. His children were born in North Preston. His will was dated April 25, 1798, and the codicil (after his wife's death), November 20, 1801. (See *Norwich Probate Records*, Book 10, p. 358.)

CHILDREN:

516+   Mehitable Tyler, born Oct. 18, 1743.

517   James Tyler, born May 18, 1746; died Sept. 4, 1750.

518   John Tyler, born April 30, 1748; died May 19, 1752.

519   Abigail Tyler, born July 23, 1750; died April 19, 1789; married Captain Nathaniel Lord, of North Preston, who died June 30, 1806; they had a family, their oldest son, Hezekiah, being named in his grandfather's will.

520+   Olive Tyler, born March 22, 1752.

521+   John Tyler, born July 22, 1755.

522+ Lydia Tyler, born Oct. 5, 1758.

140 DEACON JOSEPH[4] TYLER (Hopestill[3]), born in Preston, Conn., August 4, 1711; died there April 30, 1792; married, November 22, 1750, Lucy Utley, of Stonington, Conn., born in 1726; died May 7, 1811; daughter of Samuel[3] and Hannah Frink Utley (Samuel[2] and Sarah Assbe; Samuel[1] and Hannah Hatch.) Elder Walter Hatch, the emigrant, John Frink, of Ipswich, John[2] and Valentine[1] Prentice, of New London and Roxbury, were ancestors of Lucy Utley, whose name was sometimes given in the records as " Uklie." Joseph lived on the old homestead in Preston. Children:

523 Lucy Tyler, born Sept. 26, 1756; married Asa Meech.
524+ Elizabeth Tyler, born May 27, 1758.
525+ Lydia Tyler, born Oct. 20, 1760.
526 Abigail Tyler, born May 25, 1762; married, Dec. 23, 1779, Hazard Hall (Hull?), of Ashford, Conn.
527 Desire Tyler, born April 22, 1764; died Sept. 10, 1769.
528+ Joseph Tyler, Jr., born Dec. 29, 1766.
529+ Eunice Tyler, born Sept. 20, 1768.
530 Desire Tyler, born May 11, 1772 (1770); married, April 23, 1789, David Allyn, of Groton, Conn.

141 ELIZABETH[4] TYLER (Hopestill[3]), born in Preston, Conn., November 4, 1714; baptized November 7, 1714; died ——; married, March 26, 1730, Christopher Tracy, of Preston. She was admitted to the Preston church August 8, 1735. Her children were born in Preston. Children:

531 Ruth Tracy, born May 18, 1730.
532 Desire Tracy, born March 10, 1736.
533 Christopher Tracy, born Dec. 18, 1737; died young.
534 Ammi Tracy, born Nov. 18, 1739.
535 Eunice Tracy, baptized Jan. 13, 1740.
536 Jonathan Tracy, born April 29, 1742.
537 Christopher Tracy, born Nov. 15, 1743.
538 Elizabeth Tracy, baptized Jan. 20, 1745.

146 ABIGAIL[4] TYLER (Hopestill[3]), born in Preston, Conn., October 12, 1723; married, December 17, 1745, Christopher Denison, born in North Stonington, Conn., in 1719; son of William Denison (John[2], George[1]). Children:

539   Mary Denison, born Oct. 13, 1746; baptized March 27, 1748.
540   Anna Denison, born June 1, 1748; married in Preston, Aug. 14, 1772, Jonathan Sweet.
541   Nathan Denison, born Nov. 3, 1749.
542   Amos Denison, born Dec. 20, 1751.

147   CALEB[4] TYLER (Hopestill[3]), born in Preston, Conn., May 13, 1726; died there, February 7, 1812; married, December 17, 1760, Hannah Barnes, of Groton, Conn.; she died February 16, 1816, aged 80. Children:
543+   Hannah Tyler, born Feb. 15, 1762.
544   Mary Tyler, born July 25, 1763; died April 15, 1765.
545+   Lucretia Tyler, born Nov. 12, 1764.

153   COLONEL NATHAN[4] TYLER (Nathan[3]), born in Mendon, Mass., October 31, 1729; died in Uxbridge, Mass., February 25, 1784; married, June 2, 1757, Mrs. Mary Salisbury, of Bristol, R. I., who was joint executor of his will, in 1784. She received one-third of his personal estate and a life interest in one-third of his lands. In 1756 he was a lieutenant at Fort William Henry, and also on the expedition to Crown Point, in that year. In 1758 and 1759 he was a captain of a company; he is recorded as of the train band and was on the alarm list of Mendon in the same years. He was commissioned lieutenant-colonel of the 3d Worcester County regiment, June 12, 1776, and commissioned as colonel of the same regiment, June 17, 1779. He engaged in service in Rhode Island at different times. He lived in Mendon until some time between the years 1763 and 1766, as the three elder children were born there; the next three children were born in Upton, Mass., and the two younger in Uxbridge. Here he seems to have bought the tanyard property of Joseph Tyler, in 1775, and settled in the town as its first lawyer. He was probably the first lawyer in the south part of the county. He appears to have been a man of good standing in the community, but very little is known of his private life.

CHILDREN:
546+   Nathan Tyler, born Sept. 24, 1758.
547+   Mary Tyler, born May 29, 1761.

548+   Royal S. Tyler, born June 11, 1763.

549+   Martha Tyler, born July 5, 1766.

550   Abigail Tyler, born Oct. 20, 1768; died Jan. 31, 1774.

551   Daniel Tyler, born Sept. 15, 1772; died Jan. 11, 1774.

552   Elizabeth Tyler, born in 1775; she received £80 from father's estate, and is mentioned in her brother Nathan's will.

553   Benjamin Tyler, born in 1778; received one-half of his father's lands.

154 CAPTAIN JOHN[4] TYLER (Nathan[3]), born in Mendon, Mass., September 27, 1731; died there, September 27, 1788, killed by the falling of a tree; married (1), November 30, 1763, Anna Morse, who died March 23, 1772, aged 26; married (2), April 30, 1778, widow Urana (Thayer) Bates. He was captain of a company in Colonel Joseph Read's regiment, in the Revolution, and he joined the regiment at the camp in Roxbury, January 19, 1776. The inventory of his estate was made October 29, 1788, and was £1990, 14s. He left no will. He was a farmer in Mendon, where his children were all born. Children, by first marriage:

554   Anna Tyler, born Sept. 5, 1764; died, unmarried, in Sutton, Mass., in 1791; her will was filed Aug. 18, 1791, and her brother Dr. John Tyler, of Westboro, was named as executor.

555+   John Eugene Tyler, born April 10, 1766.

CHILDREN, by second marriage:

556+   Joseph Tyler, born Feb. 12, 1779.

557+   Abigail Tyler, born Dec. 15, 1781.

558+   Nathan Tyler, born Feb. 22, 1784.

559+   Aaron Tyler, born June 8, 1786.

560+   Mary Tyler, born July 10, 1789; died early; married John H. Reed, of Northbridge, Mass., born October 8, 1775; son of Thomas Reed. He moved to Snow Hill, S. C., and taught in an academy and died there April 27, 1828. They had a daughter, and after the mother's death the child was taken by Aaron Tyler, the mother's brother, where she died early, s. p.

155 DORCAS[4] TYLER (Robert[3]), born in Mendon,

Mass., September 23, 1722; married, in Upton, Mass., January
28, 1739, Ebenezer Fisk, born in Wenham, Mass., July 2, 1716;
died in 1804; son of Ebenezer Fisk, descended from Symond,
Lord of the Manor of Stadhaugh, Suffolk, England. He was
among the first settlers of Shelburne, Mass., but resided also
in Upton, Grafton and Hardwick, Mass.; was the first town
constable of Shelburne, in 1768. Among his descendants were
seven ministers. Children:

561   Dorcas Fiske, born Oct. 17, 1740.
562   Elizabeth Fiske, born Jan. 28, 1743.
563   Jonathan Fiske, born Sept. 17, 1746; married Hannah
       Rice.
564   Ebenezer Fiske, born Sept. 9, 1749; married Sarah
       Barnard.
565   Levi Fiske, born Sept. 16, 1751; went through the
       Revolution.
566   Abigail Fiske, born Oct. 7, 1755; married, Nov. 26,
       1782, Samuel Barnard, and moved in 1793, to Waits-
       field, Vt.
567   John Fiske, born in Grafton, Sept. 27, 1757; married
       Anna Leland.
568   Simeon Fiske, born in Hardwick, July 15, 1762; mar-
       ried Dinah Whitcomb.
569   Moses Fiske, born Sept. 13, 1764; married Hannah
       Batchelor.

156 ZILPHA[4] TYLER (Robert[3]), born in Mendon,
Mass., March 22, 1724; married (1), Daniel Fisk (Daniel,
Samuel, William, John, William, Robert, Simon, Simon, William, Symond), born in Wenham, Mass., June 17, 1718; died
in the Revolutionary army; he lived in Upton and Holliston,
Mass.; married (2), —— Aldrich. The Upton records give
the death of widow Zilpah Aldrich as occurring June 10, 1806,
at the age of 82. Children, by first marriage:

570   Robert Fisk, born Feb. 24, 1746; married Mary Hall.
571   Zilpha Fisk, born April 16, 1753; married, Jan. 26,
       1792, Peter Forbush, of Upton, who was in the
       Revolution.
572   Hannah Fisk, born in Upton, March 28, 1756; died
       July 17, 1837; married in Upton, Jan. 27, 1778,
       Isaac Nelson, son of Lieutenant Jonathan Nelson,

of Upton and Ann Jones his wife. Isaac was in the
Revolution; killed by the fall of a tree Dec. 12, 1812;
had five children (Anna, Syntha, Zilpha, Jonathan,
Lois). *Zilpha Nelson,* married Colonel Elijah Stoddard, of Upton, an important man in Worcester
county; they had eight children, of whom *Isaac Nelson Stoddard,* was the second; he married Martha
Le Baron Thomas, of Plymouth, and they had twelve
children, of whom *Francis Russell Stoddard* was fifth;
he married Mary Frances Baldwin, and has a daughter, May Baldwin (Stoddard) Yeomans, and a son,
Francis Russell Stoddard, Jr.

573   Submit Fisk, born Oct. 27, 1758; married, June 25,
       1778, William Putnam, of Upton.
574   Daniel Fisk, born 1759; died Jan. 22, 1841; married
       (1), Hannah Rockwood; married (2), Hannah
       Palmer.

157 ELIJAH[4] TYLER (Robert[3]), born in Mendon,
Mass., November 8, 1727; married, September 14, 1749, Ruth
Owen, born in Braintree, Mass., October 9, 1727; daughter of
Benjamin and Hannah (Adams) Owen, of Quincy, Mass.;
Ruth was first cousin to President John Adams, and through
the Adams family was descended from John Alden and Priscilla
Mullen. Elijah was a soldier in the French and Indian wars,
in 1755, as a sergeant in a company commanded by Captain
John Fry, on the expedition to Crown Point, and again, 1758,
enlisted in Captain Nathan Tyler's company. He resided in
Upton, where all his children were born, but in 1772 he was
in Chesterfield, Mass., and he removed to Windham County,
Vt., in 1800, with son Stephen and grandson Ephraim.

CHILDREN:

575   Anna Tyler, born Sept. 24, 1750; married, Aug. 16,
       1769, Amariah Taft.
576+   Nathan Web Tyler, born Oct. 14, 1752.
577+   Stephen Tyler, born June 9, 1754.
578   Catherine Tyler, born Sept. 10, 1756; married Isaac
       Bullard, who was in the Revolution and who removed
       to Montrose, Pa.
579   Eunice Tyler, born Dec. 10, 1758.

580   Ruth Tyler, born Feb. 27, 1761; married John Bullard, who was in the Revolution, and in 1836 resided in Buckland, Mass.

581   Hannah Tyler, born May 4, 1763; married —— White.

582+   Moses Tyler, born June 10, 1766.

583+   Sally Tyler, born in 1768; baptized in Chesterfield, Mass., Sept. 27, 1772.

584+   Simeon Tyler, born in 1770.

158 HANNAH[4] TYLER (Robert[3]), born in Mendon, Mass., November 8, 1729; married, February 4, 1755, Francis Nelson, born in Rowley, Mass., September 10, 1722; son of Deacon Samuel Nelson; moved to South Upton (then part of Mendon), with father, in 1734. His emigrant ancestor came from Rowley, Yorkshire, England, in December, 1638. He was constable and collector for Rowley in 1751; selectman in 1752, and highway surveyor. The children were born in Upton. Children:

585   Stephen Nelson, born April 29, 1756; died Feb. 1, 1829; married Azuba Taft, daughter of Matthew Taft, and moved to Buckland, Mass.; had three children.

586   Anna Nelson, born June 30, 1757; married John Brown, of Uxbridge; had two daughters.

587   Elijah Nelson, born Jan. 9, 1759; moved to Buckland, Mass., and had a son.

588   Asa Nelson, born Nov. 10, 1760.

589   Joseph Nelson, born Jan. 10, 1763; died April 27, 1843; married Abigail Dean, Dec. 24, 1789, who died Nov. 26, 1824; he remained at home with his father and had six children.

590   Hannah Nelson, born March 18, 1770; married Daniel Alexander, of Upton.

591   Abigail Nelson, born May 6, 1774; married John Taft, born Feb. 6, 1773; moved to Ohio.

172 LIEUTENANT JOSEPH[4] TYLER (Joseph[3]), born in Sutton, Mass., May 21, 1738; died in Townshend, Vt., in 1815; married, January 31, 1761, Ruth Reed, born in 1733; died in Townshend, July, 1825; daughter of Deacon Samuel Reed, of Uxbridge, Mass. He was in the French and Indian Wars from Uxbridge, and in the Revolutionary War he was

in Captain Fletcher's company at "Ti" and Bennington, and in the last-named battle he was disabled and returned home, and was granted a life pension. He settled in Townshend, Vt., and began his "clearing" in 1763, and built a log hut in the dense woods; he was the first settler. For the first three years he returned to Uxbridge winters. All the fifteen families in the place turned out with hand sleds to help his family in from Brattleboro, when they came in 1767, and drew them over the ice of the river to their home, as there was no path. He was one of fifteen to form the first Congregational church. In 1775 he was nominated by Cumberland County representatives as first major of a regiment of Minute Men, confirmed by New York Committee of Safety, in 1776; he was a delegate from Townshend on the committee of safety June, 1776-1777. In 1781 he was a member of the Vermont board of war. He favored and worked for the sovereignty of Vermont and was on committee of eleven to secure signers in opposition to Great Britain. He was a very conscientious, stern man and made many enemies. Great Britain set a price on his head. He was appointed justice of the peace by the state, twenty years from 1786. He was the first town clerk of Townshend, at its first meeting, May 30, 1771, and afterwards town treasurer, selectman and representative to the Vermont General Assembly. His home was in the east part of the town. The three elder children were born in Uxbridge, the others in Townshend.

Children:

592+ Lydia Tyler, born Aug. 7, 1762.

593 Zacheus Tyler, born May 1, 1764; died in Townshend, in 1771, aged 7.

594+ Betsey Read Tyler, born Sept. 1, 1766.

595 Ruth Tyler, born Aug., 1767; died in Townshend, July, 1791.

596+ Joseph Tyler, born April 11, 1771.

597 Mehitable Tyler, born June 9, 1774; died, s. p., in Cambridge, Vt., November, 1843; married Thaddeus Murdock.

173 TIMOTHY[4] TYLER (Joseph[3]), born in Sutton or Uxbridge, Mass., May 21, 1742; died, probably in Townshend, Vt., in 1775; married (1), in Westmoreland, N. H., July 3,

1769, Sarah White, of Putney, Vt., born June 3, 1742; and died s. p.; daughter of Thomas White, of Leominster, Mass.; married (2), December 10, 1774, Susanna Fisher (or Fish), of Mendon, Mass. A splinter in his hand caused his death before the birth of his son. He moved to Townshend, where he had several real estate transactions, about 1770. Child:

598+ Timothy Tyler, born in Mendon, May 11, 1775.

174 MEHITABLE⁴ TYLER (Joseph³), born in Uxbridge, Mass., December, 1744; married, November 18, 1771, Ezra Holbrook, of Townshend, Vt., where he cleared a large farm. He was at the battle of Bennington. She was an expert needlewoman. The children were all born in Townshend. Children:

599   Abner Holbrook, a farmer, married Sarah Lee, and had seven children.

600   Sally Holbrook, married Reuben Nichols and had seven children.

601   Arbe Holbrook, shoemaker and farmer; married Philena Hazelton, and had nine children.

602   Jared Holbrook, married Chloe Dunton; had six children.

603   Mehitable Holbrook, died unmarried; a teacher many years.

604   Ursula Holbrook, died unmarried, was the housekeeper at home.

605   Ezra Holbrook, twin to Ursula, died in young manhood.

176 SOLOMON⁴ TYLER (Joseph³), born in Uxbridge, Mass., September 23, 1757; died there, November 7, 1810; married (1), February 17, 1781, Mary Archer, of Uxbridge; born in 1761; died there, July 17, 1808; daughter of Benjamin Archer; married (2), June 28, 1809, Jerusha (Wood) Newell, born in 1765; died September 26, 1834; widow of Solomon Newell. He was a farmer and resided in Uxbridge, where the children were all born. He was in the Revolution, in 1780, in Captain Thaddeus Read's company, in Colonel Nathan Tyler's 3d Worcester County regiment. Children, by first marriage:

606+ Joseph Tyler, born Jan. 8, 1782.

607+ Kelita Tyler, born Feb. 5, 1784.
608+ Melinda Tyler, born Feb. 7, 1786.
609+ Royal Tyler, born Aug. 2, 1788.
610+ Parker Tyler, born Nov. 14, 1790.
611 Emery Tyler, born Aug. 30, 1792; died Jan. 25, 1814.
612+ Benjamin Tyler, born Feb. 22, 1796.
613 Mary Tyler, born Oct. 25, 1797; died March 30, 1798.
614+ Timothy Tyler, born July 16, 1799.
615+ Solomon Tyler, born July 18, 1802.
616+ Mary Tyler, born April 17, 1804.

CHILD, by second marriage:
617+ Newell Tyler, born April 12, 1810.

178 CAPTAIN EBENEZER[4] TYLER (Ebenezer[3]), born in Attleboro, Mass., March 31, 1714; died at sea; he was a sea-captain; married, November 16, 1740, Anne Crawford, daughter of Captain John Crawford. He had 50 acres in Attleboro, and a home lot in Providence, from his father. They lived in Providence, R. I. In 1744, Captain John Crawford gave Ebenezer a deed of 150 acres in Providence, "being lot bought by grantor's father from William Olney; also 80 acres," etc. In 1759 Ebenezer deeds to his wife "for love," etc., house and lot. In 1796, "Ann Tyler, widow of Ebenezer, mariner, late deceased," "for love," etc., in a series of deeds, grants real estate in Providence to her four daughters.

CHILDREN:
618 Martha Tyler, was unmarried in 1796.
619 Hannah Tyler, unmarried in 1796; probably died, aged 75, Sept. 26, 1824, as recorded in Providence *Gazette*.
620 Amy Tyler, married, Sept. 24, 1769, Dexter Brown, of Providence, R. I., son of William Brown.
621 Mary Tyler, married, May 4, 1766, James Arnold.

180 PHEBE[4] TYLER (Ebenezer[3]), born in Attleboro, Mass., July, 1718; died in Ashford, Conn., in 1807; married Ichabod Ward, of Ashton, Mass. When she was over 14 years old, her father being dead, she chose Hezekiah Peck, of Attleboro, as her guardian. She had 100 acres of land from her father's estate, in Ashford, Conn. Child:

622   Molly Ward, born in Attleboro, March 8, 1752; married, Jan. 7, 1773, at Ashford, Conn., Dr. Thomas Huntington, born in Norwich, Conn., Jan. 13, 1745; son of John Huntington.

181 CATHERINE[4] TYLER (Ebenezer[3]), born in Attleboro, Mass., May 19, 1721; died in Middlefield, Mass., August 4, 1810; married David Robbins, born in Attleboro, July 21, 1717; son of John Robbins. She had 140 acres of land in Ashford, Conn., from her father. Catherine chose her uncle, Samuel Tyler, as her guardian, December 21, 1736. The children were born in Attleboro. Children:

623   Priscilla Robbins, born June 4, 1741.
624   Job Robbins, born May 27, 1743.
625   David Robbins, born July 25, 1745.
626   Sarah Robbins, born July 29, 1747.
627   Betty Robbins, born Sept. 20, 1749.
628   Hannah Robbins, born Sept. 2, 1751.

183 CAPTAIN JOHN[4] TYLER (Ebenezer[3]), born in Attleboro, Mass., September 19, 1724; died there January 11, 1794; married, October 10, 1745, Anna Blackington, born in 1722; died August 23, 1793; daughter of Pentecost Blackington, Jr., of Attleboro, and Rebecca Figgett. John had the homestead in Attleboro at his father's decease, and his wife had a legacy of £200 from her father's estate. On an order for wages, dated July 5, 1775, he appears as a captain in the Revolutionary army. He marched on the Lexington Alarm, April 19, 1775, and he also marched on the alarm of the battle of Bunker Hill, in which battle he was a participant. The Tyler families of Attleboro furnished ten men for the Revolution. In 1774 he was one of seven judges of a " Superior and Inferior Court to hear and determine controversies that have arisen or may arise in this town." His children were born in Attleboro.

CHILDREN:
629+   John Tyler, born April 25, 1746.
630+   Elizabeth Tyler, born Jan. 14, 1747.
631+   Nanne Tyler, born July 14, 1754.
632   Phebe Tyler, born Aug. 19, 1756; died unmarried, Nov. 26, 1818; joined the 2d Congregational church in Attleboro in 1800.

633+   Experience Tyler, born July 12, 1758.
634+   Ebenezer Tyler, born Sept. 8, 1760.
635+   Othniel Tyler, born April 4, 1763.

184   LIEUTENANT JOB⁴ TYLER (Ebenezer³), born
in Attleboro, Mass., June 18, 1727; died in Ashford, Conn.,
February 24, 1800; married, October 6, 1757, Martha Chaffee,
born in 1734; died April 8, 1796; buried in Westford Village,
Ashford. He was probably lieutenant of the 10th company
of the Alarm list of the 5th regiment of the Connecticut militia,
in 1777. His military career is not very well known. His
father left him 200 acres of land in Ashford, Conn., about
1736, and when he became a man he probably removed there.
At all events, he is "Job Tyler of Ashford, Conn.," when his
own will was dated, September 24, 1796. His inventory is
$1,161.85, and includes 84 acres of land and buildings. He
probably gave land to his sons during his lifetime.

CHILDREN:

636   Ebenezer Tyler, born Dec. 27, 1757; probably died
          young.
637+   Samuel Tyler, born April 12, 1759.
638   David Tyler, born Aug. 8, 1761; died aged 18 or 19.
639+   Comfort Tyler, born Feb. 22, 1764.
640+   Job Tyler, born March 12, 1770.
641+   John Tyler, twin to Job.
642   Catherine Tyler, born Feb. 12, 1773; married (1), be-
          fore 1796, —— Bingham; married (2), ——
          Thompson; married (3), —— Seymour, perhaps of
          Ashford; she had two daughters.
643+   William Tyler, born Oct. 4, 1775.
644   Martha Tyler, born ——; died 1852; married, after
          1796, Samuel Chapman, perhaps of Ashford; had
          several children; she resided in Onondaga County,
          N. Y.

185   HANNAH⁴ TYLER (Ebenezer³), born in Attleboro, Mass., December 15, 1728; married Ebenezer Freeman,
born in Attleboro, April 7, 1727; died there September 8, 1775;
son of Ralph and Sarah (Capron) Freeman. She had £100
from her father's estate. Her children were born in Attleboro.
Children:

645   Anne Freeman, born May 1, 1750; died June 15, 1750.
646   Eunice Freeman, born April 10, 1752.
647   Catherine Freeman, born Feb. 15, 1755.
648   James Freeman, born Dec. 12, 1757.
649   John Freeman, born May 23, 1760.
650   Toby Freeman, born Sept. 2, 1763.
651   Hannah Freeman, born Sept. 17, 1766.
652   Ebenezer Freeman, born Sept. 29, 1771; died Aug. 31, 1775.

186   WILLIAM[4] TYLER (Ebenezer[3]), born in Attleboro, Mass., February 22, 1732; died in Providence, R. I., November 2, 1816; married Mehitable Potter, born June 5, 1741; died June 23, 1812; daughter of Joseph Potter of Providence. William was a hatter and lived in Providence, where he sold a lot of land, in 1761, for £1200. He received from his father's estate 209 acres of land in Ashford, Conn. His children were born in Providence. Children:

653+   Catherine Tyler, born Nov. 12, 1762.
654   Joseph Tyler, born March 14, 1766; died July 20, 1772.
655   Phebe Tyler, born Nov. 30, 1770; died July 12, 1772.
656   Joseph Tyler, born Nov., 1772; died April 28, 1843, s. p. in Providence; married (1), Mary ——; married, (2), a widow. He was a hatter.
657+   Phebe Tyler, born Feb. 16, 1775.
658   Betty Tyler, born March, 1777; died Oct. 26, 1778.
659+   Betsey Tyler, born in 1780.
660+   John Tyler, born Dec. 7, 1784.
661+   Phila B. Tyler, born Dec. 31, 1787.
662   Phineas Tyler, died in New York City about 1850; married (1), Phila Benson; married (2), Miss Welch, of Eliot, Maine; think he lived in Kittery, Maine, a long time; had children.
663+   William Tyler.
664   Sallie Tyler, married (1), —— Spears; married (2), —— Cornell; had a daughter by first husband, and a son and daughter by second husband.
665+   Nancy Tyler, born July 15, 1784.
666   Mehitable Tyler, married Michael Anthony, a sea cap-

tain of Cincinnati, and they had three sons and two
daughters.

203   LIEUTENANT MOSES[4] TYLER (Samuel[3]),
born in Attleboro, Mass., May 4, 1722; died there, October 9,
1804; married (1), Patience Ide, born April 26, 1724; died
November 15, 1756; daughter of Benjamin and Elizabeth
(Black) Ide; married (2), January 28, 1758, Thankful Read,
of Attleboro, died August 25, 1816, aged 83; daughter of
Captain Daniel and Elizabeth (Ide) Read. He was lieutenant
of the 1st company of the 4th regiment of the Bristol County
(R. I.), militia, in 1776. Early in life he was sergeant in the
Attleboro company of militia, and belonged to the train band
and alarm list. His will was dated July 9, 1793, and probated December 4, 1804. The inventory of the estate was
$3409.51. He lived in Attleboro and all his children were
born there.

CHILDREN, by first marriage:
667+   Chloe Tyler, born July 14, 1745.
668   Mary Tyler, born Oct. 4, 1746; probably died young.
669   Patience Tyler, born April 2, 1748; probably died
       young.
670   Samuel Tyler, born Aug. 5, 1749; probably died young.
671+   Moses Tyler, born May 20, 1751.
672   David Tyler, born June 16, 1754; died young.

CHILDREN, by second marriage:
673   Thankful Tyler, born Jan. 5, 1759; published in 1784
       to Timothy Perry, of Westford, (?); perhaps resided
       in Wrentham. She had £9 left her in father's will,
       being in addition to other previous gifts.
674+   Zelotes Tyler, born April 8, 1760.
675+   Zuriel Tyler, born Jan. 22, 1762.
676+   Rufus Tyler, born March 28, 1764.
677+   David Tyler, born Aug. 13, 1766.
678+   George Tyler, born Oct. 12, 1768.
679   Huldah Tyler, born Oct. 31, 1772; had £9 left her in
       her father's will, in addition to other previous gifts.
680+   Judson Tyler, born June 4, 1776.
681   Tirzah Tyler, born March 30, 1780; had £21 left her
       in her father's will, in addition to previous gifts from
       him.

207   NATHAN[4] TYLER (Samuel[3]), born in Attleboro, Mass., June 24, 1730; died there, December 28, 1790; married, March 22, 1753, Rebeckah Esty, daughter of Samuel Esty, of Stoughton, Mass.   In 1757 he belonged to the Attleboro company of militia, and to the train band.   He was a private in the 4th Bristol county regiment, 1776-1777.   His estate was probated April 1, 1791, and the inventory was £21, 19s.   His son Samuel acted as administrator.   The children were born in Attleboro.   Children:

682+ Mary Tyler, born April 26, 1755.

683   Hannah Tyler, born Nov. 12, 1756; published Jan. 26, 1778, to Samuel Holmes.

684   Nathan Tyler, born Sept. 2, 1758; died April 29, 1777.

685   Samuel Tyler, born March 18, 1761; died Sept. 11, 1796; his widow, Lucy Tyler, married (2), Nov. 28, 1799, David Smith, of Attleboro.   Samuel was in the Revolution, the service being on an alarm in Rhode Island, in 1780.   He was an inn-keeper.

686+ William Tyler, born Aug. 4, 1764.

687+ Thomas Tyler, born June 17, 1768.

688   Elizabeth Tyler, born April 19, 1770; married in 1792, Thomas Tingley, Jr., who was probably born in Attleboro, July 17, 1769, and died in Harford, Pa., Dec. 19, 1847.

208   HULDAH[4] TYLER (Samuel[3]), born in Attleboro, Mass., November 14, 1733; died October 7, 1780; married, March 22, 1763, Amos Ide, born in Attleboro, November 25, 1729; died February 5, 1810; son of John and Mehitable (Robinson) Ide (Nicholas of Rehoboth).   After his wife's death, he was, perhaps, published (2) to Hannah Holmes, April 16, 1781.   The children were born in Attleboro.   Children:

689   Huldah Ide, born Dec. 22, 175–; died May 7, 1758.

690   Amos Ide (Ensign), born April 10, 1756; died March 31, 1816; married Sarah Metcalf and had five children.

691   George Ide, born Sept. 17, 1758.

692   Abijah Ide, born Oct. 30, 1761; died April 27, 1776.

211   COLONEL EBENEZER[4] TYLER (Samuel[3]),

born in Attleboro, Mass., March 25, 1740; died January 29, 1811; married, May 4, 1762, Hannah Read, of Attleboro; born July 7, 1744; died September 18, 1822; daughter of Captain Daniel and Mary (White) Read. He was first lieutenant in the Revolution. In 1786, he was captain in the militia: in 1790 major, and in 1799 colonel. He served six years as major-general of the Massachusetts militia. He was at the Concord fight as a " Minute man." His sword, captured from a British surgeon, is now in the possession of his descendant, General Mitchell, of Bangor. He was three times deputy to the General Court of Massachusetts. He died suddenly, being found in the barn, on the mow, with his pitchfork in his hand, where he had gone to feed the cows. His will was dated August 7, 1804, and probated July 2, 1811. His wife and son Samuel were executors. Samuel to have all lands, buildings, etc., and to pay debts and legacies. His wife had the usual provision, and his other children were left small sums of money, having received some portions of their shares previously. His children were all born in Attleboro.

CHILDREN:

693+   Walter Tyler, born June 20, 1763.
694+   Lucinda Tyler, born May 10, 1765.
695   Rowland Tyler, born Feb. 15, 1767; died Oct. 1, 1775.
696   Abijah Tyler, born Jan. 22, 1769; died Oct. 1, 1775.
697   Leander Tyler, born March 28, 1771; died Sept. 26, 1775.
698   Nancy Tyler, born Jan. 1, 1774; died July 28, 1793; married, May 26, 1793, Calvin Sweet.
699+   Ebenezer Tyler, born Feb. 9, 1776.
700+   Lavinia Tyler, born March 25, 1778.
701+   Rowland Tyler, born Feb. 2, 1780.
702+   Abijah Weld, twin to Rowland.
703   Leander Tyler, born Jan. 22, 1782; died July 26, 1790.
704+   Crawford Tyler, born April 8, 1784.
705+   Samuel Tyler, born Dec. 7, 1785.
706+   Sylvia Tyler, born Jan. 24, 1788.
707+   Hannah Tyler, born Sept. 17, 1789.

FIFTH GENERATION

234 MARY[5] TYLER (John[4]), born in Tolland, Conn.,
January 25, 1722; married, February 23, 1741, Abea Crane,
of Tolland. They moved to Alstead, N. H. She and her son
Isaac are mentioned in her brother Isaac's will. The children
were born in Tolland. Children:

708   Joshua Crane, born Nov. 21, 1742.
709   Isaac Crane, born March 6, 1745; married Miss Put-
       nam, of Warren, Mass., and settled in Vermont; had
       a large family.
710   Mary Crane, born Oct. 28, 1747.
711   Abea Crane, born Feb. 8, 1751.
712   Eleazer Crane, born Aug. 28, 1753; died Dec. 27, 1857.
713   Joseph Crane, born May 19, 1759.
714   Eunice Crane, born July 3, 1762.
715   John Crane, born Oct. 10, 1766.

235 SARAH[5] TYLER (John[4]), born in Tolland, Conn.,
February 18, 1724; died there in 1776, while nursing her
brother John; married (1), May 24, 1744, David Burroughs,
of Stafford, Conn.; married (2), —— Benton; married (3),
—— Lewis; married (4), —— Stafford; married (5), ——
Leach; married (6), —— Olcott. Child, by first marriage:
716   David Burroughs, born in Stafford.

CHILDREN, by second marriage:
717   John Benton.
718   Isaac Benton.
719   Sarah Benton, married —— Mason.
720   Abigail Benton.

236 ANNAH[5] TYLER (John[4]), born in Tolland,
Conn., March 12, 1727; died August 19, 1803; married, June
27, 1751, Jonathan Ladd, of Tolland, born March 5, 1728;
died August 27, 1810; son of Jonathan and Susannah (Kingsbury) Ladd, of Norwich, Conn. The children were born in
Tolland. Children:

721   Anna Ladd, born Aug. 27, 1752; died young.
722   Eliab Ladd, born April 21, 1754; married Susalla Lathrop; had a family.
723   Abijah Ladd, born Feb. 27, 1756; married Huldah Fuller, and had a family.
724   John Ladd, born April 3, 1758; married Esther Wood and had a family.
725   Sarah Ladd, born April 27, 1760.
726   Jonathan Ladd, born June 15, 1762; died Aug. 21, 1762.
727   Anna Ladd, twin to Jonathan; died Aug. 21, 1762.
728   Jonathan, born March 21, 1764.
729   Ruth Ladd, born March 30, 1767.

237   MOSES[5] TYLER (John[4]), born in Tolland, Conn., February 25, 1730; died about 1777; married Widow Tryphena (Keyes) Hinds, of Warren, Mass. Moses has a deed from John Davies, of Western, May 5, 1764, interest in four lots in Shrewsbury, Mass., the consideration being £38, 10s. He was probably a private in the Revolution and appears on a return of Captain Harwood, of Colonel Learned's regiment, dated October 7, 1775. Abner Tyler (his brother) was appointed guardian of the children, who were all minors at the time of the death of Moses. Moses lived in Warren and the children were born there. Children:

730+   Moses Tyler, born in 1764.
731+   John Tyler, born in 1766.
732+   Isaac Tyler, born Nov. 16, 1767.
733   Sarah Tyler, born in 1770; published, Oct. 8, 1789, to Rufus Barrett, of West Brookfield, Mass. In 1784 she chose —— Pattridge, of Western, as guardian. They moved to Canada.
734+   Tamar Tyler, born in 1773.

238   RUTH[5] TYLER (John[4]), born in Tolland, Conn., February 28, 1732; died in North Brookfield, Mass., April 26, 1814; married (1), Deacon Jonathan Bond, of North Brookfield; born in Watertown, Mass., April 22, 1736; moved to Boylston, Mass., where he died in 1784; son of Deacon Jonathan Bond, of Watertown; married (2), October 11, 1809, Roger Bruce, of North Brookfield; born September 30, 1734;

died May 11, 1818; they had no children; (he married [1],
Zeruiah Thurston, who died s. p., March 25, 1809). When a
widow, Ruth made her home with her son, Jonathan Bond.
The three elder children were born in Sturbridge, Mass., and
the four younger in Brookfield.

CHILDREN, all by first marriage:

735   Jonathan Bond (Deacon), born March 17, 1760.
736   Joseph Bond, born March 18, 1762; died Oct. 16, 1781.
        (*See Harvard College Oration by Harrison Gray
        Otis.*)
737   Solomon Bond, born May 9, 1764.
738   Mary Bond, born Aug. 28, 17—; married and died
        soon after.
739   Sarah Bond, born March 14, 1771; married Abijah
        Pierce, of Boylston, and had two children.
740   Ruth Bond, twin to Sarah; married John Bond, of
        Boylston, and died soon after leaving a son, Tyler
        Bond.
741   Eunice Bond, married John Gale, of Stratford, Conn.

239 PRUDENCE[5] TYLER (John[4]), born in Tolland,
Conn., November 26, 1735; married John Dunton, of Stur-
bridge, Mass. The children were born in Sturbridge.
Children:

742   Abner Dunton.
743   John Dunton.
744   Prudence Dunton.
745   Elizabeth Dunton.

240 LIEUTENANT ABNER[5] TYLER (John[4]), born
probably in Tolland, Conn., in 1738; died in Western, Mass.
(now Warren), March 1, 1819; married, December 1, 1774,
Bethiah Muzzey, of Spencer, Mass., born June 22, 1754; died
October 22, 1850; daughter of John Muzzey, of Spencer, Lexington and Rutland, the leading citizen of these places. Abner
was commissioned as second lieutenant, May 31, 1776, and
again, in the same regiment, 4th Worcester County, April 9,
1778. He was executor of his father's will. In 1897, his
only living male descendant, John W. Tyler, was residing in
Warren, Mass. The children were born in Warren. Those
who married, lived to average 77 years. Children:

746   John Tyler, born Aug. 30, 1775; died Nov. 29, 1799.
747+   Daniel Tyler, born May 12, 1777.
748   Sarah Tyler, born Feb. 18, 1779; died Sept. 25, 1859;
       married Robert Field; had a son and daughter.
749   James Tyler, born Jan. 24, 1781; died May 5, 1782.
750+   Olive Tyler, born Oct. 2, 1782.
751   James Tyler, born Oct. 28, 1784; died Oct. 25, 1871;
       Married Huldah Gleason, who died first; they had one
       child who died young. John Tyler, of Warren, peti-
       tioned, Aug. 27, 1870, showing that James was in-
       sane. His estate was distributed among his brother
       Abner and sisters Ruth and Lucy and his nephews and
       nieces.
752   Moses Tyler, born Oct. 6, 1786; died Nov. 6, 1786.
753+   Ruth Tyler, born March 24, 1788.
754+   Abner Tyler, born March 8, 1790.
755+   Amos Tyler, born Aug. 14, 1791.
756   Lucy Tyler, born Aug. 7, 1793; died Oct. 13, 1890;
       married Stephen Gleason; had a son and daughter.
757+   Jonas Read Tyler, born July 20, 1795.

241   JOHN[5] TYLER (John[4]), born in ——; died in
Tolland, Conn., May 30, 1780; married, February 18, 1773,
Thankful Williams. He settled in Tolland, where he and his
wife were members of the Baptist church. He was on the
Tolland committee formed December 8, 1777, to provide for
families during the Revolutionary War. His estate was probated in Stafford, Conn. In the records the name is spelled
" Tiller." The children were born in Tolland. Children:
758   Sarah Tyler, born Jan. 22, 1774.
759   Jerusha Tyler, born April 27, 1775.
760   Ruth Tyler, born Sept. 8, 1778.
761+   John Tyler, born Aug. 28, 1780.

243   MOSES[5] TYLER (Moses[4]), born in Chester, N. H.,
in 1735; died in Whitestown, Oneida County, New York, in
1829, at the home of his son Nathaniel; he lived in Thetford,
Vt., and about 1800 he went to Whitestown. The name of his
wife is not known. He was in the Revolution. The exact
order of the births of the children not known. Children:
762   Perry Tyler; moved to Texas.

763+   Asa Tyler.
764+   Dean Merrill Tyler.
765+   Nabby Tyler.
766+   Nathaniel Tyler.
767   Job Tyler; died Sept. 9, 1821.
768+   Daniel S. Tyler, born (probably) in Thetford, Vt., Dec.
           17, 1787.
769   John Barber Tyler, who resided in Pulaski, N. Y.
770   Nannie Tyler; married Rice E. Derby.
771+   Isaac Tyler, born in Thetford, Aug. 16, 1800.

245 ADONIJAH⁵ TYLER (Moses⁴), born in Chester,
N. H., in 1739; died in Hopkinton, N. H., October 12, 1812;
married (1), Mary Abbott, of Concord, N. H.; married (2),
widow Davis, of Hopkinton, N. H. (See *History of Henniker,
N. H.*) He moved to Hopkinton, N. H., from Henniker, N. H.,
about 1771, and had a large farm on the Contoocook River.
Tyler's Bridge (where now is Tyler's railway station on the
Boston & Maine Railway) was named for him. Children, by
first marriage:

772+   James Tyler, born April 12, 1760.
773+   Rachel Tyler, born March 2, 1762.
774+   Miriam Tyler, born March 22, 1764.
775+   Jeremiah Tyler, born April 9, 1766.
776+   Simeon Tyler, born March 20, 1768.
777+   Moses Tyler, born April 9, 1770.
778+   Polly Tyler, born June 4, 1773.
779+   Sarah Tyler, born March, 1775.

CHILD, by second marriage:
780+   Phineas Tyler.

246 JEPTHAH⁵ TYLER (Moses⁴), born in Chester,
N. H., in 1741; died ——; married Molly ——. He resided
in Henniker, N. H. His name appears on a muster roll (1761)
of a company under the command of Captain Francis Peabody.
In 1775, he served three months and a half, as a private in
Colonel John Stark's regiment. In 1777, he marched from
Pembroke, N. H., in July, in Captain Samuel McConnell's
company, Colonel Stickney's regiment and General Stark's
brigade, and joined the Northern Continental Army at Ben-

nington and Stillwater.   He had the rank of first sergeant.   In
1778, Sergeant Tyler was in an expedition to Rhode Island.

CHILDREN:

781   Annie Tyler.
782+   Jepthah Tyler, born in 1777.

247   ABIGAIL⁵ TYLER (Moses⁴), born in Chester,
N. H., in 1743; died in 1826; married William Eastman, of
Haverhill, N. H.   The children were born in Haverhill.
Children:

783   Miriam Eastman; married John Barber.
784   Stephen Eastman; married Lydia Boyd.
785   Ruth Eastman; married John Kimball.
786   Isaac Eastman; married Esther Leach.

248   JOSHUA⁵ TYLER (Moses⁴), born in Hopkinton,
N. H.; died February, 1829; married Rebecca Usher.   He
lived for a time in Pembroke, N. H., and removed to Thetford,
Vt., about 1785, taking with him three sons and two daugh-
ters.   He was in the Revolutionary War, serving in 1776 in
Captain Samuel McConnell's company of Colonel Daniel Moor's
regiment; he received £6 bounty.   In 1777, he marched to
Saratoga in Captain Rand's company, same regiment (*N. H.
State Papers*, Vol. 14).   The children were born in Pembroke.
Children:

787+   John Tyler, born March 28, 1773.
788+   Joshua Tyler.
789+   James Tyler, born in 1780.
790+   Rebecca Tyler.
791   Lucretia Tyler; married Asa English, of Tunbridge,
       Vt.; no children.

251   LUCRETIA⁵ TYLER (Moses⁴), born in Pembroke,
N. H., in 1748; died September 16, 1815; married, April 23,
1769, Moses Eastman.   Children:

792+   Hannah Eastman, born Jan. 5, 1770.
793   Salome Eastman, born Aug. 3, 1771; married ——
       Wilmarth.
794   Charles Eastman, born Dec. 11, 1774; married (1),
       Sally Bradly; married (2), —— Chamberlain.

795   Nancy Eastman, born Dec. 11, 1778; married (1),
       Amos Brown; married (2), —— Virgin.
796   Warren Eastman, born Oct. 2, 1781; unmarried.
797   Lycurgus Eastman, born Jan. 3, 1784; married Sally
       Langly.
798   Lucretia Eastman, born Sept. 6, 1789.

       261 BENJAMIN TYLER[5] READE (Martha[4]), born
in Boston or Marblehead, Mass.; married Mary Appleton
Dodge, of Ipswich, Mass., who died in 1830; he was a cabinet-
maker and innholder. Children:
799   Benjamin Tyler Reade, Jr., known as " Squire "; he
       had a son bearing the same name who was, at one
       time, treasurer of the Eastern Railway in Massachu-
       setts.
800   (Hon.) William Reade, baptized June 9, 1776; died
       suddenly, Feb. 18, 1837; married, Nov. 13, 1800,
       Hannah Hooper, born Aug. 1778; died May 16,
       1855; daughter of Robert Hooper, of Marblehead.
       He was Representative to Congress from 1811-1815.
801   Polly Reade; married Hon. William Hooper, of Marble-
       head.
802   Rebecca Reade; married Rev. David Jewett.
803   Martha Reade; married William Ropes, one of the
       noted merchants of Boston.

       263 JOHN[5] TYLER (Abner[4]), born in Boxford, March
13, 1745; died February 17, 1813, while on a visit to his sons
in Bakersfield, Vt.; married Rachel Crosby, born September 15,
1751; died April 6, 1817; daughter of David Crosby, of
Billerica, Mass. He was a farmer and lived in Brookfield,
Mass. His son John was appointed administrator of his estate.
The inventory was $3,962.18. Children:
804   Royal Tyler, born Aug. 30, 1772; married, Sept. 19,
       1793, Phebe Doane, of Brookfield. He removed to
       Bakersfield, Vt., and thence to Geneva, N. Y.
805   Dr. Eli Tyler, born March 1, 1774; died in Malone,
       N. Y., unmarried. He lived for a time in Bakers-
       field, Vt.
806+   Molly Tyler, born July 10, 1776.
807+   Sally Tyler, born Sept. 20, 1778.

808+   John Tyler, born Nov. 20, 1780.
809+   Abner Tyler, born Aug. 4, 1785.

264   GIDEON⁵ TYLER (Abner⁴), born in Brookfield,
Mass., July 8, 1747; died in West Brookfield, in 1832; married,
September 1, 1776, Esther Hill, of West Brookfield, who died
there. He was a farmer. The children were born in Brookfield. Children:
810   Nathan Tyler.
811+   Phineas Tyler.
812   Warren Tyler; died young, s. p.
813   Abner Tyler; died young, s. p.
814   Theodore Tyler; died young, s. p.
815   Joshua Tyler.
816   Amos Tyler; married Mrs. Latherby.
817+   Polly Tyler.
818   Esther Tyler, born in 1784; died in North Brookfield,
       March, 1853; married (1), Thaddeus Dodge, of West
       Brookfield; married (2), Ephraim Dewing, of North
       Brookfield; no children.

266   MOLLY⁵ TYLER (Abner⁴), born in Brookfield,
Mass., September 1, 1753; died in Chesterfield, N. H., December 16, 1842; married, May 9, 1775, Samuel Hamilton, born in
Ireland, 1752; died in Chesterfield, February 12, 1810; son of
a linen merchant, who settled in Chesterfield between 1780 and
1785, where he was a weaver of linen cloth. (See *Hist. of
Chesterfield, N. H.*, Randall.) The children were probably
all born in Chesterfield. Children:
819   John Hamilton, born July 11, 1775; settled in Wind-
       ham, Vt., where he was killed by falling from a
       bridge.
820   Hannah Hamilton, born Dec., 177—; married Joseph
       Hill and removed to Madison, Ohio.
821   Hance Hamilton, born March 18, 1780; married Betsey
       Mark, of Gilsum, N. H.; removed to Western, Vt.
822   Loammi Hamilton, born May 11, 178—; married ——
       Wilder; moved to Northampton, Mass.
823   James Hamilton, born October, 178—; married Rebecca
       Bacon, of Richmond, N. H.; removed to Fabius, N. Y.
824   Samuel Hamilton, born Jan. 22, 1787; died, s. p. Oct.

19, 1878; married Polly McCurdy, of Surry, N. H.,
who died March 12, 1872, aged 83.

825   Ara Hamilton, born May 22, 1789; died July 24, 1865;
married (1), in 1815, Sally Robertson, who died Dec.
11, 1823, s. p.; married (2), in 1824, Almira Fullam,

826   Fanny Hamilton, born July 1, 1791; died aged 22,
unmarried.

827   Uri Hamilton, born April 27, 179—; moved "west."

828   Amadella Hamilton, born August, 1796; moved to Ohio,
where married Verannus Allen.

267 MOSES[5] TYLER (Abner[4]), born in Brookfield,
Mass., March 16, 1756; died in West Brookfield, March 8,
1825; married (published September 25, 1778), Rebecca Trow-
ant; born in 1759; died February 17, 1816. He had eight
months' service in 1775 in Captain Peter Harwood's company,
Colonel Ebenezer Learned's Mass. regiment, dated Brookfield,
November 21, 1775. In 1778 he was surety with his brother
John on the bond which Captain Thomas Hale, gent., gave for
£300 each, as guardian to Abigail, Martha and Joshua Tyler,
children of Abner, deceased.

CHILDREN:

829+   Betsey Tyler, born April 25, 1780.

830+   David Tyler, born Aug. 20, 1781.

831   Hannah Tyler, born Feb. 9, 1783; died unmarried, in
West Brookfield, May 24, 1878.

832+   Polly Tyler, born Feb. 20, 1785.   ,

833   Moses Tyler, born April 28, 1787; died Jan. 12, 1807.

834+   Eli Tyler. born March 25, 1789.

835   Melinda Tyler, born Sept. 7, 1791; died Feb. 1, 1872;
married —— Willys, of Hartford, Conn.

836   Patty Tyler, born in 1793; died Oct. 8, 1796.

837   Fanny Tyler, born 1795; died 1800.

838   Warren Tyler, born Sept. 11, 1797; died June, 1822,
in Natchez, Miss.

839   Fanny Tyler, born March 12, 1800; died Sept. 15, 1805.

268 DOCTOR JOSHUA[5] TYLER (Abner[4]), born in
Brookfield, Mass., August 12, 1758; died in Chesterfield, N. H.,

June 11, 1807; married, in 1780, Judith Ayers, of Brookfield, Mass., born January 12, 1763; died in Chesterfield, August 11, 1854, daughter of Onesiphorus and Anna (Goodale) Ayers (Jabez, Samuel, Captain John of Ipswich). He went to the center village of Chesterfield between 1776 and 1781; sworn in as a freeman May 14, 1781. He built a house there. He was in the Revolution and supposed to be a private in 1776, in Captain Ezekiel Knowlton's company of Colonel Dyke's regiment of Mass. militia; name is spelled " Tiler "; and the same man appears as a private, service December 16, 1776, to March 1, 1777. (*Abstracts of Rolls*, Vol. 20, page 137.) He may have enlisted July 30, 1777, in Daniel Gilbert's company in Colonel Job Cushing's regiment for service at Bennington. (*Various Service*, Vol. 19, page 131.) According to the records in Brookfield he was in the Battle of Bennington, and Half Moon Service, July 13, 1777. The children were born in Chesterfield.

CHILDREN:

840+ Joshua Tyler, born Aug. 16, 1781.

841+ Judith Tyler, born Dec. 4, 1782.

842+ Jason Tyler, born Jan. 21, 1784.

843   Ayers Tyler, born Sept. 15, 1785; died 1787.

844   Patty Tyler, born Jan. 14, 1787; married, 1808, Joshua Kelley.

845   Anna Ayers Tyler, born Sept. 8, 1789; died April 14, 1868, aged 79.

846   Betsey Tyler, born Aug. 29, 1791; died 1871, aged 80; married (1), —— King; married (2), —— Atwood; married (3), —— Comings.

847   Buckley O. Tyler, born May 13, 1793; died 1794.

848+ Joseph Warren Tyler, born Dec. 9, 1795.

849+ Buckley Olcott Tyler, born Feb. 13, 1798.

850   Fanny S. Tyler, born Sept. 14, 1799; died in Chesterfield, about 1837, unmarried.

851   Royal Tyler, born Jan. 21, 1801; died 1803.

852   Rolston Tyler, born Aug. 14, 1804; died in infancy.

853+ Rolston Goodell Tyler, born Aug. 7, 1805.

272 JOHN[5] TYLER (Gideon[4]), born in West Boxford, Mass., April 1, 1751; died January 18, 1823; married, in 1791, Mercy Adams, born October 16, 1756; died November 15,

1832. He resided on the old Tyler farm in West Boxford. His real estate was valued at $8,103. at the time of his death, and his personal estate at $2,340.79. The Boxford homestead was valued at $5,460. His widow was administratrix. He was a private in Captain James Sawyer's company of Colonel James Frye's regiment, and was in camp in Cambridge, 1775. Children:

854   Rebecca Tyler, born Sept. 19, 1791; died Sept. 24, 1797.
855   Mercy Wood Tyler, born Feb. 26, 1793; died, unmarried, April 17, 1880.
856+   John Tyler, born Feb. 24, 1795; died Nov. 30, 1827.
857+   Mehitabel Tyler, born May 5, 1797; died April 8, 1891.
858   Rebecca Tyler, born May 25, 1799; died Sept. 5, 1803.

273   JONATHAN[5] TYLER (Gideon[4]), born in West Boxford, Mass., April 1, 1751; died June 26, 1840; married, June 15, 1780, Martha Symonds, born in 1759; died February 10, 1825. He had land from his father's estate in Boxford, and a portion of salt marsh in Rowley. He marched on the alarm of April 19, 1775, from Boxford, in Captain John Cushing's company. He enlisted July 1, 1778, in Captain Benjamin Edgell's company, Colonel John Jacob's regiment, and was discharged September 12, 1778. He also appears to have re-enlisted in the same company, and to have served until the end of the year. Children:

859   Mary Tyler, born 1782; died, s. p., Feb. 10, 1827; married, Nov. 23, 1806, Samuel Thurlow, of Newburyport, Mass.
860   Mehitable Tyler, born April 3, 1785; married, Oct. 7, 1807, Rev. Moses Welch, born Feb. 28, 1783; died 1853; several years a home missionary.
861   Sally Tyler, born 1787; died single, Aug. 24, 1856.
862+   Betsey Tyler, born 1789.

277   STEPHEN[5] TYLER (Gideon[4]), born in West Boxford, Mass., June 9, 1760; died November 25, 1812; married Catherine Baxter. He is buried in the cemetery in Boxford and his widow moved to New Hampshire. He served two months and ten days in 1777 in Captain Samuel Johnson's company of Colonel Titcomb's regiment, the service being in Rhode Island. Children:

863   Dean Tyler, born Nov. 3, 1791; moved to Ohio in 1833.

864   Catherine Tyler, born July 8, 1793; died aged 3 years.

865   Stephen Tyler, born Jan. 24, 1795; a lawyer in New Orleans, where he died in 1823. Admitted to the bar in 1820.

866   Catherine, born 1797; living, unmarried, 1833.

867   Nancy Tyler, born March 20, 1799; married —— Davis.

287   SARAH⁵ TYLER (Samuel⁴), born in Boxford, Mass., April 9, 1724; died in 1774; married Samuel Tenney, born in Bradford, Mass., May 24, 1725; son of Samuel and Sarah (Worcester) Tenney, descended from Thomas, of Rowley. They resided in Littleton, Ashburnham and Acton, Mass., where he lost most of his property through the depreciation of continental currency. In 1786 he removed to Hancock, N. H., where he died February 11, 1795. He married a second wife. Children, by first marriage:

868   Amos Tenney, born Sept. 29, 1746; died July 30, 1756.

869   Abigail Tenney, born Feb. 24, 1748.

870   Silas Tenney, born April 18, 1750; died Aug. 5, 1756.

871   Samuel Tenney, born May 26, 1752; died Sept. 9, 1753.

872   Samuel Tenney, born June 4, 1754; died Aug. 19, 1775; resided Groton, Mass.

873   Daniel Tenney, born July 7, 1756; died March 24, 1812; married Sally Shattuck, Pepperell, Mass.; had three children.

874   Sarah Tenney, born May 12, 1760; died Dec. 25, 1760.

875   Amos Tenney, born Nov. 23, 1761; died April 1, 1848; married Mary Chapin and had eleven children; lived in Acton, Mass., and Hancock, N. H.

876   Sarah Tenney, born May 23, 1764.

877   Silas Tenney, born July 5, 1766; resided Wilmot, N. H., and died Jan. 1, 1834.

878   Isaac Tenney, born June 9, 1768.

290   ABIGAIL⁵ TYLER (Richard⁴), baptized in East Boxford, Mass., April 21, 1728; died, a widow, June 25, 1813, aged 86; married, Nov., 1749, George Carlton, of Boxford. The children were born in Boxford. Children:

879   Betty Carlton, born Nov. 18, 1750; married Reuben
       Gragg, who died in 1796 in Boxford. They had one
       son and two daughters.
880   Abigail Carlton, born March 15, 1752.
881   Joseph Carlton, born Feb. 10, 1754; killed at Battle of
       Bunker Hill.
882   Enos Carlton, born Jan. 4, 1756.
883   Richard Carlton, born Feb. 12, 1758; died Dec. 24,
       1763.
884   Amos Carlton, born June 22, 1760; died March 11,
       1762.
885   Mehitable Carlton, born April 13, 1766; married Israel
       Foster, of Boxford.

    295 BETTY[5] TYLER (Nathaniel[4]), born in Methuen,
Mass., September 1, 1745; married, July 8, 1769, Daniel Cross,
of Methuen. Children born there. Children:
886   Daniel Cross, born Aug. 26, 1770.
887   Isaac Cross, born Dec. 5, 1771.
888   Samuel Cross, born April 12, 1773.
889   Eunice Cross, born March 17, 1775.
890   Jesse Cross, born April 12, 1777.
891   Elizabeth Cross, born Feb. 22, 1779.
892   Charlotte Cross, born Feb., 1781.
893   Anna Cross, born March 11, 1783.
894   Abigail Cross, born March 26, 1785.
895   Israel Cross, born Jan. 8, 1788.

    296 NATHANIEL[5] TYLER (Nathaniel[4]), born Octo-
ber 4, 1747; died in Springfield, Pa., in 1829; married, February 22, 1770, Abigail Andrews, of Boxford, Mass. He lived
in Methuen and moved to Sempronious, Cayuga County, N. Y.,
and probably went to Herkimer County, and then moved to
Springfield, Pa. He had eight months' service in 1775, in
Captain Charles Furbush's company of Colonel Ebenezer
Bridges' regiment. The four elder children were born in Boxford. Children:
896   Nathaniel Tyler, born July 7, 1772; probably died
       early; nothing was known of him by Daniel Tyler
       (No. 2300) who furnished many records.
897   Daniel Tyler, born April 14, 1774; probably died early,
       as Daniel (No. 2300) did not know of him.

898   Betsey Tyler, born Dec. 17, 1775; married David Thompson, of Sempronious, N. Y.; removed to Springfield, Pa.; had eight children, seven of whom had families.

899+ Andrews Tyler, born Nov. 17, 1779.

900   Joseph Tyler; married Polly ———, of Herkimer, N. Y.; had eight children, and removed to Indiana before 1823.

901   John Tyler, died single, killed by the falling of a tree.

902   Fanny Tyler; moved to Springfield, Pa.

298 JESSE⁵ TYLER (Nathaniel⁴), born March 8, 1752; moved to Coventry now (since 1840), Benton, N. H., where he died; married, February 17, 1778, Lucy Webber, of Methuen, Mass., whose mother was of the Kimball family of Haverhill. He was in the Revolution. The children were born in Methuen. Children:

903+ Lucy Tyler, born Oct. 5, 1778.

904+ Elisha Tyler, born July 28, 1781.

905+ Kimball Tyler, born Sept. 9, 1782.

906   Daniel Tyler, born Oct. 18, 1784; died, unmarried, about 1830, in home of brother Samuel, in Coventry, N. H., where he resided.

907+ Betsey Tyler, born Oct. 14, 1786.

908   Persis Tyler; died July 20, 1792.

909   Polly Tyler, born May 15, 1791; died same day.

910+ Jesse Tyler, born Aug. 1, 1792.

911+ Hepsibeth Tyler, born April 4, 1796.

912   Persis Tyler, twin to Hepsibeth, died s. p. early; married Young Clifford; resided Haverhill, N. H.

913+ Samuel Tyler, born March 20, 1798.

299 SIMEON⁵ TYLER (Nathaniel⁴), baptized January 27, 1754; died in Camden, Maine, September 21, 1840; married, October 13, 1779, widow Hannah (Merrill) Wright, of Methuen, who died in Camden, 1835. He was in Captain Davis' company, Colonel Frye's regiment, in 1775, and was at the Lexington fight and at the Battle of Bunker Hill, in the thickest of the fight. In 1776 he was a corporal and in 1778 a sergeant, and in this latter year his company was detached to guard and fortify forts in and near Boston. In 1779 he

served a short time at Castle Island. He was a Revolutionary
pensioner. (See *Rev. Pension Rolls, Waldo County, Maine.*)
He lived a while in Belfast, Maine, and owned land where fac-
tories now stand. He moved to Camden and he and many of
his descendants are buried in the old cemetery there, under the
brow of Mt. Megunticook. The children were born in Camden.

CHILDREN:

914+   Abel Tyler, born Aug. 8, 1780.
915   Hannah Tyler, born March 28, 1782; probably died
          young.
916+   Rhoda Tyler, twin to Hannah.
917+   Simeon Tyler, born Jan. 7, 1784.
918   Dudley Tyler, born Dec. 23, 1785; a carpenter at Lin-
          colnville, Maine; went to Ohio or Minnesota.
919+   Samuel Tyler, born Dec. 17, 1787.
920+   Coburn Jonathan Tyler, born Feb. 10, 1792.

   300 DANIEL[5] TYLER (Nathaniel[4]), born in Dracut,
Mass., September, 1756; died aged about 82; married, April
26, 1781, Mary (Polly) Carter, of Methuen, Mass., who died
in Windsor, Mass., November 3, 1819, in her 63d year. He
was in the Revolution. (See *Pension Book*, p. 48, No. 3.)
He resided in Dracut, Methuen, Pelham, Windsor, Mass.,
Wyndham, N. H., and Gibbonsville (Watervliet), N. Y. In
1832 he was in Windsor where he had been for about 30 years.
The six younger children were born in Pelham. Children:

921   Persis Tyler.
922+   Isaac Tyler, born Feb. 8, 1784.
923+   Daniel Tyler, Jr., born March 16, 1788.
924   Polly Tyler, twin to Daniel.
925   Sally Ann Tyler, born March, 1791; married —— Wil-
          son, of Rome, N. Y.; had sons who owned a foundry
          there.
926+   Moses W. Tyler, born May 27, 1794.
927+   Eunice Tyler, born Sept. 2, 1796.
928   Aaron Tyler, born July 23, 1798; died s. p. June 20,
          1871; estate probated in Pittsfield, Mass.; married,
          July 9, 1857, Jeannette Rice, of Cheshire, Mass.,
          daughter of Holden and Sophia (Whalen) Rice, who
          survived him. He resided in Windsor on his father's
          farm and was both farmer and storekeeper.

301 POLLY⁵ TYLER (Nathaniel⁴), born in Methuen, Mass., in 1770; died in 1847; married, April 8, 1788, Samuel Kimball, of Methuen, born November 11, 1750; died June 19, 1825. The children were born in Dracut. Children:

929 Samuel Kimball, moved to Genesee, N. Y.

930 Tyler Kimball, resided in New York City.

931 Mary Kimball, married Jonathan Lynde, of Melrose, Mass.; had four children.

932 Hannah Kimball, married J. E. Gowan, of Stoneham, Mass.; had two children.

933 Clarissa Kimball, married Haskell Alexander; resided s. p. St. Louis, Mo.

934+ Ahigail Kimball, born March 1, 1799.

935 Jacob Kimball, resided Melrose, Mass., s. p.

936 Jonas Kimball, married and had three children.

937 Martha Kimball, married Joseph Richardson, of Lowell, Mass.; had three children.

306 DANIEL⁵ TYLER (David⁴), baptized in Boxford, Mass., August 11, 1745; time of marriage and name of wife unknown. He went with his parents to Piermont, N. H., and returned to Hebron, Conn., where he resided in 1781. The children were born in Piermont. Children:

938 Daniel Tyler; perhaps resided in Gerry, Mass.

939 Ebenezer Tyler, probably died in 1827 in Chautauqua County, N. Y. The administrators of his estate were John Tyler and Asahel Lyon; no kin given.

940 David Tyler.

941 Jonathan Tyler, born in 1766; died in 1826 (?) in Chautauqua County, N. Y.; a Revolutionary veteran.

942 Nellie Tyler.

943 Sarah Tyler.

944 Hannah Tyler, married —— Wilson, of Colchester, Conn., living in 1854.

945 Abigail Tyler, married —— Webster, of Lebanon, Conn.

307 EBENEZER⁵ TYLER (David⁴), born in Boxford, Mass., August 8, 1747; died in Saybrook, Ohio, in 1823; married Jerusha Chapman, who died in 1834. He moved with his father to Lebanon, Conn., in 1751; thence to Piermont, N. H.,

in 1768; then to Rutland, Vt.; then to New York State, and in 1816 to Ohio. His estate was probated in Jefferson, Ohio. He was in the Revolution from Piermont in Captain Chandler's company, Colonel Jonathan Chase's regiment, in 1777. The children were all born in Piermont, probably, although the two younger may have been born in Lawrence, N. Y. Children:

946+   Joseph Tyler, born Feb. 2, 1772.
947   Esther Tyler, born Jan. 13, 1775; died s. p., Jan. 1,
        1863; married, Oct. 16, 1794, —— St. Clair.
948   Patty Tyler, born March 29, 1777; died, unmarried, in
        Saybrook, Ohio, March 22, 1839.
949   Jerusha Tyler, born Jan. 30, 1780; died Sept. 4, 1826;
        married, March 3, 1807, ——; resided Spring-
        field, Pa.
950+   Samuel Tyler, born July 2, 1782.
951+   Oliver Tyler, born Feb. 25, 1788.
952   Asenath Tyler, born June 1, 1790; died in Lawrence,
        N. Y., Feb. 16, 1819; married, Jan. 8, 1816, in Ohio,
        —— Pierce; one daughter.
953   Elmira Tyler, born May 12, 1792; married, March 30,
        1813, —— Babcock; lived in Springfield, Pa.
954+   Hubbard Tyler, born July 5, 1794.
955+   Amasa Tyler, born March 9, 1798.

308   DAVID[5] TYLER (David[4]), born in Boxford, Mass., November 4, 1747; baptized November 12, 1749; died ——; married (1), June 10, 1773, Judith Davis, born November 15, 1751; died August 7, 1801; married (2), June 21, 1803, Sarah Brigham, born Dec. 22, 1747; widow of Ephraim Brigham. This record is taken from the old family Bible. David was drafted from Piermont, N. H. (where he had gone with his father), October 3, 1777, and with others, refused to go to war, whereupon the lieutenant, John Weed, addressed the colonel of the regiment into which they were to be placed, and begged that " they may be Delt with as ye law Directs." He resided in Piermont, where his children were born.

CHILDREN, all by first marriage:
956   Aaron Tyler, born Jan. 18, 1774; died in Piermont,
        Oct. 11, 1777.
957   Mercy Tyler, born Jan. 23, 1775.

958   Judith Tyler, born Sept. 26, 1777; died March 22, 1817.

959   (Rev.) David Tyler, born Feb. 6, 1780; was a Methodist preacher near Buffalo, N. Y.; has sons in the railway business.

960   Aaron Tyler, born April 18, 1782.

961+   Jesse Tyler, born March 5, 1785.

962+   John Howard Tyler, born Aug. 5, 1787.

963   Phebe Tyler, born June 4, 1789.

964   Anna Tyler, born May 13, 1791.

965   James Porter Tyler, born Sept. 4, 1793; married Philura Crocker, of Lebanon, N. H.; resided in St. Johnsbury, Vt.

966   Samuel D. Tyler, born Feb. 18, 1798; became a Mormon and moved to Utah.

309   JONATHAN[5] TYLER (David[4]), born in Lebanon, Conn., January 1, 1752; died in Piermont, N. H., June 28, 1848; married, 1774, Sarah McConnell, who was aged twelve years and six months; born in Pembroke, N. H., in 1762; died November 29, 1815. This was the first marriage in Piermont, and the officiating clergyman was Rev. Peter Powers. Her family came to Piermont six months before her marriage, and she came into the town with them astride a horse. He came to Piermont with his father in 1768, from Lebanon, Conn., and was an original character, of whom many stories were told. In 1769 wild game was exceedingly abundant in Piermont; moose " yarded " on the meadows that winter; bears, wolves and deer were ever present. Jonathan gave the name of " The Northern Army " to a pest of worms which nearly destroyed all their crops in 1781 (see the story of the pigeons under No. 84). He served in the Revolution and when the army retired from Ticonderoga on the approach of Burgoyne, he was taken prisoner. He was held for a time on the west side of Lake George. Soon after they were allowed to go to the east side to help build a block-house, and with two companions he made his escape; they nearly perished from hunger, for four days while in the woods west of the Hudson River, having only leaves, twigs, buds and roots to live on; and after they crossed the river they had the same privations. He was in Captain House's company, Colonel Warner's regiment, in July

1777. He had a pension of $96 a year. (See *History of
Coos County, N. H.*) He and his wife are buried in the old
cemetery in Piermont, and the children were born in Piermont.

CHILDREN:

967+ Daniel Tyler.
968+ William Tyler.
969   Hannah Tyler, married Jonathan Hartwell, of Comp-
      ton, Quebec. She had two sons and three daugh-
      ters.
970+ Clarissa Tyler, born July 5, 1794.
971   Lydia Tyler, married (1), Samuel Davis; married (2),
      John Hartwell, who died July 2, 1833, in his fiftieth
      year; they lived on the old Jonathan homestead in
      Piermont and had two sons and two daughters; mar-
      ried (3), ——— Boynton.
972   Lucy Tyler, married Amos Giles, and died s. p.
973   Aaron Tyler, simple minded and died single.
974   Polly Tyler, died aged 90; married Samuel Danforth, of
      Pittsford (or Pittsfield), N. H.; had two sons and
      three daughters.
975   Betsey Tyler, died, unmarried, at about 20 years of age.
976   Sarah Tyler, married Lawson Drury, who settled in
      French, Scioto County, Ohio, in 1816; she had among
      her children a doctor and a minister.
977+ Theodosia Tyler, born April 11, 1800.
978+ Amos Tyler, born April 11, 1802.
979+ Eliza Montgomery Tyler, born Sept. 14, 1804.

312 LIEUTENANT DUDLEY[5] TYLER (Dudley[4]),
born in Rowely, Mass.; baptised December 2, 1739; died in
Georgetown, Mass., 1822; married (1), 1762, Sarah Spofford,
born March 4, 1744; daughter of Captain (Deacon) Abner
and Sarah (Colman) Spofford, of Georgetown; married (2),
Ruth ———, who died in 1822, aged 63. He was in active
service in the French and Indian Wars in 1757, 1759, and later
campaigns. He was seven years in the Revolution and was
in the Battle of Bunker Hill; during the time from 1775-1782
his name occurs with frequency on the Revolutionary rolls.
He was promoted from ensign to first lieutenant; was lieutenant

in a company of Colonel Thomas Nixon's 6th Massachusetts regiment; was wounded at the Battle of Princeton, January 3, 1777. He left the camp at White Plains without a formal discharge and thus lost his pension. In 1757-1760 he owned the Francis Brocklebank place in Rowley. He died, however, in the almshouse. The children were born in Rowley.

CHILDREN:

980   Dudley Tyler, born 1763; baptized June 3, 1764; died 1765.

981+   Joseph Tyler, baptized April 13, 1766.

982   John Tyler, baptized April 3, 1768.

983   Phebe Tyler, baptized Aug. 5, 1770.

984   Dudley Tyler, baptized April 23, 1773.

313 THOMAS[5] TYLER (Dudley[4]), born in Rowley, Mass.; baptized February 22, 1741; died November 4, 1776; married Mary ——. He was on the Alarm List and belonged to the Train Band in 1757. He marched on the Lexington Alarm, and was in camp in Cambridge, May 17. His name appears on the Coat Rolls for December 26, 1775, and he was in the Continental Army in 1776. His name appears on a receipt dated March 14, 1777, " he being deceased." Children:

985   Barnabas Tyler, born Sept. 6, 1769; married, Feb. 28, 1799, Mehitable Bradley, of Amesbury, Mass. He was a householder in Haverhill, in 1799.

986+   Dudley Tyler, born March 6, 1771.

987+   Thomas Tyler.

316 JOB[5] TYLER (Dudley[4]), born in Rowley, Mass.; baptized August 28, 1748; died June 18, 1831; married (1), 1774, Abigail Swan; married (2), June 21, 1786, Anna Pike, born 1765; died 1819. He lived in Haverhill and was a householder there in 1798, rated at $180. In 1787-1788 and 1789 he was chosen surveyor of lumber. He is said to have built the first toll bridge across the Merrimac River. He moved to Canaan, N. H., in 1803. Children, by first marriage:

988+   Joseph Tyler, born May 17, 1775.

989+   Phebe Tyler, born Nov. 29, 1776.

990+   Mary Tyler, born May 23, 1778.

991+   Anna Tyler, born Oct. 27, 1780.

992   Abigail Tyler, born Sept. 27, 1784; married James
        Blaisdell, of Canaan, N. H.

CHILDREN, by second marriage:

993   Fanny Tyler, born June 27, 1787; died in infancy.

994+   John Tyler, born June 2, 1789.

995   Elizabeth Tyler, born April 5, 1790; died April 8, 1860;
        married Elisha Miner.

996   Fanny Tyler, born March 29, 1792; married Amos
        Miner.

997+   Sally Parker Tyler, born March 24, 1794.

998   Lucy Tyler, born July 24, 1796; died 1869; married
        James Morse, and moved to Wisconsin in 1853.

999+   Job Colman Tyler, born March 1, 1799.

1000+   James Pike Tyler, born June 23, 1801.

1001   Elsey Tyler, born July 14, 1803; died in Canaan,
        Aug. 29, 1814.

1002   Theodore Tyler, born April 12, 1806; died in Beverly,
        Mass., Jan. 19, 1837, probably, unmarried.

1003+   Caroline B. Tyler, born Nov. 20, 1808.

319   THEODORE[5] TYLER (Dudley[4]), born in Rowley, Mass.; baptized January 22, 1758; died at sea, April,
1799; married, December 7, 1785, Susanna Hunt, who died in
Newburyport, Mass., March 15, 1835, aged 70. He was in
the Revolution and was drafted in 1775. In 1776 he was hired,
with others, for two months in February, for 40 shillings L. M.
per man. He was in Captain Jonathan Evans' company of
Colonel Wade's Essex County Massachusetts regiment, beginning with January 1, 1778. In July, 1778, he appears to have
been in Captain Jonathan Foster's company of the same regiment. The last roll was made up to January 1, 1779. The
company was stationed at Middletown, R. I. The children
were born in Newburyport.

CHILDREN:

1004   Susanna Tyler, born Sept. 19, 1786; married, Nov. 5,
        1807, John Cook, Jr., of Newburyport.

1005   Phebe C. Tyler, born in 1788; died in East Haverhill,
          Mass., Jan. 5, 1874; she was blind and unmarried.
1006   Elizabeth Woodwell Tyler, born June 10, 1790; mar-
          ried, Sept. 20, 1808, James Barker, of Newburyport.
1007   Mary Ann Tyler, born April 2, 1792; married, May
          20, 1810, Paul Bishop, of Newburyport.
1008+   William Hunt Tyler, born Sept. 14, 1796.

    320 BRADSTREET[5] TYLER (William[4]), born in
Willington, Conn., June 11, 1725; died there in 1805; married
Sibel ———.   His will was probated in Stafford, Conn., Decem-
ber 5, 1805; dated January 5, 1795, and is signed "Broad-
street Tyler, of Willington, Conn."   The will mentions his wife
"Sibel," "my sons Broadstreet and James," who had the farm
of 120 acres, inventoried at $990, and names his daughters.
He appears with the rank of private on the roll of Captain
Jacob Gould's company, which marched on the Lexington
Alarm, April 19, 1775.   He also served a little over a month in
Captain John Robinson's company, Major Gage's regiment,
which marched to reinforce the Northern Army.   The children
were born in Willington.

CHILDREN:

1009+   Broadstreet Tyler, born in 1758.
1010   James Tyler.
1011   Hannah Tyler, single in 1795.
1012   Sarah Tyler, married before 1795.
1013   Dolly Tyler, single in 1795.
1014   Isabel Tyler, married before 1795.

    322 WILLIAM[5] TYLER (William[4]), born in Willing-
ton, Conn., June 22, 1730; died in Hamilton, Chenango County,
N. Y., in 1809; married Zerviah (probably) Root.   He was in
Partridgefield (which, until 1804, consisted of the present towns
of Peru and Hinsdale), before January 4, 1782, at which date
he buys land there.   He sold land there October 17, 1793, and
"Zereah" also signs; again, August 27, 1795, he sells lands,
"Zerviah" signing.   His last deed on record in Pittsfield,
Mass., is dated Sept. 22, 1803, wherein he is described as
"lately of Partridgefield and now of Hamilton, Chenango
County, N. Y."   His estate was probated in Morrisville, N. Y.

The two elder children were born in Willington and the third
and fourth in Partridgefield (Peru).

CHILDREN:

1015   (Lieutenant) Rufus Tyler, born in 1752 or 1762;
        was early at Partridgefield, where he bought land
        April 2, 1785; he died in Lebanon, N. Y.; estate
        probated in Morrisville, N. Y., in 1835; he married
        Welthea or Wealthy ——, who probably died s. p.
        before him, as the records indicate his only heirs
        to be his brothers and sisters. He was a party to
        22 land grants in Partridgefield between the first
        one and May 12, 1800, which is the date of his last
        grant recorded in Pittsfield. In the grant of June
        28, 1798, he is described as " Lieutenant "; in that
        of 1799 as " taverner "; he was licensed as " inn-
        holder " in 1796. He enlisted in the Revolutionary
        Army from Willington in 1777 (see *Pension Book*,
        page 50). He was the first hotelkeepeer in the
        present village of Hinsdale. He moved to Leba-
        non, N. Y.

1016   Esther Tyler, born 1764; married John Henry and
        moved to Hamilton, N. Y.

1017+   Roswell Tyler, born Oct., 1772.

1018+   Asahel Tyler, twin to Roswell.

1019   Nathan Tyler, moved to Yates County.

1020   Samuel Tyler, moved to Michigan about 1836.

1021   Katura Tyler, married Floyd Fargo and moved to
        Monroe County, N. Y.

1022   Mercy Tyler, married John Reed.

326 JONATHAN[5] TYLER (William[4]), born in Will-
ington, Conn., April 12, 1744; married (1), April 12, 1764,
Honora Hatch, of Willington, Conn., who died in Strafford,
Vt.; married (2), Mrs. Alice (Cole) Spaulding, of Royalton,
Vt., who died aged 85. He moved to Hartland and Strafford,
Vt. The eldest child was born in Willington. Children, by
first marriage:

1023+   Job Tyler, born April 14, 1765.

1024   Phebe Tyler, born Sept. 7, 1767. (This child is doubt-
        ful; did not go to Vermont.)

1025+   Derias Tyler, born about 1774.

337   ABRAHAM[5] TYLER (Job[4]), born in Boxford,
Mass., June 9, 1735; died in Bradford, Mass., April 4, 1815;
married (1), April 29, 1756, Abigail Stickney, born June 27,
1738; died August 3, 1779; married (2), June 4, 1780, Jerusha
(Coburn) Mersay; died November 26, 1811; sister of David
Coburn, who married her stepdaughter, Sarah; married (3),
February 25, 1812, widow Annie (Stickney) Peabody, of Bradford, sister of his first wife. He was a sergeant in Captain John
Cushing's company of Colonel Samuel Johnson's 4th regiment
of Essex County, Massachusetts militia, which marched on the
alarm of April 19, 1775.   Children, by first marriage:
1026   Sarah Tyler, born Sept. 24, 1756; died Nov., 1844;
        married, March 29, 1818, David Coburn, of Box-
        ford.
1027+   Abigail Tyler, born May 1, 1758.
1028+   Hannah Tyler, born Sept. 13, 1759.
1029   Mary Tyler, born Oct. 16, 1761; died May 16, 1762.
1030+   Molly Tyler, born Feb. 16, 1763.
1031+   Priscilla Tyler, born Feb. 18, 1765.
1032+   Abraham Tyler, born Oct. 15, 1766.
1033   Infant, born 1767; died the same day.
1034+   Isaac Tyler, born Nov. 20, 1767.
1035+   Jacob Tyler, born Feb. 17, 1769.
1036+   Elizabeth Tyler, born July 18, 1771.
1037+   Job Tyler, born Nov. 4, 1772.
1038+   William Tyler, born Oct. 10, 1774.
1039+   Joseph Stickney Tyler, born April 15, 1776.
1040+   Parker Tyler, born April 7, 1778.

CHILD, by second marriage:
1041   Moses Coburn Tyler, born Oct. 13, 1780; died at sea,
        in the West Indies, in 1803.

338   PHINEAS[5] TYLER (Job[4]), born in Boxford,
Mass., November 22, 1736; the first person baptized in West
Boxford Church, December 12, 1736; died in Leominster,
Mass., August 6, 1817; married (1), February 14, 1758, Han-
nah Foster, of Andover, Mass., born April 9, 1739; died June
3, 1769; daughter of Joshua and Mary (Barker) Foster;

married (2), December 6, 1770, Elizabeth Barker, born April 27, 1747. He was dismissed to the church in Leominster in 1793. He was a drummer in Captain Henry Ingalls' company on the expedition to Crown Point in 1755; also in 1757, he was in the second company of Boxford, and probably belonged to the train band. He appears with the rank of a private on the Lexington Alarm roll of Captain Nathaniel Lovejoy's company, Colonel Samuel Johnson's 4th regiment of Essex County, Mass. militia. The elder children were born in West Boxford, and the younger children in Leominster, beginning with Elizabeth.

CHILDREN, by first marriage:

1042   Phineas Tyler, born May 13, 1759; died Nov. 23, 1762.

1043   Nathan Tyler, born Nov. 6, 1761; died March 9, 1763.

1044+ Phineas Tyler, born Feb. 14, 1765.

CHILDREN, by second marriage:

1045+ Simeon Tyler, born Aug. 15, 1771.

1046+ Samuel Tyler, born Feb. 28, 1773.

1047   Hannah Tyler, born Aug. 9, 1775; died, unmarried, in Leominster, June 18, 1813.

1048+ Elizabeth Tyler, born Jan. 28, 1778.

1049   Mehitable Tyler, born Nov. 29, 1782; died, unmarried in Leominster, Sept. 26, 1822.

1050   Nabby Tyler, born Jan. 15, 1787; died March 27, 1814, unmarried.

1051   Stephen Tyler, born Aug. 28, 1789; died young.

1052+ Daniel Tyler, born Aug. 18, 1791.

339 MOSES[5] TYLER (Job[4]), born in Rowley, Mass., September 18, 1738; died in Lancaster, Mass., February 11, 1824; married (1), August 3, 1763, Hannah Tyler, of Rowley, born September 3, 1741; daughter of Asa and Hannah (Peabody) Tyler (No. 91); married (2), probably in 1783, Sarah Lindall, who died March 11, 1822. In his will, dated December 16, 1822, and probated March 2, 1824, he is named as "Yeoman." He resided in Lunenburg. Previously he had lived in Bradford, where he was a member of the school committee, 1793-1803. Moses and his brothers, Phineas and Joshua, owned a large section of land in the southern part of Lunenburg, and in 1900 their residences remained much the

same as when they were alive. The elder children were born in Rowley, and the younger in Bradford.

CHILDREN, by first marriage:

1053   Hepsibah Tyler, born July 24, 1764; not mentioned in her father's will, so probably died, s. p., before 1822; published, May 7, 1798, to Ashael Houghton, of Lunenburg.

1054+   Nathan Tyler, born Dec. 10, 1766.

1055   Phebe Tyler, born Jan. 28, 1773; died young.

1056   Phebe Tyler, born March 16, 1775; married Eleazer Hartwell; was a widow in 1822.

1057   Hannah Tyler, born Dec. 6, 1779; unmarried in 1822.

CHILDREN, by second marriage:

1058   Moses Tyler, born in Bradford, Mass., 1784; died in Lunenburg, June 12, 1846, aged 62.

1059+   Zebediah Tyler, born July 21, 1787.

1060+   Ancill Tyler, born March 29, 1790.

340   ELIZABETH[5] TYLER (Job[4]), born in Boxford, Mass., February 27, 1740; died in Rindge, N. H., March 20, 1812; married, January, 1762, Lieutenant Joseph Mulliken, of Bradford, Mass., who died March 27, 1812; she removed with her father's family to Rindge in 1794. Children:

1061   Joseph Mulliken, born in Rindge, in 1774; died Sept. 9, 1818; was graduated from Dartmouth College in 1802; principal of New Ipswich Appleton Academy, 1803-1807; received degree of M. D. in 1817.

1062   Benjamin Mulliken.

1063   Samuel Mulliken, a school-teacher.

1064   Leonard Mulliken, a musician, who died about 1820; removed to Shelburne, Vt., where he was the leader of a band.

1065   Rebecca Mulliken, married, Nov. 18, 1794, William Hodgskins; she died 1798.

1066   Betsey Mulliken, married, Nov. 25, 1788, Nathaniel Carlton, of New Ipswich, N. H., and Lunenburg, Mass.

1067   Rachel Mulliken.

1068   Fanny Mulliken.

341 HANNAH[5] TYLER (Job[4]), born in West Boxford, Mass., October 4, 1741; died in Bradford, Mass., April 24, 1824; married, October 15, 1765, Joshua Hardy, of Bradford, who died June 3, 1814. The children were born in Bradford. Children:

1069   Zebediah Hardy, born Sept. 24, 1766; died Oct. 3, 1766.

1070   Hannah Hardy, born Jan. 8, 1768; died Jan. 29, 1736; married Jacob Hardy; one of her sons became Rev. Seth Hardy.

1071   Joshua Hardy, born June 27, 1770; died Aug. 26, 1843; married Mary Goss; one of his sons was named "Tyler."

1072   Rhoda Hardy, born April 3, 1772; died Oct. 20, 1837.

1073   Frances Hardy, born Jan. 13, 1775; married Samuel Tyler, No. 1046.

1074   Abel Hardy, born April 12, 1777; died Nov. 20, 1801.

1075   Tyler Hardy, born Oct. 22, 1780; died Oct. 16, 1801.

1076   Jerusha Hardy, born April 15, 1783; married Flint Tyler, No. 1097.

1077   Phineas Hardy, born June 12, 1785; died in 1854; married Olive Parker.

1078   Betsey Hardy, born June 25, 1787; died Nov. 8, 1803.

342 ASA[5] TYLER (Job[4]), born October 23, 1743; married, June 23, 1768, Elizabeth Tyler, of Rowley, Mass., No. 353, born April 22, 1746. He was one who signed the town Declaration of Independence in 1776. He moved to Boxboro, Mass., and thence to Westmoreland and Rome, N. Y. In Rome, at the first town meeting in 1796, he was elected a fence-viewer; and in 1797 was overseer of the highways. The children were baptized in Rowley. Children:

1079+   Hannah Tyler, baptized Dec. 2, 1770.

1080   Peggy Tyler, baptized Sept. 22, 1771.

1081+   Asa Peabody Tyler, born June 9, 1773.

343 DEACON BRADSTREET[5] TYLER (Job[4]), born in Boxford, Mass., August 27, 1745; died there April 5, 1842; married (1), April 13, 1769, Mary Foster, of Andover, Mass., born March 22, 1750; died August, 1785; married (2), Mrs. Eunice Adams, of Newbury, Mass., who died June 22, 1798,

aged 44; married (3), December 27, 1798, Mrs. Mary Bacon, who died May 20, 1820, aged 62. He appears with the rank of private on the roll of Captain Jacob Gould's company, which marched on the Lexington Alarm, April 19, 1775. He also served in Captain John Robinson's company, which marched to reinforce the Northern Army. The children were born in Boxford.

CHILDREN, by first marriage:

1082+ Joshua Tyler, born Oct. 6, 1776.

1083+ Mary Tyler, born Jan. 13, 1779.

1084 (Capt.) John Tyler, born April 29, 1781; died Nov. 12, 1872; did not marry. He was in the War of 1812. His military title came from his connection with the militia. He left a legacy to the church in West Boxford, for the support of the gospel in that society. After the settlement of his estate, the fund was found to amount to about $30,000.

1085 Infant, born Nov. 3, 1784; probably died very young.

CHILD, by second marriage:

1086+ Bradstreet Tyler, Jr., born Oct. 13, 1794.

CHILD, by third marriage:

1087 Aaron Tyler, born 1801; died 1803.

344 JOSHUA[5] TYLER (Job[4]), born in Boxford, Mass., January 27, 1747; died in Leominster, Mass., March 27, 1825; married December 5, 1776, Ismenia Kimball. He moved to Rindge, N. H., and thence to Leominster. In Rindge, in 1776, he signed the town's Declaration of Independence. He was in Captain Rand's company, Colonel Moor's regiment, in 1776, and in the same company and regiment joined the northern Continental Army under General Gates, in 1777; discharged, October 18, 1777, at Saratoga. The children were born in Rindge. Children:

1088 Rebecca Tyler, born Sept. 4, 1777; died in Leominster, May 30, 1807; married, Nov. 26, 1796, Elisha Cooledge, of Leominster; they had a daughter, who died at the age of 19.

1089+ Joshua Tyler, Jr., born Feb. 3, 1779.

1090+ Betsey Tyler, born March 9, 1782.

1091   Mercy Tyler, born April 19, 1784; married, June 26,
        1806, Asa Bancroft, of Groton, Mass.   They moved
        to Canada, and had twelve children.

1092+   Phebe Kimball Tyler, born Sept. 6, 1785.

1093+   Thomas Tyler, born July 14, 1787.

1094+   Ismena Tyler, born Sept. 20, 1789.

1095   Grata Tyler, born Aug. 12, 1793; married (1), Jan.,
        1814, Luther Johnson, of Lancaster, Mass., who
        died April 24, 1822; married (2), May 29, 1738,
        Benjamin Farwell; she had two children by first
        marriage.

1096+   Elsa Tyler, born May 28, 1796.

   346 PARKER⁵ TYLER (Job⁴), born in Boxford,
Mass., January 31, 1752; died in Townsend, Mass., October 13,
1837; married (1), January 29, 1782, Hannah Flint, who died
in Leominster, Mass., October 13, 1802; married (2), November 12, 1803, Lucy Giddings, of Lunenburg, Mass.   He moved
to Rindge, N. H., thence to Sterling, Mass., in 1791; then to
Leominster, to Wilton, N. H., and again to Rindge in 1818,
and in 1837 to Townsend, Mass.   He was in the Revolution,
serving in Captain Richard Peabody's company, Colonel Edward Wigglesworth's regiment, stationed at Ticonderoga in
August to October, 1776, and probably all the next winter;
was on the pension rolls in 1831 and 1833.   He was a carpenter and farmer.

                  CHILDREN, by first marriage:

1097+   Flint Tyler, born Nov. 2, 1782.

1098   Apphia Tyler, born Nov. 22, 1784; died Sept. 29,
        1806; married, June 4, 1806, William Abbott, of
        Wilton, N. H.

1099+   Hannah Tyler, born Oct. 20, 1786.

1100+   Parker Tyler, Jr., born Oct. 7, 1788.

1101+   Seth Payson Tyler, born April 29, 1791.

1102+   Putnam Tyler, born Sept. 20, 1793.

1103   Louisa Tyler, born Nov. 19, 1795; died Jan. 17, 1889;
        married John Hodgman, of Townshend, Mass., who
        died in 1853; then she lived with her sister, Mrs.
        Wilder, in Rindge; no children.

1104   Laura Tyler, twin to Louisa; died March 17, 1877, in Enfield, Mass.; married Joseph Simonds, of Groton, Mass., who died Feb. 10, 1871; she resided in Petersham, Mass.; no children.

1105+   Miriam Tyler, born Jan. 23, 1798.

1106+   Levi Tyler, born Oct. 22, 1800.

CHILDREN, by second marriage:

1107+   Apphia Tyler, born Nov. 6, 1806.

1108+   Asa Tyler, born July 31, 1809.

347   FRANCES[5] TYLER (Job[4]), born in Boxford, Mass., in 1754; died there, November 2, 1844; married, March 21, 1782, Lemuel Wood, of Boxford, who died July 1, 1819, aged 78. The children were born in Boxford. Children:

1109   Lemuel Wood, born April 29, 1783; married —— Cook; died in Bangor, Maine; had a family.

1110   Fanny Tyler Wood, born Dec. 10, 1784; married Joseph Eaton, of Harpswell, Maine; ten children.

1111   Charlotte E. Wood, born Dec. 28, 1786; married Samuel Bates, of Dedham, Mass.; had children.

1112   Mary Chadwick Wood, born July 22, 1789; married —— Hutchinson; had children.

1113   Aaron Wood, born Jan. 2, 1791; died Oct. 24, 1794.

1114   Daniel Wood, born Feb. 10, 1793; married Abigail Stickney[7] Tyler, No. 2621.

1115   Aaron Wood, born Oct. 27, 1797; died Nov. 2, 1868, unmarried.

349   MARGARET[5] TYLER (Asa[4]), born in Rowley, Mass., June 12, 1735; died March 26, 1786; married, May 24, 1757, Lieutenant Jedediah Stickney; born April 1, 1735, in Boxford, Mass.; died April 8, 1809. (He married (2), in 1796, Sarah Herrick.) He was a soldier, and assisted in removing the Arcadians, May 28, 1755. Was a member of the First Foot company of Boxford, 1757. As "Ensign" marched on the day of the battle of Lexington, and saw service in the Revolutionary War. Children:

1116   Ancil Stickney, born Aug. 11, 1758; died young.

1117   Nathan Stickney, born Aug. 7, 1760; married (1), R. Phelps; married (2), A. Phelps; married (3), H. Burpe.

1118   Ancil Stickney, born June 3, 1762; married Mehitable
        Perley, June 27, 1793; died in 1835; was in the
        Revolutionary War.
1119   Apphia Stickney, born Sept. 13, 1764; married Jonas
        Warren, April 27, 1784.
1120   Betty Stickney, born Aug. 1, 1766; died unmarried,
        Feb. 21, 1788.
1121   Peggy Stickney, born Aug. 30, 1768; married Oliver
        Peabody, Sept. 13, 1792.
1122   Hannah Stickney, born July 14, 1773; died in Box-
        ford, Jan. 18, 1845; married, Nov. 12, 1793, Nathan
        Peabody, born April 12, 1770; died Nov. 24, 1809;
        son of Deacon Moses and Hannah (Foster) Pea-
        body.
1123   Rebecca Stickney, born Oct. 8, 1775; died unmarried,
        April 14, 1795.
1124+   Asa Tyler Stickney, born Nov. 17, 1777.

351 LUCY[5] TYLER (Asa[4]), born in Rowley, Mass.,
October 1, 1739; married Thomas Ames, of Boxford, Mass.
(published March 12, 1761); moved about 1778 to Rindge,
N. H.   He was a member of the Second church in Boxford,
where his children were baptized.   Children:
1125   Molly Ames, born May 2, 1762.
1126   Priscilla Ames, born Sept. 4, 1763.
1127   Sarah Ames, born Dec. 8, 1765.
1128   Jeremiah Ames, born July 14, 1771; married, April
        29, 1798, Sally Platts, daughter of Captain Joseph
        Platts.   He moved to Morristown, N. Y., where he
        had a family.
1129   Thomas Ames, born Oct. 13, 1776.
1130   Hannah Ames, born in Rindge, Feb. 25, 1780.
1131   Charlotte Ames, born in Rindge, March 9, 1784; mar-
        ried Joseph Platts, son of Captain Joseph Platts.
        His descendants live in Waltham, Mass.

354 CAPTAIN ASA[5] TYLER (Asa[4]), born in Rowley
Village (now West Boxford), Mass., December 21, 1748; died
in Blenheim, N. Y., April 9, 1808; married, 1780, Martha
Dodge, born September 6, 1756; died December 1, 1803. He
appears first in Revolutionary records in the year 1775 as

corporal on the Lexington Alarm roll of Captain Meghill, and then as sergeant in Captain Gridley's company in the same year; in January, 1778, he was commissioned as second lieutenant in Captain Jeremiah Putnam's company, Colonel Nathaniel Wade's regiment. In 1779 he sold "Scraggy Pond" in Rowley, accepting quite a large sum in Continental currency, to show his loyalty and confidence in the government, of which his close friend, Robert Morris, was treasurer. Finding himself impoverished by the repudiation of this currency, in 1783 he moved to Suffield, Conn., where his four younger children were born. In 1801 he moved to Blenheim and purchased a "lease farm." He was appointed postmaster, which position he retained until his death. He gave the ground for a church where he and his wife are interred. Through his wife he was great uncle to George Peabody, the philanthropist, and uncle to General Henry Leavenworth of the War of 1812. The family Bible, with a chest full of Continental money, were burned in Barrytown, N. Y., in 1872. The two elder children were born in Rowley Village.

CHILDREN:

1132   Clarissa Tyler, born 1780; married Henry Kent; one child (Clarissa, who married —— Howell.)

1133   Henry Putnam Tyler, born Aug. 4, 1782; died in Philadelphia, 1860; he married in 1855, at the age of 70 a girl of 23. He was for many years a bookkeeper in Philadelphia; two daughters (Emma, born 1856; married [1], a Japanese and had one daughter; married [2], —— Brink and had a son, Victor; Laura, born 1859; died 1868.)

1134+   Nathan Peabody Tyler, born Feb. 16, 1784.

1135+   Asa Tyler, born Feb. 25, 1789.

1136   Laura Tyler, born 1791; died 1792.

1137   Patty Tyler, born 1792; died 1794.

367 PHEBE[5] TYLER (Jonathan[4]), born probably in Haverhill, Mass., about 1740; married Abijah Buck, born in Newbury, Mass., in 1777, the second year of the settlement, he moved from New Gloucester, Maine, to Buckfield, Maine (Oxford County), a town named for him and his two brothers, who also were early settlers there. His father-in-law, Jonathan

Tyler, accompanied him to the new town, where he was a man of note. The children were born in New Gloucester except the youngest. Children:

1138   Elizabeth Buck, born July 1, 1763.

1139   Ellen Buck, born Jan. 8, 1765.

1140   Phebe Buck, born Dec. 17, 1766.

1141   John Buck, born Dec. 27, 1768; married Molly ——; had two sons and two daughters.

1142   Rebekah Buck, born Dec. 15, 1772.

1143   Abijah Buck, born March 1, 1777.

1144   Jonathan Buck, born in Buckfield, Feb. 5, 1782.

368   JONATHAN[5] TYLER, JR. (Jonathan[4]), born, probably in Haverhill, Mass., July 6, 1742; married Mercy Hackett, daughter of Henry Hackett, of New Gloucester; born December 10, 1743. They grant their interest in her father's estate, £6, June 13, 1775, to Moses Hackett of New Gloucester. Moses Hackett, as administrator of the estate of Jonathan Tyler, late of New Gloucester, July 11, 1783, deeds to James Rider, of North Yarmouth, for £99, 15s, 50 acres in New Gloucester. It is probable that the estate here administered upon was that of Jonathan[5]. He had a grant of land from his father on the 20th of June, 1767, of 60 acres in New Gloucester, for which he paid £10, 13s, 4d. He enlisted in Captain Merrill's company, Colonel Phinney's regiment of Foot, May 15, 1775. (*Coat Rolls 8 Months Service*, Vol. 56.) In a letter to his wife, dated Boston, June 25, 1777, signed by himself, he states that he has been sick with the small pox, entered the hospital April 29 and left it June 18, 1777, and went to Boston. (*Resolve*, 1820, chap. 101.) (See also *Books, Enlisted Men and Officers*, Vol. 27.) The children were born in New Gloucester.

CHILDREN:

1145   Mary Tyler, born July 30, 1767; died unmarried, in her native place, March 6, 1846.

1146+   Mercy Tyler, born April 16, 1773.

1147   Jonathan Tyler, born March 17, 1776.

369   NATHANIEL[5] TYLER (Jonathan[4]), born probably in Haverhill, Mass., about 1744; died in 1809; married Rebecca Sherloc (probably Sherlock).

The placing of this line is conjectural; no record of birth

found; names of children indicate descent from Moses[2] (Job[1]), in fact is the only possible line of descent my records will allow. From only two of Moses'[2] sons does it appear he could come, that is Joshua[3] and Jonathan[3]. In Joshua's line we have nothing to show he had Tyler grandsons, or that any of his line went to Maine. It is probable that this line comes from Jonathan[3], Moses[2], Job[1]. We know that Jonathan[3], like his brother James, went to Maine, and Jonathan[4] was at New Gloucester, Maine, by 1763, before the first proprietor's meeting down to 1773. Jonathan[4] was at Haverhill, Mass., in 1743, where probably was born his son Jonathan[5], 1742, and where Nathaniel[5] may have been born. It is but a short distance from New Gloucester, Maine, to the Augusta, Maine, region where the children of Nathaniel largely settled. Two of Nathaniel's children went to Bethel, Maine, which is about as far northwest from New Gloucester as Augusta is to the northeast. Jonathan[3] had brothers: Nathaniel, Jonathan, Ebenezer and Joseph, and Nathaniel[5] gives four of his sons these same four names. The names of Nathaniel, Jonathan and Joseph recur in the names of the grandchildren of Nathaniel[5]. Jonathan[3] had a brother Joshua, and this name appears among Nathaniel's grandchildren, while David and Asa, names also occurring in the seventh generation of Nathaniel's line, are names found among the grandchildren of Moses[2] (Job[1]), the father of Jonathan[3].

In 1775 we find the name of Nathaniel Tyler among five new names added to Augusta taxpayers, when General Arnold ascended the Kennebec to go to Quebec. In a return of men enlisted into the Continental Army, from Colonel Joseph North's 2d Lincoln County regiment, dated Gardnerstown, February 2, 1778, occurs the name of Nathaniel Tyler, from Hallowell, Maine, who enlisted for three years. In 1780 Nathaniel Tyler was a soldier at Fort Halifax. " Nathaniel and wife Rebecker " join in a deed of land, February 4, 1793, as shown in the *Wiscasset Register of Deeds*, Vol. 24, p. 18. In 1797 Nathaniel owned land, horses and cattle in Augusta. The eldest child was born in Sidney, Maine; the fifth, sixth and seventh children were born in Augusta, Maine.

CHILDREN:

1148+ Nathaniel Tyler, Jr., born 1785.

1149+   Jonathan Tyler.
1150+   Ebenezer Tyler.
1151+   Eleazer Tyler.
1152+   Thomas Sherlock Tyler, born Feb. 8, 1798.
1153+   Elias Tyler, twin to Thomas S.
1154+   Joseph C. Tyler, born in Augusta.
1155+   Rachel Tyler.
1156+   Hannah Tyler.
1157+   Ruth Tyler.
1158+   Betsey Tyler.
1159   Susannah Tyler, died in Augusta, Me., unmarried.
1160+   Rebecca Tyler.
1160a   Daniel Tyler.

370 JOSEPH[5] TYLER, JR. (Joseph[4]), born in Haverhill, Mass., April 8, 1749; died in Billerica, Mass., January 29, 1834; he is buried in a tomb on School Street in Lowell, Mass.; married, July 10, 1779, Abigail Spalding, of Chelmsford, Mass., born March 15, 1759; died December 21, 1849; daughter of Colonel Simeon Spalding. The children were born in Newburyport, Mass., except the eldest and youngest. Children:

1161   Joseph Tyler, born in Salisbury, Mass., July 16, 1781; died March 1, 1851, unmarried; buried in the family tomb. Representative from Lowell to the General Court, 1833-1835; Lowell City Council in 1837, and probably other years.
1162+   John Tyler, born April 8, 1783.
1163   Fanny Tyler, born March 6, 1785; died Dec. 29, 1787.
1164   George Tyler, born April 8, 1787; died, unmarried, Dec. 10, 1827; buried in the family tomb.
1165   Moses Tyler, born March 27, 1789; died in Nashua, N. H., Oct. 21, 1849, s. p.; married Lydia Hale, born Dec. 26, 1815; daughter of Moses Hale. They lived in Nashua, and had a daughter (Harriet), who died at the age of 8 years.
1166   James Tyler, born July 6, 1791; died Feb. 8, 1849, unmarried, and is buried in the family tomb.
1167+   Philip Tyler, born April 9, 1793.
1168+   William Tyler, born in Cambridge, Mass., Aug. 14, 1795.

371   PHEBE⁵ TYLER (Joseph⁴), born in Haverhill,
Mass., March 23, 1750; died February 12, 1780; married,
March 16, 1773, Joel Spalding (as the name was then spelled),
born March 12, 1743; died July 26, 1823; son of Colonel
Simeon and Sarah (Fletcher) Spalding, whose sister Abigail
married Joseph Tyler, No. 370. He was in the Revolutionary
War; was at the surrender of Burgoyne; represented Chelmsford in the General Court several years and was a member of
the first Constitutional Convention of Massachusetts. In 1791
he married (2), widow Rebecca (Pierce) Corey, a sister of
Governor Benjamin Pierce, of New Hampshire, who was father
of Franklin Pierce, President of the United States. The children were born in Chelmsford.

CHILDREN:

1169   Silas Spalding (or Spaulding) died in infancy.
1170+   (Capt.) Jonathan Spalding, born June 12, 1775.
1171   Otis Spalding, died in infancy.
1172   Phebe Spalding, born Dec. 26, 1779; married, Dec.
        28, 1800, Joseph Butterfield Barnum, of Dracut,
        Mass.; they both died, Dec. 5, 1857, s. p.

372   MARY⁵ TYLER (Joseph⁴), born in Haverhill,
Mass., November 17, 1754; died in Portland, Maine, 1850;
married, in 1772, Captain Jonathan (or Joseph) Stevens, of
Bradford, Mass., born March 21, 1747; died 1800; a shipbuilder of Bradford, where the children were born. Children:

1173   Polly Stevens, born March 19, 1773; was unmarried.
1174   Joseph Stevens, born Jan. 29, 1775; lived in Portland,
        Maine.
1175   Jonathan Stevens, born Jan. 15, 1778.
1176   John Stevens, born May 7, 1780.
1177   Jacob Stevens, born Jan. 19, 1783.
1178   James Stevens, born June 16, 1785.
1179   Jeremiah Stevens, born Jan. 20, 1788; was a sea-cap-
        tain of Portland, Maine.
1180   Ignatius Stevens, born June 3, 1790.
1181   Louis Stevens, born Aug. 23, 1793.
1182   Jonathan Ignatius Stevens, born Nov. 9, 1797.

374   NATHAN⁵ TYLER (Joseph⁴), born in Haverhill,

Mass., in 1757; died in Middlesex Village, Mass., November 2, 1829; married in Dracut, Mass., July 31, 1788, Polly Wood, of Chelmsford, Mass.

The Merrimack River, by J. W. Meader (1869) says: "In the navigation of the river and auxiliary canals, the family of Tylers bore an important and conspicuous part, and are historically connected with the river and with Lowell. Mr. Nathan Tyler owned nearly all the land from the head of the Pawtucket (or Navigation) Canal to the Merrimack, and as far down as the mouth of the Concord, the manufacturing companies making their first land purchase of him. . . ." He resided near the foot of Pawtucket Falls, and carried on a saw and grist mill; which was swept away by the "Great Freshet" (1810). "For three generations the Tylers of Lowell have been intimately connected with the Merrimack and its canals; in their younger days in the lively times of East Chelmsford, as fishermen, lumbermen and boatmen; and in maturer years in many high positions of responsibility and trust. . . ."

Mr. Nathan Tyler owned a large tract of land in Lowell, a part now covered by the Boot corporation, and the whole of that covered by the Massachusetts, Prescott and Middlesex as far south as Massic Falls on the Concord, with also a considerable territory on the west of Central Street, between Merrimac and Market Streets, a large and valuable part of which, covered by Tyler block, is still in the family. Nathan's house, subsequently the residence of Jonathan[6], was on the north side of Merrimac Street between the canal and Bridge Street, and was built of lumber sawed at Tyler's mill below Pawtucket Falls. The family became widely separated and is now represented in Lowell by female members. "Tyler Park" contains abount 80,000 feet of land, with ample streets surrounding it.

Ignatius Tyler was appointed administrator of his estate, and the inventory was $14,610.55, and was made December 8, 1829. The children were born in Middlesex Village, Mass.

CHILDREN:

1183   Otis Tyler, born Oct. 2, 1788; died ibid, 1849; did not marry.

1184   (Lieutenant) Jonathan Tyler, born Jan. 17, 1790;

died in Lowell, Mass., Oct. 14, 1877; married in Chelmsford, April 4, 1816, Ciril S. Butterfield, daughter of Captain Benjamin Butterfield. He owned the heart of the present city of Lowell, Mass., property now owned by John Tyler Stevens. Lieutenant Tyler lived in the mansion built by his father; he had no children.

1185+ Nathan Tyler, Jr., born Jan. 25, 1792.
1186+ Silas Tyler, born June 2, 1795.
1187 Mary Tyler, born April 1, 1797; died in Middlesex Village, May 17, 1746; unmarried.
1188+ William Tyler, born Feb. 11, 1799.
1189+ Samuel Tyler, born June 1, 1801.
1190 Betsey Tyler, born Aug., 1803; died in Middlesex Village, Oct., 1857; married, Aug. 12, 1841, Edmund Swett, of Chelmsford, Mass.; no children.
1191+ Ignatius Tyler, born July 5, 1804.
1192+ Fanny Tyler, born July, 1807.

375 MOSES[5] TYLER (Joseph[4]), born in Rowley, Mass., in 1758; died in Billerica, Mass.; married (1), ——; married (2), May, 1783, Sarah Lindell, of Bradford, Mass. Child:
1193 Moses Tyler, Jr., born in Bradford, July 1, 1784.

379 SARAH[5] TYLER (Joseph[4]), born in Chelmsford, Mass., October, 1768; died in Newburyport, Mass., October 6, 1831; married, January 20, 1794, Joseph Granger, of Newburyport, born in Andover, Mass., December 7, 1765; died in Newburyport, March 21, 1847 (see the *Granger Genealogy*). The children were born in Newburyport. Children:
1194 Fanny Granger, born Oct. 19, 1794; died in 1856; married in 1813, Jonathan Coolidge.
1195 Sarah Granger, born April 18, 1796; died May, 1846; unmarried.
1196 Joseph Granger, born Sept. 25, 1797; married (1), Harriet J. Granger; married (2), Mary H. Granger; lived in Calais, Maine.
1197 Mary S. Granger, born July 5, 1799; married Bailey Chase, of Newburyport.
1198 Farnham Granger, born June 2, 1801; died in Sydney,

Australia, in 1837; married Lydia Riley, of New York, who died in 1864.

1199   George T. Granger, born Aug. 10, 1804; married in 1828, Lucy Pulsifer; he moved to Galveston, Texas, and had a son and a daughter.

1200   Daniel Granger, born Sept. 19, 1806; married (1), Elizabeth A. Pearson; married (2), Mary Ann (Danforth) Pearson, widow of Jabez Pearson; no children; lived in Newburyport.

383   JAMES[5] TYLER (Abraham[4]), born in Scarboro, Maine, June 21, 1747; died in Saco, Maine, April 7, 1813; married Lydia Stone, of Limington, Maine. He lived in the north part of " Pepperellboro," now Saco, near " Heath Meeting House." He enlisted May 9, 1775, in Captain Abraham Tyler's company, Colonel Edmund Phinney's regiment, and served until September 29, 1775. He was a corporal. (*Mass. Archives*, Vol. 215.) His father grants him, June 26, 1775, in the consideration of £200, 170 acres at Blue Point, being a part of the Sir William Pepperell purchase. His father is supposed to have deeded him land which included the homestead. James sold the old homestead March 11, 1813, to Abia Chamberlain for $2000. But it was really an exchange for lands situated in Gray, Maine. The children were born in Pepperellboro, now Saco.

CHILDREN:

1201+   Mehitable Tyler, born April 20, 1779.

1202   Eliza (or Elsa) Tyler, born Nov. 9, 1780.

1203   Elizabeth Tyler, born Jan. 7, 1782; intentions published Sept. 28, 1801, to Thomas Seavey, of Scarboro.

1204+   Hannah Tyler, born March 7, 1784.

1205   Allison Tyler, born Nov. 3, 1785; died in Pepperellboro, Nov. 7, 1789.

1206+   James Tyler, born Jan. 1, 1787.

1207   Louisa Tyler, born Jan. 7, 1789; married George Simpson, of Saco; both died s. p. in advanced age.

1208+   Abraham Tyler, born March 7, 1793.

1209   Abigail Tyler, born June 7, 1795; married Samuel Rice.

388   COLONEL ANDREW[5] TYLER (Abraham[4]), born

in Scarboro, Maine; baptized there June 18, 1758; died in
Frankfort, Maine, November 24, 1844; buried on the farm and
grave marked with a double stone, inscribed " A Patriot of
'76 "; married, August 4, 1782, in Scarboro, Hannah Seavey,
born July 11, 1762; died in Frankfort, December 30, 1838.
He was a farmer and built the first frame house in the Frankfort region. In the rear is old " Tyler Mountain," where is
his large quarry of granite; the landscape is very bold. A
part of the old farm, 300 acres, is still owned in the family
and called "Hillside Farm." He was in the Revolution, a
private in his father's company in 1775, and served during
the intervening years in other companies until 1780, reaching
the rank of sergeant; was in camp at Valley Forge in January,
1778, and at the surrender of Burgoyne. Appointed a lieutenant in the militia by Governor John Hancock, in 1789;
Lieutenant-Governor Samuel Adams appointed him captain
of the militia in 1794; Governor Caleb Strong, of Massachusetts, appointed him major in 1803, and Governor James
Sullivan, of Massachusetts appointed him lieutenant-colonel in
1807. He was highway surveyor of Frankfort in 1818; selectman and assessor in 1807; also land surveyor. The children
were born in Frankfort.

CHILDREN:

1210   Mary Tyler, married Elisha Thayer, of Winterport,
        Maine. They had a son (Tyler) who became a
        physician, married and had a family.
1211+   Andrew Tyler, born Sept. 30, 1793.
1212   Abigail Tyler, died, unmarried, Oct. 15, 1811.
1213   Ann Eliza Tyler, died, unmarried, July 3, 1849.
1214+   Sally Tyler, born April 15, 1798.
1215   Clarissa Tyler, born 1805; died March 28, 1839, un-
        married.

396 DOMINICUS[5] TYLER (Abraham[4]), born in Scar-
boro, Maine; baptized there February 15, 1767; married in
Scarboro, January 26, 1797, Rebecca Carl. He moved to
Frankfort, Maine. Benjamin Nason, of Biddeford, grants
Dominicus, July 31, 1789, 10 acres at " Blew Point." He
had from his father, March 26, 1795, for £12 18s, 2¼ acres on
Dunston Landing Road. Also, September 22, 1803, a tract in
Scarboro, from his father " in consideration of 4 years labor

heretofore received." He granted to Benjamin Millikin, his wife "Rebeker" joining, December 5, 1804, a marsh on Dunston River, about 40 rods north of "Tyler's Bridge," called Goosebury Island. He had 20 acres from his father, October 5, 1805, for $250, lying at "Tyler's Bridge," the right being reserved for Abraham's daughter Hannah, probably unmarried, to take wood for one fireplace, during her life. (*Portland, Maine, Registry of Deeds*, Books 22, 47 and 48.) His peculiar name doubtless comes from the fact that his father, in one of his numerous marriages, took one of the Jordan family as a wife, and his father had a business transaction with " Dominicus Jordan " at one time, from whence the name probably comes. The male line in this family threatens to become extinct.

CHILDREN:

1216+   John Tyler.
1217   Royal Tyler, died, unmarried, in Frankfort, Maine, aged 85.
1218+   Allison Tyler, born in 1800.
1219+   Sally Tyler.
1220+   Mehitable Tyler.
1221+   Abigail Tyler.
1222+   Elsie Tyler.
1223   Betsey Tyler, married —— Metcalf, a farmer of Frankfort, and her son (Captain William Metcalf) resided in Farmington, Maine.

397   SARAH[5] TYLER (Abraham[4]), born in Scarboro, Maine, April 3, 1768; died February, 1820; married, October 7, 1787, Peletiah Marr, born June 19, 1765; settled in Plantation of Little Ossipee, where he died November 27, 1826; son of Dennis and Sarah (Hutchins) Marr. Children:

1224   Peletiah Marr, born Sept. 17, 1791; died ibid.
1225   Isaac Marr, born Sept. 16, 1792; married (1), Sally Stone; married (2), Elizabeth Edgecomb; married (3), Eliza Morton.
1226   Lavinia Marr, born April 13, 1793; married. Dec. 31, 1818, Samuel Wiggin, who died in 1825.
1227   William Marr, born Oct. 20, 1794; died aged 1 week.
1228   Adaline Marr, born April 13, 1796; married, Nov. 11, 1817, Rev. Andrew Hobson.

1229   Dennis Marr, born Oct. 24, 1799; died May 1, 1830.
1230   Sally Marr, born Jan. 10, 1802; died May 1, 1829.
1231   Parker Marr, born July 29, 1803.
1232   Tyler Marr, born March 5, 1805.
1233   William Marr, born Oct. 20, 1806; died July 5, 1828.
1234   Martha Marr, born Nov. 17, 1808; died Aug. 30, 1837.
1235   Rebecca Marr, born June 17, 1809.
1236   Lydia Marr, born Nov. 17, 1812; died Dec. 15, 1835.

399   CAPTAIN ABRAHAM[5] TYLER (Abraham[4]),
born in Scarboro, Maine, October 20, 1770; married Sally
Small. He was in the Revolution, his name being on the Pension Rolls. He removed to Limington, Maine, and was there
in 1792. He had a land grant from his brother David, August
10, 1809, of 70 acres for $475. He being then at Bowdoin-
ham, Maine. He was a sea-captain. The children were born
in Scarboro. Children:
1237   Sally Tyler, died in Scarboro Dec. 21, 1795.
1238   Sarah Tyler, baptized in the First church, Scarboro,
        Dec. 14, 1804; married James Watson. They had
        a large family, and one son (James) resided in
        Sangerville, Maine.
1239   Anna Tyler, married —— Briggs, and died s. p.
1240+   Benjamin Tyler.
1241   Phebe Tyler, married —— Caswell, and had a family.
1242   John Tyler.
1243   Daniel Tyler.

400   JOHN SMITH[5] TYLER (Abraham[4]), born in
Scarboro, Maine, October 2, 1772; died in Pownal, Maine, Octo-
ber 18, 1840; married (1), January 8, 1790, Lucy Trickey,
who died October 2, 1830, aged 59; daughter of Zebulon and
Rebecca (Stillings) Trickey, of Falmouth, Maine, and grand-
daughter of Zebulon and Eleanor (Libby) Trickey, of Kittery,
Scarboro, and Falmouth, Maine; married (2), Sarah Lord, who
died s. p. Before 1800 he was at Hiram, Maine, living on the
Stephen Ridlon place, near "Tyler Hill," with his brother
Daniel, removing to Pownal in 1797.

CHILDREN, by first marriage:
1244+   William Tyler, born in Cape Elizabeth, Maine, Jan. 9,
        1791.

1245+   Rebecca Tyler, born July 30, 1792.
1246+   Zebulon Tyler, born March 12, 1794.
1247   Eliza Tyler, married (1), —— Sylvester; married (2),
        Abner Dennison.
1248+   Eveline Tyler, born Oct. 2, 1798.
1249   Mary Tyler, born in Pownal; died young.
1250+   John Tyler, born Oct. 2, 1803.
1251   Anis Tyler, born 1806; died in 1856, unmarried.
1252+   Lucy Tyler.
1253+   Sophia Ann Tyler.
1254   Charles Tyler, died s. p. in Durham, Maine, about
        1885; married (1), Sarah Libby, a widow of Pow-
        nal; married (2), Anuah ——, a widow of Scar-
        boro, Maine. He resided in Levant, Maine, then
        moved to Durham.

401   DAVID[5] TYLER (Abraham[4]), born in Scarboro,
Maine; baptized July 20, 1774; will dated November 14, 1861;
probated in Belfast, Maine; married (1), March 2, 1791,
Rhoda Libby, born June 17, 1772, daughter of Major Josiah
and Eunice (Libby) Libby, of Scarboro; married (2), Nancy
——, who survived him. (For account of the Libby Family
see *Collections of Maine Historical Society*, Vol. iii, p. 68.)
He settled in Freedom, Maine, and lived also in Bowdoinham.
For $300, June 17, 1809, Joseph Jackson, Mariner, of Bow-
doinham, granted to David Tyler, of Bowdoinham, " yeoman,"
70 acres of land adjoining Dean Tyler's property, who was his
brother. David sold the same land, August 10, 1809 (no
wife joining), for $475 to Abraham Tyler, of Bowdoinham,
" yeoman." (See *Wiscasset, Maine, Reg. Deeds*, Vols. 74 and
75.) Before 1800 he lived, with his brother, John Smith Tyler,
on the Stephen Ridlon place in Hiram, Maine.

CHILDREN, by first marriage:
1255   Annie Tyler, married Benjamin Bither.
1256   Polly Tyler, married —— Strout.
1257   Martha Tyler, married —— Marshall.
1258   Rhoda Tyler, married —— Glidden.
1259   Artemesia Tyler, married March 11, 1829, Jacob
        Fogg; married (2), —— Taylor.
1260+   Eunice Tyler.
1261+   Orville Tyler, born in Freedom, Maine, 1806.

CHILDREN, by second marriage:

1262   Josiah Tyler, born in Unity or Freedom, Maine; died
        about 1890; was a farmer; he married and had chil-
        dren; one a son, died and left a widow in Bradford,
        Maine.
1263+   Major Tyler.
1264   Horace C. Tyler, died intestate; married Sarah L.
        ———; he lived in Freedom and the inventory of his
        estate amounted to $5,507.18. His wife was ad-
        ministratrix and apparently there were no children.

404 DANIEL⁵ TYLER (Abraham⁴), born in Scarboro,
Maine, February 5, 1780; died in Gorham, Maine, September
26, 1822; married Mary Higgins, of Standish, Maine, daughter of Enoch F. and Miriam (Dean) Higgins; she probably
died a widow in Belfast, Maine, April 1, 1856, aged 76. He
was a lawyer and magistrate. He removed to Gorham. The
male line is nearly out. The children were born in Gorham.
Children:
1265   Sally Tyler, born May 15, 1804; died May 10, 1809.
1266+   Lendell Tyler, born Aug. 28, 1805.
1267+   Mary E. Tyler, born July 2, 1807.
1268   Daniel Tyler, born April 28, 1809; died unmarried.
1269+   Sally Tyler, born Aug. 16, 1811.
1270   Allen Tyler, born April 2, 1814; died unmarried.
1271+   Emily Tyler, born May 27, 1818.
1272   Abraham Tyler; died unmarried.
1273+   Martha Tyler.

405 SAMUEL⁵ TYLER (Abraham⁴), born in Scarboro,
Maine, in 1781; died in Saco, Maine, where he resided, January
22, 1809; married (published) August 17, 1799, Lydia Josse,
of Saco. He cut his knee in the woods and bled to death, after
crawling three miles. His widow and children moved in 1820
to Hartford, Maine, where she died January 2, 1854. The
children were born in Saco. Children:
1274+   John Tyler, born March 27, 1800.
1275+   Grace Tyler, born Sept. 9, 1802.
1276+   James Josse Tyler, born April 12, 1805.
1277+   Dorcas Tyler, born Aug. 2, 1807.

409   CAPTAIN JOSEPH[5] TYLER (Royall[4]), born in Scarboro, Maine; baptized March 29, 1752; will dated November 25, 1825; estate probated in Alfred, Maine; married June 22, 1784, Jane March Small, born June 19, 1765; daughter of Colonel Samuel and Anna (Libby) Small, of Scarboro. He moved to Limington, Maine; at one time resided in Standish, Maine; later returned to Scarboro. and was received in the First Congregational church, September 29, 1808.   He was in the Revolution.   He was commissioned captain after the war by Governor Increase Sumner, of Massachusetts.   His son Daniel was administrator of his estate.   Joseph was a friend of Alexander Hamilton, on whose death, in 1804, he, with some others, made his coffin.   The children were born in Scarboro, except the youngest.   Children:

1278+   Mary Stevens Tyler, born Oct. 13, 1785.
1279+   Benjamin Tyler, born June 19, 1787.
1280+   Anna Tyler, born Nov. 2, 1788.
1281+   Elizabeth Tyler, born April 10, 1791.
1282+   Joseph Tyler, born Oct. 10, 1792.
1283+   Martha Tyler, born Dec. 30, 1794.
1284+   Abraham Tyler, born March 7, 1798.
1285+   Samuel Tyler, born March 7, 1800.
1286+   James Tyler, born Feb. 28, 1801.
1287+   Jane Tyler, born May 12, 1802.
1288+   Daniel Tyler, born in Limington (probably), May 4, 1806.

412   SAMUEL[5] TYLER (Royall[4]), born in Scarboro, Maine, April 21, 1762; died in Westport, Maine, January 6, 1827; married, December 15, 1783, in Edgecombe, Maine, Martha Dunton, born December 21, 1764; perhaps the daughter of Samuel Dunton, whose land bounded land that Samuel Tyler bought.   Cornelius Tarbox, of Edgecombe, grants land to Samuel, March 15, 1787, " being at a place called Hell Gate Cove on the river," etc.   John Hall, of Georgetown, Maine, July 25, 1787, sold to Samuel for £5 land on Squam Island (now Westport), 100 acres, "being at Hell's Gate and bounded by Samuel Dunton's and Nathaniel Knight's land," etc.   (*Wiscasset Deeds*, Vols. 20 and 21.)   The children were born in Edgecombe, Maine, except the two younger, who were born in Westport.

CHILDREN:

1289+   James Tyler, born June 6, 1785.

1290   Phebe Tyler, born Oct. 20, 1786.

1291   Martha Tyler, born April 9, 1791; published, Nov. 25, 1812, to Smith Rogers, both then of Bath, Me.

1292   Bethiah Tyler, born Feb. 25, 1793; married —— Crawford; she had two daughters and a son.

1293   Samuel Tyler, born Feb. 23, 1795; died young.

1294   Betty Tyler, twin to Samuel; married James Collins, of Gardiner, Maine, and had two sons and three daughters. (One is Captain Jason Collins, of the steamer " Kennebec.")

1295   Apphia Tyler, born June 11, 1797; married —— Whitten, of Freeport, Maine; had four sons.

1296   Royal Tyler, born April 21, 1799.

1297+   Ezra Tyler, born May 27, 1804.

1298   Samuel Tyler, born Jan. 15, 1808; died May 27, 1831, probably unmarried. For $500 he grants, April 29, 1831, to Ezra Tyler and Bethiah Crawford, of Westport, interest in the estate of Samuel Tyler, deceased, of Westport.

414   JAMES[5] TYLER (Royal[4]), born in Scarboro, Maine; baptized October 13, 1782; died in Portland, Maine, July 16, 1849; married Sarah Jordan, of Cape Elizabeth, Maine, daughter of Captain and Sarah (Grundy) Libby Jordan (who married (3), Abraham Tyler, the uncle of James). The children were born in Portland. Children:

1299+   Martha Tyler.

1300+   Melinda Tyler.

1301   James Tyler, died, unmarried, in New Orleans, La.; he was a master mariner.

1302   Clement Tyler, died, unmarried, in New Orleans; was a master mariner.

1303   Sarah Ann Tyler, died aged 14.

1304   Louisa Tyler, married Fred W. Bemis.

1305   Charles Tyler, died about 1855 in San Francisco, unmarried; he was a seaman.

1306+   Simon Houston, born in Gorham, Maine, in 1820.

1307   Matthew Tyler, died unmarried.

417   JACOB[5] TYLER (Jacob[4]), born May 27, 1752;

died, in Methuen, Mass., March 6, 1810; married, September 26, 1782, Ruth Marsh, of Haverhill, Mass., born November 9, 1760; died February 15, 1812. He lived in Methuen, Mass. He was a private in Lieutenant Peter Poor's company of Andover, that marched, Wednesday, April 19, 1775, on the Alarm, from Andover to Cambridge, 55 miles. On Saturday, May 27, 1775, Jacob Tyler, Jr., and 15 other men were engaged with the enemy at Chelsea, Mass., and also on Sunday, May 28th, in which they drove the British from a schooner and set fire to it and destroyed it. Four men were wounded. They were a detachment from Captain Poor's company. He joined Captain Benjamin Farnum's company as a private. They were in the Battle of Bunker Hill. He died intestate and his widow administered upon the estate. His real estate was inventoried at $4,364, and his personal property at over a thousand dollars. Each of the children received about $660 in the distribution.

CHILDREN:

1308+   Ruth Tyler, born Aug. 9, 1785.

1309+   Lydia Tyler, born June 25, 1787.

1310+   John Tyler, born Sept. 12, 1790.

1311   Benjamin Marsh Tyler, born June 29, 1792; died s. p. in Franklin, N. H., in 1847; married, Nov. 26, 1835, Mary Ware, of Andover, N. H. He was educated in the military school in Norwich, Conn.; afterwards a teacher there, at Taunton Hill, in Andover, N. H., and later master of "Noyes' School" during its brief existence. His work had so impressed the people of Franklin and surrounding towns that when the school was broken up on account of the contesting of Mr. Noyes' will, "The Instructor's School" was built for him, organized in 1830, on a Normal basis with a regular course of training. He had large classes of teachers and attracted scholars from afar. When the records of New England school work are adequately made up, Mr. Tyler will have an honored place. "No citizen of Franklin has ever had a larger or better influence."

1312   Jacob Tyler, born April 9, 1794; died in Methuen, Mass., Dec. 22, 1856; married Sally Currier, who died Aug. 7, 1850; no children. He was a farmer.

1313+   Sally Tyler, born April 4, 1796.
1314   James Tyler, born July 11, 1797; died in Pelham,
        N. H., Nov. 7, 1875; married, July 10, 1834 or
        1835, Elizabeth Wyman, born Sept. 7, 1816; daugh-
        ter of Edward and Hannah (Cutter) Wyman. He
        was a farmer and lived in Pelham.
1315+   Varnum Tyler, twin to James.
1316+   Jeremiah Tyler, born Jan. 16, 1799.

419 LYDIA[5] TYLER (Jacob[4]), born in Haverhill,
Mass., in 1756; died ———; married, August 26, 1778, Nathan
Swan, of Methuen, Mass., who married (2), Lydia's sister
Sarah; he was born September, 1758. She received her portion of her father's estate at her marriage. Children:
1317   Nathan Swan, born May 17, 1780.
1318   Lydia Swan, born Dec. 21, 1782.

420 SARAH[5] TYLER (Jacob[4]), born in Haverhill,
Mass., September, 1758; married (second wife) Nathan
Swan, widower of her sister Lydia; born September, 1758. She
was to receive jointly, with her sister Phebe, the residue of her
mother's estate. Child:
1319   Sarah Swan, baptized in North Andover, in 1791.

425 JEREMIAH[5] TYLER (Moses[4]), born in Woburn,
Mass., November 20, 1755; died in Lowell, Mass., at home of
daughter, Mrs. John Locke, September 2, 1835; married widow
Anna Munroe, who died March 18, 1781; he married again, but
the name of his wife is not known; she died in 1798. He was
in the Revolution in Captain Edmund Munro's company of
Colonel Timothy Bigelow's 15th Massachusetts Bay Regiment;
he served in the early parts of the years 1778 and 1779, and at
some period he enlisted for three years. His name is on the
Pension Rolls. In 1821 he was living in Ashby, Mass. The
children were born in Woburn. Only those who survived their
father are enumerated. Children:
1320   John Tyler (?).
1321+   William Tyler, born Oct. 1, 1789.
1322+   Benjamin Tyler.
1323   Jonas Tyler, resided in Franconia, N. H., where he
        was a hotel-keeper, and where he died about 1850.
        There is a strong probability that he had sons.

1324+   Fanny Tyler, born April 3, 1785.

426 MOSES[5] TYLER (Moses[4]), born in Andover, Mass., September 12, 1757; died, while living with his son Moses in Harvard, Mass., later than 1840; his will was dated March 29, 1839; married, in Boston, Mary Cotton, who died in Harvard, October 24, 1838, aged 80. He was in the Revolution, enlisting from Woburn, in Captain Abishar Brown's company of Colonel Josiah Whitney's regiment, in 1776; also in Captain Samuel Fay's company, Lieutenant-Colonel Webb's regiment in 1781, in the three months' series; also on the roll of same company as late as January, 1784. He was a pensioner, as late as 1840. He kept a retail store in Boston, and is in the directory for the year 1812. He removed to Harvard, Mass. Children:

1325+   Mary Tyler, born in Boston, Feb. 2, 1797.
1326   Moses Tyler; his father resided with him in Harvard in 1840.

427 JONATHAN[5] TYLER (Moses[4]), born in Woburn, Mass., June 14, 1760; died there February 14, 1833; married, May 1, 1781, Rhoda Bruce, born January 22, 1761; died December 5, 1828; daughter of John and Mehitable Bruce. In 1776 he was in Captain Abishar Brown's company and in camp in Hull, Mass. He is thought to have been a pensioner at the time of his death. His son Joseph declined to administer his estate, but later became surety for Benjamin Wyman, of Woburn, who was appointed administrator. Jonathan was a cordwainer. He was also, probably, a storekeeper in Boston in the retail business, and his name appears in the directory of 1796. The children were born in Woburn. Children:

1327+   Jonathan Tyler, Jr., born Sept. 17, 1782.
1328   Polly Tyler, born July 19, 1793; died young.
1329   Sally Tyler, born March 25, 1785; married, Sept. 17, 1818, Abijah Stearns.
1330   Isaac Tyler, born in 1787; drowned June 24, 1788, aged 16 months.
1331   Infant, born 1788-9; died July 14, 1789, aged under 1 year.
1332   Susanna Tyler, born April 21, 1790; married ———— White, and moved to Vermont.

1333+ Mary Tyler.
1334   Eliza Tyler, died unmarried.
1335+ Hannah Tyler, born Sept. 25, 1793.
1336   Moses Tyler, born in 1794; went to Albany, N. Y.
1337   Isaac Tyler, went to St. Joseph, Mo.
1338+ Joseph Tyler, born in 1798.
1339   Infant, died April 12, 1803.
1340   Clarissa Tyler, born in 1801; died Dec. 3, 1860, un-
       married.
1341+ Rhoda Bruce Tyler, born Dec. 14, 1802.

429 ELEANOR[5] TYLER (Moses[4]), born August 7,
1764; married, December 14, 1788, Elisha Fuller, of Charlestown, Mass., born October 8, 1760. The children were born
in Charlestown. Children:

1342   Hannah B. Fuller, born Oct. 13, 1790.
1343   Abigail T. Fuller, born Sept. 10, 1791.
1344   Elisha D. Fuller, born Oct. 25, 1793.
1345   Freeman H. Fuller, born June 7, 1799.
1346   William P. Fuller, born March 2, 1802.
1347   Charles C. Fuller, born Aug. 9, 1805.
1348   Isaac B. Fuller, born Feb. 2, 1808.

432 JONAS[5] TYLER (Moses[4]), born in Woburn, Mass.,
May 31, 1733; died in Charlestown, Mass., June 26, 1853;
married (1) (published November 11, 1804), Rebecca Adams,
born in Winchendon, Mass., March 30, 1781; died s. p. May
28, 1806; married (2), February 6, 1810, in Lexington, Mass.,
Ruhamah Bridge, who died January 10, 1864, aged 82. He
was a dealer in West India goods, and resided in Charlestown,
where the children were born.

CHILDREN, by second marriage:

1349   George Washington Tyler, born Feb. 5, 1813; died
       s. p. in Leavenworth, Kan., Aug. 22, 1870; married,
       Nov., 1855, Mrs. Louisa (Elms) Drake, the divorced
       wife of the historian Drake. Was graduated from
       Harvard Law School in 1857, and was admitted to
       practice the same year. Early in life he was a com-
       mission merchant in Boston, where in his store, his
       brother John fell and died. George Tyler was well

educated and brilliant; had a large library which
was open for the use of young men. He was an
early editor on the Boston *Herald*. Removed to
Leavenworth, Kan.

1350   John Francis Tyler, born Sept. 10, 1815; died unmarried March 3, 1837, the result of a fall in the store
of his brother George in Boston.

1351   Rebecca Adams Tyler, born March 23, 1817; died
unmarried in Charlestown July 1, 1890.

1352+   Benjamin Franklin Tyler, born April 4, 1821.

1353   Anne (or Annie) Tyler, born April 28, 1823; died unmarried in Charlestown, Aug. 16, 1898.

1354   (Captain) Jonas Kendall Tyler, born March 25, 1825;
died there May 2, 1898; married, Dec. 24, 1874,
Mrs. Lydia Maria (Preston) Walsh, who died s. p.
Sept. 7, 1888. He received a good education. He
enlisted in the Mexican War, in Boston, June 5,
1846, at the age of 21 attaining the rank of lieutenant. He was admitted to practice law at the
Suffolk County, Massachusetts Bar, July 5, 1853.
In June, 1861, he recruited a company for the
Civil War, going out for three years as its captain,
which became a part of the 29th Regiment of Mass.
Volunteers. He wrote for the " Boston Herald "
in its early days and was always a great reader.
His temperament led him to take life easily and
probably prevented him attaining the place his abili-
ties entitled him to reach. His will was proved May
26, 1898. He left to his nephew, John Tyler, the
" swords, pistols and accoutrements to the same,
belonging, worn and used by me in the Mexican and
Civil Wars." His residence was at 252 Bunker
Hill Street, Charlestown. His nephew John was
executor.

444   MOSES[5] TYLER (Moses[4]), born in Boston, Mass.,
November 26, 1734; died September 16, 1811; interred in
" Tyler's Point " cemetery, Barrington, R. I.; married, July
17, 1760, Elizabeth Adams (perhaps he had a first wife, who
died soon); born in 1738; died November 7, 1811. He was
called " Esquire." In 1761 he bought his house in Boston on

"King's Lane" of Peter Barbour. Moved to Warren and Barrington, R. I., soon after, where are recorded the births of his children. He appears on a list of officers commissioned for the 3d regiment of militia in the County of Bristol, July, 1771. His rank was lieutenant in Captain Jacob Ide's company, Colonel George Leonard's regiment. He was on the committee of correspondence, March 21, 1774, restricting the tea importation from Great Britain. In 1776 and 1777 he was a deputy from Barrington the General Assembly; he was a justice of the peace. He built ships on "New Meadow Neck" near Kelley's Bridge and also called "Tyler's Point," a narrow and short tongue of land bounded by tidewater, and reached by bridge from Barrington Center and by a second bridge from Warren. The old cemetery there, now neglected, contains three generations of Tylers, side by side. There stood the first Baptist church (erected in 1663), until 1700. In 1778, when the British and Hessians invaded Warren and burned many buildings, Mr. Tyler was conspicuous in his efforts to prevent their invading Barrington. He prevented the landing of two Hessians, who came over in a boat, killing one, whose musket, 110 years old, was shown at the Centennial anniversary of the town. Mr. Tyler bequeathed the gun to his grandson, Sylvanus Haile Bowen. On the lock plate is stamped the English crown and the initials G. R. (Georgius Rex) and date, 1760. The Tyler homestead on "Tyler's Point" passed to John[6] and John[7] Tyler, and originally included all the land between the two rivers. The children were born in Warren, except the youngest.

CHILDREN:

1355+   Hannah Tyler, born April 4, 1764.
1356   Elizabeth Tyler, born Feb. 24, 1766.
1357+   Mary Tyler, born Feb. 18, 1768.
1358+   John Tyler, born Nov. 26, 1769.
1359   Sarah Tyler, born in Barrington, Dec. 19, 1771; died June 7, 1785; buried in the cemetery at Tyler's Point.

446   SARAH[5] TYLER (Moses[4]), born in Boston, Mass., April 12 (or 2), 1738; died in January, 1791; interred in Copp's Hill burying-ground; married, May 22, (or 2), 1759,

Robert Breck, born in Boston, February 17, 1735; died in 1783 and interred in Copp's Hill burying-ground.   He was in the cooperage business, and had a fine residence at the North End on Love Street, with a silver plate on the door.   He was a Revolutionary patriot.   The children were born in Boston. Children:

1360   Luther Breck, born March 15, 1762; a mariner and never married; was captured by the British in the War of 1812; escaped and recaptured, and died in Dartmoor Prison, England.

1361   Isabella Breck, born July 31, 1763; died Nov. 1, 1847; married, Sept. 20, 1789, Jonathan Stoddard, born in Boston, Sept. 2, 1766; lived in Boston and died Aug. 20, 1827.

1362   Sarah Breck, baptized June 9, 1765; died unmarried.

1363   Robert Breck, baptized Sept. 9, 1766; died unmarried.

1364   Moses Breck, baptized April 3, 1768; died in Plymouth, Mass., May, 1807.

1365   Deborah Breck, born May 6, 1769; married W. Blake, May 9, 1795; died s. p.

1366   Joseph Breck, born Oct. 10, 1771; died in Littleton, Mass, June 27, 1822; married, Oct. 12, 1809, Lucy Everett, of Roxbury; they had at least four children.

1367   Hannah Breck, born April, 1772; died young.

1368   Ann Breck, born July 30, 1774; died young.

1369   Hannah Breck, born in 1776; died unmarried.

1370   Samuel Breck, born Feb. 27, 1778; died suddenly in Boston, March 20, 1809.

448   HANNAH[5] TYLER (Moses[4]), born in Boston, Mass., June 24, 1742; married, January 9, 1766, Alden Bass, " mariner."   Children:

1371   Hannah Bass, married — — Eaton.

1372   Mary Bass, married ——— Colburn. See No. 3332.

1373   Moses Bass.

1374   Joseph D. Bass.

1375   Deborah Bass, left children.

449   CAPTAIN ELISHA[5] TYLER (Moses[4]), born in Boston, Mass., April 16, 1744; died there, January 21, 1808;

married, March 27, 1766, by Rev. Andrew Eliot, Dorcas Page, who died in Boston, December 28, 1770, aged 29, and was interred in Copp's Hill burying-ground. He was a shipwright and mariner and was styled "Esquire." His will speaks of him as "Late of the Bay of Honduras—formerly of Boston (Dorchester)." Will probated March 28, 1808; son Elisha was legatee; brother Edward was executor. (*Boston Probate Records.*) Children:

1376+ Hannah Luther Tyler.

1377 Elisha Tyler, born March 3, 1767; died unmarried. He was a "mariner."

450 ELLIS[5] TYLER (Moses[4]), born in Boston, Mass., September 16, 1745; died there, November 5, 1788; married, April 6, 1769, in Boston, Abigail Luther Parkman, who died in Harvard, Mass., about 1817, aged 68. He was a tailor and shipwright. In 1779 he was steward on the ship *General Putnam*, commanded by Daniel Waters, Esq.; in 1780 he held the same rank on board the ship *Viper*, commanded by William Williams; in 1781 he was steward on the brig *Prospect*, commanded by Joseph Vesey. He was five feet eight inches in height, and was of a dark complexion. His wife was executor, and his will was probated January 10, 1786. His children were born in Boston. Children:

1378+ Edward Tyler, born Nov. 10, 1776.

1379 Ellis Callender Tyler, died in Harvard, Mass., unmarried, aged 46. His brother Edward administered upon his estate, and gave bond, July 14, 1817. It was distributed among his surviving brothers and sisters.

1380 Hannah Luther Tyler, married, Sept. 29, 1791, Samuel Pearce, a baker, of Boston.

1381 Abigail (Nabby) Tyler, married Lawrence Gray, mariner, July 24, 1793; no children recorded in Boston.

1382+ Sarah (Sally) Tyler.

452 MABEL[5] TYLER (Daniel[4]), born in Canterbury, Conn., June 30, 1724; died February 21, 1792; married, November 1, 1749, Hon. Seth Paine, Jr., born in Pomfret, Conn., May 21, 1719; died there, February 24, 1762: he and his wife

are buried in the old Brooklyn, Conn., yard; he was the son of Seth and Mary (Morris) Paine. He was a skilful surveyor and a leading man in his community. For several years he was representative to the General Assembly and a member of the United States Constitutional Convention, in January, 1788, and voted to "ratify." He was both a merchant and farmer. Was admitted to the Congregational church January 1, 1758. (See *Paine Family Records.*) The children were born in Pomfret.

CHILDREN:

1383 Seth Paine, born Aug. 23, 1750; married —— Lester, of Preston, Conn., a farmer, who moved to Tunbridge, Vt., and died in 1820; they had two sons and three daughters.

1384 Mary Paine, born May 4, 1753; died Nov. 23, 1765.

1385 John Paine, born March 28, 1755; a farmer; died unmarried, in Winsor, Vt., 1785.

1386 Elijah Paine, born Jan. 21, 1757; died in Williamstown, Vt., April 21, 1842; married Sarah Porter; was graduated from Harvard College in 1781; settled in Montpelier, Vt., in 1785, and in 1790 was on the committee to settle the boundary between New York and Vermont; was a member of Congress from 1795-1801; in 1801 was appointed Judge of the United States District Court in Vermont; had four sons and two daughters.

1387 Ebenezer Paine, born Aug. 23, 1758; died Aug. 17, 1826; married Sarah De Croe; moved to Edenton, N. C.; had two boys and a girl.

1388 Sarah Paine, born April 4, 1760; died in Troy, N. Y., 1832; married in 1781, Judge Isaac Cushman, who died June 2, 1842.

1389 Amasa Paine, born May 28, 1762; died in Troy, N. Y., Dec. 25, 1823; married, Sept. 9, 1787, Elizabeth Homer; was two years at Yale College; was graduated from Harvard College in 1785; a lawyer; they had one son and six daughters.

1390 Anne Paine, born March 20, 1764; died in Guildhall, Vt.; married —— Denison.

1391 Daniel Paine, born Jan. 29, 1767; moved to Randolph, Vt., in 1798, where he died Feb., 1811; married

Mehitable Lester; was a farmer. they had three sons and four daughters.

454 ASA⁵ TYLER (Daniel⁴), born in Canterbury, Conn., March 5, 1731; died ——; married Antis ——; moved to Brooklyn, Conn. Children:

1392   Alemeron (or Alleman) Tyler, born March 12, 1767; died Dec. 26, 1768.

1393   Alemeron Tyler, born Feb. 6, 1769; died Jan., 1772.

1394   Henrietta Maria Tyler, born Nov. 6, 1771; living in 1811.

1395   Alvan Tyler, born Jan. 26, 1773; living in 1811.

1396   Bernice Tyler, born Jan. 20, 1775; probably died before 1813.

1397   Tabitha Tyler, born Dec. 26, 1776; married —— Stowell.

1398   Asenath Tyler, born Dec. 10, 1779; living in 1811.

1399   James Tyler, born Dec. 20, 1781; probably died before 1813.

1400+   Alcemon Tyler, born Oct. 16, 1784.

1401   Jabez Tyler, born June 6, 1786; living in 1811. .

455 AMY⁵ TYLER (Daniel⁴), born in Canterbury, Conn., December 10, 1733; died September 13, 1811, in Hampton, Conn.; married, in Canterbury (afterward Brooklyn, Conn.), November 27, 1760, Aaron Goodell, born in Pomfret, Conn., July 26, 1733; died in Chaplin, Conn., March 28, 1823. son of Ebenezer Goodell (Thomas, Zachariah, Robert). He was a farmer and lived in Mansfield, Conn., where the children were born. Children:

1402   Olive Goodell, born Nov. 28, 1761; married Rev. Jesseniah Holmes and moved to New York state. He was a Baptist minister and they had 19 children.

1403   Anne Goodell, born Feb. 6, 1764; married James Eaton, of Chaplin, Conn.; had a son (Edwin) who had a family.

1404   Zilpha Goodell, born April 25, 1765; married, Dec. 15, 1791, Andrew Burnham, who died in Mansfield, Feb. 11, 1810, and afterwards she moved to Ohio and joined the Shakers; they had five children who died young.

1405   Isaac Goodell, born April 10, 1770; died in Chaplin,
       Conn., May 1, 1856; married, Nov. 27, 1804, Chloe
       Hammond, born April 15, 1772; died Jan. 27, 1870.
       He was a farmer and had two sons and two daugh-
       ters. From his son (Walter) who was a prominent
       man, is descended the genealogist, Rev. Isaac Good-
       ell, of Haverhill, Mass., who is the author of the
       Goodell Genealogy.

1406   Theda Goodell, born 1773; died in Chaplin, in 1775;
       was the first white child buried there.

456   LUCY[5] TYLER, born in Canterbury, Conn. (afterward Brooklyn, Conn.), November 13, 1735; married, February 1, 1759, Abijah Goodell, of Pomfret, Conn., where the
children were born; he was born June 27, 1736; son of Jacob
Goodell (Thomas, Zachariah, Robert).   Children:

1407   Huldah Goodell, born March 1, 1760.
1408   Elisha Goodell, born April 20, 1765.
1409   Elijah Goodell, born April 23, 1766.
1410   Nathan Goodell, born May 26, 1768.
1411   Lucy Goodell, born March 6, 1772.
1412   Molly Goodell, born Feb. 26, 1774.

459   CAPTAIN JAMES[5] TYLER (Daniel[4]), born in
Canterbury, Conn., July 25, 1743; died 1784; administrator
appointed October 5, 1784; married (1), (published September
15, 1769), in Bridgewater, Mass., Sarah Shurtleff, born in
Bridgewater, November 5, 1749; died in Canterbury, Conn.,
March 11, 1781, daughter of William and Sarah (Kingman)
Shurtleff; married (2), April 11, 1782, Mehitable Scarborough.
Captain Daniel Tyler, of Pomfret, Conn., was appointed administrator. The inventory was filed November 2, 1784, Seth
Paine and Jabez Allyn being the appraisers. The amount was
£566, 3s, 7d. It included his " silver-belted sword, and other
arms and ammunition; 21 silver buttons; 6 large silver spoons
and 12 small ones; 22 cream and Delph plates; one note against
Asa Tyler of £28, 7s, 9d." Captain Daniel Tyler was chosen
guardian of the children; at sixteen years of age Joseph Tyler
chose Ebenezer Scarborough, of Brooklyn, as his guardian.
Captain James' residence was in Canterbury, Conn.

CHILDREN, by first marriage:

1413 William Tyler, baptized Dec. 16, 1770; died July 13, 1773.

1414 Sarah Tyler, born July 16, 1772; married —— Eddy.

1415+ James Tyler, born Sept. 16, 1774.

1416 Joseph Tyler, born June 12, 1776; in 1785 he is mentioned in the settlement of his father's estate, but he is not named in his grandfather Gen. Daniel Tyler's will, in 1797, and probably died before that time, but later than 1792, when he chose his guardian.

1417 Anne Tyler, born Jan. 26, 1779; died, unmarried, Feb. 21, 1796. The administrator of her estate was her brother, Dr. James Tyler, and it was distributed May 2, 1797, to her brothers Joseph and Dr. James and sister, Mrs. Sarah Eddy; it amounted to about £60.

1418 Elisha Tyler, baptized Feb. 4, 1781; died before date of grandfather's will.

CHILDREN, by second marriage:

1419 Hitty Tyler, born Feb. 5, 1783; died before date of grandfather's will.

1420 Patty Tyler, born June 18, 1784; died before date of grandfather's will.

460 ELIZABETH[5] TYLER (Daniel[4]), born in Canterbury, Conn., December 15, 1744; married, February 28, 1765, Increase Hewit. Child:

1421 Thomas Hewit, born before Oct., 1797. mentioned in Daniel Tyler's will.

462 CAPTAIN DANIEL[5] TYLER (Daniel[4]), born in Canterbury, Conn., May 21, 1750; died in Brooklyn, Conn., April 29, 1832; married (1), April 15, 1771, Mehitable Putnam, born in Pomfret, Conn., October 21, 1749; died in Brooklyn, November 28, 1789; daughter of General Israel and Hannah (Pope) Putnam; married (2), in Brooklyn, June 10, 1790, Mrs. Sarah (Edwards) Chaplin, born in Elizabethtown, N. J., July 11, 1761; died in Brooklyn, April 25, 1841; widow of Benjamin Chaplin, and daughter of Timothy Edwards, son of

President Jonathan Edwards. She inherited many of the traits of her distinguished ancestry. Captain Tyler was graduated from Harvard College in 1771. He served as adjutant to his father-in-law, General Putnam, in 1775 and in many campaigns. In 1777, he and thirty-five others obtained leave to form an independent Matross company, to be commanded only by the commander-in-chief or by majors or brigadier-generals of the State of Connecticut. This company was ordered to rendezvous in Greenwich, in 1780, and they did efficient work when New London and Rhode Island were threatened. He was Captain of Artillery in 1778. When the town of Brooklyn was organized, June 26, 1786, Daniel was one of the selectmen. He was among the heaviest of the tax-payers, and served on the committee for the first grammar school. By 1795 he had a fine farm under cultivation. Captain Tyler engaged extensively in business, receiving and discharging large quantities of produce. In the church struggle of 1816, "Old Captain Tyler" held up the orthodox banner and was supported by the majority of the church. His will was dated April 24, 1832. The nine elder children were born in Pomfret, Conn.; the two younger in Brooklyn, Conn.

CHILDREN, by first marriage:

1422+   Molly Tyler, born Aug. 1, 1772.

1423+   Pascal Paoli Tyler, born May 15, 1774.

1424   Daniel Putnam Tyler, born March 1, 1776; died, unmarried, in Whitesboro, N. Y., Jan. 18, 1798. He was graduated from Yale College in 1794; became a lawyer.

1425   Septimus Tyler, born Sept. 12, 1779; died May 26, 1782, in Pomfret.

1426+   William P. Tyler, born Oct. 7, 1782.

1427+   Betsey Tyler, born June 18, 1784.

1428   Septimus Tyler, born June 7, 1788; died Sept. 17, 1817, of yellow fever while on frigate *Congress,* on passage home from bearing government dispatches to Hayti, in the War of 1812; he was graduated from West Point; he was commissioned Assistant Quarter-Master General in the War of 1812.

CHILDREN, by second marriage:

1429+   Sarah Pierpoint Tyler, born April 25, 1791.

1430+   Edwin Tyler, born Nov. 24, 1793.
1432+   Daniel Tyler, born Jan. 7, 1799.
1431+   Frederick Tyler, born May 7, 1795.

464   ZILPHA⁵ TYLER (Daniel⁴), born in Canterbury, Conn., June 28, 1758; died in Brooklyn, Conn., September 22, 1784; married, in 1777, Thomas Merritt, Jr., of Brooklyn, born in Scituate, Mass., April, 1754; died in Rowley, Mass.; son of Thomas and Jane (Nichols) Merritt. The children were born in Brooklyn. Children:

1433   Eunice Merritt, born April 15, 1778; married Joseph Scott; is mentioned in her grandfather Tyler's will.
1434   Joseph Merritt, died Aug., 1782, in infancy.
1435   Septimus Merritt, born June 27, 1782; probably died young.
1436   Infant daughter, born and died Sept. 19, 1784.

466   PHINEAS⁵ TYLER (John⁴), born in Canterbury, Conn., May 17, 1738; died in Brookfield, Vt., October 31, 1796; married, November 19, 1766, Lucy Hyde. He moved to Brookfield, where, February 5, 1800, he took a life lease of property owned by his son Asahel. His administrator was Daniel Tyler(?), who as such, gave deed to land at Brookfield, November 22, 1856, the last Tyler entry there. His children were born in Canterbury. Children:

1437+   Asahel Tyler, born July 6, 1768.
1438+   John Tyler, born July 15, 1770.
1439   Molly Tyler, born Sept. 4, 1772.
1440   Elijah Tyler, born Feb. 12, 1775.
1441   Zilpah Tyler, born Sept. 2, 1777.
1442   Amasa Tyler, born July 10, 1780.
1443   Lucy Tyler, born Oct. 12, 1782.

471   OLIVER⁵ TYLER (John⁴), born in Canterbury, Conn., January 2, 1754; died in East Randolph, Vt., September 18, 1834; married, January 4, 1775, Abigail Warren, who died July 20, 1836, aged 83. He was in the Revolution in the militia, in Saratoga, in Captain Clark's company, Colonel Latimer's regiment, in 1777. He is mentioned in the Pension Rolls. He removed to Vermont from Tolland, Conn., in 1781, and was a farmer and hotel-keeper. The three elder children

were born in Canterbury, and the three younger in East Randolph. Children:

1444+   Zerviah Tyler, born March 16, 1776.

1445   Polly Tyler, born Dec. 6, 1778; married Joel Allen, of Greenfield, Mass., and had two children.

1446+   Perley Tyler, born in 1779.

1447   Joseph Tyler, born Jan. 5, 1782; died, unmarried, Jan. 1, 1833.

1448   Sophia Tyler, married Daniel Martin, of Bradford, Vt., and had four or five children.

1449+   Orris Tyler, born Dec. 26, 1783.

478   MARY[5] TYLER (Moses[4]), born in Preston, Conn., September 12, 1730; died June 15, 1800; married (1), March 15, 1749, Elijah Boardman, born March 13, 1720, in Preston; son of Wait John and Mary (Billings) Boardman; descended from Daniel and Thomas of Ipswich, Mass.; married (2), May 28, 1760, Benjamin Coit, born March 28, 1731; died April 21, 1812; son of Colonel Samuel and Sarah (Spalding) Coit; his first wife was Abigail Billings, by whom he had four children. He was buried in the Coit tomb in Griswold, Conn. He was State Representative in 1772, 1773, 1778; and Judge of the County Court, etc. Children, by first marriage, born in Preston:

1450   Henry Boardman, died young.

1451   Jonas Boardman.

1452   Elijah Boardman.

1453   John Boardman.

1454   Frances Boardman.

CHILDREN, by second marriage, born in Preston:

1455   Henry Coit, born Dec. 11, 1761; died unmarried, 1790.

1456   George Coit, born Sept. 19, 1763; died in London, Eng., Sept. 28, 1787.

1457   William Coit, born Aug. 21, 1766; married Hannah Corning.

1458   Abigail Coit, born Aug. 20, 1768; married Nathaniel Shipman.

1459   Martha Coit, born Oct. 16, 1770; married Dwight Ripley.

1460   Betsey Coit, born Oct. 29, 1772; married Rev. Jonathan Pomeroy.

1461   Thomas Coit, born Feb. 7, 1775; lost at sea on journey to Europe; vessel never reported.

480   ELISHA⁵ TYLER (Moses⁴), born in Preston, Conn., August 5, 1734; died there March 26, 1809; married, December 31, 1755, Hannah Lester, who died February 23, 1813, in the 82d year of her age. They are buried in the old Pachaug cemetery. He was executor of his father's will and is mentioned thus: " I give to my son . . . the horse I usually ride, my best saddle and bridle, my largest Bible, and a sixth part of my library, my silver shoe buckles, my gold sleeve buttons together with all my wearing apparel both woollen and linen and my best walking cane. . . . Moreover, I give to my said son, my negro man Quam, enjoining it on my said son to take all proper and tender care of him, inasmuch as said negro hath faithfully served me many years." The children were born in Preston.

CHILDREN:
1462+   Moses Tyler, born Aug. 16, 1761.
1463+   Hannah Tyler, born July 23, 1764.

482   SARAH⁵ TYLER (Moses⁴), born in Preston, Conn., September 30, 1738; died there, May 26, 1827; married, April 17, 1755, Seth Smith. The children were born in Stonington, Conn. Children:
1464   Moses Smith, born Jan. 9, 1756; died Jan. 17, 1777.
1465   Parker Smith, born Nov. 2, 1758.
1466   Sabra Smith, born March 18, 1762.
1467   Chester Smith, born June 24, 1764. (Hon. Samuel O. Prentice, of Hartford, Conn., is a descendant of Chester.)
1468   Shubael Smith, born March 17, 1769.

483   ESTHER⁵ TYLER (Moses⁴), born in Preston, Conn., December 9, 1740; died in Rutland, Vt., September 16, 1787; married, October 1, 1759, Captain Nathaniel Gore, of Coventry, Conn., born April 21, 1739; died in Rutland, September 9, 1813. Captain Nathaniel was descended from John Gore of Cambridge, Mass., who came from England about 1648. Nathaniel was a sergeant and had seven days' service

at the time of the Lexington Alarm, in Captain William Belcher's company. Commissioned July 6, 1775, as lieutenant of the 8th company of the 8th Connecticut regiment, Colonel Jedediah Huntington, afterwards the " 17th Continental." He was taken prisoner at the battle of Long Island, and sent to the *Jersey* prison ship, where his sufferings permanently impaired him.

CHILDREN:

1469   Sally Gore, died young.
1470   Esther Gore.
1471   Sally Gore.
1472   Nathaniel Gore.
1473   Almary Gore.
1474   Frederick Gore.
1475   Polly Gore.
1476   Jesse Gore.

491   MAJOR SAMUEL[5] TYLER (James[4]), born in Preston, Conn., August 21, 1734; died there, March 20, 1820; married, March 17, 1757, Judith Brown, who died July 5, 1821, aged 86. He was appointed major in May, 1777, and transferred to the 27th regiment from the 8th regiment of the militia, January, 1780. The regiment was composed of men from Preston, Groton and Stonington. The children were born in Preston. Children:

1477+   James Tyler, born Aug. 3, 1763.
1478+   Bishop Tyler, born Jan. 27, 1767; died April 12, 1844.
1479+   Esther Tyler, born July 17, 1769.
1480+   John Brown Tyler, born Nov. 9, 1773.
1481+   Amy B. Tyler, twin to John Brown.

509   JOSEPH[5] TYLER (Joseph[4]), born in Preston, Conn., April 11, 1748; died August 17, 1824; buried in the old Brooklyn, Conn., cemetery; married, January 9, 1772, Anne Freeman, born 1750; died November 12, 1812, in her 61st year, and buried beside her husband. Children:

1482+   Daniel Tyler, born in 1773.
1483   Zipporah Tyler, born in 1775; died unmarried, May 29, 1835; buried in Scotland, Conn.
1484+   Joseph Tyler, born in 1777.

1485   Polly Tyler, born Aug. 23, 1780; died May 15, 1801.

1486+   Steavens Tyler, born in 1782.

1487   Nancy Tyler, born in 1785; died, unmarried, Oct. 3, 1806.

513   LIEUTENANT JAMES[5] TYLER (Joseph[4]), born in Preston, Conn., May 18, 1757; married, November 22, 1786, Clarinda Punderson. He resided in Preston and Jewett City, Conn. He was first lieutenant of the 4th company of the 6th battalion, Wadsworth's brigade, under Colonel Chester, in 1776, from Windham county. Children:

1488   Harriet Tyler, born in 1788; died April 5, 1799.

1489   (Capt.) James Tyler, born July 21, 1789; died, unmarried, in Jewett City, Conn., in 1864. He was in the War of 1812.

1490   Clarina Tyler, born Aug. 1, 1791; died, unmarried, in 1822.

1491   Sophia Tyler, born in 1793; died Sept. 17, 1794.

1492   Sophia Tyler, born Oct. 13, 1795; died, unmarried, in Jewett City, Conn., in 1861.

1493   (Rev.) Joseph Punderson Tyler, born Sept. 14, 1797, in Griswold, Conn.; died, unmarried, in North Bridgewater, Mass., Dec. 26, 1844. He was graduated from Brown University in the class of 1823; studied at Andover Theological Seminary; was ordained to the ministry of the Congregational church, June 3, 1828. He became a home missionary on Long Island, in 1828, and an agent of the American Home Missionary Society. He preached in eastern Connecticut and on Long Island from 1828-1834, when he became the pastor of the church in West Gloucester, Mass.; he was acting pastor in Voluntown and Sterling, Conn., in 1835-1836; preached in Chilmarth, Mass. and Little Compton, R. I., between 1836 and 1841.

1494+   Harriet Tyler, born Jan. 15, 1800.

1495   Prudentia Tyler, born in 1803; died Nov. 26, 1804, aged 16 months.

1496   Prudentia Ann Tyler, born 1806-1807; died Jan. 9, 1810.

1497   Infant, died April 30, 1822.

514   ZURIAH⁵ TYLER (Joseph⁴), born in Preston, Conn., August 25, 1759; died in Plainfield, N. H., May 27, 1846; married Gideon Woodward.   He was in the Revolution. Children:

1498   Erastus Woodward, born April 18, 1791; died in Grinnell, Ia., July 29, 1870; married Sarah Gilson, and had ten children (among them Tyler Woodward, President of the United States National Bank, Portland, Ore.).

1499   Sarah Woodward, born Aug. 25, 1793; died, s. p., Aug. 22, 1886; married John Daniels.

1500   Frederick Woodward, born Dec. 6, 1795; died Dec. 1, 1861; married Lucy Fay and had a family.

1501   Henry Woodward, born Jan. 23, 1798; died April 26, 1873; married Jane Cornell and had a family.

1502   Sophia Woodward, born June 3, 1800; died Sept. 3, 1890; married Sylvanus Bryant; had a family.

516   MEHITABEL⁵ TYLER (John⁴), born in North Preston (now Griswold), Conn., October 18, 1743; died January 3, 1816; married, February 6, 1766, John Coit, of Preston, born June 4, 1741; died March 3, 1808; son of Samuel and Sarah (Spa[u]lding) Coit.   He marched on the Lexington Alarm as a sergeant.   Children:

1503   Lydia Coit, born Dec. 13, 1766; married James Lord.

1504   (Capt.) Nathaniel Coit, born May 5, 1768; married (1), Betsey Morgan, of Preston; married (2), Mrs. John Prentice.

1505   Sarah Coit, born May 1, 1770; married James Rogers, Norwich, Conn.

1506   Olive Coit, born Feb. 22, 1772; died in Sutherland, Mass., in 1840; married (1), May 29, 1793, Colonel Moses Tyler, No. 1462; married (2), 1835, Rev. J. Dorrance, of Sutherland, Mass.

1507   John Coit, born Dec. 20, 1773; married Betsey Coit, daughter of Wheeler Coit; he was a merchant in New York City and a cotton trader.

1508   Sophia Coit, born Oct. 14, 1775; married Roland Burbank, of West Springfield, Mass.

1509   James Tyler Coit, born Oct. 1, 1778; died in Saint Mary's, Ga., where he went on mercantile pursuits.

1510   Rebecca Coit, born Feb. 2, 1783; died, s. p. about 1820, drowned while crossing a river; married (1), March 27, 1805, her cousin Daniel T. Coit, No. 1512, son of Daniel and Olive (Tyler) Coit, No. 520; married (2), Joseph Williams.

1511   (Hon.) Roger Coit, born Jan. 25, 1786; married (1), Oct. 7, 1808, Frances Coit, who died in Plainfield, Conn., Sept. 26, 1843; daughter of Daniel and Mercy Coit; married (2), Feb. 25, 1845, Mrs. Eliza Coggeswell. (See *Coit Genealogy*.)

520   OLIVE[5] TYLER (John[4]), born in North Preston, (now Griswold), Conn., March 22, 1722; died November 18, 1782; married, November 29, 1781, Daniel Coit, born in Preston, Conn., January 28, 1757; died October 11, 1790; son of Benjamin and Abigail (Billings) Coit. He was received into the church July 6, 1783. (He married (2), August 31, 1786, Mercy Brewster, who survived him, and married, in her turn, William Coggeswell, of Plainfield, Conn., May 22, 1791.) Daniel Coit served during a part of the Revolution and died at the early age of 33. Olive Tyler Coit is buried in the old Pachaug, Conn., cemetery.

CHILDREN:

1512   Daniel Tyler Coit, born Oct. 28, 1782; died Jan. 28, 1808; married, March 27, 1805, his cousin, Rebecca Coit, No. 1510, who died June 17, 1841, aged 58. They had a son, named for his father, who was a distinguished physician in Boston, but left no children.

1513   Olive Tyler Coit, twin to Daniel, died of consumption, Nov. 20, 1798, aged 16.

521   CAPTAIN JOHN[5] TYLER (John[4]), born in North Preston (now Griswold), Conn., July 22, 1755; died there, April 6, 1836; married (1), February 11, 1780, Mary Boardman, born in North Preston (now Griswold), Conn., about 1759; baptized May 4, 1760; died there September 13, 1818; in the 59th year of her age; daughter of —— and Mary Boardman, of North Preston; married (2), May 29, 1822, Esther (Chesebro) Moss, a widow, born in Stonington,

Conn., August 26, 1776; died September 28, 1849. Captain Tyler was commissioned May 28, 1784, by Governor Matthew Griswold, as captain in the third company in the eighth regiment of Connecticut.   Children, by first marriage:

1514+   Joseph Coit Tyler, born Feb. 5, 1781.
1515+   Mary Tyler, born Oct. 26, 1782.
1516+   Olive Tyler, born Nov. 29, 1784.
1517+   John Tyler, born Sept. 17, 1789 (perhaps 1787).
1518+   Henry Coit Tyler, born Aug. 9, 1791 (perhaps 1792).
1519+   Dwight Ripley Tyler, born June 30, 1795.
1520+   Thomas Spaulding Tyler, born Jan. 7, 1798.
1521+   Abby Tyler, born July 31, 1800.

522   LYDIA[5] TYLER (John[4]), born in North Preston (now Griswold), Conn., October 5, 1758; died in Preston, February 24, 1787; married (as third wife), August 7, 1777, General Samuel Mott, of Preston; born in Westerly, R. I., October 31, 1736; died in Preston, May 16, 1813; son of Jonathan Mott. (He married (1), Abigail Rossiter, of Preston, who left a family; he married (2), Abigail (Ayer) Stanton, of Preston). He rendered distinguished service in the Revolutionary War, as a colonel and as a general. Mrs. Lydia Mott is buried in the Pachaug cemetery. The children were born in Preston.

CHILDREN:

1522   John Tyler Mott, born Sept. 15, 1778; married, Nov. 30, 1810, Dolly Ayer, daughter of Captain Nathan Ayer, of Preston; had three sons and five daughters.
1523   Lucy Mott, born May 29, 1779; died unmarried, and was buried in Preston.
1524   Samuel R. Mott, born Aug. 7, 1782; died in infancy.
1525   Lydia Mott, born Dec. 24, 1784; she died unmarried, and was buried in Preston; she is not mentioned in General John Tyler's will of 1798.

524   ELIZABETH[5] TYLER (Joseph[4]), born in Preston, Conn., May 27, 1758; married, August 17, 1775, William Brown, of Poquetannock, Conn. The children were born in Preston.   Children:

1526   Elizabeth Brown, born Aug. 1, 1776.
1527   William Wilbur Brown, born June 6, 1779.

1528   Tyler Brown, born June 18, 1781.
1529   Lucy Brown, born June 10, 1785.
1530   Erastus Brown, born May 17, 1787.
1531   Ansel Brown, born May 21, 1789.
1532   Harry Brown, born Aug. 7, 1795; died June 13, 1801.
1533   Mary Brown, born June 9, 1798.

525 LYDIA[5] TYLER (Joseph[4]), born in Preston,
Conn., October 20, 1760; died January 27, 1799; married, December 7, 1780, Frederick Witter, of Preston, born August 13,
1752; died December 6, 1801; son of William and Hannah
(Freeman) Witter.   Hannah Freeman was the daughter of
Joseph Freeman (Joseph[2], John[1]), and was descended from
Elder William Brewster, through her mother, Hannah Brewster.   Mr. Witter was commissioned ensign of the 1st company,
8th regiment, Connecticut militia in 1783; lieutenant in 1784
and captain in 1787.   He left a large property.

Children:

1534   Lydia Witter, born March 27, 1783, in Preston; died
        in Litchfield, Conn., March 9, 1850; married, Dec.
        4, 1800, Gilbert Button, descended from No. 116,
        born Nov. 23, 1778; had eleven children (Lydia,
        Maria, Julia, Harriet, Emily, Lucy, Nancy, Gilbert,
        Rosina, Minerva, Louisa).   *Emily* married Chester
        Spaulding, of Sheffield, Mass., who at her death mar-
        ried her sister Julia; Emily had twelve children, of
        whom the sixth, *Rhoda Jane Spaulding*, married
        Hayden Marcus Truesdell, and had three children
        (Arthur E., Mary Belle and Jennie E.),   Arthur
        married Elizabeth G. Leonard, and has one son
        (Leonard W.) and Mary B. married Harry Lyman
        Bradley, and has two children (Hayden S. and
        Jeannette).
1535   Lucy Witter, born Dec. 28, 1785; married Elisha
        Searles, and moved to Chautauqua Co., N. Y.
1536   Betsey Witter, married William Park; settled in Bur-
        lington, N. Y.; seven children (Betsey, Harry,
        Phebe, John, Mary, Byron, Isaac).
1537   Polly Witter, born Aug. 21, 1789; died Sept. 9, 1828;
        married, 1806, Frederick Bailey; removed to Brook-

lyn, Penn.; twelve children (Mary, Frederick, Lodo-
wick, Sally, Isaac, William, James, Esther, Robert,
Henry, Eliza, Lavinia).

1538   Hannah Witter, married Avery Button and lived in
Connecticut; seven children (Almira, Erasmus, Abigail, Sabra, Hamilton, Samuel, Albert.)

1539   Anna Witter, born 1794; died May 22, 1849; married
(1), Aug. 30, 1812, Allen Button; married (2),
George Phillips; nine children by first marriage
(Allen, Joseph, Anna, Edwin, James, Roswell, Frederick, Frances, Henry.)

1540   Minerva Witter, born 1796; died Dec. 27, 1818.

1541   Eunice Witter, born Jan. 1, 1799; married Avery
Bolles; settled in Pennsylvania; a daughter (Mrs.
Harriet Bolles Baker) is living.

528   CAPTAIN JOSEPH[5] TYLER (Joseph[4]), born in
Preston, Conn., December 29, 1766; died November 11, 1807;
married, April 1, 1787, Lucy Kimball; born March 17, 1767;
she married (2), June 20, 1813, Daniel Meech; she died March
17, 1853; Zerviah Witter was his first wife. Joseph lived on
the old Hope homestead in Preston. He had the title of captain, perhaps in the militia. Children:

1542   Stephen Tyler, born Feb. 5, 1788; died single, Dec.
31, 1873. He lived on the old Hope homestead and
was a rhymester.

1543+ Asa Kimball Tyler, born March 29, 1790.

1544+ Joseph Tyler, born June 22, 1792.

1545+ Polly Tyler, born Sept. 16, 1794.

1546+ Daniel Meech Tyler, born March 31, 1797.

1547+ Charles Tyler, born Nov. 21, 1799.

1548+ Lydia Tyler, born May 26, 1802.

1549+ Oliver Spicer Tyler, born Aug. 3, 1804.

1550+ Guerdon Kimball Tyler, born Oct. 1, 1806.

529   EUNICE[5] TYLER (Joseph[4]), born in Preston,
Conn., September 20, 1768; died February 16, 1849; married,
December 31, 1789, Captain Oliver Spicer, of Preston, who
died November 22, 1839, aged 73; buried in Preston City.
The children were born in Preston. Children:

1551   Eunice Tyler Spicer, born Oct. 7, 1790.

1552   Oliver Spicer, born April 9, 1792; died July 27, 1793.

1553   Lucinda Spicer, born May 4, 1794.

1554   Abera Spicer, born April 23, 1797.

1555   Athelia Spicer, born Oct. 14, 1800.

1556   Diana Spicer, born March 25, 1804.

1557   Joseph Tyler Spicer, born Aug. 12, 1809; died Oct. 14, 1810.

543   HANNAH[5] TYLER (Caleb[4]), born in Preston, Conn., February 15, 1762; died in Norwich, Conn., October 8, 1846; married, November 12, 1777, Joseph Ames, of North Stonington, Conn., born about 1752; died February 8, 1836; buried in the homestead burying-ground, which has since been obliterated. He was a private in the Revolutionary War. The children were born in North Stonington. Children:

1558   Caleb Tyler Ames, born Sept. 5, 1778; died Aug. 18, 1813; married, 1798, Phebe Hewitt, of Preston, Conn.; had three sons and five daughters.

1559   Rebecca Ames, born Jan. 7, 1780; died March 1, 1832; married, 1798, Erastus Safford, of Preston, who later married (2), Phebe Parks and moved to Van Buren, N. Y., where most of the family reside; had four sons and five daughters by first marriage.

1560   Elijah Ames, born March 8, 1782; died in New London, Conn., 1849; married Mary Moore. He was sheriff and custom officer; had eight sons and five daughters.

1561   Keziah Ames, born May 14, 1784; died 1859; married Colonel David Moore, of Preston; had three daughters and one son.

1562   William Ames, born May 7, 1786; died Aug. 14, 1839; married Phebe Baker; had three sons and five daughters.

1563   Nancy Ames, born Oct. 26, 1787; died unmarried, Aug. 18, 1831.

1564   Joseph Ames, born Oct. 28, 1790; died in Canaan, Pa., in 1849; married Gertrude Schenck; daughter of Colonel John Schenck, who raised a regiment for the Revolution; had eight sons and three daughters.

1565   Alfred Ames, born May 25, 1792; left home early, not
        heard from again.

1566   John Tyler Ames, born Feb. 27, 1794; died June 13,
        1794.

1567   Hannah Tyler Ames, born Aug. 29, 1795; died in
        Norwich, April 13, 1885; married Benajah Gus-
        tine, of Pennsylvania; they had a daughter who
        lived in Norwich.

1568   Bradford Ames, born July 8, 1797; died Sept. 22,
        1798.

1569   Henry Clinton Ames, born April 1, 1799; killed in a
        mill in 1848; married Betsey Moore; had four sons
        and four daughters.

1570   Rufus Ames, born Sept. 25, 1801; married (1), Eunice
        Burdick, of Westerly, R. I.; married (2), Betsey
        Burdick; had one son and two daughters by first
        marriage.

1571   Erastus (or Erastmus) Darwin Ames, born Feb. 14,
        1804; died in 1849; married, 1828, Sarah Packer,
        of Lebanon; they had two children who died young.

        545 LUCRETIA⁵ TYLER (Caleb⁴), born in Preston,
Conn., November 13, 1764; died in Unadilla, April 22, 1855;
married, November 16, 1780, Rev. Reuben Palmer, Sr., who
died August 15, 1822. He was a prominent minister in Montville, Conn., where all his children were born, and where he was
succeeded by his son Rev. Reuben Palmer, Jr. The descendants
largely engaged in quilt manufacturing in the vicinity. In
this line are numerous ministers and professors. Mr. Palmer
was a man of humor. When his 17th child was born he re-
marked: "I am thankful for this child, and her name shall
be Thankful."

CHILDREN:

1572   Hannah Tyler Palmer, born Dec. 25, 1781; died Jan.
        18, 1868; married, March, 1798, Nehemiah Lamb.
        who died May 10, 1850.

1573   Sally Palmer, born Oct. 16, 1783; died April 13, 1823;
        married, Sept. 1, 1803, Christopher Green.

1574   Reuben Palmer, born Dec. 26, 1784; died July 22,
        1869; married, March, 1805, Mary Comstock, who
        died March 22, 1833. He succeeded his father in the

pulpit in Montville, and became a Doctor of Divinity.

1575 Lucretia Palmer, born April 25, 1786; died Dec. 30, 1871; married, April 18, 1809, Samuel Fox, who died Dec., 1861.

1576 Mary Palmer, born Dec. 25, 1787; died Sept. 8, 1873; married, Dec. 17, 1814, Roswell Caulkins, who died Dec., 1861.

1577 Caleb Palmer, born March 14, 1790; died Jan. 14, 1876; married, Jan. 26, 18—, Lucy Fox.

1578 Tyler Palmer, born March 4, 1792; married, Jan. 15, 1815, Lydia Cook, who died Sept. 20, 1873.

1579 Gideon Palmer, born Oct. 23, 1794; died July 12, 1854; married, July 11, 1813, Mercy Turner.

1580 Joshua Palmer, born Oct. 13, 1795; died Oct. 3, 1819; married, Jan. 1, 1813, Hannah Caulkins.

1581 Gershom Palmer, born Aug. 6, 1796; died Nov. 13, 1796.

1582 Samuel Palmer, born Feb. 11, 1798.

1583 Rhoda Palmer, born Oct. 18, 1799; died June 4, 1872; married, May 22, 1818, Elisha Hurlburt, born Jan. 3, 1791.

1584 Peter Palmer, born May 12, 1803; died Jan. 18, 1892.

1585 Acsha Palmer, born May 12, 1803; died Oct. 9, 1828; married, Sept. 22, 1820, Samuel W. Palmer.

1586 Lois Palmer, born Dec. 19, 1804; died Jan. 24, 1844; married, Dec. 12, 1837, Seth A. Warner.

1587 Emma Palmer, born Dec. 30, 1807; died Jan. 24, 1871; married, Dec. 12, 1838, Job Bullock.

1588 Thankful B. Palmer, born Jan. 29, 1809; married, Feb. 6, 1831, Wells Westbrook.

546 NATHAN[5] TYLER (Nathan[4]), born in Mendon, Mass., September 24, 1758; died in Uxbridge, Mass., November 4, 1792; published in Uxbridge, December 12, 1788, to Nancy Mann, of Wrentham, Mass., a sister of Dr. James Mann, and daughter of David Mann; (she married (2), Colonel Moses Whitney, of which marriage there were six daughters.) Her father having died, upon the early death of her first husband, Nathan Tyler, she sold her home in Uxbridge and moved to the old Mann homestead in Wrentham. Nathan Tyler was 14

years old when his father moved to Uxbridge. He entered
Harvard College and was graduated in 1776. He was a private
in Captain Thaddeus Read's company, Colonel Nathan Tyler's
regiment, July 28 to August 7, 1780. *Rhode Island Service*,
Vol. 3. He was classmate and chum of his future brother-in-
law, Dr. James Mann. He practiced law in Uxbridge and
died at the early age of thirty-five of lung fever. He was a
candidate for Congress at the time of his death and his con-
stituents raised a monument with a highly eulogistic inscription
enclosed by an iron fence, which long stood on Uxbridge common, but it is now removed and preserved elsewhere. His
will, dated October 6, 1792, was probated November 27, 1792.
Inventory was £365.

CHILD:

1589+   Mary Welles Tyler, born in Uxbridge, Mass., April
        2, 1792.

   547 MARY[5] TYLER (Nathan[4]), born in Mendon,
Mass., May 29, 1761; published November 12, 1784; married,
February 18, 1785, Ezekiel Morse, born in Sutton, Mass., September 12, 1749, son of Dr. Benjamin Morse (Benjamin, Benjamin, Anthony of Newbury, Mass.). By her grandfather
Tyler's will Mary received the " best case of draw(er)s."
Children:
1590   Mary Tyler Morse, married Hon. Septimus G. W.
        Huntington, son of Rev. Mr. Huntington, and
        brother of Governor Huntington. She was precep-
        tress of an academy in Coventry, Conn.
1591   Abigail Morse, married Horace Briggs.
1592   Royal Tyler Morse, born Aug. 12, 1793; married in
        1827, Eunice Adams; had two daughters and a
        son.
1593   Benjamin F. Morse, married Susan C. Lethbridge, of
        Franklin.

   548 REV. ROYAL S.[5] TYLER (Nathan[4]), born in
Mendon, Mass., June 11, 1763; died in Salem, Conn., April
10, 1826; married (1), Polly ——, who died in Canterbury,
Conn., March 13, 1792; married (2), in Thompson, Conn.,
June 10, 1793, Lydia Watson, who died in Ohio City, O., Au-
gust, 1834, aged 64; daughter of Joseph Watson, of Thomp-

son. Mr. Tyler was graduated from Dartmouth College in 1788 (?); studied theology with Rev. Nathaniel Emmons, D.D., of Franklin, Mass.; ordained in Andover, Conn., July 4, 1792, where he built a fine house, still standing; he was dismissed from this church May 20, 1817; settled in Salem, Conn., in 1818, whence dismissed in 1824. He was interested in several revivals. In extreme youth he served as a private in various companies in his father's regiment, the service occurring in the years 1776-1780 and 1782. The three elder children born in South Coventry, Conn., and the younger in Andover, Conn.

CHILDREN:

1594   Samuel Lockwood Tyler, born Nov. 16, 1794; died in Florence, Ala., Oct. 5, 1822; was graduated from Brown University in 1820; he taught in the academy in Florence.

1595+   Royal Wells Tyler, born July 25, 1796.

1596+   George Washington Tyler, born June 27, 1798.

1597+   Abigail Watson Tyler, born Nov. 25, 1801.

1598   Nathan Tyler, born July 14, 1803; died in Meadville, Pa., March 5, 1833; leaving a son (Eliphalet); he was a lawyer.

1599+   Benjamin S. Tyler, born about 1805.

1600   Lydia Tyler, born in 1807; died in Salem, Conn., Nov. 27, 1825, aged 18.

1601+   Gideon Wells Tyler, born Aug. 15, 1810.

549 MARTHA[5] TYLER (Nathan[4]), born in Upton, Mass., July 5, 1766; was published in Uxbridge, Mass., December 12, 1788 to Dr. James Mann, born July 22, 1759, whose sister married Martha's brother Nathan. He was descended from William Mann, who came to Cambridge, Mass., from Kent County, England. Dr. Mann was a classmate of Nathan[5] Tyler, his brother-in-law. He was assistant surgeon in the Revolution, and practiced medicine in Boston. Was a chief surgeon in the War of 1812, and later stationed at Fort Independence, Boston, and then at Governor's Island, New York, where he died November 7, 1832. Mrs. Mann was very intellectual and a poetess.

CHILDREN:

1602   Mary Ann Mann, married Thomas C. Williams, who

was interested in the early coal fields of Pennsylvania; she died, s. p. in Brooklyn, N. Y.

1603   Nancy Brewster Mann, died early; was very intellectual and a poetess.

1604   Caroline Mann, died, unmarried, in Brooklyn, N. Y.

1605   Harriet Mann, resided, unmarried, in Brooklyn.

1606   William Hill Mann, interested in early Pennsylvania coal fields. He married Miss Lawton, of New York, whose father was once " King of Wall Street," and moved to Wisconsin; had three children.

555 DOCTOR JOHN EUGENE[5] TYLER (John[4]), born in Mendon, Mass., April 10, 1766; died in Boston, June 25, 1821; married, June 25, 1801, Hannah Breck Parkman, born in Westboro, Mass., October 22, 1788; died September 6, 1834; daughter of Breck and Susanna (Brigham) Parkman, of Westboro; Mr. Parkman was the son of Rev. Ebenezer and Hannah (Breck) Parkman. Dr. Tyler was graduated from Harvard College in 1786; practiced medicine in Westboro, Mass., and entered mercantile life later, in Boston. In 1820, for $300 John E. Tyler, merchant of Boston, has " $\frac{1}{2}$ of land " in Jefferson, Maine, from Silas Piper, of Harlem, Maine. (*Wiscasset Register of Deeds*, Vol. 116.) He and Joseph Tyler had a grant from Benjamin Moor, in Surry, Maine, 1802. (*Hancock County, Maine, Register of Deeds*, Vol. 15.) The children were born in Westboro.

CHILDREN:

1607+   Hannah Parkman Tyler, born Sept. 25, 1803.

1608   Susanna Brigham Tyler, born July 12, 1806; died Nov. 9, 1821.

1609+   Anna Sophia Tyler, born Jan. 28, 1809.

1610+   Sarah Augusta Tyler, born June 11, 1811.

1611   John Breck Tyler, born May 6, 1813; died March 29, 1818.

1612   Charlotte Catherine Tyler, born Oct. 8, 1815; died Dec. 6, 1816.

1613   Maria Tyler, born Sept. 8, 1817; died Jan. 27, 1819.

1614+   John Eugene Tyler, born Dec. 9, 1819; died March 9, 1878.

556 JOSEPH[5] TYLER (John[4]), born in Mendon,

Mass., February 12, 1779; died in Charleston, S. C., October 20, 1843; married, February 7, 1805, Elizabeth Ann Milliken, born in Ellsworth, Maine, June 24, 1784; died in Charleston, S. C., September 30, 1824; daughter of Thomas and Mary (McKinney) Milliken. He had lived in Boston, and sailed from that port October 29, 1821, on the *Diana*, David Higgins, Master, with family, for Charleston, where they arrived November 7, 1821, after a very rough and tempestuous passage. The children were born in Boston. Children:

1615   Eliza Ann Tyler, born Jan. 23, 1806; died in infancy.

1616   John Marcellus Tyler, born Oct. 15, 1807; died, s. p. Nov. 8, 1831.

1617+   Elizabeth Ann Tyler, born Sept. 12, 1810.

1618   Joseph Alonzo Tyler, born Nov. 8, 1812; died Nov. 30, 1822.

1619   Caroline Mary Tyler, born June 17, 1816; died Jan. 21, 1897, s. p.

1620   James Henry Tyler, born March 18, 1818; died May 14, 1820.

1621   Benjamin Palmer Tyler, born Nov. 23, 1819; died, s. p., Sept. 30, 1852.

557 ABIGAIL[5] TYLER (John[4]), born in Mendon, Mass., December 15, 1781; died in Lisbon, Conn., in 1806; married (certified April 17, 1805, by Rev. David Long), Rev. Levi Nelson, born in Milford, Mass., August 8, 1779; died in Lisbon, Conn., in 1855, aged 77, and in the 52d year of his ministry; son of Seth Nelson, descended from Thomas. (He married (2), Mary Hale, she died, s. p.) He attended Brown University and Williams College, but ill health prevented graduation. In 1803 he was a Home missionary in Oneida and Lewis counties, New York. He was a Congregationalist, and in Lisbon, Conn., was ordained December 5, 1804.

CHILD:

1622   Daughter, who married in January, 1826, and died, s. p., in June, 1826.

558 DEACON NATHAN[5] TYLER (John[4]), born in Mendon, Mass., February 22, 1784; died in Providence, R. I., March 11, 1838; married (1), June 26, 1811, Elizabeth Brooks

of Petersham, Mass., who died in Boston, October 11, 1816; daughter of Aaron Brooks, Sr.; married (2), June 10, 1819, Mary Ward, born in 1790; daughter of Daniel and Damaris (Stevens) Ward, of Petersham. He lived on the Upton road in Mendon, in a house that was taken down before 1898; he was the last of the old stock living in Mendon. He removed to Boston about 1834, and was a deacon in the Park Street church, Boston. In the *Registry of Deeds* in Wiscasset, Maine, is recorded a transaction between Nathan and his brother Aaron of Bath, Maine, by which he bought one-half a mill for $1500. Later he seems to have acquired full title to the mill. The three elder and the three younger children were born in Mendon.

CHILDREN, by first marriage:

1623+ Fisher Ames Tyler, born March 26, 1812.

1624 Mary Elizabeth Tyler, born June 13, 1813; died April 25, 1835; married, Sept. 14, 1831, Rev. Arthur Granger, of Medfield, Mass., who died in Providence, R. I.; one child who died.

1625 Henry Tyler, born May 19, 1815; died in Petersham, Sept. 28, 1815.

1626 Henry Brooks Tyler, born in Boston, August 17, 1816; died there April 23, 1817.

CHILDREN, by second marriage:

1627 Abigail Nelson Tyler, born in Boston, April 27, 1820; died in Providence, R. I., June 30, 1840.

1628 Sarah Ann Tyler, born Jan. 7, 1824; died April 13, 1825.

1629 Susan Ann Tyler, born April 17, 1826; died, unmarried, in Madison, Wis., June 12, 1864.

1630+ Catherine Barnard Clapp Tyler, born Sept. 7, 1829.

559 AARON[5] TYLER (John[4]), born in Mendon, Mass., June 8, 1786; died in Griggsville, Ill.; married Elizabeth Ober, of Beverly, Mass., who died in Griggsville, March 3, 1850. He lived for a time in Bath, Maine, and then moved to Griggsville. He gave to his brother Nathan, May 10, 1831, his wife Elizabeth, joining, one-half of a saw mill in Georgetown, Maine, on "Robbin Hood's Cove," for $1500. Later Nathan ac-

quired full title to the mill. *Wiscasset Deeds*, Vol. 153. The two elder children were born in Mendon. Children:

1631   Abigail Anna Tyler, born Jan. 10, 1809; died Dec. 10, 1809.

1632+ Thomas Stephen Tyler, born Aug. 27, 1810.

1633   Ruth Allen Tyler, born May 29, 1812; died, unmarried, Nov. 12, 1885; well educated; a teacher.

1634   Elizabeth Ober Tyler, died unmarried; was a teacher.

1635   Aaron Tyler, died in infancy.

1636   Urania Bates Tyler, died aged 17.

1637+ Aaron Tyler.

1638   George William Tyler, born in Bath, Maine; married Isabel McDonald, of San Francisco, Cal., where he was a merchant and died, s. p. 1874; his widow was living in 1897.

1639+ Joseph Alonzo Tyler, born in Bath, Maine, in 1834.

1640   Anna Maria Tyler, married George Pratt, of Cohasset, Mass., or Griggsville, Ill.; s. p.

1641   Nancy Ober Tyler, died aged 18.

1642   Mary Ellen Tyler, resided, unmarried, a teacher and preceptress, in St. Louis, Mo.

1643   Abigail Nelson Tyler, resided, unmarried, an invalid, in St. Louis.

576 NATHAN WEB[5] (Elijah[4]), born in Upton, Mass., October 14, 1752; died in Columbus, N. Y., March 24, 1830; married, in Goshen, Mass., March 28, 1776, Olive Patch, of Chesterfield, Mass., born May 19, 1756; was living in Columbus in 1837, aged 80. The Massachusetts rolls show that he went to Quebec in 1775; he was in the Revolution according to the *Pension Book*, page 55, No. 4. He marched on the Lexington Alarm. He resided awhile in Chesterfield, Mass., and moved to Norwich, N. Y., and about 1820 to Columbus, N. Y. He was a farmer. Child:

1644+ Elijah Tyler, born in Westhampton, Mass.

577 STEPHEN[5] TYLER (Elijah[4]), born in Upton, Mass., June 9, 1754; died in Wilmington, Vt., April 27, 1833; married (1), August 12, 1788, Anna Stevens, who died June 2, 1799; married (2), January 21, 1801, Sarah Alvord, who died March 13, 1817; she was born in South Hadley, Mass.,

March 14, 1767; daughter of Gideon and Sarah (Montague) Alvord. He marched on the Lexington Alarm; a private on the roll of Captain Robert Webster, General Seth Pomeroy's 2d Hampshire County regiment, which marched from Chesterfield, April 21, 1775. He served six days and then enlisted in the army. In May, 1792, Stephen Tyler, of Westhampton, Mass., had a grant of 50 acres in that place from Elisha Alvord, of Northampton, for £35. *Probate Records of Northampton*, Book 4. The four elder children were born in Buckland, Mass., the four younger in Wilmington, Vt.

CHILDREN, by first marriage:

1645+   Benjamin Owen Tyler, born Sept. 24, 1789.
1646+   Ephraim Tyler, born April 19, 1791.
1647+   Eli Tyler, born May 20, 1793.
1648   Betsey Tyler, born May 20, 1795; died in Wilmington, Dec. 10, 1803.
1649+   Chester Grennell Tyler, born in Westhampton, Mass., Nov. 19, 1797.

CHILDREN, by second marriage:

1650   William Tyler, born March 19, died March 20, 1802.
1651   Stephen Tyler, born Oct. 9, 1803; died the same day.
1652   Ebenezer Tyler, born Oct. 6, 1804.
1653   Anson Lyman Tyler, born Nov. 8, 1808; early moved to New York and died near Rochester.

582   MOSES[5] TYLER (Elijah[4]), born in Upton, Mass., June 10, 1776; died April 11, 1854; married, November 15, 1791, Sarah Cook, of Hadley, Mass. He moved to Wilmington, Vt., about 1800, with brother Simeon and brother-in-law Bullard; in 1807, he moved to Montrose, Pa., where he was a deacon in the Presbyterian church. At the age of 74 he was living in Bridgewater, Pa., with his son Moses. In 1777, from September to the last of November, was a private in Captain John Banister's company, Colonel Job Cushing's 6th Worcester County regiment. Again, in 1779 he served from August to the last of December in Captain Thomas Hovey's company, Colonel Nathan Tyler's 3d Worcester County regiment. The service was in Rhode Island, in that year. (*Mass. Archives.*) The male line in this family is extinct. The seven younger

children were probably born in Montrose. Order of birth uncertain in some cases.

CHILDREN:

1654+   Hannah Tyler, born in Hadley, Mass., Feb. 24, 1795.

1655+   Moses Coleman Tyler, born in Wilmington, Vt., April 7, 1802.

1656   Parmelia Tyler, born in Wilmington, Jan. 31, 1804; died Aug. 10, 1888; married William Sloan. (Their daughter Ann married David Quick, of East Rush, Pa.)

1657+   Emma Tyler, born probably in Wilmington, in 1806.

1658+   Emily Tyler, born in 1807.

1659   Melinda Tyler, married Thomas Carrier. (Among their children were Sarah, Prudence, Lucinda, Moses. Benjamin, Sylvester, Eldad.

1660   Eunice Tyler, born in 1810; married Chauncey Tubbs.

1661   Eliza Tyler, born in 1812.

1662   Sally Tyler, married Joseph Beebe. They had eight children. (Owen, Angeline, Hiram A., William L., Ezra, Joseph, Hannah, Elizabeth.)

1663   Clarissa Tyler, married Jason Potter. They had four children. (Alonzo, Isaiah, Emmeline, Dennison.)

1664   Benjamin Owen Tyler, born in 1819; died young.

583   SALLY[5] TYLER (Elijah[4]), born in Upton, Mass., in 1768; baptized in Chesterfield, Mass., September 27, 1772, (no record of birth exists); married Job Walker, of Dover, Vt. Children:

1665   William Walker.

1666   Calvin Walker.

1667   Elijah Walker.

1668   Mary Walker.

584   SIMEON[5] TYLER, (Elijah[4]), born in Upton, Mass., September 9, 1770 (probably no record of birth); died in 1850, aged 80; married, November 24, 1796, Betsey Brewster, of Hampton, Mass. (published April 9, 1796); daughter of Nathan Brewster. He moved to Vermont soon after 1800 and lived for a few years in Wilmington, Vt.; in February, 1807, he moved, with his brother Moses and brother-in-law, Isaac Bullard, to Montrose, Pa. The two elder children were

born in Westhampton, Mass.; the four younger in Montrose, and the others in Wilmington.   Children:

1669+   Simeon Tyler, born Dec. 6, 1797.
1670+   Betsey Tyler, born Dec. 6, 1799.
1671+   Ansel Tyler, born Feb. 14, 1803.
1672+   Harvey Tyler, born April 1, 1804.
1673+   Abigail Tyler, born Aug. 19, 1806.
1674   Rawson Tyler, born May 20, 1808; died young.
1675   Lucenia Tyler, born Jan. 19, 1810; died young.
1676   Osias Tyler, born June 20, 1813; died Feb. 7, 1848, s. p., in Bethlehem, Pa.; was in mercantile business.
1677   Brewster Tyler, born July 5, 1814; drowned, unmarried, in 1835, while rafting logs on the Susquehanna River.

592   LYDIA[5] TYLER (Joseph[4]), born in Uxbridge, Mass., August 7, 1762; died in Canton, Ohio, September, 1841; married Amos Holbrook.   Children:
1678   Joseph Holbrook.
1679   Franklin Holbrook; died in Ohio.
1680   Lydia Holbrook.
1681   Dexter Holbrook, died in Ohio; married —— Pomeroy, and had two daughters and a son.

594   BETSEY READ[5] TYLER (Joseph[4]), born in Uxbridge, Mass., September 1, 1766; died in Bernardston, Mass., June 25, 1843; married Amos Gray, of Townshend, Vt., who died March 3, 1850.   The children were born in Townshend. Children:
1682   Sophia Gray, born Sept. 14, 1786; died Sept. 20, 1850.
1683   Wyllis Gray, born Aug. 29, 1788; died Oct. 16, 1857; married Emily Newell and had two daughters and a son.
1684   Tyler Gray, born Feb. 18, 1792; died Oct. 4, 1873.
1685   Lydia Gray, born Nov. 27, 1794; died Dec. 20, 1867; married Abijah Pierce, and had three sons and one daughter.
1686   Betsey Gray, born Aug. 3, 1797; died May 5, 1867; married Samuel Fessenden; had three sons and three daughters.
1687   Ruth Read Gray, born Aug. 26, 1799; died Nov. 26, 1848.

1688   Polly Gray, born Nov. 16, 1801; died Feb. 20, 1859.
1689   (Dr.) Amos Gray, born Feb. 2, 1804; died Nov. 6,
        1884; married Jenett Noble, and resided in Dexter,
        Mich. Had one son and three daughters.
1690   Mehitable Gray, born Aug. 25, 1808; died, s. p. Dec.
        31, 1875; married Charles D. Bellamy, born May
        18, 1815; died Jan. 30, 1883.

    596   COLONEL JOSEPH⁵ TYLER (Joseph⁴), born in
Townshend, Vt., April 11, 1771; died there August 5, 1845;
married (1), January 14, 1802, Lucy Parker, of Holden, Mass.,
who died March 20, 1825, aged 45; married (2), November 7,
1827, Hannah Parker, of Putney, Vt. (not related to first
wife), who died in Brattleboro, Vt., November 20, 1860, aged
72. He was a justice of the peace in Townshend for 31 years.
The children were born there. Date of birth not known in
each case. .
                CHILDREN, by first marriage:
1691   Adaline E. Tyler, born in 1803; died, unmarried, in
        Townshend, Nov. 9, 1826, aged 23.
1692+   Moses W. Tyler.
1693   Columbus Tyler, died, s. p. 1881, aged 76 years; mar-
        ried, 1835, Mary E. Sawyer, of Sterling, Mass.,
        who died in 1889, aged about 83. He was steward
        of the McLean Asylum of Somerville, Mass., about
        forty years. He built a residence in Somerville
        when he retired, and they were among the most
        highly esteemed citizens of the place. Their estate
        was bequeathed to the Unitarian church for a par-
        sonage. Mrs. Tyler was the heroine of the verses,
        "Mary Had a Little Lamb." When she was a child
        in Sterling a little new-born lamb was found nearly
        dead, one day, and she nursed it back to life, sitting
        up all night to keep it alive. At her brother's sug-
        gestion they took the lamb to school, one day, hav-
        ing considerable trouble to get it over a high stone
        wall. They had high seats, boarded up, in the
        schoolroom, and Mary placed the lamb inside this
        enclosure, at her feet, on a shawl. When she went
        out to the place for recitation the clatter of little
        hoofs was heard on the floor, and the lamb appeared.

The teacher laughed outright and the children giggled, but Mary was very much ashamed and led the lamb to a shed outside in the schoolyard, where it stayed until she went home. A young man named John Roulstone, visiting the school that day, was greatly pleased with the incident. The next day he brought three stanzas which he had written. Two stanzas have been added since then, by another hand. From the lamb's fleece, Mary's mother knit two pairs of stockings, which were kept until Mrs. Tyler was about 80 years of age. The ladies of Boston were then raising money for the preservation of the Old South Meeting-house, and Mrs. Tyler contributed these stockings, which were unraveled and small pieces of the yarn sold, thus realizing a considerable sum from the pair of hose.

1694+ Ferdinand Tyler, born in 1808.

1695 Kelita R. Tyler, born in 1810; died, unmarried, in Townshend, Nov. 4, 1832, aged 22.

1696 Lucy Parker Tyler, born Jan. 3, 1813; died in Boston, Dec. 4, 1886; she was an invalid; largely through her pains a fund was created to keep up the cemetery in Townshend.

1697+ Joseph Curtis Tyler, born Oct. 8, 1814.

1698 Jerome W. Tyler, died, s. p., in Boston, 1893; married ———; was in business with his brother Joseph in Boston.

1699 Hanson L. Tyler, born in 1818; died in Townshend, Dec. 19, 1827, aged 9.

CHILD, by second marriage:

1700 Horace P. Tyler, born in 1830; died in Townshend, Dec. 28, 1831, aged one year.

598 TIMOTHY[5] TYLER (Timothy[4]), born in Mendon, Mass., May 11, 1775; married Eunice Rawson. He settled on a farm in Townshend, Vt., and later, in 1811, moved to Speedsville, Tompkins County, New York, and lived on a farm in " Rawson Hollow," where he died in 1866, aged 91. Children, born in Townshend:

1701 Eunice Tyler, died in infancy.

1702+ Hiram Ward Tyler, born March 3, 1802.
1703 Cynthia Taft Tyler, born Feb. 23, 1804; died in 1882, aged 78, unmarried.

606 JOSEPH[5] TYLER (Solomon[4]), born in Uxbridge, Mass., January 8, 1782; died there December 13, 1862; married (1), June 23, 1809, Trial Taft, who died August 18, 1815, aged 39; married (2), Mrs. Sophia (Alvord) Robinson, who, in later life, left her Tyler husband and resided with her daughter, Caroline (Robinson) Jackson. He resided in Townshend, Vt., Dimock, Pa., and Uxbridge, Mass.

CHILDREN, by first marriage:
1704+ Mary Almira Tyler, born in Charlton, Mass., Jan. 30, 1811.
1705 Taft Tyler, born in 1815; died May 26, 1830.

CHILDREN, by second marriage:
1706+ Hiram Tyler.
1707+ Sophia Tyler.

607 KELITA[5] TYLER (Solomon[4]), born in Uxbridge, Mass., February 5, 1784; died September 15, 1862; married, October 8, 1801, Eleazer Keith, of Thompson, Conn., born January 12, 1780; died there in 1850. The children were born in Thompson. Children:
1708 Joseph Damon Keith, born Dec. 5, 1802; married (1), Lucy Bundy; married (2), Hannah Bates; two children.
1709 Silence Matilda Keith, born Aug. 31, 1804; died March 19, 1826; married Hezekiah Bugbee; one son.
1710 Noah Keith, born Jan. 11, 1807; died Oct. 17, 1808.
1711 George Washington Keith, born July 26, 1809; married Mary Spaulding; two children.
1712 Luther Tyler Keith, born April 26, 1813; died May 17, 1884; one son and a daughter.
1713 Almira Keith, born Aug. 16, 1815; married Frederick Botham, a lawyer, of Southbridge, Mass.; died May 27, 1884.
1714 William Judson Keith, born June 16, 1818; married Rebecca Sophia Hartshorn, of Southbridge, Mass.; two sons.

608   MELINDA⁵ TYLER (Solomon⁴), born in Uxbridge, Mass., February 7, 1786; died December 13, 1863; married October 26, 1806, John Weld, of Charlton, Mass., born August 9, 1780; died December 30, 1857. The children were born in Uxbridge.   Children:

1715   Mary Weld, born Oct. 16, 1807; died Sept. 28, 1844; married, May 30, 1830, Daniel Seagraves, of Uxbridge, Mass.; five children.

1716   Tyler Weld, born Oct. 6, 1809; died, unmarried, July 23, 1870.

1717   Dolly Weld, born Oct. 7, 1812; died, unmarried, Sept. 21, 1887.

1718   John Weld, born May 17, 1815; died, unmarried, Aug. 22, 1837.

1719   Solomon Weld, born Oct. 3, 1821; died, unmarried, Aug. 17, 1842.

1720   Leonard Upham Weld, born Aug. 25, 1826; died Sept. 14, 1829.

1721   Otis Weld, born March 30, 1829; married, July 1, 1855, Mrs. Isabella (Anderson) McGilvery; resided s. p. in Bloomington, Wis.

609   ROYAL⁵ TYLER (Solomon⁴), born in Uxbridge, Mass., August 2, 1788; died in Dimock, Pa., February 27, 1841; married (1), Mary Southwick, of Mendon, Mass.; married (2), Sybil Fordham, of Pennsylvania. The three elder children were born in Uxbridge; the others in Dimock.   Children:

1722+   Sylvanus Tyler, born Oct. 19, 1811.
1723+   Moses S. Tyler, born Oct. 18, 1814.
1724+   Mary Tyler, born Feb. 13, 1819.
1725+   Louisa Southwick Tyler, born Dec. 16, 1820.
1726   Anna Tyler, born May 22, 1822; died Nov., 1872; married, in 1841, William Haverly, and went to Kansas. She left a family of nine children.
1727+   Royal Tyler, born Jan. 16, 1825.
1728+   James Tyler, born June 11, 1827.

610   PARKER⁵ TYLER (Solomon⁴), born in Uxbridge, Mass., November 14, 1790; died June 28, 1853; married (1), in Uxbridge, December 9, 1810, Huldah Taft; married (2),

Lovey Wright of Ohio. He moved to Copley, Ohio. After
his second marriage he moved to Indiana as a pioneer, about
the year 1840, and settled on Grand Prairie, eight miles northwest of Williamsport, the county seat, where he laid out the
" Old Tyler Place," noted for big apple orchards and fine
fruit, and a south line row of walnut trees, intended originally
for a fence. He was a natural mathematician, a Whig in politics, and a religious man.

CHILDREN, by first marriage:

1729   Huldah Tyler, married —— Borlund, of Copley, Ohio.
1730   Mary Tyler, died in infancy.

CHILDREN, by second marriage:

1731+   William H. Tyler, born in Copley, Jan. 22, 1825.
1732+   Martha Tyler.
1733+   George Clinton Tyler, born in Copley, Nov. 1, 1828.
1734+   James Tyler.
1735+   Hiram Tyler.
1736+   Harriet Tyler.
1737   Homer C. Tyler, lived in West Lebanon, Ind.; one
         son (Roy Homer).
1738   John Quincy Adams Tyler, resided, s. p., Alvin, Ill.

612   BENJAMIN^5 TYLER (Solomon^4), born in Uxbridge, Mass., February 22, 1796; died in Wadsworth, Ohio,
March 20, 1875; married, June 8, 1820, Olive Brown Bartlett,
who died August 21, 1874. The two elder children were born
in Copley, and the others in Wadsworth. Children:

1739+   Benjamin Tyler, born March 22, 1821.
1740+   Joseph Tyler, born Aug. 14, 1822.
1741   Solomon Tyler, born Nov. 6, 1824; lived in Hampton,
         Iowa; a blacksmith and land speculator.
1742   Mary Tyler, born Sept. 29, 1826; died Oct. 25, 1826.
1743+   Rosina Tyler, born Oct. 5, 1827.
1744   Abraham Tyler, born July 6, 1831; died Aug. 17,
         1832.

614   TIMOTHY^5 TYLER (Solomon^4), born in Uxbridge, Mass., July 16. 1799; died in Smithfield. R. I., March
29, 1870; married (1), Phebe Bates, of Smithfield, where he

settled; married (2), Mrs. Sally Arnold. The children were born in Smithfield. Children:

1745+   Albert Tyler, born Nov. 16. 1823.
1746+   Charles E. Tyler, born Feb. 8, 1835.

615 SOLOMON⁵ TYLER (Solomon⁴), born in Uxbridge, Mass., July 18, 1802; died in Indiana while visiting his children, December 17, 1878; married April 6, 1828, Lucretia Cook, of Mendon, Mass., born December 19, 1796; died October 4, 1872. He moved to Copley, Ohio, where he was a farmer. Children:

1747+   Cynthia Tyler, born June 14, 1829.
1748   Ransom Tyler, born Nov. 11, 1831; died Aug. 1, 1832.
1749   Ransom Tyler, born May 29, 1833; died May 9, 1835.
1750+   Lemuel Tyler, born Aug. 13, 1835.
1751   Malcom Tyler, born May 10, 1839; had a daughter (Esther), residing in Akron, Ohio, and a son (William).

616 MARY⁵ TYLER (Solomon⁴), born in Uxbridge, Mass., April 17, 1804; died in Charlton City, Mass., May 7, 1893; married, January 30, 1831, Caleb Torrey, of Charlton City, who started manufacturing in what is now a large industry. Children:

1752   Henry Clay Torrey, born Nov. 11, 1831; is a carriage-maker in Central Village, Conn.
1753   George Edwin Torrey, born Oct. 2, 1834; died Sept. 22, 1837.
1754   Mary Louisa Torrey, born April 22, 1837; married, Oct. 1, 1854, Henry Brown, of Charlton, Mass.
1755   George Torrey, born June 10, 1839; lives in Central Village, Conn.; a carriage-maker.
1756   Emily Torrey, born Aug. 26, 1841; married Rensalaer Sayles, of Uxbridge, Mass.
1757   Edwin Tyler Torrey, born Nov. 4, 1844; a farmer and lives in Southbridge, Mass.

617 NEWELL⁵ TYLER (Solomon⁴), born in Uxbridge, Mass., April 12, 1810; died in Worcester, Mass., May 20, 1891; married (1), October 16, 1834, Watie H. Bates, of Bellingham, Mass., born in 1813; died June 20, 1887; married

(2), Sybil Bates (sister of Watie), of Mendon, Mass., born
October 19, 1841; died August 20, 1894; they were daughters
of Peter and Sybil (Hill) Bates. He was a farmer, merchant
and manufacturer. He held office in Uxbridge; 1860-1861
was in the State Legislature. He was a founder of the Free
Baptist church in Worcester.

CHILDREN, by first marriage:

1758   Dolliver Tyler, born in Mendon, Aug. 19, 1837; died
      in Sturbridge, Mass., Sept. 5, 1843.

1759+ Minerva Tyler, born in Uxbridge July 9, 1847.

629 DEACON JOHN[5] TYLER (John[4]), born in Attleboro, Mass., April 25, 1746; died in Ararat, Pa., May 27,
1822; married, June, 1768, Mercy Thacher, born December
27, 1752; died January 14, 1835; daughter of Rev. Peter
and Bethiah (Carpenter) Thacher, of Attleboro; descended
from a long line of Rev. Peter Thachers, all eldest sons, inter-
rupted only by Rev. Thomas Thacher, the famous first pastor
of the Old South Church, Boston; also a descendant of Thomas
Hinckley, Governor of Plymouth Colony.

Prof. W. S. Tyler says of her: " My grandmother Tyler
was a very remarkable woman. For many years she was the
chief physician of all the settlers in Susquehanna County.
Mounting her horse astride with the doctor's saddlebags, she
would ride fast as the fastest to meet an emergency—a confine-
ment or any extreme sickness—in any part of the country.
And so often did she ride from Harford to Ararat carrying on
horseback all sorts of heavy luggage—a dye-tub, a big brass
kettle, etc., etc.—that it became a common saying that ' she
brought her loom on horseback, in her lap, with her grand-
daughter in it weaving.' (See *History Susquehanna County*,
passim). And she could minister to the souls as well as the
bodies of her patients, for her Christian faith and activity was
fully equal to her personal energy and efficiency." The *Lexington Alarm Rolls* state that John Tyler, Jr., of Attleboro,
was a private on the Lexington Alarm Roll of Captain Moses
Wilmarth's first company, Colonel John Daggett's 4th Bristol
County regiment, which marched from Attleboro April 19,
1775, and served eleven days. In *Daggett's History of Attleboro*, there is service attributed to John Tyler and John Tyler,

Jr., in April, 1775, in Caleb Richardson's company, Colonel
Timothy Walker's regiment. In 1776 the same history noted
that John Tyler, Jr., is on a committee to give notice of persons using "India Tea" after March. John Tyler, a sergeant, served in Captain Richardson's company, which marched
into the State of Rhode Island, between April 21 and May 25,
1777, "to hold the line until men could be raised for two
months for that purpose." His name appears again on the
muster roll of the Attleboro troops as a member of Captain
Ebenezer May's company, August 22 to September 24, 1778.
Harford, Susquehanna County, was settled in 1790 by the
"Nine Partners," by which name the place was generally known
until 1807. Deacon John Tyler went there in the autumn of
1794. He was nearly fifty years old when he moved to this
almost unbroken wilderness. "Five of his children were grown
up and had already migrated to Pennsylvania. . . . The
four younger children, among whom was Joab . . .
"moved" in the family caravan. A huge canvas-covered
wagon, drawn by oxen, was their vehicle by day, and much of
the way, their tent by night. A cow, led or driven alongside,
furnished no inconsiderable part of their daily food and drink.
They were weeks in performing a journey that now can be
accomplished in 24 hours. Deacon John's was the first frame
house built in the town. A "reading meeting" was established
by vote of the people in 1794, and John Tyler was chosen to
conduct it. But for ten years there were no taxes, military
duties, civil rulers, or church organization. In 1800 a Congregational church was organized consisting of seven members,
all of whom were Tylers, Thachers and Carpenters. In 1803
John Tyler was chosen one of the first deacons, and public
worship was now held in his house, sometimes also in his barn.
In this house also was the first school. In 1807, on petition
of the inhabitants, the settlement was constituted a town and
election district under the name of Harford, so called after
Hartford, Conn., but varied in the spelling to agree with the
pronunciation. In 1810, John Tyler removed still further into
the wilderness and pitched his tent on a lofty tableland, which,
from its commanding elevation, was called by him, and has
ever since born the name of Ararat. There also a Congregational church was soon established, of which he became one of
the first deacons. The children were all born in Attleboro.

1760+   Mercy Tyler, born Nov. 5, 1769.
1761+   Mary Tyler, twin to Mercy.
1762+   Polly Tyler, born Sept. 15, 1771.
1763+   Nanny Tyler, born Aug. 31, 1773.
1764+   John Tyler, born Feb. 23, 1777.
1765+   Job Tyler, born Aug. 22, 1779.
1766+   Achsah Tyler, born April 20, 1782.
1767+   Joab Tyler, born July 23, 1784.
1768+   Jabez Tyler, born March 13, 1787.

630 ELIZABETH[5] TYLER (John[4]), born in Attleboro, Mass., June 14, 1747; died November 17, 1821; married (1), Daniel Carpenter, born in Attleboro, September 29, 1744; died there April 14, 1803; son of Obadiah Carpenter (Obadiah, William, William from London, Eng., 1638, to Weymouth, Mass.); married (2), (second wife), Thomas Sweet. Her children were born in Attleboro.

CHILDREN, by first marriage:
1769   John Carpenter, born Sept. 1, 1766; died March 2, 1838; married (1), Feb. 21, 1793, his cousin, Polly Tyler, No. 1762; married (2), June 1, 1813, Lydia Pattie, born June 28, 1784; died March 3, 1861.
1770   (Capt.) Daniel Carpenter, born April 2, 1768; died Sept. 3, 1835; married, March 5, 1795, Alice Richardson, born in 1770; died Jan. 28, 1844; daughter of Daniel Richardson. He was a farmer and a captain in the militia.
1771   Ezra Carpenter, born May 11, 1770; died Feb. 27, 1821; married, June 17, 1795, Molly Follet; resided in Harford and Herrick, Pa.; had four children.
1772   Betsey Carpenter, born March 28, 1772; died Jan. 24, 1835; married, in 1793, Samuel Thacher, born Oct. 28, 1768; died Oct. 9, 1833; son of Rev. Peter Thacher, of Attleboro. He was one of " nine partners " of Harford, Pa.; had nine children.
1773   Samuel Carpenter, born May 22, 1774; died Nov. 1, 1775.
1774   Remember Carpenter, born Feb. 8, 1776; died Dec. 1, 1845; married, Oct. 11, 1801, Betsey Read, who died Dec. 1, 1845; daughter of David Read, of Attle-

boro. He was a deacon in the church, and resided
in Pawtucket, R. I.

1775   Ebenezer Carpenter, born Oct. 25, 1781; died June
25, 1849; married, Aug. 17, 1806, Clarissa Kent;
he resided, a farmer, in Pawtucket, R. I.

1776   Jesse Carpenter, born Sept. 20, 1785; died June 7,
1857; married, Dec. 19, 1805, Philena Richardson,
who died Dec. 19, 1862; daughter of Daniel Richardson, of Attleboro.

1777   Nancy Carpenter, born Aug. 11, 1786; died March 17,
1864; married, Feb. 19, 1804, Spencer Blanding, a
farmer, who resided in Hillsdale, Pa.; son of Simeon
Blanding; had one son.

1778   Samuel Carpenter, born Jan. 12, 1789; died March 3,
1859; married, Oct. 19, 1815, Nancy Ingraham,
born Sept. 12, 1794. He was a manufacturer and
president of the Attleboro bank; also a captain in
the militia; had two children.

1779   Eliza Carpenter, born Nov. 1, 1792; died March 12,
1825; married, Feb. 11, 1819, Benjamin Bowen, a
farmer, of Pawtucket, R. I.

631 NANNE[5] TYLER (John[4]), born in Attleboro,
Mass., July 14, 1754; died January 17, 1816; married, April
16, 1778, Peter Thatcher, who died in Attleboro, December 4,
1814, aged 62. He was a farmer and lived in Attleboro, and
the children were born there. Children:

1780   Peter Thatcher, born March 30, 1779; died Sept. 20,
1863; married (1), May 7, 1804, Salona Dunham;
born June 11, 1780; died Oct. 31, 1824; married
(2), Jan. 12, 1826, Susan (Carpenter) Peatt, born
Aug. 20, 1796; had eight children.

1781   Mercy Thatcher, born Feb. 16, 1783; married (1),
Timothy Balcom, of Attleboro; married (2), Ebenezer Tiffany, of Pawtucket, R. I.

1782   Phebe Thatcher, born May 22, 1786; married Elias
Ingraham, of Attleboro; she died Dec. 25, 1870,
aged 84.

1783   Ona Thatcher, born March 24, 1788; died Aug. 6,
1788.

633 EXPERIENCE[5] TYLER (John[4]), born in Attle-

boro, Mass., July 12, 1758; died in Smithfield, R. I., June 2, 1833; married Philip Briggs. Children:

1784 (Dr.) Tyler Briggs.

1785 John Briggs.

634 MAJOR EBENEZER[5] TYLER (John[4]), born in Attleboro, Mass., September 8, 1760; died in Pawtucket, R. I., October 15, 1827; married (1), Mary French, who died in Attleboro October 3, 1804, aged 44; daughter of Joseph French; married (2), Mrs. Rachel (Deane) Forbes, born in Norton, Mass., November 24, 1773; died March 5, 1834, aged 60, s. p. He resided in Attleboro and Pawtucket. He was at the head of the Attleboro Manufacturing Company, which became, in 1809, The Tyler Manufacturing Company. The Major was a very capable man and it was a prosperous business concern for many years. At the time of the Revolution there were two Ebenezer Tylers in Attleboro, possibly three. One served as a private and one as a lieutenant, in the war. He who became "Major" was one of these. When Captain Richardson marched into the State of Rhode Island "to hold the line till men could be raised for two months for that purpose," Ebenezer Tyler and Ebenezer Tyler, Jr., responded, and remained in the company which was raised to replace this company. The private marched on the Lexington Alarm, April 19, 1775, and served at intervals for about a month at a time, in 1777, 1778 and 1780; the lieutenant served a short time in 1777, from May to October, 1778, and in the summer of 1780. Major Ebenezer Tyler probably served as a captain in the "South Company" of the town militia. An Ebenezer Tyler, of Attleboro, was in Captain Moses Wilmarth's company in Rhode Island from March to August , 1781. Major Tyler's will was dated October 10, 1823; probated November 6, 1827. His wife Rachel had life interest in the land, house, barns and buildings situated in Pawtucket, furniture, etc., and pew No. 40 in Catholic Baptist meeting-house in Pawtucket. His daughter Nancy, wife of Daniel Greene, had lands in Pawtucket. The children of his daughter, Lucinda Richardson, deceased, received $1,000 each. A legacy was made to Rachel Tyler Dean, "Niece of my beloved wife Rachel." His son William Tyler, was residuary legatee and executor. His wife, Rachel, left her property by will to the Deane family.

CHILDREN, by first marriage:

1786+   Lucinda Tyler, born Nov. 6, 1785.
1787+   William Tyler, born Jan. 7, 1789.
1788   Joseph Tyler, born Jan. 21 (or 22), 1791; died Aug. 25, 1813.
1789+   Ann (or Nancy) Tyler, born July 19, 1794.
1790   Infant son, born and died Dec. 9, 1796.

636 OTHNIEL[5] (John[4]), born in Attleboro, Mass., April 4, 1763; died August 9, 1846; married (published in Uxbridge, Mass., December 24, 1788), Olive Taft, of Uxbridge. He was graduated from Brown University in 1783. He became a lawyer, being admitted to the Suffolk bar before 1807. Resided in Sudbury, Mass. He joined the Second Congregational church in Attleboro by a letter from Wayland, Mass., January 5, 1840. On the pay-roll and muster roll of Captain Alexander Foster's company, Colonel Thomas Carpenter's first regiment of Bristol County, Mass., militia, he appears a private. The service was 17 days in Rhode Island, July 27 to August 12, 1778 (*Rhode Island Service*, Vol. 2).

CHILDREN:

1791   Royal Tyler, died unmarried before 1846.
1792+   George Tyler.
1793   Mary Ann Tyler, died unmarried.

637 SAMUEL[5] TYLER (Job[4]), born in Ashford, Conn., April 12, 1759; died in September, 1825, in Marcellus, Onondaga County, N. Y., a week after his return from visiting his sick brother, Comfort, from disease contracted in Montezuma; married Deliverance Whiting, who died in 1862, aged 94. He was in the Revolution, probably, but his record is not known. In 1792 or 1794 he removed to Onondaga County, and settled in "Tyler Hollow," which was named for him. The town of Marcellus and Onondaga County were organized in 1794, and he was among the very earliest settlers in the town. In 1797 he was appointed supervisor, and was the first justice of the peace in 1798. Some of the first courts of common pleas and general sessions held in the county, from 1794 to 1803, were held in his house. He was one of the incorporators of the Skaneateles turnpike in 1806. He built saw,

grist and fulling mills in "Tyler Hollow." The eldest child
was born in Ashford, the others probably all in "Tyler Hollow," which was included in the town of Marcellus, N. Y.
This family were all large men, averaging six feet. Samuel
gave to each of his sons a farm in "Tyler Hollow."

CHILDREN:

1794+   Samuel Tyler, born April 2, 1785.

1795   Artemesia Tyler, married Seth Dutcher, of Lysander,
        N. Y. She had a large family (three of them were
        named Mary, Lorraine and Seth).

1796   Ebenezer Tyler, born 1792; drowned in his 14th year,
        in the mill sluice of his father's mill.

1797+   David Tyler, twin to Ebenezer.

1798+   Job Tyler.

1799+   Comfort Tyler.

1800+   James Tyler.

639   COLONEL COMFORT[5] TYLER (Job[4]), born in
Ashford, Conn., February 22, 1764; died in Montezuma, N. Y.,
August 5, 1827; married (1), 1786, Deborah Wemple, a half-
sister of General Herkimer; she died soon after marriage; married (2), Betsey Brown. He claimed to be a descendant of
Wat Tyler, the Revolutionist in the time of Richard II. He
received a good education and entered the American army in
1778 and served at West Point. In 1783 he removed to Canghuawaga, N. Y., on the Mohawk River, where he went on
General James Clinton's expedition to establish a boundary
line between New York and Pennsylvania. At the age of 24, he
became a member of the famous "Lessee Company." It was
travel through the wilderness, of New York State, in connection
with this company, which awakened Mr. Tyler's thoughts to
the beauty and fertility of the new country, and he resolved
to settle there. In the spring of 1788, in company with Major
Danforth, he pushed ahead 50 miles into the wilds and began
the first permanent settlement of Onondaga County. He felled
the first tree and constructed the first piece of turnpike road
west of Fort Stanwix (Rome). The early settlers ground their
corn in wood mortars. The oak stump which (hollowed out)
answered for Colonel Tyler's grist-mill was standing (sound)
in 1845. He was a favorite with the Indians, who called him

" To-whan-la-gua," meaning " one that is double," capable of
two states in life; *i. e.*, could act the rôle of laborer or play the
gentleman.   He was the first salt manufacturer (in a com-
mercial sense) in this region.   The year of his arrival, he was
shown a salt spring by Indians, who had, for their own uses,
been taught by the Jesuits a primitive mode of procuring salt.
Before that time the spring had been held in superstitious awe,
as accursed by a demon, who made its waters bitter.   Mr.
Tyler took an iron kettle of 15 gallons capacity and in 9 hours
had made 13 bushels of salt.   This was the natal day of our
American salt trade.   Colonel Tyler was surveyor of the Cayuga reservation, leading promoter of the original Seneca Turnpike Road and Cayuga Lake Bridge, an active worker in
establishing schools and churches; justice for the town of
Manlius in 1794; same year he was the first supervisor, until
1798.   Was sheriff of Onondaga County; the first postmaster,
and afterwards, from 1799 to 1802, was appointed county
clerk.   In the years 1796-1797, was in the legislature; he
obtained the charter for the Cayuga Bridge Company, in which
the famous Aaron Burr was a leading stockholder.   This Burr
acquaintanceship was the beginning of the only shadow chap-
ter in Colonel Tyler's remarkable biography.   On December 6,
1805, Colonel Tyler landed at the island of poor, beguiled
Blennerhasset, with 4 boats and 30 men, some of whom were
armed.   (The going armed would not seem in itself unusual
in a pioneer region.)   This affair, greatly impaired Colonel
Tyler's fortunes and blighted his political prospects.   Colonel
Tyler, whenever charged with treasonable intent, always indig-
nantly denied it; but the episode embittered and saddened the
remainder of his life.   He said to his little grandchild—" whenever persons refer to this matter, you are to tell them, whatever
might have been contemplated, *you know that no harm to our
country was intended by Mr. Tyler.*"   In 1811 he moved to
Montezuma, N. Y., where he became deeply interested in the
Cayuga (Salt) Manufacturing Company.   To make the town
more accessible, he superintended the building of two long
bridges over the Seneca and Clyde Rivers, with a 3-mile turnpike over Cayuga marshes.   Later he lived a few years at
Hoboken, N. J., to superintend the draining of salt meadows.
In the War of 1812 he served as assistant commissary general
(with the rank of colonel) to the Northern Army.   After the

war the Erie Canal policy engaged his most earnest attention. He labored equally with the most zealous until success was assured. Colonel Tyler's affability, sympathy, animation, originality, knowledge of human life and nature, united to an ever-present benevolence, caused his society to be sought and delightfully esteemed; his home was the constant scene of cordial hospitalities. He had great capacity for achievement, both in range and degree. Comfort's remains were removed to Syracuse by a grandson, many years after his death, and rest in a tomb in the chief cemetery of the city.

CHILD, by first marriage:
1801+ Deborah Wemple Tyler, born March, 1787.

CHILD, by second marriage:
1802+ Mary Tyler, born in 1788.

640 JOB[5] TYLER (Job[4]), born in Ashford, Conn., March 12, 1770; died March, 1836; married Charlotte Utley. He is supposed to have gone to Onondaga County, N. Y., and some of the family think he died in Montezuma, N. Y. It is believed that his children were all born in Onondaga County, N. Y. Children:
1803+ Lora Tyler, born Jan. 4, 1792.
1804+ Oren Tyler, born Aug. 21, 1795.
1805+ Asher Tyler, born May 10, 1798.
1806+ Chauncey Tyler, born Dec. 27, 1800.

641 JOHN[5] TYLER (Job[4]), born in Ashford, Conn., March 12, 1770; died February 19, 1845; married Clarissa Chapman, born May 26, 1777; died April 7, 1841, aged 64. He lived on his father's place one mile from Westford Village (Ashford), Conn. He went to New York state with his brothers, but returned to Ashford, where he is buried. Tradition says that he was one of the projectors of the Erie Canal with DeWitt Clinton, but this honor was shared, at least, with his brother Comfort. The children were born in Ashford, Conn. Children:
1807 Catherine Tyler, born Aug. 11, 1800; married Marlin More. They had five children (Emeline, Clarissa, Harriet, Asher, Dexter).

1808   Betsey Tyler, born June 6, 1802; married Palmer
        Converse. They had eight children (Palmer, Tyler,
        Fielder, Elnathan, Jared, Sterry, Lorraine, Mary
        Jane).
1809+ John Tyler, born Oct. 3, 1805.
1810+ George Tyler, born March 19, 1810.
1811   Harriet Tyler, born Aug. 19, 1811; died March 2,
        1813.

    643 WILLIAM[5] TYLER (Job[4]), born in Ashford,
Conn., October 4, 1775; died in Marcellus, N. Y., September,
1825; married Prudence Brown, of Scotch parentage, who died
about 1845. He removed to New York state with his brothers,
and resided in Marcellus. William and his brother Samuel
received word one day that their brother Comfort was at the
point of death and they went to see him in his home in Montezuma, N. Y., and stayed about a week. There was much sickness in Montezuma, and the two brothers, after their return to
Marcellus, were taken with a fatal illness and each lived only
about a week. Comfort, however, on whose account they had
made their last journey, lived for two years after their death.
The records of William's children are rather meager, in some
instances, and the order of their seniority, as well as many matters of family interest, is determined by a letter from Mrs.
Genevieve (Tyler) Dresser, a granddaughter. The children
were probably born in Marcellus.

1812   William Tyler, probably died in infancy.
1813   Elsie Tyler, married —— Holcomb, and has two
        daughters, who were living, very aged, in Pavilion
        Center, N. Y., in 1904.
1814+ Augustus Tyler.
1815   Betsey Tyler, married William Smith, and resided
        near Horner, N. Y.; she had three sons, one who
        lived in Rochester, N. Y., and another in School-
        craft, Mich.; the latter had a son and a daughter.
1816   Erastus Tyler went west and later south, and died,
        unmarried, of the cholera.
1817   Lavinia Tyler, married (1), Erastus Buck; married
        (2), —— Hawkins. She lived in Mount Vernon,
        Ohio, and had a daughter by her first marriage, also
        a son, who lived in Fort Wayne, Ind.

1818   John Tyler, married and had a child, but they all died early in Syracuse.

1819   Charles Tyler, was with Pike on his expedition, ascending the top of the mountain afterward called Pike's Peak. He was an old-time Californian, making and losing several fortunes. He died unmarried, about 1874. He lived in Burr Oak, Mich., at one time.

1820   Ann Tyler, married Henry Williams, and had a daughter (Mary), who lived in Cedar Rapids, married to —— White.

1821+ George Tyler, born July 11, 1817.

1822   Hiram Tyler, was a partner of his brother George in business in Syracuse for many years. He moved to Burr Oak, Mich., and resided in the family of his brother George. He was a brilliant society man in Syracuse, and Burr Oak, and died, in 1880, unmarried.

1823   Mary Tyler, died, s. p. in 1847; married John Sutphen.

1824   Laurens Tyler, was a musician, and educated by his brother George with West Point in view, and Laurens passed a brilliant and successful examination. But that year another candidate from the same district also stood the same test, and lots were drawn, but Laurens did not draw the prize. He also was in business with his brother George. He died in Almo, Kansas, leaving one daughter.

653 CATHERINE[5] TYLER (William[4]), born in Providence, R: I:, November 12, 1762; died March 29, 1807; married Major Jabez Gorham, born July 15, 1760; died May 27, 1802. Children:

1825   Jabez Gorham.
1826   John Gorham.
1827   Bethiah Gorham.
1828   Catherine Gorham.
1829   Hannah Gorham.
1830   Benjamin Gorham.
1831   Sarah Gorham.
1832   William Field Gorham.

657 PHEBE[5] TYLER (William[4]), born in Providence,

R. I., February 16, 1775; died January 29, 1837; married
Philip Peckham, born 1772; died March 9, 1802.   Children:
1833   Philip Peckham.
1834   Mary Peckham, married William Sheldon, of Providence, R. I.

659 BETSEY⁵ TYLER (William⁴), born in Providence, R. I., 1780; died March 8, 1850; married (1), Stephen
G. Williams; married (2), John Viall.

CHILDREN, by first marriage:
1835   Stephen Williams.
1836   William Williams.
1837   Elizabeth Williams.
1838   Martha Williams.
1839   Anthony Williams.

CHILDREN, by second marriage:
1840   James Viall.
1841   Mehitable Viall.
1842   Ann Viall.

660 JOHN⁵ TYLER (William⁴), born in Providence,
R. I., December 7, 1784; died there January 7, 1832; married Emily Cory, of East Greenwich, R. I., born August, 1792;
died in Providence, April 29, 1874; daughter of Captain Oliver
and Rebecca Cory. He was a hatter in Providence. The
eighth child was born in Pawtucket; the others in Providence.
Children:
1843   William Tyler, died young.
1844   Rebecca C. Tyler, born Dec. 31, 1811; died Feb. 5,
1899; married, Dec. 23, 1832, Eleazer Holbrook, of
Brimfield, Mass., who died, s. p., Aug. 5, 1834.
1845+   John Tyler, born April 26, 1813.
1846   Mary W. Tyler, born June 12, 1815; died in Norwich,
Conn., Dec. 19, 1890; married B. Holbrook Aldrich,
of Foster, R. I., who died Feb. 9, 1891.   They had
seven children (George W., Phila A., Willard L.,
James T., B. Holbrook, Jr., Cassius M., Harvey C.).
1847   William Tyler, died young.
1848+   James R. Tyler, born Feb. 28, 1820.

1849   Emily Tyler, died young.
1850+ Ebenezer C. Tyler, born May 19, 1823.
1851+ Albert D. Tyler, born Feb. 21, 1826.
1852   Phila Ann Tyler, born 1828; died 1832.

661 PHILA B.⁵ TYLER (William⁴), born in Providence, R. I., December 31, 1787; died September 9, 1858; married, October 12, 1807, Barney Merry, born in Scituate, R. I., May 29, 1784; died in Pawtucket, R. I., December 18, 1847; son of Samuel and Abigail Barney. Children:
1853   Almira Merry, born Jan. 31, 1809.
1854   Mehitable Merry.
1855   Samuel Merry.
1856+ Elizabeth Merry, born Oct. 17, 1815.
1857   Benjamin Merry.
1858   George Merry.
1859   Joseph Merry.

663 WILLIAM⁵ TYLER (William⁴), born in Providence, R. I.; went to sea and never returned; married Hannah Lowell, daughter of Abner Lowell, first keeper of Plum Island Light, below Newburyport, Mass. Children:
1860   Catherine Gorham Tyler.
1861   Mary (or Polly) Tyler.
1862   William Tyler, died young.

665 NANCY⁵ TYLER (William⁴)), born in Providence, R. I., July 15, 1784; died September 24, 1857; married (1), Samuel Merry, of Pawtucket, R. I., brother of Barney Merry; married (2), Galen Pope.

CHILD, by first marriage:
1863   Abby Merry, married (1), John Harwood; married (2) Gilbert Smith.

CHILD, by second marriage:
1864   Catherine Pope, married Matthew Ingraham, of Providence, R. I., and had two daughters and a son.

667 CHLOE⁵ TYLER (Moses⁴), born in Attleboro, Mass., July 14, 1745; married (published October 3, 1767),

Elijah Bates, who died January 22, 1821, aged 74. She received £1, 12s by her father's will in addition to other gifts. They lived in Thompson, Conn., where the children were born. Children:

1865   William Bates, born about 1770; married Sally Joslin; had two sons and two daughters.

1866   Tyler Bates, born in 1772; died July 10, 1848; married Polly ——, who died July 23, 1848, aged 72. He lived in Thompson; had five sons and seven daughters.

1867   Elijah Bates; married and had four daughters.

1868   Chloe Bates, born in 1775; died March 6, 1854, aged 79; married Ezekiel Rhodes, of Thompson, who died Feb. 1, 1829, aged 55; had six sons and four daughters.

1869   Holman Bates.

1870   Jacob Bates.

1871   Alfonso Bates.

1872   Fannie Bates, married Stephen Brackett, of Southbridge, Mass., and had two sons and two daughters.

1873   George Bates.

1874   Daughter, married —— Martin.

1875   Daughter, married —— Ballard.

671   "SQUIRE" MOSES[5] TYLER (Moses[4]), born in Attleboro, Mass., May 20, 1751; died suddenly in Richmond, N. H., of apoplexy, while sitting on a rock in a field, November 9, 1818; married, September 9, 1777, Mary Scott, born December 25, 1757; died May 14, 1827; daughter of John Scott, of Richmond. He removed to Richmond in 1775 and bought lots five and six in range 12, where he built buildings that were standing in 1880. His home overlooked Mount Monadnock to the east. Four generations of Tylers have lived here. In the inside finish of his house there was not a knot in the boards. An uncut horse-block of hewn stone stands beside the path. The History of Richmond speaks of him as a man of more than ordinary attainments, who had superior qualifications for business, and calls attention to the town records which he kept for many years, as proof of his ability. He was a wonderfully good land surveyor; was a justice of the peace, conveyancer, and representative for several years to the General Court; he

held numerous town offices. He carried on farming in the same way that he conducted all his other business, in which he was exceedingly orderly and methodical. His disposition was rather peculiar, but he seems to have been a man of strength of character. He was large, physically, weighing over 300 pounds. It is said that the only plan extant of the town of Richmond was made by him. His children were born in Richmond.

CHILDREN:

1876+ Chloe Tyler, born July 1, 1778.
1877   Melinda Tyler, born Aug. 12, 1780; married Asa
       Bancroft, of Warwick, Mass., and moved to Plain-
       field, Vt.; had sons and daughters; two sons were tea
       merchants in Boston.
1878   Mary Tyler, born Aug. 9, 1782; married John Griffin,
       of Essex, Vt.
1879   Aaron Tyler, born July 30, 1784; died Jan. 24, 1796.
1880+ Moses Tyler, born Aug. 29, 1786.
1881   Benjamin Tyler, born May 21, 1789; died May 12,
       1796.
1882+ John Tyler, born May 31, 1791.
1883   Patience Tyler, born July 17, 1795; married Samuel
       Atherton, son of Jonathan Atherton, and died s. p.;
       they moved to Attleboro, Mass.

674 ZELOTES[5] TYLER (Moses[4]), born in Attleboro, Mass., April 8, 1760; died a widower, June, 1840; married (published November 1, 1791), December 7, 1791, Molly Robinson, who died in Attleboro before her husband. She joined the Second Congregational church in Attleboro, in 1813. He appears to have gone to Smithfield, R. I. He was a private in the Revolution from Attleboro, going out on the alarms in Rhode Island in 1777, 1778 and 1780, and was a Revolutionary pensioner. He was executor of his father's will, received the real estate, and was to pay the legacies and debts. The children were born in Attleboro.

CHILDREN:

1884   Truman Tyler, born Aug. 27, 1792; he resided in
       Concord, Mass., and was living in 1842.
1885   Nancy Tyler, born Feb. 2, 1794; died July 29, 1830.

1886   Leafa Tyler, born Nov. 11, 1796; died, unmarried, July 24, 1842. Her will was probated Sept. 6, 1842, in Lancaster, Mass.

1887   Sally Tyler, born Feb. 4, 1798; married Leonard Holmes, of Attleboro, and had a family.

1888   Mary Tyler, born July 16, 1800; died, unmarried, in Attleboro, where living in 1842.

1889+   Simeon Stillman Tyler, born Oct. 22, 1803.

1890   Louisa Tyler, born Aug. 13, 1806; died Dec. 24, 1845; married David T. Stanley, of Attleboro; had children.

1891+   Orville Tyler, born July 22, 1808.

675 ZURIEL[5] TYLER (Moses[4]), born in Attleboro, Mass., January 22, 1762; baptized on the 31st of the month in Oldtown; died of cancer, in Essex, Vt., February 9, 1838; published, March 19, 1785, to Chloe Bragg, of Wrentham; married Mehitable Bassett, born in 1765; died in Colchester, Vt., May 19, 1849, at home of her daughter Roxey. He removed to Essex, Vt., where he was a farmer and owned a mill and farm, and was a lister and surveyor, in 1798. He had £26, 10s from his father's estate in addition to previous gifts. He was a private in the Revolution in 1779 and 1780, on the alarms in Rhode Island. He was buried in Essex Center. The youngest child was born in Colchester, Vt., and the others in Essex, except the eldest, whose birthplace is unknown.

CHILDREN:

1892   Achsah Tyler, born Sept. 3, 1794; died, in New Salem, Mass., Jan. 29, 1804.

1893+   Daniel Tyler, born Nov. 26, 1795.

1894+   Rodney Tyler, born Sept. 30, 1797.

1895+   Roxey Tyler, born Feb. 12, 1800.

1896   Irene Tyler, born Aug. 13, 1803; died Feb. 25, 1899, s. p., in Colchester, aged 95 years; married (1), Dec. 3, 1831, Barney Fisher, son of Calvin Fisher, who died in Colchester Sept. 14, 1862; married (2), Aug. 8, 1865, Joseph Lane, a widower, from whom she was divorced through trouble over her property; married (3), May 7, 1877, Rev. Richard Trick, a widower, born in England; died June 19, 1893.

1897+   Orlin Tyler, born Oct. 11, 1804.
1898+   Ruby Tyler, born Jan. 23, 1809.

676 RUFUS[5] TYLER (Moses[4]), born in Attleboro, Mass., March 28, 1764; died at his sister's home in Wrentham, Mass., in 1816; married, October 22, 1787, Dorothy Allen, of Rehoboth, Mass., who died in 1813, aged 44. He was a blacksmith, and resided in Richmond, Rehoboth and Orange, Mass. The four elder children were born in Richmond. Children:
1899   Relief Tyler, born Feb. 12, 1805; died Aug. 29, 1893; married, Jan. 1, 1829, Captain James Rhodes, born in Thompson, Conn., Dec. 31, 1808; died May 15, 1875; son of Ezekiel and Chloe (Bates) Rhodes; had one son.
1900+   Dolly Tyler.
1901+   Sally Tyler.
1902+   Esther Tyler, born May 9, 1801.
1903+   Nancy Tyler.
1904   Betsey Tyler, died early, unmarried.
1905   Rufus Tyler, died aged 15 or 16.

677 DAVID[5] TYLER (Moses[4]), born in Attleboro, Mass., August 13, 1766; died in Essex, Vt., January 5, 1832; married (1), Hannah ——, who died March 24, 1812, aged 40; married (2), Mary Stone, who died June 9, 1835, aged 55; she moved to Chicago. He was lister and surveyor in Essex, in 1798. He received £26, 10s, from his father's estate, in addition to other gifts.

CHILDREN, by first marriage:
1906   Hannah Tyler, born Dec. 10, 1794; married George Gates.
1907+   David Tyler, born in Essex, Jan. 6, 1797.
1908   Nancy Tyler, born March 7, 1799; died in Pages' Corner, Vt., March, 1840.
1909   Amos Tyler, born Aug. 5, 1802 (children recorded at Essex: Hannah, Lucy, and David).
1910   Mary R. Tyler, born Sept. 24, 1807; died in Essex, Nov. 30, 1889; married Loyal Daniels, of Essex.
1911   Maria Tyler, born Aug. 6, 1810; died, unmarried, in Essex, Aug. 17, 1871.

CHILDREN, by second marriage:

1912   Julia Tyler, born Aug. 26, 1813; died in Essex, June
        18, 1895.
1913+   Samuel Tyler, born April 8, 1815.
1914   Fanny Tyler, born March 4, 1818; died June 20,
        1884; married —— Brigham, of Essex.
1915   William Tyler, born July 15, 1822; died early; went
        to Wisconsin.

678 COLONEL GEORGE[5] TYLER (Moses[4]), born in
Attleboro, Mass., October 12, 1768; died February 25, 1862,
aged 94; married, February 16, 1800, in Thompson, Conn.,
by Rev. Lorenzo How, Esther Joslyn, born in Thompson, June
2, 1782; died October 4, 1851. He was an early settler of Essex, Vt.. where he went in 1788, and became a man of influence. In his youth, he bought a year of his time, and his
father gave him a year. In addition to previous gifts his
father's will gave him £26, 10s. In the War of 1812 he was
a colonel at Plattsburg, N. Y. He often went from Essex,
Vt., to Richmond, N. H., on horseback. to visit his brother
Moses (he was a great horseman), and was costumed in continental style, viz.: suit of velvet, with knee-breeches, shoe
buckles and cocked hat. He had 300 acres of land in Vermont,
and was a farmer and stock-dealer, taking horses and cattle
to the Boston market. He went security for friends through
whom he lost much, and removed, with his wife and all his
family except two sons. to Alexandria, Licking County, O.
The children were born in Essex.

CHILDREN:

1916+   Erastus Tyler, born Nov. 14, 1802.
1917+   Lorin Tyler, born Dec. 27, 1804.
1918   Betsey Tyler, born July 20, 1807; died in Alexandria,
        O., April 1, 1876; married (1), 1829, Roswell M.
        Butler, born 1804; died 1830; married (2), 1848,
        in Alexandria, James Remington, born 1809; died
        1888. Son: William H. Butler.
1919+   George Rising Tyler, born March 20, 1810.
1920+   Lyman Early Tyler, born June 18, 1812.
1921+   Cassius Tyler, born Aug. 2, 1815.
1922+   Emeline Tyler, born Feb. 22, 1818.

1923+ Foster Tyler, born July 5, 1820.
1924+ Joel Lafayette Tyler, born Sept. 17, 1823.

680 JUDSON⁵ TYLER (Moses⁴), born in Attleboro, Mass., June 4, 1776; died in Alexandria, Licking Co., O., July 25, 1855; married (1), Prudence Woodworth, who died in Granville, O.. July 7, 1838; married (2), Mrs. Abigail Stratton. He was a carpenter and went to Essex, Vt., with three older brothers when young; moved to Ohio in 1833, and settled in Granville, Licking County. In addition to previous gifts, he received £22 from his father's estate. The children were born in Essex. Children:

1925 Charlotte Emily Tyler, born April 19, 1816; died, s. p., March, 1890; married, June 25, 1852, Lyman W. Rose. In her early days she was a schoolteacher.

1926+ Rufus A. Tyler, born April 18, 1818.

1927 Burnham W. Tyler, born Feb. 2, 1820; married Jerusha J. Barrack, of Alexandria, O.

1928+ Sarah Abigail Tyler, born April 16, 1827.

682 MARY⁵ TYLER (Nathan⁴), born in Attleboro, Mass., April 26, 1755; married, November 14, 1776 (published June 18, 1776), Allen Claflin, born in Attleboro, November 8, 1754; son of Ebenezer and Bethiah (Tiffany) Claflin. The children were born in Attleboro. Children:

1929 Nathan Claflin, born Sept. 15, 1778.
1930 William Claflin, born April 4, 1780.
1931 Leonard Claflin, born April 29, 1785.
1932 Sally Claflin, born Nov. 12, 1786.
1933 Polly Claflin, born Oct. 15, 1788.

686 WILLIAM⁵ TYLER (Nathan⁴), born in Attleboro, Mass., August 4, 1764; died in Livingston County, N. Y., in 1847; married in Massachusetts, Hope Brown; she died at the home of her daughter Hannah, in Geneseo, N. Y., aged 93. At 16 years of age William entered the Revolutionary army for six months, and January 12, 1781, he enlisted as a private for three years from Lanesboro, Mass., in Captain Abraham Watson's company, Colonel John Greaton's 3d Massachusetts Bay regiment. He is described in the old military records as being

five feet, six inches tall; dark complexion, dark eyes, and black hair. He saw service in the State of New York. He was a farmer, and lived in Lanesboro and Cheshire, Mass., and before 1800 moved to Newport, on West Canada Creek, Herkimer County, N. Y. He is buried in Geneseo, N. Y., and his grave is marked by a stone. His children were born in Cheshire and Newport. The dates of their births are not known in each case.

CHILDREN:

1934   Mahala Tyler, married —— Conant or —— Conough.

1935+ Lovina Tyler, born in Cheshire, Feb. 22, 1789.

1936   Lydia Tyler, married Abraham Harris.

1937   Dexter Tyler, died young of consumption.

1938+ Samuel Tyler, born in 1794.

1939+ William Tyler, born in Newport, N. Y.

1940   Rufus Tyler, died near Dunkirk, N. Y.

1941   Hannah Tyler, married —— White, moved to Geneseo, N. Y., and died s. p.

1942   Olive Tyler, married Isaiah Hall; moved to Michigan.

1943+ Thomas Tyler, born in Newport.

1944+ Benjamin Brown Tyler, born in Newport, Sept. 10, 1810.

1945   Lucy Tyler, born in Newport, 1813; married —— Waite, Geneseo, N. Y.

687 THOMAS[5] TYLER (Nathan[4]), born in Attleboro, Mass., June 17, 1768; died in Adams, Mass., July 10, 1834; married, in Adams, in 1792, Mrs. Mary Blakely; born in Adams, November 8, 1770; died there, August 5, 1846. He was a blacksmith and highly respected. The children were born in Adams. Children:

1946   Nathan Tyler, born March 8, 1794; died May 6, 1795.

1947+ Henry Tyler, born July 26, 1795.

1948+ Lucy Tyler, born April 27, 1797.

1949+ Duty Sayles Tyler, born March 23, 1799.

693 WALTER[5] TYLER (Ebenezer[4]), born in Attleboro, Mass., " Monday," June 20, 1763; died March 5, 1846; married (published March 23, 1790), to Bathsheba Sweet, daughter of Captain Henry Sweet, son of John and grandson

of Henry Sweet, of Attleboro. She joined the Oldtown, Mass., church, October 1, 1806. He passed his last years with his brother Samuel. The male line is extinct. He was in the Revolutionary War, in Captain Samuel Robinson's company, Colonel Isaac Dean's 4th Bristol County, Mass. regiment, four days in August, 1780, on the Alarm at Tiverton, R. I. Child:

1950 Augustus Clement Tyler, died in Harpersfield, Ohio, in 1831. His will mentions his " wife Clarisa "; his " mother Bathsheba deceased," and " father Walter Tyler." A letter to Harpersfield failed to bring out any further information.

694 LUCINDA⁵ TYLER (Ebenezer⁴), born in Attleboro, Mass., " Friday," May 10, 1765; died August 13, 1802; married (published April 14, 1787), Henry Sweet, born in Attleboro, June 26, 1761; died February 21, 1828; son of Captain Henry and Mrs. Bathsheba (Balcom) Alexander Sweet. He married (2), Nabby Green, daughter of Roland Green, of Mansfield, who died June 11, 1843; they had one child, Rolandus Green Sweet. Lucinda's children were born in Attleboro. Children:

1951 Hannah Sweet, born May 8, 1788.
1952 Lauretta Sweet, born May 21, 1790; died June 22, 1869.
1953 Harriet Sweet, born May 21, 1793.
1954 Henry Hannibal LaFayette Sweet, born Nov. 1, 1796.

699 EBENEZER⁵ TYLER (Ebenezer⁴), born in Attleboro, Mass., " Wednesday," February 9, 1776; was drowned, in the Penobscot River, Maine, May 13, 1800, aged 25 years; married, in Orrington, Maine, September 8, 1799, Lavinia Brewer, born in Worcester, Mass., November 23, 1778; daughter of Colonel John Brewer, for whom New Worcester Plantation, Maine, afterward Orrington and later Brewer, Maine, was named; he was descended from Josiah and Hannah (Woolson) Brewer, of Weston, Mass. Her mother was Martha, daughter of Ezra Graves, of Sudbury; she was the fifth of nine children. She married (2), in 1818, Bradshaw Hall, of Castine, Maine, long Registrar of Deeds for Hancock County, Maine. She survived her second husband also, and passed

her last days with her daughter Lucinda, and died in Orono, Maine.

CHILD:

1955+   Lucinda Tyler, born in Brewer, Maine, June 4, 1800.

700   LAVINIA⁵ TYLER (Ebenezer⁴), born in Attleboro, Mass., " Tuesday," March 25, 1778; married, January 12, 1807, Dr. Abijah Draper. They lived in West Roxbury, Mass.   Children:

1956   (Dr.) Abijah Weld Draper, born Jan. 25, 1808; died Feb. 9, 1874; married (1), Jan. 20, 1839, Lydia Frances Swain; born in Nantucket, Mass., Jan. 18, 1812; died in West Roxbury, April 29, 1846; married (2), April 26, 1848, Mrs. Sarah Hawes (Hewins) Reynolds, born in South Boston, March 19, 1819; had three sons and one daughter.

1957   Augusta Draper, born July 21, 1810; died Sept. 4, 1877; married, Nov. 25, 1847, Chauncey Woodward, who died Feb., 1872; she had two sons and one daughter.

1958   Amanda Draper, twin to Augusta; died April 26, 1879.

701   ROWLAND or ROLAND⁵ TYLER (Ebenezer⁴), born in Attleboro, Mass., " Wednesday," February 2, 1780; died in Bangor, Maine, October 18, 1872; buried in Dixmont; married (1), March 28, 1804, Sally Ginn, born February 20, 1784; died March 12, 1834; daughter of William H. Ginn, a shipbuilder of Ellsworth, Maine; married (2), Mrs. Daggett. Mr. Tyler went to Penobscot County in 1796, which was then known as Hancock County. He taught school in Bangor several terms and also in Hampden, Maine. He followed the business of architect and builder and had charge of building the old City Hall in Bangor, which was replaced in 1893. He was appointed agent for Dr. Dix and took charge of his property interest in the township of Dix, now Dixmont. He was in the War of 1812, and kept up his military interest afterward, being many years a major in the militia. He was a very rigid temperance man, a deacon of the church, and long a justice of the peace. An old pupil said about 1890, " If there ever was a true, noble gentleman, Rowland Tyler was

one." He was a faithful member of the Methodist church. After his first marriage he bought a farm in Dixmont and lived there until about 1840, when he removed to Bangor. After marrying Mr. Daggett's widow, a tavern, built by Mr. Daggett about 1820, came into his possession. There he kept the "Tyler Stand" tavern, and gave it to his son Lyman at his death. He always took a leading part in the affairs of the section where he lived and matters of dispute were referred to him for settlement. The children were born in Dixmont.

CHILDREN:

1959   Mary Anne Tyler, born Feb. 26, 1805; died April 20, 1830, unmarried.

1960+   Harriet Augusta Tyler, born Nov. 24, 1806.

1961   Sally Ginn Tyler, born Feb. 5, 1808; died May 9, 1854.

1692   Hannah Reed Tyler, born Dec. 12, 1809; died April 9, 1886; married Captain Nathan Lowe, of Deer Isle, Maine, who died after a disaster to a boat. They had several children.

1963   Frederick Tyler, born Sept. 15, 1812; died, s. p., June 22, 1835; married, Feb. 25, 1835, Diadamia P. Emery, born in Fairfield, Maine, June 7, 1813, daughter of Samuel and Diadamia (Johnston) Emery; she married (2), Nov. 28, 1839, Joseph Emery.

1964+   Lucinda Tyler, born Aug. 25, 1814.

1965   Lyman Tyler, born May 15, 1816; died March 14, 1886; married, Jan. 1, 1844, Lucetta Libby, born July 11, 1815, in Waterport, Maine, daughter of David and Hannah (Knight) Libby, of Carmel, Maine. Lyman was a builder and contracted for many buildings. He owned the "Tyler Stand," in Bangor, and 360 acres, and three other farms aggregating 260 acres; he also kept a store, and had teams on the road collecting eggs. In 1855 he retired from the "Tyler Stand" to his farm-house on the opposite side of the road and hired a man to carry on the hotel. After that he spent his winters in Boston handling produce of all kinds, which was forwarded from his store in Bangor and from Prince

Edward Island. He left a large estate, and his widow died two years later; their only child, a daughter, died before she was seven years old.

1966+ Caroline Herrick Tyler, born April 3, 1818.

1967+ Louisa Elvira Tyler, born Sept. 11, 1820.

1968   Rowland Abijah Tyler, born June 3, 1822; probably died before 1897; resided in San Francisco, Cal., unmarried.

1969   Lafayette Tyler, born Aug. 15, 1824; died Sept. 15, 1826.

1970   Lavinia Draper Tyler, born Jan. 28, 1829; died March 4, 1830.

702 DOCTOR ABIJAH[5] WELD TYLER (Ebenezer[4]), born in Attleboro, Mass., February 2, 1780; died, drowned in Penobscot River, Maine, August 22, 1807; married Fanny Richardson, born December 11, 1780; died August 18, 1861; daughter of Abiathar Richardson. She joined the Congregational church in Attleboro, March 5, 1815; she presided in the home of her brother-in-law Samuel Tyler, after his first wife's death. Dr. Tyler moved to a place near Hampden, Maine, in the early part of the nineteenth century. The children were born in Attleboro. Children:

1971   Abijah Weld Tyler, born Aug. 25, 1802; died March 9, 1803.

1972+ Louisa R. Tyler, born in 1804.

1973   Abijah Weld Tyler, born in 1805; died in Charlestown, S. C., Aug. 21, 1838, unmarried.

704 CRAWFORD[5] TYLER (Ebenezer[4]), born in Attleboro, Mass., "Thursday," April 8, 1784; died in Milford, N. H., March 9, 1850; married Martha Clark (?), who died October 3, 1860, aged 70. He moved to Milford, N. H., and his first tax in that town was in 1813. He appears on a deed as a witness between Ephraim Murch and wife, and Rowland and Abijah Tyler, of Hampden, Maine, the same dated December 14, 1804. His will, dated February 16, 1850, shows him to have been a millwright. Children:

1974   Nancy Tyler, born in Milford, in 1813 and died there, Dec. 9, 1813.

1975   Martha C. Tyler, born in Milford, 1815; died May 12, 1839.

1976   Ebenezer Tyler, moved to Illinois and married; mentioned only in father's will.

1977   Eveline Tyler, born in 1817; died Dec. 16, 1884; married, April 19, 1843, George H. Whitney, of Grafton, Mass., who died Oct. 13, 1884, aged 79. They had one daughter, who died aged about ten. Eveline is mentioned in her father's will.

1978   Henry S. Tyler, born in 1819; died Aug. 26, 1820.

1979   Henry C. Tyler, born in 1822; died Jan. 28, 1823.

1980   Mary Ann Tyler, born in 1823; died Dec. 11, 1824.

1981+   Humphrey M. Tyler, born in Ipswich, N. H., Dec. 8, 1825.

1982   Harriet C. Tyler, born in 1828; died Oct. 29, 1829.

1983   Henrietta Tyler, probably twin to Harriet, died Nov. 8, 1849.

1984   Harriet E. Tyler, born in 1831; died July 31, 1849.

705 SAMUEL[5] TYLER (Ebenezer[4]), born in Attleboro, Mass., December 7, 1785; died November 20, 1850; married (1), Betsey Samson, who died in 1828; married (2), Charity Willard, who died in Attleboro, April 2, 1859, aged 53. He was an enterprising, influential man in Attleboro, and a pious church-member. His will mentions him as "a depraved worm of the dust." His four elder daughters were baptized in Oldtown, Mass., October 23, 1825.

CHILDREN, by first marriage:

1985+   Eunice Doggett Tyler, born April 3, 1813.

1986   Elizabeth Samson Tyler, born May 30, 1818; died, s. p., April 25, 1863; married, Jan. 5, 1854, Atherton Wales, of Attleboro, who married (1), Louisa R. Tyler, No. 1972.

1987   Hannah Read Tyler, born Jan. 6, 1823; married Alexander Thompson, of St. Johnsbury, Vt., and died s. p.

1988   Ann Frances Tyler, born June 18, 1825; married, in Providence, R. I., Nov. 25, 1857, Charles Lincoln Heywood, of Concord, Mass.; born in Lunenburg, Mass., April 17, 1827; died, s. p., in 1883; son of Lincoln and Rebecca Heywood. He was superintendent of the Fitchburg Railroad for twelve years.

He resigned to travel abroad and for leisure to develop his railroad patents, of which he had ten. His snow-plough was generally and widely adopted, while his bridge-guard saved many brakemen from death. He owned two mills in Acton. He was a philanthropist and had a class in the Sunday-school of the Charlestown State Prison for many years, and he was especially interested in the welfare of young boys. The American Humane Society employed him to look after the transportation of animals, the last year of his life. His widow resided in Providence in 1898.

CHILDREN, by second marriage:

1989   Harriet Amanda Tyler, born May 10, 1837; married Edward Deane, of Attleboro; resided, s. p., in Providence, R. I., in 1898. She was a teacher before her marriage. She and her brother were baptized in Oldtown, Mass., Nov. 30, 1838.

1990+   Samuel Willard Tyler, born May 14, 1838.

707   SYLVIA[5] TYLER (Ebenezer[4]), born in Attleboro, Mass., January 24, 1788; married, April 29, 1816, Tristam Bird, of Dorchester, Mass. The children were born in Dorchester. Children:

1991   Charles Bird.
1992   Henry Bird.
1993   Hannah Bird.
1994   Loretta Bird.

707   HANNAH[5] TYLER (Ebenezer[4]), born in Attleboro, Mass., "Thursday," September 17, 1789; died August 19, 1825; married, June 10, 1810, General Nathaniel[5] Guild; born June 23, 1775; died August 25, 1845 (Aaron[4], Nathaniel[3], Samuel[2], John[1]). He was an architect and lived in Dedham, where he was on the school board for fifteen years; also town treasurer and collector of taxes, and treasurer of the First church. He was a brigadier-general, and a member of the Ancient and Honorable Artillery Company. Children:

1995   Lucinda Guild, born Sept. 7, 1811; married, Nov. 30,

1843, Gorham D. Pearson, who died March 31, 1885, in West Roxbury, Mass. She removed to Walpole.

1996 Nathaniel Tyler Guild, born Nov. 9, 1813; died in Quincy, Mass., July 4, 1881; married, June 3, 1841, Mary Green, of Melrose, Mass. An engineer on B. & W. Railway, and depot master in Grantville, Mass.; no children.

1997 Edward Guild, born Aug. 29, 1816; died Aug. 29, 1886, unmarried.

1998 Henry Guild, born Nov. 29, 1818; married Louisa P. Frobisher; had a family; was a manufacturing jeweler in Boston.

1999 Samuel Foster Guild, born April 30, 1824; died July 5, 1879; married, Jan. 8, 1849, Hannah M. Usher, South Boston; had four children; was a gold refiner.

SIXTH GENERATION

730   MOSES[6] TYLER (Moses[5]), born in Warren, Mass.,
August 8, 1763; died May 13, 1806; married, 1785, Sarah
Patrick, born December 22, 1766; died September, 1827;
daughter of Thomas and Sarah (Johnson) Patrick. Her will
was probated in Springfield, Mass. After the death of Moses
Tyler, David Hoar sold real estate belonging to the three
younger children. The elder children were born in Warren,
the three younger in Brimfield, Mass. Children:

2000+   Thomas Tyler, born Jan. 26, 1787.
2001+   Tryphenia Tyler, born March 14, 1789.
2002+   Sarah or Sallie Tyler, born June 2, 1791.
2003+   Moses Tyler, born May 10, 1797.
2004+   Horatio Tyler, born Sept. 7, 1801.
2005   John Tyler, born Nov. 20, 1803; moved to Buffalo,
        N. Y., and died Feb. 22, 1824, unmarried.
2006   Eliza Tyler, born March 3, 1806; married William
        Tucker, a gunsmith of Brimfield. They had two
        sons.

731   DOCTOR JOHN[6] TYLER (Moses[5]), born in Warren, Mass., in 1766; died March 24, 1853; married (1), Olive
Goodwin, of Simsbury (now Bloomfield, Conn.); married (2),
March 20, 1833, Ann Brown in Hartford, Conn. He was in
the Revolution, enlisting March 1, 1782, in Cram's Massa-
chusett's artillery; engaged previously at Mud Island Fort,
Pennsylvania. He appears on a list of pensioners in 1840.
His residence was in Simsbury. His widow was interested in
preserving Tyler records. Children:

2007   Olive Goodwin Tyler; married James Bidwell, of
        Bloomfield, and died s. p.
2008+   John Keyes Tyler.

732   ISAAC[6] TYLER (Moses[5]), born in Warren, Mass.,
November 16, 1767; died there, June 11, 1847; married, March
20, 1794, Bethiah Cutler, born in Warren, May 15, 1772; died

there, August 11, 1848; daughter of Captain Joseph Cutler,
and descended from James Cutler, of Watertown, Mass., 1634.
In 1782 his uncle Isaac Tyler became his guardian. His
estate was probated October 12, 1847, and his son-in-law,
Timothy James was appointed administrator. The children
were born in Warren. Children:

2009+ Cutler Tyler, born Nov. 19, 1794.
2010+ Keyes Tyler, born Sept. 29, 1796.
2011+ Lydia Tyler, born Feb. 6, 1799.
2012+ Isaac Tyler, born June 1, 1801.
2013+ Bethiah Tyler, born June 4, 1803.
2014 Mary Tyler, born Aug. 29, 1805; died Nov. 30, 1806.
2015+ Reuben Tyler, born Feb. 11, 1808.
2016+ Rebecca Tyler, born Aug. 10, 1809.
2017+ Mary Tyler, born Nov. 3, 1811.
2018+ Tryphena Tyler, born Feb. 26, 1814.
2019+ Moses Tyler, born Nov. 15, 1816.

734 TAMAR[6] TYLER (Moses[5]), born in Warren,
Mass., 1773; died in Hardwick, Mass., September 11, 1864;
married Marcus Marsh, of Hardwick, Mass., who died May 10,
1823, aged 52. In 1787 she chose Daniel Hodges, of Western,
as her guardian. The eldest child may have been born in
Warren, but the others were born in Hardwick. Children:

2020 Zenas Marsh, born about 1793.
2021 Triphena Marsh, born in 1798; died unmarried, Jan.
7, 1843.
2022 Marcus J. Marsh, born about 1800; married Amelia
Dexter, and had three sons (Marcus, Moses, Addison.)
2023 Mary Marsh, born about 1801; died Jan. 24, 1873;
married —— Bartlett.
2024 Tyler Marsh, born about 1802; died Jan. 8, 1875.
2025 Sally Marsh, born about 1813; died unmarried, Dec.
2, 1873.

747 DANIEL[6] TYLER (Abner[5]), born in Warren,
Mass., May 12, 1777; died October 5, 1851; married (1), January 6, 1803, Abigail Cutler; born in Warren, October 31,
1778; died December 24, 1811; daughter of Lieutenant Ebenezer Cutler; married (2), April 20, 1813, Lucy Dunbar, of

Ware, Mass., who died October 10, 1813, aged 30; married (3), April 2, 1817, Sarah Jones, of Worcester, Mass., who died September 3, 1848, aged 67. His will, dated September 1, 1848, was filed October 14, 1851. His son David R. Tyler was made residuary legatee and executor. John appealed from the probate, but without avail. The children were born in Warren. The male line will be extinct with the death of John Warren[8] Tyler.

CHILD, by first marriage:

2026+   John Tyler, born Dec. 4, 1803.

CHILDREN, by third marriage:

2027   Bethiah Tyler, born Dec. 24, 1818; died Nov. 25, 1891; married Warren Lincoln, of Warren, who died May 18, 1878, aged 64; they had children.

2028+   David Richards Tyler, born Jan. 12, 1821.

750 OLIVE[6] TYLER (Abner[5]), born in Warren, Mass., October 2, 1782; died August 5, 1846; married, June 1, 1806, Thomas Cheney Hodges, born May 19, 1784; died in Homer, O., 1872; son of Daniel Hodges (George, William, John, William.) The children were born in Warren, except the two younger. (See *Hodges Family of New England.*) Children:

2029   Cassandana Hodges, born April 28, 1807; died in Cleveland, O., Feb., 1883; married (1), Aug. 5, 1838, Dr. John Baxter, who died in Brandon, O., Jan., 1848; married (2), Jan., 1854, Arthur Greer, of Mt. Vernon, O. She had two sons and a daughter (Thomas, Harris, Ruth.)

2030   Ruth Hodges, born Oct. 26, 1808; died, s. p., July 10, 1834, in New Harmony, Ind.; married in New York City, March 25, 1831, Dr. John Baxter, who married (2), her sister Cassandana; he was a son of John and Elizabeth (Marshall) Baxter.

2031   George Holland Hodges, born April 5, 1810; died Oct. 31, 1888, in Homer, O.; married (1), Jan. 1, 1849, Catherine Phinney, born in Vermont, April 4, 1828; died Sept. 10, 1859; married (2), April, 1868, Julia Ann Jones, daughter of Nelson and Mary Ann (Babbs) Jones, of Utica, O., living in

Homer, O., in 1894; he had three sons and a daughter by his first marriage (John, George, William, Augusta.)

2032 Lucien Hodges, born April 23, 1813; died Aug., 1872, in Richwood, O.; married, Dec. 24, 1837, in Grafton, Mass., Sarah H. Phillips; they had four sons and a daughter (James, Charles, Henry, Albert, Mary.)

2033 Rachel Rich Hodges, born June 1, 1815; died unmarried, Sept. 10, 1887, in Warren.

2034+ Mary Josephine Hodges, born Oct. 11, 1817.

2035 Olive Cheney Hodges, born in Palmer, Mass., March 5, 1820; married, in Springfield, Mass., Feb. 18, 1873, Franklin Drury, of Warren, born there 1799; died there, s. p., Jan. 1, 1889; son of Winsor and Alice Drury. Mrs. Drury was living in Johnstown, O., in 1893.

2036 Augusta Hodges, born in Palmer, July 25, 1822; died s. p., in Brookfield, Mass., Oct. 6, 1853; married, Sept. 2, 1846, Leonard Warren, of Warren.

753 RUTH⁶ TYLER (Abner⁵), born in Warren, Mass., March 24, 1788; died January 17, 1883; married, April 23, 1812, Pardon Allen; born in Wardsborough, Vt., July 5, 1785; died in Warren, April 6, 1847. The children were born in Warren. Children:

2037 Abner Tyler Allen, born Feb. 9, 1813; married Eunice Shepherd; resided in Willoughby, O., in 1898.

2038 Daniel Cutler Allen, born Aug. 11, 1814; married Delia Baker.

2039 Harvey S. Allen, born April 9, 1816; married Lucy Cheetum; had one son and two daughters (Aylmer, Ruth, Clara.)

2040 Amasa I. Allen, born April 4, 1818; married Wealthy Homes.

2041 Olive Allen, born March 14, 1820; married Thomas Dencon.

2042 George Allen, born Sept. 24, 1821.

2043 Pardon Allen, born March 30, 1824; married, Dec. 27, 1849, Lydia Ann Greenough, of Salem, Mass., born in Chester, N. H., Aug. 17, 1827; lives in

South Warren and has two sons and a daughter (Henry, Harrison, Cora.)

754   ABNER[6] TYLER, JR. (Abner[5]), born in Warren, Mass., March 8, 1790; died in Springfield, Mass., August 28, 1876; married, April 15, 1825, Lucretia Allen, born in Wardsboro, Vt., November 5, 1786; died in West Brookfield, Mass., October 11, 1848; daughter of Abner and Lucy (Brooks) Allen, of Warren, and descended from James Allen, of Medfield, Mass. He settled in Pepperell, Mass., where he managed the estate of Col. William Prescott. He returned to Warren, and thence removed to West Brookfield, but his later years were spent with his daughter, Mrs. Bardwell. The male line in this family is extinct. The children were born in Pepperell.

CHILDREN:
2044+   Lucy Brooks Tyler, born Dec. 8, 1828.
2045   Amos Edward Tyler, born March 31, 1831; died April 12, 1849, while in the academy in Marlboro, Mass.

755   AMOS[6] TYLER (Abner[5]), born in Warren, Mass., August 14, 1791; died in Palmer, Mass., January 15, 1829; married, April 1, 1824, Betsey Drury, of Brimfield, Mass., born August 4, 1796; died January 25, 1863. His estate was probated in Springfield, Mass., 1829, Case No. 11451. The administrator was Isaac Tyler, and James Tyler was surety, both living in Western. The male line is extinct. The children were born in Warren. Children:
2046+   Maria S. Tyler, born Oct. 15, 1824.
2047   Sarah J. Tyler, born May 3, 1826; died in Warren, Oct. 1, 1843.
2048+   Julia Ann Tyler, born March 4, 1828.

757   JONAS[6] READ TYLER (Abner[5]), born in Warren, Mass., July 20, 1795; died October 10, 1871; married, May 11, 1825, Susan Crabtree, born October 9, 1805; died December 26, 1890. He settled on a farm in Warren, now occupied by his grandchildren, where he proved himself to be an excellent farmer. The male line is extinct. The children were born in Warren. Children:
2049+   Sarah Tyler, born Jan. 13, 1827.

2050   Abner Tyler, born July 5, 1828; died unmarried, July
        5, 1881.
2051+   Ruth Tyler, born April 28, 1833.

761   JOHN[6] TYLER, JR. (John[5]), born in Tolland,
Conn., August 28, 1780; settled on the old Tyler place near
Willimantic River, where he died, 1846; married Almira Baker;
born April 16, 1784; died in Somers, Conn., April 5, 1864;
daughter of John and Elizabeth (Dimick) Baker. The family
are said to have been members of the Baptist church in Tolland. None of the family now live there. All the children
were born there, but the exact order of birth is not known.
Children:
2052+   John M. Tyler, born in 1806.
2053   Sylvester Tyler, died s. p.
2054+   Nathan Tyler.
2055   Amelia Tyler, died unmarried; buried in North Haven,
        Conn.
2056+   Julia Ann Tyler, born in 1816.
2057   Sarah Tyler, born about 1816; died about 1850, in
        Indianapolis, Ind.; married, about 1845, ———
        Wheeler, and had two daughters.
2058   Almira Tyler, born 1820; died unmarried, in Somers,
        Conn., Jan. 10, 1877, aged 57.

763   ASA[6] TYLER (Moses[5]), born probably in Thetford, Vt., 1782; died while on a visit to his son in Coldwater,
Mich., in 1863; married Hannah Gates. He went to Whitestown, N. Y., with his father about 1800; thence to Mexico,
N. Y., in 1802, where he cleared a farm. The children were
probably all born in Mexico. Children:
2059   Lucinda Tyler.
2060+   Saxton Gates Tyler.
2061   Lewis Tyler, probably moved to Coldwater, Mich.
2062   Alphonso Tyler, born in 1811; went in 1848 to Hebron,
        Ill., where he died in 1889, s. p.; married; no chil-
        dren.
2063+   Beulah Tyler, born in 1813; married William Mark-
        ham.
2064   Philena Tyler, married ——— Halsey; resided in 1897
        in Mexico, N. Y.

2065   Lydia Tyler.
2066   Cordelia Tyler, married ——— Bickard; resided in 1897
        in Olds, Mich.
2067   Dotha Tyler.
2068   Arsaville Tyler.
2069   Celinda Tyler, married ——— Stone.
2070   Lucy Ann Tyler.

764 DEACON DEAN MERRILL[6] TYLER (Moses[5]),
place and date of birth unknown; died in Portland, Mich.,
through an accident, July 13, 1848; married Phebe Post. He
lived for a time in Mt. Morris, N. Y., and then moved to
Portland, Mich., where he was a deacon in the Baptist church,
1840-1848. He was dismissed to the church in this place from
that of Walled Lake, Mich. He was the oldest constituent
member of the Portland church and its only deacon. He was
universally respected in his community. Children:

2071   Isaac E. Tyler, married Elizabeth ———. (His
        daughter Amelia married ——— Smith, and her son
        [Dr. Dean Tyler Smith], lived in Jackson, Mich.).
2072   Dean Merrill Tyler, Jr.
2073   Emerson Tyler.
2074   Laura Tyler, married ——— Crawford; resided Owosso,
        Mich.
2075   Betsey Tyler, married ——— Brown; resided in Port-
        land, Mich.
2076   Sarah Tyler, married ——— Briggs.
2077   Caroline Tyler, married ——— Briggs; the two sisters
        married brothers.
2078   Phebe Tyler, married ——— Morehouse.

765 NABBY[6] TYLER (Moses[5]), born probably in
Thetford, Vt.; married Byron Hawley. Child:
2079   Loren Hawley, who lived in Pulaski, N. Y.

766 NATHANIEL[6] TYLER (Moses[5]), time and place
of birth unknown; died in Whitestown, Oneida County, N. Y.,
March 20, 1876; married Beulah Gates. He was in the War
of 1812. He lived in Sackett's Harbor, N. Y., farming, and
was a Baptist deacon. His father died at his home. The
children were born in Whitestown. Children:

2080+ Oliver H. P. Tyler, born Oct. 12, 1817.
2081+ Moses Merrill Tyler, born July 14, 1819.
2082+ James Tyler, born April 25, 1821.
2083+ Job Tyler, born Nov. 25, 1824.
2084+ Jane Tyler, born Feb. 2, 1827.
2085+ Nathaniel Tyler, born April 8, 1829.
2086 William Wirt Tyler, born Dec. 7, 1832; died unmarried, Nov. 20, 1853.

768 DANIEL S.[6] TYLER (Moses[5]), born, probably in Thetford, Vt., December 17, 1787; died in East Cleveland, O., June 8, 1843; married, in Euclid, O., October 15, 1809, Elizabeth Dille, who died in East Cleveland, September 23, 1876, aged 83. He was a drummer in the War of 1812 for a Cleveland company, and had a pension, according to the *Pension Book*, p. 67, No. 14. He had 160 acres of bounty land. Early in the nineteenth century he was a farmer in the town of Euclid. The children were born in Cleveland. Children:
2087 John Weir Tyler, born Jan. 22, 1811; died unmarried, Feb. 19, 1868.
2088 Henry M. Tyler, born Jan. 21, 1813; died unmarried, April 18, 1886, in Warrensville, O.
2089+ Isaac Newton Tyler, born Aug. 30, 1815.
2099 Eliza Tyler, born Oct. 27, 1817; died unmarried, Dec. 7, 1864.
2091 Almira D. Tyler, born Oct. 29, 1819; died unmarried, Sept. 7, 1855.
2092 Fanny Tyler, born March 19, 1821; died Aug. 16, 1822.
2093+ Samuel S. Tyler, born Jan. 9, 1823.
2094+ Lewis P. Tyler, born June 1, 1825.
2095 Frances Tyler, born March 16, 1827; married, June 20, 1853, P. S. Bosworth, who died, s. p., Oct. 18, 1875.
2096 Lucy Tyler, born July 21, 1829; died unmarried, in Cleveland, O., Jan. 3, 1884.
2097 Elizabeth Tyler, born Feb. 24, 1833; unmarried.
2098 Dean S. Tyler, born March 1, 1835; died unmarried, May 26, 1878.

771 ISAAC[6] TYLER (Moses[5]), born in Thetford, Vt.,

August 16, 1800; died in Leslie, Mich., August 13, 1872; married, March 30, 1823, Rebecca Rising; born in Lee, N. Y., April 20, 1805; died in Onondaga, Mich., August 10, 1888. He resided in Watertown, N. Y., and in 1837 moved to Leslie, Mich. The two elder children were born in Mexico, N. Y., and the two younger in Grass Lake, Mich. The others in Watertown, N. Y. Children:

2099+ John M. Tyler, born April 20, 1825.

2100+ Dean M. Tyler, born July 5, 1828.

2101+ Asa Lewis Tyler, born Sept. 2, 1832.

2102 Antoinette E. A. Tyler, born July 25, 1834; married, in Onondaga, Mich., Oct. 26, 1865, Lewis Garfield. She resides s. p., a widow, in Leslie, Mich.

2103+ Charlotte Adelia Tyler, born July 9, 1844.

2104 Howard J. Tyler, born July 31, 1846; died in Kalamazoo, Mich, May 25, 1864.

  722 JAMES[6] TYLER (Adonijah[5]), born April 12, 1760; died in Thetford, Vt., August 20, 1855; married, July 14, 1778, Sarah Gould, of Hopkinton, N. H. He was in the Revolution. In 1840 he lived with his son James in Thetford. The fourth to the ninth children inclusive, were born in Henniker; the two younger in Thetford. Children:

2105 Asa Tyler, moved to Rockford, Ill.

2106+ Christopher Gould Tyler, born in Hopkinton, July 10, 1779.

2107 Asher Tyler.

2108+ Mary Tyler, born Dec. 13, 1781.

2109 Joel Tyler, perhaps the singer of Philadelphia.

2110 Anna Tyler, born June 4, 1783; died July 6, 1801.

2111 John Tyler, born June 4, 1786; he was a farmer, married and had a family.

2112 James Tyler, born June 3, 1789; died s. p., in Thetford, Vt., Feb. 2, 1876; married, Dec. 1, 1814, Betsey Fletcher, born Nov. 17, 1793; died s. p., August 31, 1878; daughter of Jonathan and Betsey Fletcher. He was a justice of the peace, overseer of the poor, on the town board for many years; a man of integrity and generosity; a good natural mathematician.

2113+ Lucinda Tyler, born July 18, 1791.

2114+   Jeremiah Tyler, born Sept. 8, 1796.
2115   Candice Tyler, born March 1, 1800.

773   RACHEL[6] TYLER (Adonijah[5]), born in Chester,
N. H., March 2, 1762; died February, 1843; married Jacob
Stanley. She lived in Tunbridge, Vt., and then moved to New
York state. Child:
2116   Lucy Stanley, married —— Stewart, of Battle Creek
        House, Battle Creek, Mich.

774   MIRIAM[6] TYLER (Adonijah[5]), born in Hopkinton, N. H., March 22, 1764; died in East Canterbury, N. H.,
August 9, 1841; married, May 11, 1790, Moses Hastings, of
Hopkinton, born September 12, 1762; died in Clement Hill,
N. H., January 25, 1814. In early life she was a school-
teacher and her children graduated from academies in Bos-
cawen and Pembroke, N. H., and also became teachers. When
a widow, she joined the Shakers in East Canterbury, with four
of her children, and died there. The two elder children were
born in Clement Hill; no record of birthplace of the other
children. Children:
2117   Mary Abbott Hastings, born April 17, 1791; died
        Oct. 14, 1865; married, Feb. 29, 1816, Enoch Long,
        of Galena, Ill., a lead miner; had two children.
2118   Jeremiah Hastings, born July 26, 1793; died March
        12, 1795.
2119   Laura Hastings, born May 5, 1796; died Aug. 1,
        1836; married, Feb. 13, 1826, Joel Blood, of Water-
        town, N. Y., whose first wife was Irene H. Tyler,
        daughter of Simeon and Hannah (Rowell) Tyler,
        No. 2132. Laura had two daughters and a son.
2120   Ednah Hastings, born May 30, 1798; died in Boston,
        Mass., Jan. 12, 1892; married, May 16, 1825, Rev.
        Abiel Silver, of Contoocook, N. H., and Boston,
        Mass. He was a well-known and highly-esteemed
        minister of the Swedenborgian faith. They had
        one daughter.
2121   Maria Hastings, born June 21, 1800; died Feb. 2,
        1875; married, Oct. 6, 1829, Joseph Lee.
2122   Moses Hastings, born Oct. 7, 1802; died Sept. 4, 1826,
        in Quincy, Ill.; unmarried.

2123   Betsey McConnell Hastings, born Nov. 3, 1804; joined
        the Shakers in Sabbathday Lake, Maine, and died
        single.
2124   Harriet Hastings, born May 5, 1807; lived with the
        Shakers in Canterbury, where died Feb. 22, 1898.
2125   Charlotte Hastings, born June 5, 1809; died in Colum-
        bus, O., Feb. 8, 1839.
2126   Marcia Eliza Hastings, born Dec. 1, 1811; died
        single, Oct. 29, 1891; lived with the Shakers in
        Canterbury, where died.

775 JEREMIAH⁶ TYLER (Adonijah⁵), born in Chester, N. H., April 9, 1766; died in Orford, N. H., January,
1844; married Irene Heaton. He was in the Revolution. Lived
with his son William M. Tyler in 1840, in Thetford, Vt. In
1842 he joined the Orford Congregational church. The children were born in Thetford, Vt. Children:
2127+   Cyril S. Tyler, born Dec. 31, 1803.
2128+   Latimer Tyler, born Oct. 2, 1806.
2129+   William Monroe Tyler.

776 SIMEON⁶ TYLER (Adonijah⁵), born in Chester,
N. H., March 20, 1768; died December 24, 1855; married (1),
March 14, 1799, Hannah Rowell, born May 17, 1776; died in
Hopkinton, N. H., June 28, 1831; daughter of Nathaniel and
—— (Morse) Rowell, of Hopkinton; married (2), June 27,
1837, Susan Paige, born November 11, 1786; died March 21,
1865. All the children were by the first marriage. He was a
farmer. The children were born in Hopkinton.

CHILDREN, by first marriage:
2130   Lydia Tyler, born Aug. 29, 1801: died March 20,
        1817; buried in Hopkinton.
2131   Plumy Tyler, born May 1, 1804; died April 2, 1817.
2132   Irene Tyler, born April 4, 1806; died Aug. 27, 1808.
2133   Irene Heaton Tyler, born Jan. 15, 1809; died Feb.
        1, 1852; married, Jan. 27, 1840, Joel Blood, of
        Watertown, N. Y., whose second wife was Laura
        Hastings, daughter of Moses and Miriam (Tyler)
        Hastings, No. 2118; no children.
2134   Mary Jane Ballard Tyler, born March 29, 1813; died
        Aug. 20, 1835, unmarried.

2135+   Lucius Harvey Tyler, born Nov. 19, 1817.

777   MOSES[6] TYLER (Adonijah[5]), born in Henniker, N. H., April 7, 1770; died in Tyler's Bridge, N. H., December 21, 1857; married Betsey McConnell, of Pembroke, N. H., born January 30, 1774, of superior Scotch-Irish ancestry; she died September 9, 1866. She was received by letter from the Pembroke, N. H., church in 1801. He was a very generous and public-spirited man, and was a leading member of the Congregational church. He, with a neighbor, built the first "Tyler's Bridge" over the river. The children were born in Henniker. Children:

2136+   Nancy Tyler, born May 4, 1799.
2137+   Sarah Tyler, born Jan. 12, 1802.
2138+   Calvin Tyler (an adopted son), born March 11, 1806.

778   POLLY (MARY)[6] TYLER (Adonijah[5]), born in Chester, N. H., June 4, 1773; married Jacob Martin. They lived in Sandwich, N. H., and about 1835 moved to Gap Grove, Ill., between Dixon and Sterling, Ill. Children:

2139   Moses Tyler Martin.
2140   William Martin, married and had children.
2141   Jacob Martin, married Margaret Curtis.
2142   Eliza Martin, married (1), —— Hubbard; married (2), —— Tilton, of Gap Grove, Ill.
2143   James Martin.
2144   Simeon T. Martin.

779   SARAH[6] TYLER (Adonijah[5]), born in Tyler's Bridge, N. H., March, 1775; died February 7, 1839, in Illinois; married Robert Crowell, of Hopkinton, N. H., a cooper, and in 1839 moved to Oregon, Ill. The children were born in Hopkinton. Children:

2145   Jeremiah Crowell, was a cooper and farmer; married Betsey Bickford, of Hopkinton; they had a family.
2146   Thomas Pritchard Crowell, died young.
2147   Watts Turner Crowell, was a cooper; married Harriet Locker; lived in Springfield, N. H.; had six children.
2148   Moses Tyler Crowell, married Mary Bickford, of Hopkinton; moved to Boston, Mass., and thence to Sacramento, Cal.; had a family.

2149   Samuel Putney Crowell, went to Cuba, W. I.; probably unmarried.

2150   S. Solon Crowell, was a farmer; married in Illinois, and had six or eight children.

2151   Lorenzo Hastings Crowell, moved to Illinois; died single.

2152   Hannah Crowell, married ——— Charrice, of New Haven, Conn.

2153   Mary Crowell, married John Wilson, a farmer, of Illinois, and had three children.

2154   Sarah Ann Crowell, died Nov. 6, 1837, unmarried.

780 PHINEAS⁶ TYLER (Adonijah⁵), born in Tyler's Bridge, N. H.; died in Charlestown, Mass. He was a ship-carpenter in the navy yard in Portsmouth, N. H., and lived there. He was the only child of his father's second marriage. The name of his wife is unknown. His children were born in Portsmouth. Children:

2155   William Tyler, died about 1885, s. p.; was a ship carpenter in the Charlestown navy yard. He was married.

2156   Irene Tyler, married Paul Burbank; they both died in Sacramento, Cal., about 1885.

2157   Aramenta Tyler, married ——— Kilpatrick, of Boston, who was in the Custom House there.

2158   Amaretta Tyler, married Charles Weatherbee Nash, born Nov. 30, 1813; son of Nathaniel and Matilda (Lock) Nash, of Boston. They lost three children by scarlet fever, and others later.

2159   Maudgianna Tyler, probably never married; was an invalid and lived in Boston; made artificial flowers.

2160   Charles Phineas Tyler, died unmarried, aged 22, in Charlestown, Mass.

782 JEPTHAH⁶ TYLER, JR. (Jepthah⁵), born (probably) in Henniker, N. H., 1777; died in Lyme, N. H., November 1, 1837; married Polly Wilmot, born in 1780; died in Lyme, June 28, 1857. He lived in Lyme on " Tyler Hill "; the house was torn down about 1885. The children were born in Lyme. Children:

2161+   Jepthah Tyler, born Feb. 25, 1810.

2162   Parley Tyler, married Abby Carleton, and died, s. p.,
        April 13, 1867.
2163   Sarah Tyler, married Alfred Benton and moved to
        Maine.
2164   Hannah Tyler, married George Benton, of Maine.
2165   Lydia Tyler.
2166   Lucy Tyler, married Garten Coburn, of Lyme, N. H.
2167   Deborah Tyler, married —— Smith.

    787 JOHN[6] TYLER (Joshua[5]), born in Pembroke, N.
H., March 28, 1773; died in Thetford, Vt., September 12,
1853; married, in Grafton, N. H., November 17, 1796, Anna
Brown, born December 21, 1777; died November 10, 1872.
The children were born in Thetford. Children:
2168   Speede H. Tyler, born June 25, 1798; died May 2,
        1892, unmarried.
2169   John R. Tyler, born Feb. 10, 1801; died, s. p., Nov.
        21, 1884; his estate administered upon in Thet-
        ford, Dec. 9, 1884; married (1), Harriet Porter;
        married (2), Adeline Wilson; married (3), Sophia
        Torrey; married (4), Jeanette Morey. His wives
        all died childless.
2170+   Marie H. Tyler, born April 27, 1803.
2171   James B. Tyler, born Nov. 3, 1805; died Dec. 5, 1848,
        unmarried, in Ariston, Ill.
2172   Theodore H. Tyler, born June 11, 1807; died young
        in Thetford, Vt.
2173+   Annie G. Tyler, born July 26, 1811.
2174   Hamilton D. Tyler, born Feb. 12, 1814; died May
        28, 1859, unmarried, in Thetford; his estate was
        administered June 4, 1859.
2175   Mary M. Tyler, born Nov. 2, 1817; died July 22,
        1891; married Truman Burr, miller; born in Gran-
        tham, N. H., Dec. 14, 1809; died s. p., in Thetford,
        Oct. 8, 1883.
2176+   Lucretia J. Tyler, born Sept. 1, 1820.
2177+   Emeline F. Tyler, born May 5, 1827.

    788 JOSHUA[6] TYLER, JR. (Joshua[5]), born in Pem-
broke, N. H.; died in Thetford, Vt.; married ——. Children:
2178   William Tyler, born in Thetford; died in Manchester,

N. H.; married Lydia Howard, who died; they had one child (Alfaretta.)

2179   Nancy Tyler, born in Thetford; died, unmarried, in New York City.

789   JAMES⁶ TYLER (Joshua⁵), born in Pembroke, N. H., about 1780; died in Thetford, Vt., about 1804; his estate administered upon there November 26, 1804; married, about 1800, Sallie Taylor, who died in 1845. Child:

2180+   Orange Brigham Tyler, born in Thetford, March 28, 1801.

790   REBECCA⁶ TYLER (Joshua⁵), born in Pembroke, N. H.; married Daniel West, of Strafford, Vt., where the children were born. Children:

2181   John West.

2182   Alpa West, married Jaspar Lord, of Thetford, Vt.; she died s. p., about 1892; her husband died several years before.

2183   Daniel West, born in 1806 or 1807; died March, 1861; married Mary Fox, who died May, 1886. Believed to have lived in Thetford. Had three children (Mary J., Rebecca Tyler, Caroline M.)

2184   Asenath West, born about 1808 or 1809; married Porter Cushman, of Tunbridge, Vt., as his second wife. She died in W. Randolph, Vt. Had six children (John, Jane, Alpa, Daniel W., Eunice, Lucretia.)

792   HANNAH⁶ EASTMAN (Lucretia⁵), born January 5, 1770; died August 1, 1832; married, March 16, 1796, Stephen Ambrose. They had more than one child, but the record of only one has come to us. Child:

2185+   Lucretia Ambrose, born Jan. 15, 1799.

806   MOLLY⁶ TYLER, also called "Polly" (John⁵), born in Brookfield, Mass., July 10, 1776; died July 19, 1833; married (1), September 21, 1796, Michael Brigham, born in North Brookfield, March 2, 1772; died there August, 1802; married (2), April 17, 1805, William Bowdoin, of Ware, Mass. Her first husband was a farmer in North Brookfield, and her second husband was a farmer in Ware, and a justice of the peace. The Brigham children were born in Brookfield; the Bowdoin children in Ware. (See *Brigham Genealogy* for descendants.)

CHILDREN, by first marriage:

2186+ John Tyler Brigham, born 1795; died, unmarried, 1849; a merchant in New York City.

2187 Anna Allen Brigham, born Dec. 9, 1797; married, Sept. 21, 1819, John Gould, born Jan. 17, 1789; lived in Ware. Had eleven children.

2188 Loring W. Brigham, born Oct. 30, 1799; married, Oct. 7, 1821, Maria H. Wiswell, born Aug. 17, 1799. They lived in Ware and had eight children.

2189 Crosby Brigham, born 1802; died Sept. 25, 1803.

CHILDREN, by second marriage:

2190 Michael Brigham Bowdoin, born Nov. 2, 1806; a mason.

2191 Eunice H. Bowdoin, born Aug 4, 1808; married George Bliss, of Ware.

2192 Charles C. Bowdoin, born July 14, 1810.

2193 Sarah F. Bowdoin, born Dec. 27, 1812; married Luke Leach, a lumber manufacturer, of Orange, Mass.

2194 Caleb Strong Bowdoin, born March 26, 1815; a music teacher, unmarried.

2195 Martha M. Bowdoin, born Aug. 13, 1817; married Luther A. Erving, a merchant of Erving, Mass.

807 SALLY[6] TYLER (John[5]), born in Brookfield, Mass., September 20, 1778; died in North Brookfield, October 14, 1805; married, February 17, 1801, Silas Ball, of Brookfield. He probably moved to New York State. The children were born in North Brookfield. Children:

2196 Thomas Ball, born in 1802; died Sept. 30, 1805.

2197 Brigham Ball.

808 JOHN[6] TYLER, JR. (John[5]), born (probably) in Brookfield, Mass., November 20, 1780; died August 23, 1857; married (1), April 25, 1813, Elizabeth Hill, born in Brookfield, September 15, 1785; died November 4, 1819; married (2), April 15, 1821, Myra Bailey, of Berlin, Mass.; born November 15, 1795; died November 21, 1868. He lived in North Brookfield.

CHILDREN, by first marriage:

2198 Child, born Feb. 25, 1814; died March 16, 1814.

2199 Martha Tyler, born Feb. 7, 1815; died Oct. 6, 1817.

CHILDREN, by second marriage:

2200+   J. Bowman Tyler, born March 5, 1822.

2201   Penn Tyler, born Feb. 4, 1824; vocal music teacher;
        unmarried, in 1899, resided in Springfield, Mass.

2202+   Martha Elizabeth Tyler, born July 20, 1826.

809   ABNER[6] TYLER (John[5]), born (probably) in
Brookfield, Mass., August 4, 1785; married Deborah Tupper.
Moved to Charlestown, N. H.   Child:

2203   Robert Barkley Tyler, born Sept. 14, 1814; baptized
        in Dedham, Mass.

811   PHINEAS[6] TYLER (Gideon[5]), born in North
Brookfield, Mass.; married, March 30, 1794, Joanna Barnes,
born in North Brookfield, May 18, 1774; died in New Braintree, Mass., April 27, 1848.   The children were born in Brookfield.   Children:

2204+   Theodore Tyler, born Nov. 17, 1795.

2205+   Francis Barnes Tyler.

2206+   Isaac Tyler, born Dec. 2, 1808.

2207   Asa Tyler; died, unmarried, Sept. 20, 1878, in New
        Braintree, Mass.

2208   Louisa Tyler, married —— Kent, of Leicester, Mass.,
        and died s. p.

817   POLLY[6] TYLER (Gideon[5]), born in Brookfield,
Mass.; married Phineas Gilbert, of West Brookfield, a farmer.
The children were born in West Brookfield.   Children:

2209   Freeman Gilbert.

2210   Mary Ann Gilbert.

2211   Luther

2212   Esther Gilbert.

2213   Francis Gilbert.

829   BETSEY[6] TYLER (Moses[5]), born in West Brookfield, Mass., April 25, 1780; died in Wheeling, West Va.;
married (1) (published September 20, 1801), Abraham Howe;
born in North Brookfield, Mass., October 13, 1776; son of Eli
Howe; he was a farmer; married (2), Zadoc Hinsdale, of Hartford, Conn.; he was a hotel-keeper.   The children were born in
North Brookfield.

CHILDREN, by first marriage:

2214   Louisa Howe, married —— Tufts and died in Granby,
       Conn.

2215   Orvilla Howe, married —— Burr, of Hartford, Conn.,
       and died in New York City.

2216   Fanny Howe, married —— Williams, of Louisiana,
       and is buried in Windsor, Conn.

830   DAVID⁶ TYLER (Moses⁵), born in West Brookfield, Mass., August 20, 1781; died February 29, 1864; married Nancy Bartlett, born in North Brookfield, May 16, 1798;
died there April 29, 1866. He was a farmer and lived in
North Brookfield. His widow was administratrix and gave
bond for $14,000. The children were born in North Brook-
field. Children:

2217   Moses Tyler, born April, 1817; died in North Brook-
       field, Jan. 5, 1892; in early life was a shoe manu-
       facturer in Philadelphia; later a farmer in North
       Brookfield; one son.

2218   Warren Tyler, M. D., born Feb. 6, 1819; died in North
       Brookfield, April 18, 1891; married, Oct. 22, 1848,
       Diantha Walker, of Exeter, N. Y., born Jan. 1,
       1823; she resided there in 1901. He was assistant
       surgeon of the 36th Mass. Infantry in the Civil
       War; resigned, Oct. 22, 1863. He resided in North
       Brookfield, and had a good record.

2219   Charlotte Tyler, born in 1821; died in 1830.

2219a William Tyler, born Feb. 22, 1823; died in Toledo,
       Ohio, Sept. 8, 1845; was a captain of an Ohio river
       boat; unmarried.

2220+ Avilda Bartlett Tyler, born March 27, 1825.

2221+ Elizabeth R. Tyler, born Dec. 27, 1826.

2222   Albert Newton Tyler, born Oct. 11, 1833; drowned in
       Sturbridge, June 28, 1854; was a law student, un-
       married.

832   POLLY⁶ TYLER (Moses⁵), born in West Brookfield, Mass., February 20, 1785; died there December 7, 1862;
married, November 23, 1814, Joseph Dane, born in North
Brookfield, October 7, 1782; died in West Brookfield, April
17, 1863. He was a farmer. The children were born in West
Brookfield. Children:

2223   Joseph Dane, born April 8, 1815; died July 15, 1865; was a farmer and teacher and resided in West Brookfield.

2224   Rebecca Dane, born May 6, 1817; died in Cleveland, Ohio, Jan., 1879; married Theodore S. Lindsey, paymaster on the Lake Shore Railroad. They had a son (Theodore), who is a dentist in Cleveland.

2225   Warren Dane, born March 1, 1819; died in Wilbraham, Mass., Oct. 17, 1894; married Jane Wilson; had two sons and four daughters.

2226   Stillman Ayres Dane, born Feb. 10, 1821; died Jan. 8, 1891; married Sophronia Glazier; he resided in North Brookfield; had two daughters, and a son, who died in the Civil War, in Fortress Monroe.

2227   Emerson Dane, born July 1, 1823; died Feb. 15, 1876; married Irene Bishop; resided in North Brookfield; had a son and daughter.

2228   Lucy Ann Dane, born July 15, 1825; died Jan. 5, 1896; married (1), Otis Smith; married (2), Lewis Gleason.

2229   George Willis Dane, born Nov. 8, 1829; died in Sandusky, Ohio, May 15, 1887; married Maria R. Blanchard; he was a merchant; had a son also a merchant in Sandusky.

834   CAPTAIN ELI[6] TYLER (Moses[5]), born in West Brookfield, Mass., March 25, 1789; died July 1, 1858; married, October 8, 1819, Clarissa White, of Billerica, Mass., born in 1798; died September 21, 1871. He was a farmer and a captain in the militia. He inherited his father's farm. He lived in West Brookfield, where his children were born. Children:

2230+   George Francis Tyler, born Nov. 13, 1820.

2231   Moses Tyler, born April 5, 1822; was unmarried; resided in West Brookfield with Dwight Tyler.

2232   Warren Jerome Bonaparte Tyler, born Aug. 5, 1823; died April 26, 1826.

2233   Eli Lafayette Tyler, born June 3, 1825; resided, unmarried, a farmer, in West Brookfield.

2234   Warren Tyler, born May 29, 1827; died March 8, 1847.

2235 Lewis Cutler Tyler, born July 12, 1829; died Jan. 24, 1830.

2236+ Harriet Elizabeth Tyler, born Feb. 20, 1831.

2237+ Susan Maria Tyler, born Feb. 9, 1833.

2238 Lucy Ann Tyler, born July 20, 1835; married, Oct., 1857, John Jackson Lewis, of Franklin Falls, N. H.; a contractor; no children.

2239 Henry Edward Tyler, born July 18, 1837; died Jan. 12, 1868; married Augusta Gay; a farmer, of West Brookfield.

2240+ Charles Austin Tyler, born March 11, 1841.

2241+ Charlotte Frances Tyler, born Oct. 23, 1842.

840 JOSHUA⁶ TYLER (Joshua⁵), born in Chesterfield, N. H., August 16, 1781; died in Clara, Potter County, Pa., in 1858; married (1), Lydia Farr, who died January 13, 1805; daughter of William and Lydia (Trowbridge) Farr, of Worcester, Mass., and descended from Thomas Farr, of Dorchester; married (2), in 1810, Lois Bacon, daughter of Philip Bacon, son of Nathaniel Bacon, who was in the Revolution. Joshua finally settled in Clara, Potter County, Pa.

CHILD, by first marriage:

2242+ Dwight Tyler, born in Chesterfield, Jan. 13, 1805.

CHILDREN, by second marriage:

2243+ Joshua Tyler, born in Dummerston, Vt., Dec. 4, 1811.

2244 Elizabeth Tyler, died in Millport, Potter County, Pa.; she married ——.

2245 Royal C. Tyler, resided in Kansas.

2246 Laura Tyler, married Isaac Barnes, of Millport, Pa., where she died.

2247 George Tyler, married —— Brindle, and lived in Oswayo, Potter Co., Pa.

2248 Louisa Tyler, married, after her sister Laura's death, Isaac Barnes, of Millport.

2249 James M. Tyler, married Belinda B. Hazelton, of Independence, N. Y.; resided Shingle House, Pa.

2250 Charles F. Tyler, married Eliza Loder, and resided in Hebron, Potter County, Pa.

841 JUDITH⁶ TYLER (Joshua⁵), born in Chesterfield,

N. H., December 4, 1782; died in Burlington, Vt., March 12, 1843; married Captain Daniel Davis. The child was born in Chesterfield, N. H. Child:

2251+   Parkman Tyler Davis, born June 30, 1810.

842   JASON[6] TYLER (Joshua[5]), born in Chesterfield, N. H., January 21, 1784; died in Keene, N. H., March 10, 1843; married, 1803, Thirzy King, born May 7, 1785; died in Winchester, N. H., August 17, 1851; daughter of Colonel Samuel King, probably from Petersham, Mass. (a very prominent character, and son of Dr. Samuel King, who was in Chesterfield by 1785). Jason lived in the Center Village of Chesterfield many years; in 1831 or 1832 he moved to Swanzey, N. H., and thence to Keene, N. H. The children were born in Chesterfield. Children:

2252+   Harriet B. Tyler, born Nov. 13, 1803.
2253   Lydia F. Tyler, born Aug. 29, 1805; died in Winchester, N. H., April 25, 1875; unmarried.
2254   Malinda Z. W. Tyler, born July 23, 1807; died s. p. Oct. 19, 1865; married Martin Perry, of Swanzey, N. H., who died s. p.
2255+   Samuel King Tyler, born Nov. 3, 1810.
2256+   Mary N. M. Tyler, born Feb. 2, 1812.
2257   Jane B. Tyler, born July 3, 1814; married Lemuel Wheeler, of Troy, N. H., who died in Harmar, Ohio, Sept. 11, 1874, aged 60.
2258   Larkin W. Tyler, born Jan. 26, 1816; died 1824.
2259   Albert O. Tyler, born Feb. 20, 1819; married Emily Murdock, of Winchendon, Mass.; moved to Cincinnati in 1846, where he was a successful merchant. The U. S. gunboat *A. O. Tyler*, in the Civil War, was named in his honor; he died in Winchendon, Mass., while on a visit, Aug. 16, 1877.
2260+   Sarah Chapman Tyler, born Oct. 22, 1821.
2261+   Elizabeth H. C. Tyler, born Nov. 25, 1823.
2262+   John Larkin Tyler, born June 17, 1826.
2263   Dana A. Tyler, born Dec. 13, 1828; died Sept. 11, 1830.

848   JOSEPH WARREN[6] TYLER (Joshua[5]), born in Chesterfield, N. H., December 9, 1795; died in Hinsdale, N. H.,

November 23, 1849; married, December 8, 1823, Eleanor
Thomas, born in Hinsdale, April 8, 1804; died there September
18, 1890. He was a teacher and resided in Hinsdale, and the
children were born there. Children:

2264+ Caroline Day Tyler, born May 10, 1824.

2265+ Sophira Smith Tyler, born Oct. 17, 1825.

2266+ Pitts Cune Tyler, born March 17, 1827.

2267 Elizabeth A. Tyler, born May 6, 1828; died Sept. 6,
1829.

2268+ Elizabeth A. Tyler, born June 17, 1830.

2269 Charlotte B. Tyler, born Oct. 17, 1832; died s. p. May
23, 1856; married, Jan. 7, 1854, Albert W. Kendall,
of Hinsdale.

2270+ Orcutt B. Tyler, born June 15, 1834.

2271 Joseph W. Tyler, born March 6, 1836; died June 1,
1836.

2272 Fanny S. Tyler, born June 12, 1837; died Feb. 19,
1839.

2723+ Charles H. Tyler, born Dec. 19, 1838.

2274+ Adaline P. Tyler, born Sept. 21, 1841.

2275 Martha L. Tyler, born April 5, 1843; died in Athol,
Mass., July 3, 1898; married, March 4, 1866, Frank
Stearns, of Hinsdale, N. H., a teacher; son of John
Stearns.

2276 George Warren Tyler, born April 12, 1846; died in
Fitchburg, Mass., July 1, 1900; married, July 9,
1867, Julia Woods, of Brattleboro, Vt., born there
Dec. 2, 1843. He was in the Civil War, 14th N. H.
Volunteers. Was long connected with the Estey
Organ Works in Brattleboro, and then in the employ
of a railroad. At the time of his decease he was
superintendent of the Fitchburg cemetery.

849 BUCKLEY OLCOTT[6] TYLER, M. D. (Joshua[5]),
born in Chesterfield, N. H. February 13, 1798; died in Montpelier, Vt., May 21, 1878, aged 80; married (1), December 8,
1824, Mary Towne, of Hartland, Vt., who died in Montpelier
June 26, 1851, aged 44; daughter of Benjamin and Sarah
(Burt) Towne; married (2), May 5, 1852, Lucy Goldsmith
Russell, of Thetford, Vt., born June 22, 1812; died July 29,
1889; daughter of Peter Russell, of Thetford and descended

from the poet Oliver Goldsmith. Dr. Tyler attended lectures
at Castleton, Vt., Medical College, and at the Waterville, Me.,
Medical College. He was largely self-educated. He was graduated M. D. from Dartmouth Medical College in 1824, and
began practice that year in South Woodstock, Vt. After four
years he went to Thetford (Union Village) ; thence to Vershire,
Vt. ; he then moved to Worcester, and in 1851 to Montpelier,
Vt. ; was there partner in a drug store for five years. Later
bought an interest in the *Argus and Patriot* building, and
sold groceries. He was a Democrat in politics. The four
elder children were born in South Woodstock; the children of
the second marriage in Montpelier; others as indicated.

CHILDREN, by first marriage:

2277   Orlando Towner Tyler, born Jan. 26, 1826; died April
       26, 1826.
2278+ Cornelia Evelena Tyler, born July 26, 1829.
2279+ Frances Lestena Tyler, born April 23, 1831.
2280+ Alvaro Merrill Tyler, born June 21, 1834.
2281   Emma Josephine Tyler, born in Thetford, Oct. 16,
       1837; married, Sept. 25, 1877, Silas W. Robinson,
       of Portland, Maine, who died Dec. 4, 1888.
2282   Eugene Clarence Tyler, born in Vershire, Vt., March
       5, 1847; married, Oct. 16, 1873, Celia Conant, of
       Portland, Maine, who died, s. p., April 5, 1892.   He
       enlisted in 1861; was orderly for Lieutenant Shan-
       non on General Slocum's staff through the Penin-
       sular campaign.   He then enlisted in the 27th N. Y.
       Frontier cavalry, and was wounded; was mustered
       out June 28, 1865.   Resides in Valley Head, Ala.

CHILDREN, by second marriage:

2283+ Grace Isabella Tyler, born Oct. 3, 1853.
2284+ Charles Russell Tyler, born Nov. 2, 1856.

853   ROLSTON GOODELL[6] TYLER (Joshua[5]), born
in Chesterfield, N. H., August 7, 1805; died in Orange, Mass.,
August 14, 1882; married, February 2, 1837, Mary Jane
Dudley, of Merrimack, N. H., born there September 9, 1811;
died in Orange, June 13, 1892.   He was a farmer and moved
to Orange about 1871.   His children were born in Chesterfield.   Children:

2285+ Stella M. Tyler, born June 24, 1838.
2286 John Tyler, born Nov. 16, 1839; resided in Orange,
where he died s. p. Jan. 9, 1901; married (1),
June 20, 1891, Susan Wood, of Orange, who died
Oct. 20, 1894; married (2), Nov. 19, 1895, Mary
Flagg, of Orange, who died Sept. 3, 1898.

856 JOHN[6] TYLER, JR. (John[5]), born in Boxford,
Mass., February 24, 1795; died there November 30, 1827;
married December 24, 1824, Mary Ann Putnam, of Danvers,
Mass.; died November 15, 1844; daughter of Ebenezer Putnam
(She married [2], November, 1836, Sylvanus B. Swan, of Danvers; by this marriage she had two daughters). John Tyler
was a business man. His estate was administered August 18,
1829; his widow asked that her father might be appointed as
administrator and this was granted. The personal estate
amounted to $1,123.13, and a note states that "The title of
the Real Estate being rather doubtful, the appraisal thereof is
omitted."

CHILDREN:
2287 Mercy Ann Tyler, born in Danvers, June, 1826; died
Sept. 1, 1826.
2288 Ellen Maria Tyler, born in Boxford, April 16, 1828;
died Aug. 29, 1844, in Danvers.

857 MEHITABLE[6] TYLER (John[5]), born in Boxford, Mass., May 5, 1797; died April 8, 1891; married, September 25, 1828, Captain Enoch Wood, of Boxford, son of
Deacon Jonathan Wood, of Boxford. He was a sea-captain.
He came of one of the old and honored families of the county
and through a long and eventful life he preserved that gra-
cious spirit of courtesy which marked a gentleman of the old
school. He commanded and sailed some of the most noted ships
that ever left New England. He abandoned the sea in 1845
and spent his remaining years in old Boxford. Mrs. Wood
was a remarkable woman, with more than ordinary intellectual
ability, in addition to which she had the sterling virtues which
make a strong and self-reliant woman. The changes of the
last century did not all meet with her approval, as she was
somewhat conservative, but she enjoyed her books and took
an interest in town affairs to the end of her long life of 94

years. She had been a leading official of the Female Charitable Society of West Boxford, for many years. Their children were born in Boxford.

CHILDREN:

2289   Rebecca Tyler Wood, born Jan. 26, 1830; resides on the old Tyler farm in Boxford, unmarried.

2290   John Tyler Wood, born April 21, 1831; married, July 5, 1869, Sarah Barker, of North Andover, Mass., who died July 4, 1871; a daughter, born Jan. 30, 1871, died the same day.

2291+   Enoch Franklin Wood, born Oct. 17, 1832.

862   BETSEY[6] TYLER (Jonathan[5]), born 1789; died June 25, 1870; married, November 5, 1815, John Gage, of Pelham, N. H., who died November 1, 1865. Children:

2292   Jonathan Tyler Gage, born 1816; died June 29, 1824.

2293   John Calvin Gage, born Dec., 1817; died Jan., 1879.

2294   Martha Gage, born in 1820; died March 4, 1855.

2295   Mary E. Gage, married Walter Kimball, M. D., who died in 1880. They had a daughter who died young and two sons.

899   ANDREWS[6] TYLER (Nathaniel[5]), born November 17, 1779; married, in 1806, in Herkimer, N. Y., Elizabeth Comins. He lived in Sempronious, N. Y., and Springfield, Erie Co., Pa. Six or seven of the elder children were born in Sempronious, and the others in Springfield, Pa. Children:

2296+   Joseph C. Tyler, born June 8, 1807.

2297+   Nathaniel Tyler, born Jan. 25, 1809.

2298+   Almina Tyler, born April 23, 1811.

2299+   William P. Tyler, born Oct. 14, 1814.

2300+   Daniel Tyler, born Nov. 23, 1816.

2301   Comfort C. W. Tyler, born Sept. 30, 1818; died, unmarried, in Huntsville, Mo., in 1837.

2302+   Ira Tyler, born May 29, 1822.

2303   Hiram Tyler, born March 31, 1824; died, unmarried, in Richfield, Ill., aged 50.

2304+   Urial Tyler, born July 6, 1826.

2305   John E. Tyler, born June 15, 1829; died June 27, 1831.

2306+   Henry B. Tyler, born March 13, 1831.

903 LUCY[6] TYLER (Jesse[5]), born in Methuen, Mass., Oct. 5, 1778; married July 12, 1796, Nathaniel Kimball, of Methuen. The children were born in Methuen. Children:

2307 Elisha Kimball, born Jan. 4, 1796.
2308 Abigail Kimball, born June 28, 1798.

904 ELISHA[6] TYLER (Jesse[5]), born in Methuen, Mass., June 28, 1781; died when over 80, in Paw Paw, Mich.; married, November 11, 1811, Sally Day Webster, of Methuen, who also died in Paw Paw. He resided in Methuen and Coventry (now Benton), N. H., and moved to Paw Paw in 1845. He was a farmer. Children:

2309+ Humphrey Perley Tyler, born in West Haverhill, Mass., Aug. 1, 1813.
2310 Mary Day Tyler, married and died young, s. p.; she was a cripple.
2311+ Elisha Tyler, born in Benton, N. H., Dec. 13, 1820.
2312 Harriet Tyler, married Peter Howes, of Benton; two children.
2313 Lucy Tyler, died unmarried in Michigan.
2314 Rufus Tyler, died young.
2315 Cynthia Tyler, born in 1825; married —— Furman, a miller in Michigan and Iowa; had three children (Sophronia, Charles, George).

905 KIMBALL[6] TYLER (Jesse[5]), born in Methuen, Mass., September 9, 1782; died in Benton, N. H., August 28, 1856; married there (1), April 15, 1805, Sallie Streeter, of Llandaff, N. H., born February 28, 1784; died May 1, 1842; married (2), Dorothy Day, born September 1, 1793; died March 7, 1868. Was a butcher and cattle drover of Haverhill, Mass., and moved to Coventry (now Benton), N. H., where the children were born. These records were taken before the destruction of Benton records.

CHILDREN, by first marriage:
2316+ Relief Tyler, born Nov. 2, 1805.
2317 Lucy Tyler, born Aug. 2, 1807; died May 4, 1812.
2318+ Kimball Tyler, born Dec. 9, 1808.
2319+ Sally Tyler, born May 27, 1810.
2320+ Susan N. Tyler, born Sept. 14, 1812.

2321+   Edwin Tyler, born Aug. 20, 1814.
2322+   Alfred Tyler, born March 13, 1816.
2323   Betsey Tyler, born March 22, 1818; died May 31,
         1874; married David Howe, and moved to Stone-
         ham, Mass., in 1854; he died May 30, 1896, after
         a second marriage to Mrs. Ann Parker in 1875.
         Betsey had a daughter (Ann; died young).
2324+   Laban Tyler, born Jan. 26, 1819.
2325+   Eliza Tyler, born Oct. 16, 1821.
2326+   Moses K. Tyler, born March 14, 1823.
2327+   Charles Carroll Tyler, born July 29, 1827.
2328+   George Tyler, born May 27, 1831.
2329   Lucetta Tyler, born Jan. 9, 1832; resided, unmar-
         ried, a dressmaker in Stoneham, Mass.

    907 BETSEY[6] TYLER (Jesse[5]), born in Methuen,
Mass., October 14, 1786; married Elisha Clifford, of Haverhill, N. H. The children were born there. Children:
2330   Ransom Clifford.
2331   Emery Clifford.
2332   Plummer Clifford.
2333   Betsey Clifford.
2334   Eliza Clifford, married —— Pierce, of Lowell, Mass.

    910 JESSE[6] TYLER (Jesse[5]), born in Methuen, Mass.,
August 1, 1792; died in Benton, N. H., suddenly; married
Mary Berry, of Methuen. He was a farmer, and resided in
Benton, where the children were born. Children:
2335   Lucy Tyler, died young, unmarried.
2336   Jesse Tyler, born in 1827; married (1), Melissa M.
         Smith, of Haverhill, N. H.; married (2), Susan N.
         Harriman, of Warren, N. H. Both of his wives
         died without offspring. He resided in Plymouth,
         N. H.
2337   Lydia Tyler, married —— Hines, of Lynn, Mass.;
         had two sons and a daughter (George, Nathan,
         May).

    911 HEPSIBETH[6] TYLER (Jesse[5]), born in Methuen,
Mass., April 4, 1796; married James Rogers, of Benton, N. H.
Children:

2338   Lucinda Rogers.
2339   Hughey Rogers.

913   SAMUEL[6] TYLER (Jesse[5]), born in Methuen, Mass., March 20, 1798; married Rhoda Palmer, of Bath, N. H. He moved to Paw Paw, Mich. in 1846.   He was a farmer. Children:
2340   Jesse Tyler; died, unmarried, in railway service in Michigan.
2341   James Tyler, married; resided Dowagiac, Mich.
2342   Lucy Tyler, married John Harding, of Paw Paw.
2343   Nancy Tyler, married ——Hale; died young, s. p. in Paw Paw.
2344   Kimball Tyler.
2345   Enos Tyler.
2346   Sally Tyler.
2347   Augusta Tyler.
2348   Elisha Tyler.
2349   Samuel Tyler.
2350   Moses Tyler.
2351   Humphrey Tyler.

914   ABEL[6] TYLER (Simeon[5]), born in Camden, Maine, August 8, 1780; died September 12, 1824, in his prime; buried in Camden; married Catherine Ulmer. He was a teacher, surveyor, and by trade a mason. He was elected Master of Amity Lodge F. and A. M. of Camden, in 1815, and served one term.   He was secretary of the lodge in 1817. His children were born in Camden.   Children:
2352   Charles Alden Tyler, born June 22, 1808; died July 29, 1811.
2353+   William Stearns Tyler, born July 4, 1810.
2354+   Serena Catherine Tyler, born Sept. 6, 1812.
2355+   Charles Augustus Tyler, born Oct. 5, 1814.
2356+   Abel Dudley Tyler, born May 7, 1817.
2357   Rhoda Ann Tyler, born Sept. 1, 1819; died Aug., 1891, s. p.; married Edmund Woodmans, Jr., March 19, 1853; widower of her sister Serena.
2358+   Mary Ulmer Tyler, born March 25, 1822.

916   RHODA[6] TYLER (Simeon[5]), born in Camden,

Maine, March 28, 1782; died Aug. 30, 1869; married Alden Bass, of Camden, where the children were born.   Children:

2359   Hiram Bass, married Cornelia Kendall, of Boston, Mass. He was an attorney and justice of the peace, and was judge of probate in Waldo County, 1857-1861. He died in Camden; one son and a daughter.

2360   Mary Bass, married Joseph Mirick, of Camden.   She had four sons.

2361   Clarissa Bass, married Jonas Howe, of Camden.   She had one son and a daughter.

917   SIMEON⁶ TYLER (Simeon⁵), born in Camden, Maine, January 7, 1784; died there; married Phebe Buckman. He was a carpenter.   The children were born in Camden. Children:

2362+   Benjamin F. Tyler, born June 2, 1814.

2363   John B. Tyler, born in 1820; died, unmarried, April 9, 1848, aged 27; a boat capsized in Penobscot Bay and he was drowned with three others.

2364+   Theodore Tyler.

2365   Erastus F. Tyler, born in 1818; died unmarried, June 9, 1838, aged 20 years and six months; buried in Camden.

2366+   Edwin Tyler.

2367+   Rebecca Tyler.

2368+   Harriet Tyler.

2369   Hannah W. Tyler, died s. p., Nov. 28, 1839, aged 28 years; married Caleb S. Hobbs.

919   SAMUEL⁶ TYLER (Simeon⁵), born in Camden, Maine, December 17, 1787; died in Belfast, Maine, February 4, 1829; married March 30, 1814, Lucy Keen, of Rockland, Maine, who died August 11, 1874; after Samuel's death she moved to Rockland, Maine, where the children were brought up; later she married Mr. Simonton, and by this marriage a son was born named Gilman Simonton.   Samuel was in the War of 1812, stationed at Castine, Maine, and his name is on the *Pension Book*, page 69.   He was a master mason and resided in Belfast, and the children were born there.   Children:

2370+   Alden Lorenzo Tyler, born May 18, 1820.

2371+   Samuel Henry Tyler, born March 4, 1824.

2372   Dudley Tyler, died in infancy.

2373+   Susan Rosella Tyler, born March 26, 1816.

2374+   Margaret Fidelia Tyler, born March 26, 1816.

2375+   Lucy Ann Tyler, born Feb. 2, 1822.

920   COBURN JONATHAN[6] TYLER (Simeon[5]), born in Camden, Maine, February 10, 1792; his grave-stone says " died December 7, 1873, aged 83 years "; married (1), Clarissa Smith, from whom divorced; married (2), September 7, 1834, Deborah Norton Conant, who " died August 20, 1887, aged 81 years "; she was a widow; had two husbands lost at sea. He is on the *Pension Book* for the War of 1812, p. 67. He was a manufacturer and inspector of lime. The children were born in Camden.

CHILDREN, by first marriage:

2376   Sumner S. Tyler, died in New York, Nov. 22, 1841, aged 16 years, 10 months and 22 days.

2377+   Alonzo Tyler.

2378   Julia Ann Tyler, married Thomas Welch, of New Orleans, La., who died; resided a widow in Rodney, Mass.; had three children (Stanley, Benjamin, Margaret).

CHILDREN, by second marriage:

2379+   Simeon Coburn Tyler, born Feb. 12, 1836.

2380   Ada Anna Tyler, died April 26, 1848, aged 4 years, 7 months and 12 days.

2381   Hannah W. Tyler, died Oct. 4, 1842, aged 1 year, 7 months.

922   ISAAC[6] TYLER (Daniel[5]), born in Pelham, Mass., February 8, 1784; died in Eden, N. Y., 1855; will dated April 18, 1855, and probated in Buffalo, N. Y., June 29, 1855; his son Aaron residuary legatee and executor; married Clarissa Green, of Pittsfield, Mass. He was in the War of 1812. Children:

2382   Aaron Tyler, lived in Garden City, Minn.

2383   Sally Tyler, married Roswell K. Wilson.

2384   Mary Tyler, married Lorence Carr.

2385   Moses Tyler.

923   DANIEL[6] TYLER (Daniel[5]), born in Pelham, Mass., March 16, 1788; married Olive Alger. He moved to Plainfield, Ill., then to Bridgewater, Mass. Children:

2386   Daniel Tyler.
2387+ William Tyler.
2388   Aaron Tyler.
2389   Olive Tyler.
2390   Percy Tyler.
2391+ Julia Tyler, born April 5, 1825.

926   MOSES[6] W. TYLER (Daniel[5]), born in Pelham, Mass., May 27, 1794; died in Albany, N. Y., August 13, 1846; his estate was probated in Albany, January 28, 1847, his son being administrator; married (1), Abigail Ann Alger, of Bridgewater, Mass.; married (2), 1837, Eliza Alger, of West Troy, N. Y. He resided in Pittseld, Mass., for a time; he moved early to Gibbonsville, N. Y. (Watervliet), with his father where he was village trustee from 1827-1831 inclusive. He moved to West Troy, N. Y., and later to Albany, where he was an assessor for the second ward in Albany.

CHILDREN, by first marriage:

2392   Ann Eliza Tyler, born 1817; died unmarried in the forties.
2393+ Mary Ann Tyler, born in Pittsfield, Mass., Aug. 24, 1820.
2394   Sarah Tyler, born Feb. 20, 1825; died unmarried.
2395   Daniel Tyler, died young.
2396   Moses Tyler, born Nov. 8, 1826.
2397   Edildia Tyler, born June 2, 1828.
2398   Julia F. Tyler, born 1830; married Robert Smith, Brockton, Mass.

CHILD, by second marriage:

2399+ Levinus A. Tyler, born in West Troy, Aug. 25, 1839.

927   EUNICE[6] TYLER (Daniel[5]), born in Pelham, Mass., September 3, 1796; died in Dalton, Mass.; married, in Windsor, Mass., July 3, 1814, Alpheus Barden. Children:

2400   Daniel Barden, born 1817; resides in Garfield, N. Y.
2401   (Dr.) Denison Barden, resides in Philadelphia, Pa.

2402   Daughter, married Henry Tillerson; resides in Dalton.
2403   Almira Barden.
2404   Aaron Tyler Barden, died; his widow resides in Dalton.
2405   Eliza Barden.
2406   Elvira Barden.

934   ABIGAIL[6] KIMBALL (Polly[5]), born in Dracut,
Mass., March 1, 1799; died December, 1879; married Simeon
Smith, born April 18, 1798; died September, 1865; probably
son of Simeon Smith, to whom Simeon Tyler, by deed, March
29, 1781, then at Camden, Maine, conveys his land in Methuen.
Children:
2407   Jacob Tyler Smith, born April 28, 1834; died Aug.
        18, 1878; married Mary J. Leavitt; one child died
        in infancy.
2408   Simeon Blood Smith, born Jan. 8, 1837; died May 28,
        1881; married Mary J. Fuller; had three sons, all
        of whom are residents of Denver, Colo.
2409   Abigail Ober Smith, born July 7, 1841; died Oct. 7,
        1886; married, March 29, 1870, C. A. E. Spamer,
        of Baltimore, Md.; had two daughters and a son,
        and two infants who died.
2410   Samuel Tyler Smith, died young.

946   JOSEPH[6] TYLER (Ebenezer[5]), born in Piermont,
N. H., February 2, 1772; died in Waverly, Iowa, October 13,
1853; married, September 28, 1792, Mehitable Ladd.   He
moved from Piermont to Waterbury, Vt., and in 1805 to North
Lawrence, St. Lawrence County, N. Y.; he then moved to
Iowa.   The four elder children were born in Piermont; the
fifth and sixth in Waterbury, and the nine younger children
probably in Lawrence.   Children:
2411+   Asa Ladd Tyler, born Sept. 14, 1794.
2412   Thirza Tyler, born April 15, 1796; married Luther
        Martin; both died in Michigan; they had no chil-
        dren; she was blind.
2413   Arza Tyler, born Oct. 10, 1797; killed by lightning
        about 1832; she married and had a family.
2414+   George Washington Tyler, born March 30, 1800.
2415   Alexis Tyler, born Nov. 19, 1801; probably died
        young.

2416   Jerusha Tyler, born April 17, 1803; married Thomas Lake, and had a family.

2417+   Truman Murry Tyler, born in Rutland, Vt., Aug. 30, 1804.

2418+   Richard Harrison Tyler, born Sept. 9, 1806.

2419   Hannah L. Tyler, born Feb. 10, 1808; married, 1827, Rev. Mr. Meecham, a Mormon; had a family.

2420+   John L. Tyler, born April 10, 1810.

2421   Hiram L. Tyler, born July 23, 1812; died from the kick of a horse, in New York. The widow and two daughters went to Ohio with John L. Tyler.

2422   Walter B. Tyler, born Jan. 14, 1814; died in McGregor, Iowa; married Susan ———; had a family.

2423   Mary Tyler, born March 20, 1815; died young.

2424   Amasa Tyler, born May 25, 1816; married twice, and the second time to a widow with two children. He and his wife went out to spend the evening and the house and seven children burned up while they were gone. He had five daughters by his first wife.

2425   Stephen Chapman Tyler, born March 26, 1818; was an invalid and lived, unmarried, with parents; was a farmer.

2426   Asenath Tyler, born Aug. 13, 1819; died March 15, 1897; married Daniel Bronson and lived in National, Clayton County, Iowa; they had two sons.

950   SAMUEL[6] TYLER (Ebenezer[5]), born in Piermont, N. H., July 2, 1782; died in Richland City, Wis., December 16, 1871; married, February 8, 1808, Lydia Martin, born in Bradford, Vt. He was in the War of 1812, and his name is on the records of the *Pension Book*. In 1815 he moved to French Creek, St. Lawrence County, N. Y., and thence to Springfield, Pa. He then went to Ohio, and from there to Ottawa, Ill. His last place of residence was Richland City, Wis. He was a wagon-maker by trade. The three elder children were born in Bradford; the fourth and fifth in French Creek.

CHILDREN:

2427+   Ebenezer Tyler, born Jan. 1, 1809.

2428+   Maria Tyler, born April 16, 1811.

2429   Chapman Tyler, born Feb. 14, 1814; drowned in French Creek, N. Y., Sept. 20, 1816.

2430   Amasa Tyler, born March 9, 1817; at 21 he went to Canada and nothing was ever heard from him.

2431+   Hial Tyler, born April 23, 1820.

2432+   Asenath Tyler, born Jan. 25, 1823.

2433+   Lydia Tyler, born May 10, 1825.

2434+   Catherine B. Tyler, born Sept. 18, 1829.

2435+   Esther Ann Tyler, born Nov. 17, 1830.

2436   Samuel Tyler, born in Ohio, Sept. 15, 1833; died in Richland City, Wis., unmarried, May 20, 1866.

951 OLIVER⁶ TYLER (Ebenezer⁵), born in Piermont, N. H., February 25, 1788; died May, 1826; married April 20, 1815, Margaret Kincaid. He moved to Louisville, Ky., and his children were born there. Children:

2437   John Tyler.

2438   Asenath Tyler.

2439   Howard Tyler.

954 HUBBARD⁶ TYLER (Ebenezer⁵), born possibly in Lawrence, N. Y., but probably in Piermont, N. H., July 5, 1794; died in Saybrook, Ohio; estate was probated in Jefferson, Ohio, in 1886; married, February 12, 1824, ——. Children:

2440   Henry Tyler, died in childhood.

2441   Joseph Tyler, drowned, aged about 20, on Lake Erie.

2442   Elizabeth Tyler, married and had four children; is deceased.

2443   Jane Tyler, married Blake Lucas.

955 AMASA⁶ TYLER (Ebenezer⁵), born possibly in Lawrence, N. Y., but probably in Piermont, N. H., March 9, 1798; died January 24, 1877; married in Ohio, January 1, 1824, Electa Badger, of Connecticut. He went to Saybrook, Ashtabula County, Ohio, with father, where he held town offices. His estate was probated in Jefferson, Ohio, in 1879. The children were born in Saybrook. Children:

2444   Orin Tyler.

2445   Paulina Tyler, married Liberty Gary and died.

2446   Amos Tyler, probably died in Saybrook in 1894.

2447+ Ezra B. Tyler, born Feb. 23, 1835.

2448   Almond Tyler, was in the furniture business in Ashtabula.

961   JESSE[6] TYLER (David[5]), born in Piermont, N. H., March 5, 1785; married Ethelinda Brigham; born July 19, 1794; daughter of Ephraim and Sarah Brigham, of Piermont. Children:

2449   Simon Tyler.

2450   Hazel Tyler.

2451   Hosea B. Tyler, born in 1816; in 1896 he was living in Alderbrook, N. H. (P. O. Littleton); he married, ——, and had a son (James).

2452   James Tyler.

2453   Martin Tyler, perhaps moved to Lunenburg, Vt.

2454   Milo Tyler.

2455   Pierpont Tyler.

2456   Alvira Tyler.

2457   Annie Tyler.

962   JOHN HOWARD[6] TYLER (David[5]), born in Piermont, N. H., August 5, 1787; died in Pittsburg, N. H., March, 1867; married Elizabeth McConnell, born November 27, 1790; died in Compton, P. Q., January 1, 1843. He was in the War of 1812, and took part in the "Indian Stream War." He was a farmer and resided in Waterford, Vt., Compton, P. Q., and Pittsburg, N. H. Children:

2458   James Tyler, died aged one year.

2459+ Climenia Tyler.

2460+ Calvin J. Tyler.

2461   Susan McConnell Tyler, married Christopher Webster, of Compton, P. Q.; they had a son who resided in Hillhurst, P. Q.

2462+ Israel Willard Tyler, born March 20, 1820.

2463   Laura Griswell Tyler, married George Hartwell, of Lewiston, Maine; they had a son who died in Bar Harbor, Maine.

2464   Betsey Tyler, married —— West; they had two sons.

2465   David L. Tyler, born in Waterford, Aug. 3, 1825; married Sophia Woods, of Dracut, Mass., and resided in Lowell, Mass.

2466   Lucius Tyler, died young.
2467   Lucy Ann Tyler, born in Waterford March 17, 1830;
         married —— Hobart and resided in Lowell.

967   DANIEL⁶ TYLER (Jonathan⁵), born in Piermont,
N. H. He moved west. The name of his wife is unknown.
Children:
2468   Ira Tyler.
2469   Oscar Tyler.

968   WILLIAM⁶ TYLER (Jonathan⁵), born in Piermont, N. H.; killed by the falling of a tree in East Haverhill,
N. H.; his wife's name is not known. He was a farmer. The
children were born in Piermont, and are all said to have moved
" down country."   Children:
2470   Michael Tyler.
2471   Roxy Tyler; married James Cutting.
2472   Harriet Tyler, was unmarried.
2473   Sarah Tyler, was unmarried.

970   CLARISSA⁶ TYLER (Jonathan⁵), born in Piermont, N. H., July 5, 1794; died in Vershire, Vt., April 16,
1870; married, June 9, 1814, Daniel Hildreth, of Chelsea, Vt.,,
born in Pepperell, Mass., May 2, 1782; died in Chelsea, November 16, 1858; son of James and Esther (Fletcher) Hildreth.
The Hildreths originated in England and were among the
strictest of the Puritans. They were early in this country.
Daniel was a farmer and lived and died upon his farm in
Chelsea, Vt., where he was an extensive wool-grower. He first
lived in Corinth after removing to Vermont with his parents
in his early youth. His children were born in Chelsea. Children:
2474   Azro Benjamin Franklin Hildreth, born Feb. 29, 1816;
         married (1), Oct. 24, 1839, Hannah Rier, who died
         s. p., May 20, 1841; married (2), Feb. 6, 1842,
         Olive Fuller, who died Jan. 26, 1844; married (3),
         Oct. 21, 1844, Liveria Knight, who died Dec. 8,
         1890, aged 73 years, 6 months; married (4), March
         1, 1892, Mrs. Julia (Brock) Waterhouse. He was
         editor and printer for more than 35 years, and in
         1901 was the oldest journalist in Iowa. He moved

there in 1856 and settled in Charles City, and published *The Intelligencer.* He was a prominent man in Charles City; had one daughter (Mary), who died young.

2475   Almira Maria Hildreth, born Feb. 10, 1818; married Oct. 22, 1854, Edward Mason, of Corinth, Vt., born Dec. 9, 1802.

2476   George Washington Hildreth, born May 14, 1820; died in Chelsea, July 8, 1844.

2477   Daniel Elbridge Hildreth, born July 18, 1822; died in South Newbury, Vt., July 22, 1874; married, June 7, 1854, Emeline Mason; had three children.

2478   Mary Caroline Hildreth, born Aug. 5, 1824; died in Lowell, Mass., April 15, 1886; married, April 30, 1852, Charles McCoy; had seven children.

2479   Lucy Tyler Hildreth, born Dec. 6, 1826; died in Chelsea, March 3, 1842.

2480   Albert Gallatin Hildreth, born Feb. 25, 1829; married, Feb. 3, 1853, Mary M. Barnes. He lived in Boston. Several children died young; four survived.

2481   Harriet Newell Hildreth, born April 25, 1831; died in Heath, Vt., Dec. 27, 1901; married, Feb. 6, 1855, Lyman Pater, of Heath. She was early a teacher and a contributor to the periodicals of the day; prominent in church and society. Six of their children died young; one son (John) is a financial agent in Boston.

2482   Lovinia Greenleaf Hildreth, born Aug. 30, 1834; died in Lowell, Aug. 21, 1854.

2483   Amelia Brown Hildreth, born Oct. 24, 1837; died in Chelsea, May 19, 1861; married, Nov. 3, 1859, Samuel W. Burt, who died s. p.

2484   Infant son, born and died March 16, 1840.

977 THEODOSIA[6] TYLER (Jonathan[5]), born in Piermont, N. H., April 11, 1800; died March 22, 1861; married Winthrop G. Dorsey, of North Benton, N. H.; a farmer. They lived in Piermont where the children were born. Children:

2485   Sarah A. Dorsey, born March 5, 1824; married, Nov. 30, 1843, William Davis, a farmer of North Benton, N. H., thence moved to Tilton, N. H., and then

to Piermont; son of Jonathan and Merriam (Bartlett) Davis, of Northfield, N. H.; had three children (Amanda, Anna E., Winthrop G.).

2486 William Tyler Dorsey, born March, 1828; died in
North Benton, March, 1894; married Irene Davis,
of North Benton; they had a son and a daughter
(Emma, Amos).

2487 Amos Tyler Dorsey, born March, 1830; died in North
Benton in 1857; married Lizzie Brooks, of North
Benton; one son (Sprague).

978 REV. AMOS⁶ TYLER (Jonathan⁵), born in Piermont, N. H., April 11, 1802; died in Big Spring, Adams
County, Wis., August 13, 1876; married (1), February 16,
1823, in Fairlie, Vt., Lydia Bliss, of Llandaff, N. H., who died
in Compton, P. Q., June 27, 1838; married (2), January 13,
1839, in Compton, P. Q., Emogene C. Todd. He had a common school education; at 19 he was licensed to preach by the
Methodist church; in 1834 he moved to Hatley, P. Q., where,
October 21, 1836, he was ordained by the Free Baptist church,
and where he preached for years. Later in life he moved to Big
Spring, Wis. The two elder children were born in Piermont;
the others in Compton.

CHILDREN, by first marriage:
2488 Amanda Lovina Tyler, born March 21, 1824; died
in Piermont, Sept. 4, 1826.
2489+ Damon Young Tyler, born May 15, 1827.

CHILDREN, by second marriage:
2490 Amanda Melvina Tyler, born March 14, 1840.
2491 Nahum Amos Tyler, born Jan. 28, 1843; died June
29, 1845.
2492+ Roxana Cutting Tyler, born April 14, 1848.
2493+ Amos Eugene Tyler, born March 3, 1851.

979 ELIZA MONTGOMERY⁶ TYLER (Jonathan⁵),
born in Piermont, N. H., September 14, 1804; died April 9,
1877, in Wentworth, N. H.; married, February 28, 1828, Ar-
chelaus Cummings Blood, of Wentworth, where the children
were born. Children:

2494   Hannah Louise Blood, born Feb. 26, 1832; married, March 16, 1853, Nelson Ellsworth, of Pittsburg, N. H.

2495   Horatio Cutter Blood, born Aug. 5, 1838; married, Dec. 2, 1867, Hannah Emeline Chase. He was a state representative in 1893 and a selectman for 10 years in Wentworth, where he lived; they had one son (George B.).

981   JOSEPH⁶ TYLER (Dudley⁵), born in Rowley, Mass., and baptized April 13, 1766; died intestate in New-buryport, Mass.; married ———. He was a mariner. Admin-istration papers were granted to his eldest son, June 11, 1833. We have no other record of his children than the name of this son. Child:

2496   John Tyler, a cordwainer.

986   DUDLEY⁶ TYLER (Thomas⁵), born March 6, 1771; married, November 25, 1805, Betsey Kimball, of And-over, Mass., who died May 8, 1817. He resided in Haverhill, where the children were born. Children:

2497+   Joshua B. Tyler, born Nov. 16, 1803.

2498+   Charles Tyler, born June 15, 1805.

2499+   George W. Tyler, born Oct. 13, 1807.

2500   John Appleton Tyler, born Jan. 17, 1811; drowned in Andover Pond, aged 8 years.

2501+   Moses Kimball Tyler, born Feb. 2, 1814.

2502   Rufus Longley Tyler, born March 8, 1817; died in Haverhill, in infancy.

987   THOMAS⁶ TYLER (Thomas⁵), born about 1773; married, March 26, 1803, Mrs. Hannah (Winter) Eames, of Haverhill, who died April 3, 1814. He kept a tavern in West Newbury, Mass. The children were born in Haverhill. Chil-dren:

2503+   William Winter Tyler, born Nov. 30, 1803.

2504+   Ebenezer Ballard Tyler, born March 18, 1805.

2505   Chandler Henry Osgood Tyler, twin to Ebenezer; went to sea and never heard from. (See Case 55930, *Salem Probates*.)

2506+   Thomas Tyler, born Jan. 24, 1808.

988   JOSEPH[6] TYLER (Job[5]), born May 17, 1775; married, December 18, 1798, Hannah Chase, of Haverhill, Mass.   Children:

2507   Woodman Tyler, born 1800; resided in North Beverly, Mass.; died, unmarried, May 1, 1888.

2508   Wesley Tyler, born 1806; died May 26, 1860, in Salem, Mass.; married (1), Sept. 17, 1832, Harriet Butrick, who died Sept. 7, 1833; married (2), Hannah Dow; no children.

2509   Mary Tyler, married, Nov. 16, 1820, Hazen West; had three children.

2510+   Job Tyler.

989   PHEBE[6] TYLER (Job[5]), born in Haverhill, Mass., November 29, 1776; died June 16, 1849; married Nathaniel Johnson, of Haverhill, who died August 22, 1831, aged 62. The children were born in Haverhill.   Children:

2511   Joseph Johnson, married Mary Chase; 13 children.

2512   Darius Johnson, married (1), Hannah Greeley; married (2), Mrs. Miranda Bartlett; left no descendants.

2513   Nathaniel Johnson, married (1), Sarah Fuller; married (2), Charlotte Haynes; married (3), Martha ――――.

2514   Theodore Johnson, became a Mormon and moved with his two daughters (Lucy and Mary Ann) to Salt Lake City.

2515   Adeline Johnson, died in Groveland, Mass., July 15, 1830, aged 26; married John Tappan, of Newburyport, whose second wife was her sister, Mary Ann; she had one daughter (Margaret C.).

2516   Mary Ann Johnson, died in Haverhill, Mass., Nov. 27, 1886, aged 75 years and 9 months (her sister Adeline was Mr. Tappan's first wife); had a daughter (Mary A.).

2517   Hannah Johnson, married Joshua Davis; no children.

2518   Alfred Johnson, married in Middletown, Mass., and had one son.

990   MARY[6] TYLER (Job[5]), born in Haverhill, Mass.,

May 23, 1778; died June 21, 1851; married Hezekiah George, of Haverhill, who died February 24, 1851, aged 73. The children were born in Haverhill. Children:

2519   Sally George, born April 20, 1800.
2520   Joseph Tyler George, born July 9, 1801.
2521   Moses D. George, born Nov. 26, 1802.
2522   Polly George, born March 21, 1804.
2523   Hezekiah George, born March 21, 1806.
2524   Abigail Swan George, born Feb. 24, 1809.
2525   George Washington George.

991   ANNA[6] TYLER (Job[5]), born in Haverhill, Mass., October 27, 1780; died August 20, 1863; married, August 11, 1799, Moses Kelly, born in East Haverhill, Mass., December 25, 1777; died in Canaan, N. H., where he lived, October 2, 1850; son of Anthony Kelly; descended from John, of Newbury, Mass. Children:

2526   Caroline Kelly, born Feb. 9, 1800; died June 25, 1802.
2527   Ann P. Kelly, born Feb. 18, 1801; married, in 1856, Cyrus Perkins.
2528   Lois Kelly, born March 12, 1803; died young.
2529   Moses G. Kelly, born July 24, 1804; married, May 9, 1839, Lydia Pike, who died Sept. 17, 1875; he was a clothier, of Newport, N. H.

994   JOHN[6] TYLER (Job[5]), born in Haverhill, Mass., June 2, 1789; lost at sea, about 1818, on Long Island Sound; married, 1807, Sophia Miner. He was a sailor and mate on a vessel; resided in East Canaan, N. H., where the children were born. Children:

2530+   John Alexander Tyler, born Dec. 25, 1812.
2531   Allan Miner Tyler, last heard of about 1820 in New York City.
2532   Eleanor Tyler; married ―――― Weeks, of New Orleans, La. (she had a son Samuel who was a director of the U. S. Mint till he died, about 1874).

997   SALLY PARKER[6] TYLER (Job[5]), born in Haverhill, Mass., March 24, 1794; married, in Canaan, N. H., Theophilus Currier. The child was born in Canaan. Child:

2533   John Wesley Currier, born Dec. 22, 1828; lived in Sanbornton, N. H., where was selectman and a valuable citizen; he had a family.

999 REV. JOB COLMAN[6] TYLER (Job[5]), born in Haverill, Mass., March 1, 1799; died in Canaan, N. H., September 1, 1879; married (1), Julia Morse, who died in Canaan, N. H., July 13, 1863; married (2), ——. He went to Canaan with his father, when he was about four years old. He was ordained in 1831.

CHILD, by first marriage:
2534+ Elsie A. Tyler, born in Canaan, N. H.

1000 JAMES PIKE[6] TYLER (Job[5]), born in Haverhill, Mass., June 23, 1801; died in Canaan, N. H., September 26, 1879; married (1), Polly Morey, who died in 1844; married (2), 1846, Clarissa Damon, who died in March, 1873. The children were born in Canaan.

CHILDREN, by first marriage:
2535 Clarissa George Tyler, born March, 1829; died in 1856; married (1), in 1850, Joseph Palmer, of Bradford, N. H.; married (2), in 1855, Dr. J. Blaisdell, of Lawrence, Mass.
2536+ James S. Tyler, born March 29, 1832.
2537 Theodore Tyler, born Dec. 17, 1834; died Aug. 28, 1858; married, May 15, 1858, Florina Putnam.
2538+ David Morey Tyler, born May 7, 1837.
2539 Caroline Swett Tyler, born Dec. 10, 1840; married Josiah Howe, of Laconia, N. H., who died in 1882.
2540+ Colman J. Tyler, born in 1842; married Abbie Burnham and resides in Georgetown, Mass.

CHILDREN, by second marriage:
2541 Elizabeth Ann Tyler, born April 23, 1846; married G. H. Wilkinson, of Laconia, N. H.
2542 Fanny S. Tyler, born June 12, 1857; died Jan., 1893, in Concord, N. H.; married E. J. Emerson.

1003 CAROLINE B.[6] TYLER (Job[5]), born in Canaan, N. H., November 20, 1808; died in Beverly, Mass., September 19, 1883; married, January 10, 1832, in Haverhill, Rev.

Simeon Swett, of Gorham, Maine, who died August 21, 1880, aged 82. The children, from the fourth to the tenth inclusive, were born in Exeter, N. H., where he was settled for a number of years. Children:

2543   Caroline Elizabeth Swett, born in Canaan, N. H., Nov. 20, 1833; died young.

2544   Myron B. Swett, born in Newton, N. H., Sept. 4, 1834; died young.

2545   Caroline Ann Swett, born in East Kingston, N. H., Sept. 15, 1835; married, Nov. 24, 1853, —— Burnham, and had four daughters and a son (Annie, Alice, Florence, Bertha, Frederick).

2546   Christiana O. Swett, born March 20, 1837.

2547   Simeon Clarke Sweet, born Dec. 17, 1839; died young.

2548   Warren Lincoln Swett, born Nov. 29, 1841; died young.

2549   Simeon Tyler Swett, born Aug. 21, 1843.

2550   Harriet Angeline Swett, born June 6, 1845; died young.

2551   James William Swett, born Sept. 12, 1847; died young.

2552   Elizabeth Emma Swett, born May 13, 1849; married O. B. Burnham, Beverly, Mass.

2553   Angeline La Roy Swett, born Lawrence, Mass., Jan. 16, 1852; died young.

1008   HON. WILLIAM HUNT[6] TYLER (Theodore[5]), born in Newburyport, Mass., September 14, 1796; died in Calais, Maine, March, 1866; married (1), January 14, 1827, Salome Barstow Stearns, of Calais, born in Eastport, Maine, November 23, 1809; died in Calais, March 3, 1828; daughter of Elijah and Mary (Osgood) Stearns; married (2), March 9, 1830, Rebecca Laird, born in Newburyport, Mass.; died in Calais, 1873. He moved to Calais when a youth, where he became a prominent member of the Congregational church and mayor of the city in 1853 and 1854. He was a Mason of high degree. The children were born in Calais.

CHILD, by first wife:

2554   William Stearns Tyler, born 1827; died unmarried, in New York City, Aug. 22, 1854; he was for a time in Stearns' wholesale house; then in partnership with Mr. Sargeant as a wholesale druggist.

CHILDREN, by second marriage:

2555+ John Laird Tyler, born June 13, 1833.
2556   Infant, who died.

1009 BROADSTREET⁶ TYLER (Bradstreet⁵), born in Willington, Conn., in 1768; died in South Otselic, N. Y., September, 1852, aged 84; married (1), Bridget Perry; married (2), Polly Thompson. He was doubtless of the "Potter neighborhood" of Willington. He was a farmer, and moved to Vermont; stayed about a year, then went back to Connecticut; thence to Pitcher, N. Y., with three sons. He spent his last years with his son William, in South Otselic, and was interred in Pitcher. The record of his sons was found in *The Press*, a paper published in Stafford Springs, Conn., in 1892. The children were probably all born in Willington, but the order of birth is not known.

CHILDREN, by first marriage:

2557+ Dudley Tyler.
2558+ Perry Tyler.
2559+ Sally Tyler.
2560+ Ara Tyler, born June 9, 1793.
2561   Simeon Tyler, married Martha ——; went west on steamer *Erie*, which burned and only three saved, of whom he was one; went to California for gold; had a son (Adolphus).
2562+ Polly Tyler, twin to Simeon.
2563+ William Tyler, born June 11, 1798.
2564+ Ella Tyler.

CHILD, by second marriage:

2565+ Louisa Tyler.

1017 ROSWELL⁶ TYLER (William⁵), born in Peru, Mass. (formerly Partridgefield), October, 1772. He moved to New York state with his father and then went to Michigan about 1836. He had three sons and five daughters. We have meagre records of only two children. Children:

2566   Loren Tyler, was a farmer and lived in Bowne, Mich.
        He married and had children; one of the sons
        (Adin), died in 1888, leaving one son and two
        daughters.
2567   Roswell Tyler, lived in Hesperia, Mich.

   1018   ASAHEL⁶ TYLER (William⁵), born in Peru,
Mass., October, 1772; married, February 4, 1796, Sina Watkins, born in 1774. About 1800 he went to Hamilton, N. Y.,
and about 1809 to Middlesex, N. Y., where he was a first settler, a farmer, and where he put up a log hut. Their only
table was formed of shingles stuck into cracks between the logs.
The eldest child was born in Massachusetts, and the next four
in Hamilton; the others were born in Middlesex. Children:

2568+   William W. Tyler, born Jan. 14, 1797.
2569   Esther Tyler, born June 31, 1799; died Sept. 9, 1800.
2570+   Lucina Tyler, born Oct. 9, 1802.
2571   James W. Tyler, born Feb. 1, 1804; was a farmer;
        moved to Michigan and died s. p.
2572+   Asahel Watkins Tyler, born March 2, 1807.
2573+   Speda M. Tyler, born Aug. 24, 1810.
2574+   Roswell Root Tyler, born Dec. 29, 1812.
2575   Fisher Metcalf Tyler, born Sept. 30, 1815; married
        Nancy Morehouse; he moved to Naples, N. Y.; they
        had one son born there (Darwin).
2576   Huldah Maria Tyler, adopted.

   1023   JOB⁶ TYLER (Jonathan⁵), born in Willington,
Conn., April 14, 1765; died in Hatley, P. Q., August, 1857;
married (1), September 9, 1787, Sophia Leighton, born January 25, 1771; daughter of John and Hannah (Spofford)
Leighton, of Charleston, Vt.; married (2), Mehitable Tewksbury, born in Weare, N. H., November 1, 1771; died in Fayston, Vt., 1855; daughter of Jacob and Hannah (Hadley)
Tewksbury; she parted with her husband and moved to Fayston, to the home of her son Merrill, where she died; married
(3), Sally Walton, who died in 1869. Job was a farmer and
went to Hartland, Vt., with his father; in 1818 he went to
Fayston, and thence moved to Hatley, P. Q. The eldest child
was born in Hartland, as also the second wife's children; the
third wife's children were born in Hatley, with one exception.

CHILD, by first marriage:

2577+ Asahel Tyler, born Aug. 11, 1788.

CHILDREN, by second marriage:

2578+ Merrill Tyler, born in 1795.

2579 Royal Tyler, born about 1797; died in Fayston, unmarried, about 1848.

2580+ Hannah Tyler, born about 1799.

CHILDREN, by third marriage:

2581+ Hial Tyler, born 1804.

2582 Phylinda Tyler, born in 1806; died in 187–; married James Ames; had three sons (James, William, Reuben.)

2583 Caroline Tyler, born in 1808; married Alfonso Burbank. They had eight children; two of the sons (Alfonso and James) lived in Ayers Flat, P. Q., in 1898.

2584 Belinda Tyler, died in 1893, in Coaticook, P. Q.; she married —— Dearborn, and had five boys and four girls; the name of only one of her children is known (George), who lived in Coaticook.

2585 Lucinda Tyler, born in 1810; married, Aug. 12, 1834, David Griffin; their son (Edgar), lived in Strafford, Vt.

2586 Rosetta Tyler, married Simon Keneston, who died in Fayston; they had three children, two sons (Walton and Simeon, who lives in North Derby, Vt., and has the family Bible.)

2587 Sally Tyler, born in 1812; married John Hackett; two of their sons (James and Charles), live in Worcester, Mass.; another (John), lives in North Hatley; they had a daughter who married (Charles Danforth, of Greenfield, Mass.), and had two sons.

2588 Zeruiah Tyler, married Paschal Morrisett, and lived in Lowell, Mass.; he died in 1897; they had seven children (Margaret, Charles, Jane, Marshal, Lovina, Rozilla, Paschal.)

2589+ Roswell Tyler, born in Rumford, Maine, March 14, 1814.

2590+ Derias Tyler, born about 1816.

2591   Alvah Tyler, married Jane Walker; resided in 1897
in North Hatley; had ten daughters, names unknown.

1025 DERIAS⁶ TYLER (Jonathan⁵), born probably
about 1774; died May 21, 1857, aged 83; married (1), Rhoda
Bishop, of Hartland, Vt., who died in Strafford, Vt., October
9, 1799, aged 21; married (2), March 5, 1801, Lois Rowell,
of Strafford. The children were born in Strafford except the
eldest.

CHILDREN, by first marriage:

2592+ Sophia Tyler, born in Hartland, May 28, 1796.
2593   Chloe Tyler, born Feb. 6, 1798; died in Iowa; married, April 17, 1817, Daniel Munsell, of Sharon,
Vt., a daughter (Lina), married and moved to Missouri; their son died.
2594+ Lyman Tyler, born Sept. 28, 1799.

CHILDREN, by second marriage:

2595   Rhoda Tyler, born Feb. 20, 1802; died April 1, 1873;
married, Nov. 9, 1820, Roswell Robinson, of Strafford, Thetford and Sharon; one son (Edson) lives
in Sharon.
2596+ Alvah Tyler, born Feb. 17, 1804.
2597   Hannah Tyler, born April 16, 1806; died April 9,
1809.
2598+ Zeruiah Tyler, born Jan. 29, 1808.
2599+ Lucius Tyler, born May 16, 1810.
2600+ Hannah Tyler, born Nov. 3, 1812.
2601   William Tyler, born May 30, 1817; died Aug. 3, 1818.

1027 ABIGAIL⁶ TYLER (Abraham⁵), born in Box-
ford, Mass., May 1, 1758; married Richard Kimball, born in
Boxford, 1754; died in Sterling, Mass. They resided in
Rindge, N. H., until about 1790, when they removed to Utica,
N. Y., but returned to Rindge in 1804; in 1810 they went to
Sterling. The oldest child was born in Rindge. Children:
2602   Lemuel Kimball, born Oct. 23, 1785.
2603   Mary Kimball, married ―――― Powers.

1028 HANNAH⁶ TYLER (Abraham⁵), born in Box-

ford, Mass., September 13, 1759; married Jonathan Low, of
Boston, Mass. Children:

2604   Abigail Low, married —— Sumner, and died in Read-
       ing, Mass.
2605   Martha Low.
2606   Tyler Low.

1030   MOLLY[6] TYLER (Abraham[5]), born in Boxford,
Mass., February 16, 1763; died April 26, 1853, aged 90; married, December 2, 1788, John Peabody, of Boxford, born July
24, 1762; son of Captain Richard Peabody.   He settled in
Lunenburg, Mass., and was living as late as 1849.   Children:

2607   John Peabody, born Oct. 8, 1789; married Abigail
       Spaulding.
2608   Daughter, twin to John, died young.
2609   Mary Peabody, born Feb. 8, 1791; died early, unmar-
       ried.
2610   Oliver Peabody, born Jan. 2, 1792; married, Dec. 18,
       1817, Lydia Howard.
2611   William Peabody, twin to Oliver; married, July 31,
       1817, Mary Stephens.
2612   Sarah Peabody, born May 23, 1794; died 1810.
2613   Samuel Peabody, born Aug. 6, 1796; married Betsey
       Jones, April, 1819.
2614   Joseph Peabody, born Feb. 20, 1802; married, May 7
       1826, Mary Lawrence.

1031   PRISCILLA[6] TYLER (Abraham[5]), born probably in Boxford, Mass., February 18, 1765; died in Newburyport, Mass., November 26, 1859; married, April 7, 1794, Benjamin Robinson, of Boxford; born February 3, 1769; died
March 26, 1841; son of Deacon Robinson.   Children:

2615   Ruby Robinson, born Dec. 3, 1795; died Sept. 8, 1820;
       married (1), John O. Farnum; married (2), Stephen
       Pike, of Bradford, Mass.   Had one daughter by
       first marriage, and two sons by second marriage.
2616   Benjamin Robinson, Jr., born Nov. 21, 1797; died
       Sept. 27, 1855; married (1), Rebecca Foster, of
       Boxford, Mass.; married (2), —— Williams.
2617   Caroline Robinson, born Aug. 1, 1799; died 1893:
       married John Rose; had fourteen children.

2618   Louisa Robinson, born Dec. 13, 1800; died Nov. 8, 1840; married Asa Wheeler, who died Jan. 1, 1854, aged 57.

2619   Hannah Stickney Robinson, born July 22, 1803; died Feb. 24, 1852; married Manly Cole; had three sons.

2620   Samuel Granger Robinson, baptized Oct. 4, 1818; married Sally Tyler, No. 2652.

1032 ABRAHAM[6] TYLER, JR. (Abraham[5]), born probably in Boxford, Mass., October 15, 1766; died March 20, 1821; married, January 12, 1792, Hannah Bartlett, born in Uxbridge, Mass., 1768; died April 20, 1828; daughter of Jonathan Bartlett, and descendant of Josiah Bartlett, a signer of the Declaration of Independence. The eldest child was born in Boxford, the others in Portland, Maine, from which it is inferred that he took up his residence in Portland some time after 1793. He may have been the Abraham Tyler, who, with his wife Hannah, deeded for $1200, September 9, 1805, land and wharf to Enoch Ilsley, of Portland, the same being witnessed by Job Tyler and Daniel Manley. Abraham is called " cooper," also, in a record covering a transaction with Enoch Ilsley, " Trader," by which he acquires land at " Clay Cove," Portland, for $333., July 13, 1802.

CHILDREN:

2621+   Abigail Stickney Tyler, born June 8, 1793.

2622+   Caroline Bartlett Tyler, born after 1793 and before 1798.

2623+   Osborn Hull Tyler, born Oct. 9, 1798.

2624+   Phineas Parker Tyler, born Dec. 24, 1800.

1034 ISAAC[6] TYLER (Abraham[5]), born in Boxford, Mass., November 20, 1767; was accidentally drowned in Boston Harbor, January 4, 1823; married, in 1794, Dorcas Goodrich, of Newbury, Mass.; she married (2), —— Cheney, and resided in Georgetown, Mass. Isaac lived in Boxford and West Newbury. The eldest and fourth children were born in West Newbury. Children:

2625   Dean Tyler, married Mrs. Mehitable Dresser, and probably died s. p.

2626+   Josiah Goodrich Tyler, born July 26, 1797.

2627+ Orlando Tyler, born in Rowley, Mass., 1802.
2628 Mary Ann Tyler, born Feb. 20, 1807; married Jeremiah⁷ Tyler, No. 2649.
2629+ Sarah Jane Tyler, born in Rowley.

1035 JACOB⁶ TYLER (Abraham⁵), born in Boxford, Mass., February 17, 1769; died in Georgetown, Mass., about 1857, aged 88 years; married, January 23, 1794, Lavinia Barker, of Methuen, Mass. He lived in Plaistow, Atkinson and Concord, N. H., and in Boxford and Haverhill, Mass. In Concord he was janitor of the State House. Children:

2630 Solendia Tyler, born in Plaistow, N. H., July 17, 1794; died Feb. 11, 1798.
2631 Isaac Barker Tyler, born in Boxford, Mass., Nov. 19, 1795; died Jan. 24, 1815.
2632+ Lavinia Tyler, born in Atkinson, N. H., Sept. 27, 1797.
2633+ Abraham Tyler, born Oct. 22, 1799.
2634 Solendia Tyler, born in Haverhill, Mass., March 28, 1803; died unmarried, in Concord, N. H.; her will was dated Dec. 10, 1870, and her sister, Catherine T. Gerald was executrix.
2635+ Caleb Greenleaf Tyler, born Oct. 18, 1805.
2636+ Catherine Thomas Tyler, born in Concord, N. H., Aug. 25, 1808.
2637 Elizabeth Rolfe Tyler, born in Concord, N. H., Oct. 19, 1812; died there Dec. 16, 1812.

1036 ELIZABETH⁶ TYLER (Abraham⁵), born in Bradford, Mass., July 18, 1771; married, September 27, 1797, David Coburn. They moved to Keswick Ridge, New Brunswick; apparently she died, for he married (2), Molly Christy, by whom he had a son (Thomas), born about the time of David's death, who was killed by the falling of a tree in the woods, September 4, 1829, aged 56; he was a much respected citizen. The children were born in Keswick Ridge. Children:

2638 Abraham Tyler Coburn; died in 1871; married Hepsey Pickard; daughter of Frederick Pickard, of Frederickton, New Brunswick; had four daughters.
2639 David Coburn, born Sept. 17, 1806; married, Jan. 6 1833, Sarah Sloat. He settled on his father's homestead; four sons and one daughter.

2640   Phœbe Coburn; married David Pickard; had two sons
and six daughters.

2641   Deborah Coburn; married Nathaniel Perley; had one
son and four daughters.

2642   Elizabeth Coburn; married Joseph Pickard; had two
sons and one daughter.

2643   Annie Coburn; married James Pickard; had three
daughters.

1037   JOB⁶ TYLER (Abraham⁵), born November 4,
1772; died January, 1857; married, December 21, 1802, Mrs.
Phebe (Fitch) McDonald; she was living at the time of the
Civil War, and died aged over 93.   He was a salt-water
cooper, voyaging from Woburn, Mass., and going to China
and other places.   They lived in Andover and Boston, Mass.
The two elder children were born in Boston, and the three
youngest in Andover.   Children:

2644   Sophronia Tyler, born Oct. 27, 1802; died in Medford,
Mass.; married Charles Burnham; moved to Ver-
mont; had two sons, one of whom was drowned early.

2645+   William G. Tyler, born May 18, 1804.

2646+   Henry Tyler, born Dec. 25, 1809.

2647
2648 } Twins, born and died in 1807.

1038   WILLIAM⁶ TYLER (Abraham⁵), born in Boxford, Mass., October 10, 1774; died August 25, 1867; interred
in West Boxford; married, March 6, 1799, Abigail Barker, of
Methuen, Mass., who died February 11, 1862, aged 85.   The
children were born in Boxford.   Children:

2649+   Jeremiah Tyler, born June 21, 1800.

2650+   Solendia Tyler, born July 6, 1802.

2651+   Lucinda Tyler, born Nov. 26, 1805.

2652+   Sally Tyler, born Feb. 4, 1807.

2653   Child, born Jan. 1, 1809; died Jan. 6, 1809.

2654   William Tyler, born July 18, 1810.

1039   JOSEPH STICKNEY⁶ TYLER (Abraham⁵),
born in Boxford, Mass., April 15, 1776; died in 1864; married
(1), September 13, 1798, Hannah Nelson, of Georgetown,

Mass. died October 24, 1832, aged 59; married (2), Sally Burnham, of Boxford, Mass., who died in 1858 aged 78; married (3), Mrs. Sarah Esney, of Boxford, Mass., who died in 1860. He was a private in the War of 1812.

Children, by first marriage:

2655 Hannah Tyler, born and died 1799.
2656+ Hannah Tyler, born Dec. 27, 1800.
2657 Mary Tyler, born Nov. 9, 1802; died unmarried, Nov. 5, 1833, aged 31.
2658+ Abigail Stickney Tyler, born Oct. 17, 1804.
2659+ Roxanna Tyler, born Aug. 28, 1806.
2660+ Ira Stickney Tyler, born Aug. 23, 1811.
2661 Ancill Tyler, born in 1813; died Feb. 23, 1813.

1040 PARKER⁶ TYLER (Abraham⁵), born April 7, 1778; died June 19, 1856; married, March 30, 1802, Rebecca Johnson, of North Andover, Mass., who died in Salem, Mass., October 19, 1858, aged 75. He lived in Andover, Mass., and the children were born there. Children:

2662 Harriet Tyler, born March 6, 1803; died Oct. 14, 1807.
2663+ Moses Coburn Tyler, born May 7, 1805.
2664+ John Abbott Tyler, born Oct. 3, 1807.
2665 Harriet Tyler, born Dec. 31, 1809; died in Boston, Oct. 1, 1843; married, in Boston, July 14, 1842, Horace Rowley, born in Hanover, N. H., in 1810; died in Boston, July 26, 1848; buried in Copps Hill burying-ground. He was a private in Company A, First Regiment of Mass. Infantry in the War with Mexico.
2666+ Alexander Sumner Tyler, born May 14, 1812.
2667+ Leonard Tyler, born Oct. 20, 1815.
2668+ Rebecca Tyler, born May 24, 1818.
2669+ Warren Parker Tyler, born Feb. 17, 1821.
2670+ Charles Kimball Tyler, born Sept. 28, 1823.
2671+ Samuel Frye Tyler, born July 3, 1826.

1044 PHINEAS⁶ TYLER, JR. (Phineas⁵), born in West Boxford, Mass., February 14, 1765; died in the home of his son Laban in Leominster, Mass., January 21, 1847; married

(published in Lunenburg, Mass., August 30, 1788), October
16, 1788, Tabitha Hartwell, of Lunenburg, born July 14,
1768; died in Boston, Mass., March 25, 1850 (descended from
William Hartwell, who was of Concord, Mass., in 1635.) He
lived, at one time, in Jaffrey, N. H., where he built on " Tyler
Hill "; he lived in Leominster previous to going to Jaffrey, and
afterward. The fourth and fifth children were born in Jaffray
and the others in Leominster.

CHILDREN:

2672+   Moody Tyler, born Feb. 24, 1789.
2673   Stephen Tyler, born Nov. 1, 1790; died July 15, 1806.
2674+   Catherine Tyler, born Jan. 5, 1793.
2675+   Joseph Tyler, born June 16, 1795.
2676+   Phineas Tyler, born Jan. 25, 1798.
2677+   Laban Ainsworth Tyler, born June 8, 1800.
2678+   Lucy Hartwell Tyler, born April 14, 1803.
2679+   Luke Tyler, born Dec. 10, 1805.
2680+   Stephen G. Tyler, born Feb. 25, 1809.
2681   Eleazer (or Edward) Spofford Tyler, born Jan. 2,
        1813; married, Oct. 27, 1841, Martha Jane Far-
        quer; no children. He was one of the original set-
        tlers of Indianapolis, Ind., of the " mile square ";
        an early mate of noted men like Hon. William Eng-
        lish and Lew Wallace. By 1836 he was working at
        his trade in Indianapolis, that of book-binding, with
        the firm of Stacy & Williams. In 1842 he went into
        business with a partner, manufacturers of blank
        books and later formed another partnership and they
        furnished blank books and official blanks for nearly
        all the county offices in Indiana. In 1849 he made
        another change; sold out and bought out in business.
        He was a noted local musician, and organized the
        Indianapolis brass band. He was also interested in
        local theatricals. He is said never to have had an
        enemy.
2682   Harriet Newell Tyler, born March 24, 1815; died May
        18, 1815.

      1045 SIMEON[6] TYLER (Phineas[5]), born in West
Boxford, Mass., August 15, 1771; died in Leominster, Mass.,

February 12, 1858; married (1), in Leominster, February 11, 1794, Mary Pierce, born September 20, 1771; died October 15, 1814; daughter of Reuben Pierce (descended from Thomas of Charlestown, Mass.); married (2), February 16, 1816, Mrs. Alice Woods, of Leominster, who died December 8, 1855, aged 77. The children were all born in Leominster.

CHILDREN, by first marriage:

2683   Polly Tyler, born Jan. 18, 1795; died in Leominster, Sept. 21, 1850, unmarried.

2684   Amos Tyler, born Jan. 20, 1797; died s. p., July 23, 1880; married, June 13, 1831, Mary Jane Moore, born Aug. 1, 1801; died Sept. 2, 1885. He was one of the early stage drivers from Lowell to Leominster, and later a farmer. His will was filed Aug. 16, 1880, and dated May 15, 1854; no children.

2685+ Sewall Tyler, born May 3, 1799.

2686   Sally Tyler, born June 17, 1801; died Jan. 22, 1866; married, March 1, 1822, Ziba Stiles, of Leominster; one child (Mary E.).

2687+ Thirza Tyler, born April 26, 1806.

2688   Mira Tyler, born July 23, 1811; died Sept. 13, 1812.

2689+ William Tyler, born April 29, 1814.

CHILD, by second wife:

2690   Joseph Woods Tyler, born Aug. 26, 1819; died Sept. 11, 1822.

1046 SAMUEL[6] TYLER (Phineas[5]), born in West Boxford, Mass., February 28, 1773; died June 18, 1855; married, July 6, 1795, Fanny Hardy, of Bradford, Mass., No. 1065, born January 13, 1775; died June 15, 1835. The eldest child was born in Leominster, the others in Bradford. Children:

2691+ Lewis Tyler, born June 23, 1797.

2692   Francis Tyler, born March 9, 1799; died, unmarried, Sept. 14, 1857.

2693+ Frederic Tyler, born Dec. 6, 1800.

2694+ Abel H. Tyler, born July 2, 1802.

2695+ Samuel Tyler, born May 16, 1804.

2696   Alfred Tyler, born April 8, 1806; died, unmarried, May 26, 1872; was in the Civil War.

2697   Harrison Tyler, born May 20, 1808; drowned in the Merrimac River, Dec. 26, 1822.

2698+   Harriette H. Tyler, born Aug. 11, 1810.

2699   Alma Tyler, born March 16, 1812; died, unmarried, April 24, 1891.

2700+   Addison Tyler, born Aug. 10, 1813.

2701   Marietta Tyler, born Aug. 24, 1815; died Jan. 19, 1843; married Isaac Winchester, of Peabody, Mass.; has a son and a daughter.

2702+   Eri Burton Tyler, born May 19, 1818.

1048 ELIZABETH[6] TYLER (Phineas[5]), born in Leominster, Mass., December 28, 1778; died July 29, 1827; married, April 2, 1801, Asaph Spaulding, of Chelmsford, Mass., who died Jan. 4, 1843. The eldest child was born in Chelmsford, the third in Lunenburg and the others in Leominster. Children:

2703   Mira Spaulding, born June 19, 1801; died, unmarried, March 22, 1842.

2704   Sophia Spaulding, born Sept. 29, 1803; died April 7, 1867; married, March 13, 1845, Luke Woodbury, of Bolton, Mass.

2705   Eliza Spaulding, born June 15, 180–; married Jonas Walker, of Essex, N. Y.; they had two daughters and three sons.

2706   Melora Spaulding, born Sept. 2, 1808; died April 21, 1844; married William Claflin, of Framingham, Mass.; they had two daughters and a son; he married (2), Mrs. Betsey W. Jones.

2707   Asaph Spaulding, born May 20, 1809; married Martha Chase, of Leominster; they moved to Minnesota in 1856; they had two daughters and three sons.

2708   Abigail Spaulding, born Aug., 1814; married Philip Spaulding Baldwin, of Essex, N. Y.; they had two daughters and one son, who all married and had families.

1052 DANIEL[6] TYLER (Phineas[5]), born in Leominster, Mass., August 18, 1791; died in Milford, Mass., February

21, 1870; married, in Leominster, February 29, 1816, Thusa Polly, born in Harvard, Mass., August 22, 1797; died in Milford, April 4, 1884; daughter of Ebenezer and Rebecca Polly. He first moved to Hopkinton, Mass., between 1831 and 1834; thence, in 1840, to Milford, Mass., where he built a house on Purchase Road. The nine elder children were born in Leominster; the next three in Hopkinton and the youngest in Milford.

CHILDREN:

2709+ Rufus H. Tyler, born Sept. 10, 1817.

2710+ Elizabeth Tyler, born May 22, 1818.

2711 Rodolphus Tyler, born Feb. 22, 1820; died Oct. 20, 1822.

2712+ Lydia Ann Tyler, born Jan. 19, 1822.

2713+ Jane Mehitable Tyler, born Dec. 5, 1823.

2714 Caroline Sophia Tyler, born Oct. 27, 1825; died Aug. 2, 1845.

2715+ Adolphus Tyler, born Oct. 29, 1827.

2716+ Abigail R. Tyler, born Sept. 17, 1829.

2717+ Addison Hardy Tyler, born Nov. 30, 1831.

2718 George H. Tyler, born Feb. 21, 1834; died Sept. 28, 1834.

2719+ Arethusa Tyler, born March 10, 1836.

2720+ Alvan Elnathan Tyler, born Oct. 22, 1838.

2721+ Mira Eliza Tyler, born Feb. 28, 1841.

1054 NATHAN[6] TYLER (Moses[5]), born in Rowley, Mass., December 10, 1766; died in Lunenburg, Mass., August 31, 1825; married (published September 12, 1789), Relief Pearce (also called "Parce"), of Lunenburg; born 1767; died in Lunenburg, February 7, 1814. The children were born in Lunenburg. Children:

2722 Relief Tyler, born Nov. 3, 1791; married (published Nov. 9, 1822, in Lunenburg), Henry Capen, of Leominster. (See No. 2730.)

2723 Sarah Tyler, born May 28, 1794; married (published in Lunenburg, March 25, 1817), William Smith.

2724 Nancy Tyler, born Oct. 5, 1802; married (published Aug. 12, 1826, in Lunenburg), Josiah Peirce.

1059 ZEBEDIAH[6] TYLER (Moses[5]), born in Bradford, Mass., July 21, 1787; died in Lunenburg, May 12, 1854;

married (1), (intentions published October 13, 1810), Nancy
Lawson, of Lancaster, Mass., who died April 9, 1827; married
(2), September 2, 1837, Mrs. Mary Ann Stiles, of Lunenburg.
His first wife was probably a sister of his brother Ancill's wife.
The children were born in Lunenburg.

CHILD, by first marriage:
2725   Infant, born 1827; died March 3, 1827.

CHILDREN, by second marriage:
2726   John Tyler, born 1838; died July 21, 1845.
2727   Mary Elizabeth Tyler, baptized March 13, 1839.

1060 ANCILL[6] TYLER (Moses[5]), born in Lunenburg,
Mass., March 29, 1790; died in Woburn, Mass., at the home of
his daughter Mary, March 12, 1858; married (intentions published September 29, 1810), Mary Lawson, of Lancaster,
Mass.; born 1788; died June 19, 1854. He lived in his father's
house till 1819 and then removed to Lancaster, where he lived
until after the death of his wife. He was a farmer. He is
interred in the north cemetery in Lancaster, where his wife is
also laid. The eldest child was born in Lunenburg, the others
in Lancaster. Children:
2728+   Ancill Tyler, born Oct. 10, 1810.
2729+   Mary L. Tyler.
2730+   Abraham Tyler.
2731+   James Perkins Tyler, born 1818.
2732+   Moses Augustus Tyler, born 1820.
2733   Anthony Hale Tyler, born Nov. 12, 1823; died Nov.
        21, 1829.
2734   Jane Blake Tyler, born March 27, 1826; died in Wo-
        burn, Mass., June 30, 1852; married, April 16,
        1845, Joseph Buckman; born Oct. 17, 1824; died
        Sept. 26, 1853; son of Dennis and Ruth Buckman,
        of Woburn. They are both buried in Woburn; no
        family.
2735   Henry Tyler, married, Nov. 6, 1851, Eliza W. Saun-
        ders, of Stoneham, Mass.
2736+   Francis Tyler.
2737+   Ellen L. Tyler.
2738+   Clara A. Tyler.

1079 HANNAH[6] TYLER (Asa[5]), baptized in Rowley, Mass., December 2, 1770; died in Mexico, N. Y., 1863; married —— Parkhurst, of Oriskany, N. Y. The battle monument stands on their farm. They had four daughters and six sons; we have a record of only one. Child:

2739 Simeon Parkhurst. He had two sons, one a resident of Chicago, and the other a minister of Evanston, Ill.

1081 DR. ASA PEABODY[6] TYLER (Asa[5]), born June 9, 1773; baptized in Boxford, Mass., August 1, 1773; died in Rome, N. Y., January 28, 1848; married Sally Burroughs (or Barrett); born in Stafford, Conn., February 2, 1775; died April 30, 1853. In Rome he was overseer of the highways in 1810, 1818 and 1823. He was among the heaviest of the tax payers in the early days of the town; his list in 1823 was " 496 acres of first-class land, $8,602; personal, $1,142." He became a Millerite and nearly lost his reason because of the non-appearance of Christ. His children were born in Rome.

CHILDREN:

2740 Ira B. Tyler, born April 30, 1800; died in Rome Nov. 15, 1861, unmarried. He was a farmer.

2741 Cyrus Tyler, born Nov. 5, 1801; died March 21, 1813.

2742+ John Tyler, born Nov. 14, 1803.

2743 Elizabeth Tyler, born Sept. 30, 1805; died unmarried, July 25, 1826.

2744+ Jonathan Waldo Tyler, born June 25, 1807.

2745 (Dr.) James Tyler, born Aug. 14, 1809; died s. p., in Attica, N. Y., June 19, 1887; married, Sept. 1, 1840, Phebe Williams.

2746+ Ansel Tyler, born Oct. 14, 1811.

2747+ Albert Tyler, born Dec. 3, 1813.

2748+ Sarah Tyler, born Nov. 29, 1815.

2749+ Asa Norton Tyler, born June 10, 1818.

2750 Mary L. Tyler, born Sept. 12, 1822; married George Vredenburgh, of Rome, N. Y.; had two daughters (Ella and May).

1082 JOSHUA[6] TYLER (Bradstreet[5]), born in Boxford, Mass., October 6, 1776; married, 1800, Betsey Bartlett, of Newbury. He lived in West Newbury, where their child was born. He and his wife both died early, and the child was reared by the grandparents. Child:

2751+　Mary Foster Tyler, born Jan. 11, 1801.

1083　MARY[6] TYLER (Bradstreet[5]), born in Boxford, Mass., January 13, 1779; died May 2, 1846; married Deacon John Day, of Boxford; born December 10, 1776; died 1868. He was deacon of the Second church, 1814-1848. The children were born in Boxford. Children:

2752　Eunice Day, born Nov. 1, 1799; died Sept. 18, 1879; married Jonathan Chadwick, of Bradford, Mass.

2753　Mary Day, born 1802; married, Nov., 1826, Deacon Daniel K. Gage, of North Andover, Mass.

2754　Joshua Day, born 1804; died Feb. 12, 1873; married Elvira Kimball, of Bradford, Mass., born in 1807; living in 1896.

2755　John Day, born 1808; died Feb. 18, 1880; married Emily Kimball, of Bradford, Mass.

2756　Harriet Day, born in 1810; married, 1829, Hermon Kimball, of Bradford, Mass.

2757　Abigail Day, born 1813; married Guy Carleton, shoe manufacturer, of Methuen, Mass.

2758　Elizabeth Ingersoll Day, born 1815; married Albert Kimball, shoe manufacturer of Bradford, Mass.; she was living in 1896.

2759　Joanna Day, died aged 12 years.

2760　Myra Jane Day, born 1822; married Henry A. Bodwell, of Methuen, Mass.

1086　BRADSTREET[6] TYLER, JR. (Bradstreet[5]), born in Boxford, Mass., October 13, 1794; died December 2, 1862; married, June 16, 1825, Parmelia Wilkins, who died 1882, aged 85. He resided in Boxford, where his children were born. Children:

2761　Charles Bradstreet Tyler, born Jan. 5, 1827; died unmarried, 1857.

2762+　Charlotte Augusta Tyler, born Dec. 5, 1833.

1089　JOSHUA[6] TYLER, JR. (Joshua[5]), born in

Rindge, N. H., February 3, 1779; died in Leominster, Mass.,
September 3, 1824; married, May 10, 1804, Elizabeth Fairbanks, of Leominster, born May 3, 1772; daughter of Elijah
and Beulah (Carter) Fairbanks, of Leominster. He moved
from Rindge to Leominster, where the children were born. The
baptisms of all the children were recorded in Leominster, March
28, 1819. The three minor children made choice of Leonard
Burrage, of Leominster, as guardian, after the death of their
father. Children:

2763 Mary Tyler, born April 3, 1805; died in Leominster,
   unmarried, Nov. 10, 1824.
2764+ Eliza Tyler, born Oct. 8, 1806.
2765 Clarissa Tyler, born Aug. 28, 1808; died in Leominster, Sept. 14, 1825.
2766 Asa Tyler, born Dec. 21, 1810; married and had a son
   named Charles. He had a shoe store in Boston.

1090 BETSEY[6] TYLER (Joshua[5]), born in Rindge,
N. H., March 9, 1782; died February 5, 1812; married, November 27, 1806, James McCurdy, of Leominster, Mass.; he
died June 15, 1821; he married (2), his first wife's sister,
Ismena Tyler, No. 1094. His first wife's children were born
in Leominster. Children:

2767 Samantha McCurdy, born Dec. 25, 1807; married
   Dec. 25, 1831, George Patch; two children.
2768 Alonzo McCurdy, born March 14, 1810.

1092 PHEBE KIMBALL[6] TYLER (Joshua[5]), born in
Rindge, N. H., September 6, 1785; died in Jaffrey, N. H., July
13, 1869; married, September 17, 1807, Zebadiah Pierce, of
Leominster, Mass.; born 1785; died in Jaffrey, March 12,
1828. The eldest child was born in Leominster; the others in
Jaffrey, to which place he moved. Children:

2769 Reuben Pierce, born Dec. 9, 1809; died May 2, 1888;
   married, Dec. 15, 1835, Cordelia Jewell, of Pepperell, Mass.; they resided in East Jaffrey, N. H.,
   where he was a teacher. They had two daughters
   who did not marry.
2770 Rebecca Pierce, born 1810; died in Jaffrey, April 3,
   1885; married Elijah T. Smith, of Fitzwilliam, N.
   H., and moved to Rindge, N. H.; they had a son

who died young, and a daughter (Almeda), a teacher who wrote the poem for the centennial celebration of Jaffrey.

2771   Almira Peirce, born Feb. 10, 1817; died in infancy.

2772   Almira Peirce, born June, 1823; married Benjamin Davison, of East Jaffrey, N. H.; had two children who died in infancy, and a son (Arthur), who lives in Washington, N. H.

1093   THOMAS[6] TYLER (Joshua[5]), born in Rindge, N. H., July 14, 1787; died in Leominster, Mass., March 27, 1847; married, May 26, 1811, Deborah Carter; born in Jaffrey, N. H., May 1, 1787; died August 25, 1857; daughter of Jonathan Carter (Jonathan, Samuel, Rev. Samuel, Rev. Thomas). He removed from Rindge to Jaffrey and thence to Leominster. The children were born in Jaffrey, except the youngest who was born in Leominster. Children:

2773   Damaris Carter Tyler, born Sept. 2, 1814; married and resided with son in Athol, Mass.

2774   Mary Ann Tyler, born June 10, 1819; married, 1854, Samuel S. Sinclair, of Westminster, Mass.; had four children.

2775   Thomas Carter Tyler, born Jan. 3, 1821; died in Leominster, unmarried, Nov. 30, 1854.

2776+   Joel J. Tyler, born June 7, 1823.

2777   Benjamin B. Tyler, born Jan. 21, 1830; died there Jan. 4, 1847.

1094   ISMENA[6] TYLER (Joshua[5]), born in Rindge, N. H., September 20, 1789; died in Leominster, Mass., June 19, 1822; married, 1813, James McCurdy, of Leominster, who died June 15, 1821; he married (1), Betsey Tyler, sister of his second wife; see No. 1090. His second wife's children were born in Leominster. Children:

2778   Betsey McCurdy, born Aug. 29, 1813.

2779   Selina McCurdy, born July 26, 1815; died unmarried, April 4, 1899.

2780   Horatio McCurdy, born March 16, 1819; died Sept. 18, 1840.

2781   James R. McCurdy, born Aug. 21, 1821; died Aug. 1, 1847.

1096 ELSA[6] TYLER (Joshua[5]), born in Rindge, N. H., May 28, 1796; died in 1878; married Timothy Cowdrey, who died August 16, 1859. Children:

2782 Luther Cowdrey, born 1830; died Jan. 11, 1851.
2783 Adeline E. L. Cowdrey, born in 1833; married, 1851, Albert Pierce, born in 1830; had two children who died young; two sons survived (Edward T., who lived on the original Joshua Tyler place in North Leominster, Mass., and Charles A., who lived on the Phineas Tyler place in North Leominster).

1097 FLINT[6] TYLER (Parker[5]), born November 2, 1782; died in Haverhill, Mass., May 26, 1870; married, November 26, 1815, Jerusha Hardy, of Bradford, Mass., No. 1068, born April 15, 1783; died December 24, 1859. Children:

2784+ Hannah Flint Tyler, born in Bradford, Mass., June 17, 1817.
2785+ Aaron Parker Tyler, born in Wilton, N. H., Nov. 9, 1819.

1099 HANNAH[6] TYLER (Parker[5]), born in Rindge, N. H., October 20, 1786; died in Unity, N. H., September 10, 1875; married, June 14, 1804, Colonel Timothy Holt, of Andover, Mass., born September 7, 1777; died in Claremont, N. H., May 31, 1859. He was a colonel in the War of 1812. They moved to Weston, Vt., and thence to Claremont. The children were born in Weston. Children:

2786 Hannah Holt, born Oct. 28, 1805; died in Boston, Mass., Oct. 26, 1898; married (1), Oct. 24, 1824, Dr. David Pease, of Keysville, N. Y.; married (2), Henry Hannam; by first marriage she had six children, two of whom died in infancy.
2787 Maria Holt, born Sept. 27, 1809; married Thomas Richardson, of Boston, where she was living in 1896; three children, one of whom died in infancy.
2788 Dorothy Holt, born Dec. 21, 1812; died in Mound City, Miss., 1872; married Dec. 17, 1832, John B. Lovejoy; three children.
2789 Nathan Holt, born Feb. 12, 1814; died Oct. 2, 1891; married, 1837, Lavinia Webster. He was in the

Civil War. Five children, two of whom died in infancy.

2790 Lucy Tyler Holt, born Feb. 17, 1816; married Stillman White, of Weston and Ludlow, Vt.; she died in Ludlow, Aug. 2, 1898.

2791 Julia A. Holt, born Jan. 31, 1819; married, 1838, George White, a merchant of Rutland, Vt., where she died Aug. 25, 1860.

2792 Louisa J. Holt, born Dec. 23, 1821; died unmarried, in Springfield, Mass., July 28, 1842.

2793 Caroline M. Holt, born April 2, 1823; married, 1845, Albert Cowdrey, of Westmoreland, N. H.; lived in Weston, and died in Boston, June 13, 1854.

2794 Sarah J. Holt, born June 17, 1825; died unmarried, in Weston, Nov. 24, 1854.

2795 Emily A. Holt, born May 15, 1827; married, 1851, Benjamin Bickford, who died in Weston, Aug. 26, 1857.

2796 Mary E. Holt, born April 9, 1831; married Elbridge A. Smith, a baker of Unity and Newport, N. H.; as a widow she was a practising physician in Ludlow.

1100 PARKER⁶ TYLER, JR. (Parker⁵), born in Rindge, N. H., October 7, 1788; died in Lunenburg, Mass., of apoplexy, March 29, 1857; married, December 25, 1813, Abigail Buss, of Wilton, N. H., born May 29, 1791; died March 22, 1874; daughter of Silas and Hannah Buss. The fourth, fifth and seventh children were born in Jaffrey, N. H., where he appears to have lived for a time; the youngest child was born in Lunenburg, Mass. Children:

2797 Aaron Parker Tyler, born Sept. 10, 1815; died the same year.

2798 Abigail Tyler, born Aug. 29, 1817; died in 1837 of consumption.

2799 Arvilla. Tyler, born July 10, 1819; died the same year.

2800+ Parker Tyler, born July 15, 1820.

2801+ Isaac Matson Tyler, born Sept. 8, 1822.

2802 Hannah Flint Tyler, born Sept. 28, 1824; died of typhoid fever, Sept. 28, 1849.

2803+   John Pierce Tyler, born Feb. 18, 1826.
2804+   Albert Tyler, born Feb. 18, 1828.
2805+   Arvilla Anne Tyler, born Jan. 11, 1831.

1101 SETH PAYSON[6] TYLER (Parker[5]), born in
Rindge, N. H., April 29, 1791; died in Leominster, Mass.,
August 24, 1868; married (1), Sally Gray, of Wilton, N. H.,
who died April 4, 1834, in Leominster; married (2), August
22, 1836, Mrs. Susan P. Wheeler. He removed to Leominster
about 1830. His will was dated June 7, 1868; probated September 1, 1868; his youngest son was executor. The inventory amounted to $4,093.12. All his children are mentioned
in the will. They were all born in Rindge, except the youngest,
who was born in Leominster.

CHILDREN, all by first marriage:
2806   Sally Tyler, married, April 6, 1837, Josiah C. Rich-
       ardson.
2807   Chloe Ann Tyler, married, Dec. 6, 1850, George J.
       King.
2808   William Tyler, living in Oregon in 1868.
2809   (Rev.) Payson Tyler, born Jan., 1825; died in East
       Hardwick, Vt., where he preached several years;
       he had two children. He studied theology in New
       Hampton, N. H., and became a Baptist clergyman,
       preaching first in Cambridge, Vt., then in Barre
       and Conway, Mass., and later in Colchester, Water-
       bury and Newport, Vt. He was a highly respected
       minister and citizen.
2810+ Joseph Augustus Tyler, born Dec. 20, 1830.

1102 PUTNAM[6] TYLER (Parker[5]), born in either
Sterling or Leominster, Mass., September 20, 1793; died August 7, 1888; married, November 28, 1840, Lucy Seaver, of
Townsend, Mass. He lived in Wilton, Milford and Marlow,
N. H. The third child was born in Mason and the fourth,
fifth and sixth in Milford, N. H. Children:
2811   Abraham Tyler, born in Townsend, Mass., Sept. 13,
       1841; died Sept. 15, 1844.
2812   Lucy Lawrence Tyler, born in Townsend, Oct. 7,

1842; married, Aug. 25, 1868, John Adams Tyler, No. 2840.

2813   William T. Tyler, born Feb. 20, 1844; died of typhoid fever, in Washington, D. C., May 29, 1863. He enlisted Aug. 11, 1862, as a private in Company B, of the 14th N. H. Volunteer Infantry, and was mustered in Sept. 22, 1862. He was discharged for disability May 27, 1863, in Washington. (*Memorial Volume of N. H. Soldiers in the War*, 1861-1865). His residence was Marlow, N. H.

2814+   Mary Frances Tyler, born Dec. 12, 1845.

2815+   Almon Putnam Tyler, born June 25, 1847.

2816+   Julia Ellen Tyler, born July 11, 1849.

2817   Andrew Jackson Tyler, born Jan. 8, 1852; died June 16, 1867.

2818   Benjamin Franklin Tyler, born July 12, 1854; was a carpenter, unmarried and resided in Keene, N. H.

2819   Hannah Flint Tyler, born March 6, 1856; lives in Keene, N. H., unmarried.

2820   Malvina Tyler, born March 8, 1858; died Aug. 14, 1860.

2821+   Frederic Charles Tyler, born in Marlow, N. H., Jan. 20, 1862.

1105 MIRIAM[6] TYLER (Parker[5]), born in Wilton, N. H., January 23, 1798; died December 17, 1839; married, September 30, 1819, Jonathan Keyes, of Wilton, N. H.; son of Silas and Sarah (Lovejoy) Keyes, of Methuen, Mass., who was at the battle of Bennington (son of John and Abigail [Livermore] Keyes. The children were born in Wilton, N. H. Children:

2822   Edward Keyes, born Aug. 5, 1820; died Aug. 28, 1857.

2823   Silas Keyes, born 1822; died Sept. 11, 1825.

2824   Eliza Ann Keyes, born June 2, 1826; died Feb. 2, 1847; married George Lovejoy, of Milford.

2825   Maria Lovejoy Keyes, born Nov. 5, 1828; died May 13, 1860.

2826   Silas Keyes, born Feb. 28, 1831; married Lizzie Condon, of Harton, N. S.

2827   George Henry Keyes, born April 4, 1836; married

Abby A. Gutterson, of Milford; had a son (Arthur L.), who matriculated at Tuft's College.

1106 CAPTAIN LEVI[6] TYLER (Parker[5]), born October 22, 1800; died in Lyndeboro, N. H., May 25, 1870; married, September 27, 1825, Rhoda Pettengill, of Wilton, N. H., who died in 1893. They lived in Wilton and South Lyndeboro, N. H. The third and fourth children were born in Wilton, Children:

2828   Sarah B. Tyler, born Dec. 19, 1826; married, Oct. 25, 1849, Abel F. Boynton; no children.
2829+   Levi Andrew Tyler, born April 17, 1828.
2830   Rhoda Malvina Tyler, born Nov. 29, 1829; married, Dec. 14, 1852, Jonathan P. Richardson, who died in a southern prison in Virginia, Nov. 17, 1864; a son and daughter died early unmarried.
2831+   Emma F. Tyler, born June 17, 1834.
2832   Erastus F. Tyler, born Sept. 26, 1844; died Feb. 24, 1845.

1107 APPHIA[6] TYLER (Parker[5]), born November 6, 1806; died May 11, 1896; married, January 28, 1828, Frederick Adolphus Wilder, born April 16, 1804; died May 26, 1869; a farmer of Rindge, N. H.; son of Samuel Locke and Anna (Sherwin) Wilder, who removed from Boxford, Mass., to Rindge. Children:

2833   Charles A. Wilder, born Aug. 15, 1829; married, Nov. 6, 1856, Mary Manning; they resided in Rindge, and had a son (William F.).
2834   Mary Ann Wilder, born June 11, 1832; died May 7, 1839.
2835   Mary Ann Wilder, born May 15, 1846; married, Nov., 1866, Albert Emory; resided Rindge.

1108 ASA[6] TYLER (Parker[5]), born in Wilton, N. H., July 31, 1809; died in Townsend, Mass., April 18, 1870; married, March 15, 1832, Mary Adams, of Townsend, who was living in 1896 aged 83. He was a farmer and cooper; a good citizen. The children were born in Townsend. Children:

2836   Nancy M. Tyler, born April 30, 1835; died Sept. 2, 1835.

2837   Caroline L. Tyler, born Oct. 20, 1836; died June 3,
        1839.

2838   Mary Elvira Tyler, born Jan. 6, 1839; married, April
        29, 1863, Abel G. Stearns, of Townsend, Mass.; a
        teacher, member of the school board and selectman;
        no children.

2839   Asa Kendall Tyler, born July 20, 1841; married, July
        18, 1867, Sarah S. Hardy, daughter of Reuben
        Hardy, of Parishville, N. Y., and Townsend, Mass.
        He was a cooper; selectman from 1879 to 1896;
        road commissioner six years; deacon of the Congre-
        gational church since 1878.

2840   John Adams Tyler, born Jan. 25, 1844; married Aug.
        25, 1868, Lucy L. Tyler, No. 2812. Resided twenty
        years in Sandusky, O., where superintendent of
        Hodgman Manufacturing Company, resides now in
        Townsend, Mass.

2841+   Stephen A. Tyler, born April 13, 1846.
2842+   Aaron Parker Tyler, born May 31, 1850.
2843+   Lucy Ann Tyler, born Aug. 4, 1853; died Sept. 20,
        1880; married, Nov. 7, 1873, George B. Hodgman,
        of Townsend, Mass.; moved to Sandusky, O., where
        carried on business of coopering, G. B. Hodgman
        Manufacturing Company.

        1124   ASA TYLER STICKNEY (Margaret[5]), born in
Boxford, Mass., November 17, 1777; died in Orford, N. H.,
March 25, 1813; married, June 27, 1802, Mehetable Burpe.
Children:

2844   Infant, died.
2845   Ancil Stickney, born Jan. 4, 1803; unmarried.
2846   Saloma Stickney, born Dec. 1, 1810; married William
        Fowler.

        1134   JUDGE NATHAN PEABODY[6] TYLER (Asa[5]),
born in Suffield, Conn., February 16, 1784; died in Barrytown,
N. Y., December 4, 1864; married, in 1806, his cousin Persis
Lovejoy. He moved to Blenheim, N. Y., in 1801, and to Barrytown in 1840. In Blenheim he succeeded his father as postmaster and held the position until his removal. He was a member of the Legislature in 1818 from Schoharie county; became

Judge of the Court of Common Pleas of the county. He was the representative man in his vicinity, and commanded universal respect. He bought out a freighting business in Barrytown, on the Hudson, in 1840, which he and his sons successfully carried on until 1859, when he retired from active business. He was known for his strong character, unflinching integrity, and his universal gentleness and helpfulness to those around him.

CHILDREN:

2856a   Clarissa Tyler, born 1807; died young.
2857+ Phineas Lovejoy Tyler, born in Blenheim, N. Y., Jan. 29, 1809.
2857a   George Calvert Tyler, born Feb. 25, 1814; died April 17, 1865, unmarried.

1135   ASA[6] TYLER (Parker[5]), born in Suffield, Conn., February 25, 1789; died in Holland Patent, N. Y., May 12, 1843; married, May 3, 1813, Eunice Cornwell; born September 11, 1793; died March 11, 1876; daughter of Hart Cornwell. He was a farmer. His will was probated in Utica, N. Y. The children were born in Holland Patent. Children:

2848   William Fletcher Tyler, born Aug. 22, 1814; died Jan. 16, 1816.
2849+ Isabella Maria Tyler, born Sept. 25, 1816.
2850+ Helen Jenette Tyler, born Oct. 15, 1818.
2851+ Harriette Augusta Tyler, born July 27, 1821.
2852+ Jerome B. Tyler, born Dec. 9, 1823.
2853   Charles Henry Tyler, born Oct. 19, 1825; died s. p., 1862; married Margaret Shaffer. Resided in Trenton, N. Y.; will probated in Utica.
2854   Martha Dodge Tyler, born July 27, 1827; married, July 8, 1847, Lewis Benedict; one daughter (Martha, married —— Groves).
2855   Asa Tyler, born July 12, 1833; died Aug. 6, 1833.
2856+ Frances Lathrop Tyler, born Aug. 21, 1839.

1146   MERCY[6] TYLER (Jonathan[5]), born in New Gloucester, Maine, April 16, 1773; married there, November 8, 1798, Joseph Raynes, of New Gloucester; born September 26, 1774; died January 14, 1829. The children were born in New Gloucester. Children:

2857   Mary Raynes, born Jan. 20, 1799; died Sept. 21, 1800.

2858   Jonathan Raynes, born Jan. 4, 1801; died March 17, 1869; married (1), Mary Reed; had five sons; married (2) Octavia Bradford; had one son and three daughters.

2859   Orva Raynes, born Dec. 20, 1802; died in 1897 aged 94; married —— Davis.

2860   Joseph Raynes, born Feb. 17, 1804.

2861   Mary Ann Raynes, born April 3, 1807.

2862   Elvira Raynes, born Aug. 30, 1809.

2863   Susan Raynes, born Dec. 11, 1813.

1148 NATHANIEL[6] TYLER (Nathaniel[5]), born in Sidney, Maine, 1785; died in Bethel, Maine; married (1), Polly ——; married (2), Eunice Wright, of Vermont. He was in Sidney in 1819. Children:

2864   Fanny H. Tyler, born Jan. 26, 1816; married William Tyler, No. 2884; had three children.

2865   Nathan W. Tyler, born March 9, 1817; had four children.

2866+   William Tyler, born Jan. 23, 1819.

2867   Eunice Merrill Tyler, born Dec. 15, 1819; married John Merrill; resided in Windsor, Maine, and had six children.

2868+   Jonathan Tyler, born Jan. 9, 1822.

2869   Elias Tyler, born May 13, 1824; died 1842.

2870   Nathaniel Hiram Tyler, born Oct. 9, 1826; married Clara ——; had five children.

2871   David Tyler, born June 23, 1828; married Mary Susan Tyler, No. 2911; he died in Bethel, Maine; had eight children.

2872+   Lewis Tyler, born Nov. 24, 1831.

1149 JONATHAN[6] TYLER (Nathaniel[5]), born, probably about 1787; died in Windsor, Maine, May 30, 1850; married Christinia Towles. He preached some, but was never ordained. The locality in Windsor called "Tyler's Corner," was named for him. His children were born in Windsor. Children:

2873+   Samuel F. Tyler, born Jan. 20, 1810.

2874+ Asa F. Tyler, born Feb. 8, 1811.

2875+ Joshua Tyler, born Sept. 12, 1812.

2876 Hartwell Tyler, died in Windsor, unmarried.

2877 Elbridge Tyler, died in Windsor, where his will, dated March 20, 1857, mentions brothers and sisters and widow Sarah, but no children; married (1), Mrs. Nancy Peary, whose will, dated Windsor, Aug. 29, 1854, shows she was probably a widow when she married Elbridge, as she mentions as her only children, " George L., Ezekiel and Nancy J. Pera," minors; he married (2), Sarah ——.

2878 Elias Tyler, died s. p. in Windsor; married Hittie Motherwell, who also died in Windsor.

2879+ Mary Tyler.

2880 Asenath Tyler, married Stewart Merrill and had four children; she died.

2881 Hannah Tyler, married —— Merrill and died.

2882+ Betsey Tyler, born about 1824.

2883+ Eleazer Tyler.

1150 EBENEZER[6] TYLER (Nathaniel[5]), died in Gilead, Maine; married Elizabeth Robinson. Children:

2884 William Tyler; married Fanny Tyler, No. 2864; had three children.

2885+ Hannah Slade Tyler, born in Sidney, Maine, May 3, 1815.

2886+ Rebecca W. Tyler, born in Augusta, Maine, July 4, 1816.

2887 Elias Tyler, died young.

2888 Robinson Tyler, married Phebe Moore; had one child.

2889 Mary Tyler, died young.

1151 ELEAZER[6] TYLER (Nathaniel[5]), died in Vienna, Maine; married Welthy Mores; she administered upon his estate in 1837. Children:

2890 Christiana Tyler; married Charles Chamberlain.

2891 Ruth Tyler; married and had a family.

2892 Caroline Tyler.

2893 Hannah Tyler.

2894 James Tyler. Two genealogies exist either one of which is likely to belong to this man. He may have been the James, of Vienna, Maine, whose will was dated Nov. 5, 1862; wife Eliza was executrix (it names James F. and William M., minor sons, also Stephen, and daughter Martha M., who was unmarried). (*Kennebec Probate*). Or, he may have been the James of Peru, Maine, who married, April 27, 1831, Harriet Bisbee, born in Sumner, Maine, Nov. 18, 1812; daughter of John and Sarah (Philbrick) Bisbee. They had five children. (Gilbert, born Feb. 5, 1832; married, July 4, 1860, Martha Linnell; Desire, born July 14, 1834; married, Feb. 6, 1854, Andrew Abbott, who died Oct. 12, 1855; Mary E., born Jan. 27, 1840; married, April 14, 1864, Asa Jones; Harriet B., born April 4, 1844; married, April 5, 1867, Loring Hunton; Annette, born June 15, 1847; died Aug. 6, 1856.)*

2895 Elias Tyler; married and had a family.
2896 David Tyler; married and had a family.
2897 Welthy Tyler.
2898 Sterns Tyler; married and had a family.

1152 REV. THOMAS SHERLOCK[6] TYLER (Nathaniel[5]), born in Augusta, Maine, February 8, 1798; died in China, Maine, May 20 (or 26), 1861; married, February 9, 1823, Joanna Brown, born in New Hampshire, July 26, 1801; died in Augusta, Maine, January 6, 1882. He preached at the age of 28; ordained at 29 as a Freewill Baptist; blind in 1839; later his daughter, Annie R. Tyler, traveled with him. The second, third, fourth and fifth children were born in Sidney, Maine. Children:

2899+ Julia Ann Tyler, born in Belgrade, Maine, Nov. 19, 1823.
2900+ Eliza Ann Tyler, born June 21, 1826.
2901   Thomas S. H. Tyler, born June 23, 1828; died in Hallowell, Maine, April 18, 1849.
2902   Roxanna Merchant Tyler, born March 13, 1830; died in Chelsea, Maine, June 18, 1853; married in Hallowell, Maine, Sept 8, 1850, Isaiah H Hamlin; one child (Roseloen H.); died young.

* The author of this volume did not decide about this record before his decease, and both are given in the hope that it may be traced correctly.

2903+   Harriet E. Tyler, born May 13, 1832.
2904+   Annie R. Tyler, born in China, Maine, Sept. 3, 1835.

1153   ELIAS⁶ TYLER (Nathaniel⁵), born in Augusta,
Maine, February 8, 1798; died in China, Maine, where he lived;
married Abigail Webber. The children were born in China.
Children:
2905   Thomas Tyler; died in infancy.
2906   Elias Tyler; twin to Thomas, died in infancy.
2907   Daniel Tyler; died in childhood.
2908   Eliza Ann Tyler, died in China; married Charles Marsh
       of that town, and had eight children.
2909   Lucinda Tyler, died in Vinal Haven, Maine; married
       William Hopkins and had two daughters.
2910+ Daniel Willard Tyler.

1154   JOSEPH C.⁶ TYLER (Nathaniel⁵), born in Augusta, Maine; died in Gilead, Maine, 1882; married (1), Eliza
Morse, of Dixfield, Maine; died in Gilead, 1871; married (2),
Rebecca ——. He was a farmer. In the *Kennebec County
Registry of Deeds* it is recorded that in 1824 Joseph C. Tyler
of "25 Mile Pond Plantation," Kennebec County, Maine,
grants (?) to Ebenezer Tyler, of Waterborough, York County,
Maine, and Charles Tyler, of Augusta. Children:
2911   Mary Susan Tyler, married (1), Nathaniel Murry;
       married (2), David Tyler, No. 2871.
2912+ Elizabeth (Betsey) Jane Tyler.
2913   Daniel Owen Tyler, died in Palermo, Maine; mar-
       ried Elizabeth Erskins.
2914   Joseph Alva Tyler; married Emma Brand and resided
       in California.
2915   Gardiner Elanson Tyler; was shot in the Civil War
       and buried in the south; married Mary Tyler.
2916   Harriet Maria Tyler; resided in Tennessee.
2917+ Alonzo Chase Tyler, born in China, Maine, April 11,
       1836.

1155   RACHEL⁶ TYLER (Nathaniel⁵), married Rev.
Josiah Halloway. Children:
2918   (Rev.) James Tyler Halloway.
2919   Ruth Tyler Halloway; married —— Whitney.

2920   John Tyler Halloway.
2921   Seth Tyler Halloway.

1156   HANNAH[6] TYLER (Nathaniel[5]), died in Hallowell, Maine; married (1), Benjamin Young; married (2), Benjamin Slade.
        CHILDREN, by first marriage:
2922   John T. Young; married Malinda Wellman; had eight
        children.
2923   Nancy T. Young; married Captain Levi Lowe; two
        children.
2924   Eunice T. Young; died in infancy.
2925   Daniel O. Tyler Young; married Martha Crossman;
        four children.

        CHILDREN, by second marriage:
2926   Henry Coleman Tyler Slade; married Diantha Holt;
        five children.
2927   Frederick Tyler Slade; died in infancy.
2928   Robert T. Gardiner Slade; married Sarah Bean; four
        children.
2929   Lucretia C. T. Slade; married William Barry; one
        child, resides in Indiana.
2930   Anna Elizabeth Tyler Slade; married (1), J. H. Mar-
        son; had a daughter (Anna); married (2), Edward
        Button, who died in the Civil War; two children,
        who both died.
2931   Frederick William T. Slade; married (1), Sarah Mur-
        phy, who died, leaving two children; married (2),
        Lizzie Mosely; had two children.
2932   Frances E. T. Slade; married Otis Williams; had three
        children.

        1157   RUTH[6] TYLER (Nathaniel[5]), married (1), Oct.
17, 1811, Walden Sparhawk, of Augusta, Maine, who died;
married (2), Roland Sparhawk, brother of her first husband;
born 1791; died Dec. 26, 1834, of a small wound just below the
knee.   Children by first marriage:
2933   Daniel Sparhawk, went to sea.
2934+   Walden Sparhawk, born Sept. 12, 1812.

2935   Cynthia Sparhawk, married —— Bennett; three children (John, who married Ann Johnson had two
children, *Charles* and *Samuel;* Samuel, Charles).
Children, by second marriage:
2936+   Ambrose Ruel Sparhawk, born March 30, 1820.
2937   Rebecca Sparhawk, born 1822; died April, 1864, at
Gayville, N. Y.; married Henry McMaster of Augusta, Maine; two children (Frances, the eldest,
born 1850, died 1908; married William H. Williams,
a nephew of the statesman, Ruel Williams of Augusta, and had two children, *Annie Mayborn*, 1875-
1897, and *George Seth*, who married and has one
child; the second child was William H., 1861-1878).
2938   Nathaniel Sparhawk, born 1824, went to Marblehead,
Mass., married there, and his descendants live there.
2939+   Reuben Roland Sparhawk, born 1825.
2939a   Jacob A. Sparhawk, born 1830; enlisted at Rockland,
Me. 1861, in the Civil War; was taken prisoner, and
died August 15, 1861, at Richmond, Va. of wounds.

1158   BETSEY[6] TYLER (Nathaniel[5]), born probably
in Augusta, Maine; married (1), Samuel Dilling; married (2),
—— Huntoon.

Child, by first marriage:
2940   Samuel T. Dilling.

Child, by second marriage:
2941   Chesman T. Huntoon, moved to California; married,
had two children.

1160   REBECCA[6] TYLER (Nathaniel[5]), died in Michigan; married Samuel J. Wellman, of Ohio and Michigan.
Children:
2942   Rebecca Tyler Wellman, married Joseph Rowe; had
seven children.
2943   Jane T. Wellman, married Samuel Mills; six children.
2944   Joseph T. Wellman, married Mary ——; five children.
2945   (Captain) Chauncey T. Wellman, married Melvina
——; one child; resided in California.

2946 John Tyler Wellman, married Mercia Towle; two children.

1162 JOHN[6] TYLER (Joseph[5]), born in Newburyport, Mass., April 8, 1783; died in Greenbush, N. Y., March 20, 1834; married (1), Lucy Woodbury, of Mt. Vernon, N. Y.; married (2), 1812, Patience Hazard, of Hudson, N. Y.

CHILDREN, by first marriage:
2947+ John Woodbury Tyler.
2948 William Tyler; died unmarried.
2949 Porter Tyler; in 1860 was railway agent in Greenbush, N. Y.; he was married.
2950 George Tyler; died in infancy.

CHILDREN, by second marriage:
2951 Frances Tyler, born in Greenbush, N. Y., Dec., 1814, in one of the oldest houses in America, now preserved by the Albany Society of Colonial Dames. The house, built in 1642, was preserved as a fort and manor house until 1740, when it was transformed into a dwelling house. It was General Abercrombie's headquarters in the French and Indian War and near it " Yankee Doodle " was composed. On her mother's side Frances Tyler was related to Commodore Oliver Hazard Perry, the hero of Lake Erie. Miss Tyler lived in Cleveland during her last year, and was known to have been living in 1897.
2952 Abby Tyler, born in Greenbush, Jan., 1816; died in 1850.
2953 Mary Tyler; died.
2954+ Joshua Tyler.
2955 Emily Tyler; died.
2956 Lucy Tyler; died.

1167 PHILIP[6] TYLER (Joseph[5]), born in Newburyport, Mass., April 9, 1793; died in Charlestown, Mass., October 11, 1880; married, May 3, 1821, in Chelmsford, Mass., Nancy Hunting, a native of that place. The children were born in Charlestown. Children:

2957   Philip Tyler, Jr., born March 2, 1822; died Oct. 14, 1822.

2958+ Abby Tyler, born Aug. 10, 1823.

2959   Almira Tyler, born Dec. 1, 1824; died s. p. May 28, 1845.

2960   Nancy Mariah Tyler, born Nov. 15, 1826; died March 25, 1856; married, May, 1849, Charles Hurd, of Andover or Haverhill, Mass., who was a farmer; one son.

2961   Joseph Tyler, born March 6, 1829; left home Dec. 25, 1850, and probably went to Kentucky.

2962   Irena Tyler, born Jan. 26, 1831; died, s. p., Jan. 2, 1851

2963+ George Emery Tyler, born Nov. 26, 1832.

2964   Philip Hunting Tyler, born Jan. 28, 1835; married, Nov. 29, 1862, Georgianna Howard Cole; resides, s. p., in Wellesley Hills, Mass. He was in the Civil War as first lieutenant of the 3d Mass. Battery, Light Artillery; discharged Oct. 11, 1862.

2965+ Thomas Rea Tyler, born May 6, 1837.

1168 WILLIAM[6] TYLER (Joseph[5]), born in Cambridge, Mass., August 14, 1795; died in Billerica, Mass., November 27, 1861; married his cousin, Jane Spaulding, born in Wilmington, N. C., October 25, 1797; died in Peterboro, N. H., April 19, 1883; daughter of Philip Spaulding, son of Colonel Simeon Spaulding. William Tyler kept a public tavern. The children were born in Billerica. Children:

2966+ George Spaulding Tyler, born March 20, 1830.

2967+ William Tyler, born Feb. 28, 1833.

1170 CAPTAIN JONATHAN[6] SPALDING (Phebe[5]), born in Chelmsford, Mass., June 12, 1775; died April 17, 1864; married, March 11, 1819, Sarah Dodge; born August 8, 1787; died January 12, 1837; daughter of Simeon and Abigail (Cook) Dodge. He was a member of the state legislature in 1833. The children were born in Chelmsford. Children:

2968   (Doctor) Joel Spaulding, born March 2, 1820; was 40 years a doctor in Lowell, Mass., where he died Jan. 30, 1888.

2969   Jonathan Spalding, born Nov. 15, 1821; died Dec.
        27, 1826.
2970   John Spalding, born Sept. 21, 1823; died Feb. 9, 1825.
2971   Sarah Rebecca Spalding, born Sept. 10, 1825; living
        in Lowell on the old homestead near Pawtucket
        Falls, in the late '90's, with whose death the line of
        Phebe Tyler and Joel Spalding becomes extinct.
2972   George Otis Spalding, born Aug. 11, 1827; died July
        17, 1828.
2973   Jonathan Tyler Spalding, born Oct. 4, 1829; died in
        Lowell, May 26, 1872; was a merchant in Boston
        for more than 20 years.

    1185 NATHAN[6] TYLER, JR. (Nathan[5]), born in Mid-
dlesex Village, Mass., January 25, 1792; died there February
23, 1868; married (published November 3, 1838), December
2, 1838, Mary Ann Perham, of Chelmsford, Mass., born January, 1801; died December 8, 1887. He was a farmer and
cooper.   Child:
2974   Mary Elizabeth Tyler, born in Chelmsford, Sept. 9,
        1841; was unmarried.

    1186 CAPTAIN SILAS[6] TYLER (Nathan[5]), born in
Middlesex Village, Mass., June 2, 1795; died in Lowell, Mass.,
May 20, 1875; married Fannie Stanley, of Dracut, Mass.
" Mr. Silas Tyler followed the Merrimack many years as pilot,
and was connected with the Middlesex Canal for 20 years,
being for several years captain of the packet boat *Gov. Sullivan* . . . [with] the opening of the Boston & Lowell
Railway and the consequent abandonment of the canal navigation, about 1835, his connection ceased. Mr. Tyler believed
that with an enlargement this canal could have successfully
competed with the railroad. . . ." The children were born
in Middlesex Village.   Children:
2975   Silas Tyler, born June 24, 1820; died Dec. 7, 1868;
        married, in Attleboro, Mass., May 7, 1851, Maria
        Tifft, of Attleboro; daughter of John and Azubah
        Tifft; no children.
2976+   Artemas Stanley Tyler, born Nov. 2, 1824.

    1188 WILLIAM[6] TYLER (Nathan[5]), born in Middlesex Village, Mass., February 11, 1799; died in Chelmsford, Mass., February 8, 1854; married (published November 29, 1848), Mary Ann Butterfield, born in Ludlow, Vt., November 15, 1810. He lived on a farm in Middlesex Village. The children were born in Chelmsford. Children:

2977   William Otis Tyler, born Nov. 11, 1849; died in 1876.
2978+ Julia Ann Tyler, born March 16, 1851.

1189 SAMUEL[6] TYLER (Nathan[5]), born in Middlesex Village, Mass., June 14, 1803; died there April 8, 1874; married, June 13, 1850, Mary Ann D. Sanders, born in Cambridgeport, Mass., January 17, 1823; daughter of Richard and Sally (Kneeland) Sanders, who came from Abington, England, to Boston, about 1800. Samuel lived on a farm in Middlesex Village. Child:

2979   Susan Emma Tyler, born in Chelmsford, Mass., Sept. 2, 1852; resides unmarried in Lowell. In disposing of a large tract of their land in Lowell, Miss Tyler and her mother reserved a generous piece of wood and field and gave it to the city, the place to be called "Tyler Park." This territory contains about 80,000 feet, and is surrounded by ample streets.

1191 CAPTAIN IGNATIUS[6] TYLER (Nathan[5]), born in Middlesex Village, Mass., July 5, 1804; died in Bedford Springs, N. H., August 25, 1889; married (1) (published November 10, 1833), Mary Lund, of Milford, N. H., who died January, 1868; married (2), 1869, Sarah Frances Stevens, of Mt. Vernon, N. H. He "had an uninterrupted connection with the Merrimack and canals from his youth and was for a long time engaged in the lumber trade in Lowell . . . When the steamboat enterprise on the Merrimack was started . . . he was captain of the fine little freight and passenger steamer that plied between Lowell and Nashau and for some years managed an immense carrying trade via the river and the Middlesex Canal, between Concord and all northern New Hampshire and Boston. He was, like his brother Silas, long connected with the Middlesex Canal, and his employment on the river gave him a familiarity with all the canals around the falls above Lowell." The children were born in Lowell.

CHILDREN:

2980+   Frank Ignatius Tyler, born Aug. 29, 1835.

2981+   George Otis Tyler, born Sept. 18, 1838.

2982   Maria Tyler, born Nov., 1842; died June 8, 1891; married William H. Parker, of Montreal, Canada; a lumber dealer; no children.

1192 FANNY⁶ TYLER (Nathan⁵), born in Middlesex Village, Mass., July, 1807; died in Portland, Maine, February 22, 1875; married Lucius Whipple, born October 16, 1799; died February 28, 1848. The Whipples were powder manufacturers in Lowell, Mass., from 1827. Lucius was sent to Gorham, Maine, to take charge of a branch. The two younger children were born in Windham, Maine. Children:

2983   Lucius Hasham Whipple, born Feb. 12, 1829; died Feb. 23, 1858; married Charlotte Gilson.

2984   William Warren Whipple, born in Lowell, Feb. 29, 1832; married, Nov. 3, 1864, Frances Elizabeth Strout, born Dec. 1, 1842; lived in Portland, Maine, and had twin sons (Farrington H. and Clayton T.).

2985   Mary Elizabeth Whipple, born in Gorham, Maine, Sept. 23, 1835; married Ira P. Farrington.

2986   Harrison Tyler Whipple, born May 21, 1840; married, June 2, 1875, Apphia W. Judd; lived in Portland, Maine, and had two daughters (Elizabeth and Jeannett).

2987   Garaphelia Adelaide Whipple, born Sept. 20, 1841; died April 20, 1842.

1201 MEHITABLE⁶ TYLER (James⁵), born in Pepperellboro (now Saco), Maine, April 20, 1779; married Stephen Seavey, of Saco, where their children were born. Children:

2988   John Seavey, born Sept. 16, 1807.

2989   Olive Seavey, born March 13, 1809.

2990   Thomas Seavey, born Nov. 3, 1811.

2991   Caroline Seavey, born Feb. 5, 1814.

2992   Allison Seavey, born July 19, 1817.

1204 HANNAH⁶ TYLER (James⁵), born in Pepperellboro, now Saco, Maine, March 7, 1784; married, September 26, 1807, John Moulton, of Scarboro, Maine, baptized July 7, 1782; died suddenly, aged 30. Child:

2993   Mary Moulton, born Oct. 9, 1808; married Edward Milliken.

1206 JAMES⁶ TYLER (James⁵), born in Pepperellboro (now Saco), Maine, January 1, 1787; died August 2, 1858; married, February 22, 1816, Deborah Cushing, born June 12, 1791, in Exeter, N. H. He settled in " Ossipee Gore," now Freedom, N. H.   He was of more than ordinary ability; he held town offices and was state representative.   It was said of him that his judgment was clear and safe to be relied upon and that he was a judicious and successful farmer.   Children:

2994   Peter Tyler, born March 24, 1817; died in childhood.
2995+   Abram Tyler, born July 6, 1818.
2996+   John L. Tyler, born Feb. 19, 1821.
2997+   Wentworth Tyler, born Oct. 16, 1823.
2998   Lydia S. Tyler, born May 14, 1827; married Daniel Harmon.

1208 ABRAHAM⁶ TYLER (James⁵), born in Pepperellboro (now Saco), Maine, March 7, 1793; died suddenly, April, 1861; married Eunice Seavey, born March 31, 1797. The old records of " Pepperellboro " state that he was known as " Captain Abe " and was a conspicuous figure on " General Muster day," being a large man with a fine figure.   He lived at the " Heath " in Saco, where the children were born.   Children:

2999+   James Tyler, born Nov. 6, 1815.
3000   David Libby Tyler, born 1820; drowned in Penobscot River, Nov. 4, 1845, aged 25 years and 6 months. These dates are given on a stone on the farm in " Heath," Saco, no other Tyler stones there.   He was unmarried.
3001+   Andrew Tyler, born March 16, 1822.
3002+   Lydia S. Tyler, born Oct. 15, 1828.

1211 CAPTAIN ANDREW⁶ TYLER (Andrew⁵), born in Frankfort, Maine, September 30, 1793; died there intestate December 26, 1864; married, May 17, 1831, Ann Louise Wall-ing, of New York City, born March 26, 1811; died in Frankfort, intestate, July 27, 1875, aged 64 years and 4 months. Captain Andrew's estate was probated in Belfast, Maine, his widow being administratrix, with bond of $8000. The inventory of his estate was $3,448. The children were all probably born in Frankfort, except the eldest. Children:

3003+   Ann Eliza Tyler, born in New York City April 5, 1833.

3004   Matilda Stout Tyler, born Oct. 5, 1834; married, June 7, 1860, Rev. James G. Roberts, of Illinois; lives in Brooklyn, N. Y.; four children (Jacob H., Charles H., Louise, Grace S.).

3005   (Captain) Andrew J Tyler, born Feb. 8, 1836; died unmarried at sea, about 1864.

3006   Hannah Amanda Tyler, born Sept. 30, 1838; married, Jan. 3, 1872, George W. Hammatt; born in Portland, Maine, April 26, 1825; son of George and Mary Farley Hammatt, of Plymouth, Mass.; no children.

3007   Sarah Gordon Tyler, born April 7, 1840; married, Jan. 28, 1864, Edwin P. Treat, who died; was a mariner and merchant; had two sons (Edwin F. and Forrest).

3008   William Robertson Tyler, born Nov. 16, 1841; died unmarried in Frankfort Feb. 23, 1889; he left a will in which he bequeathed his right in the Tyler farm in Frankfort to his brothers and sisters; estate was probated in Belfast. He was a mariner.

3009   Charles Frederick Gordon Tyler, born Dec. 24, 1843; a mariner, unmarried; resided in Frankfort in 1897.

3010   Robert Treat Tyler, born Oct. 19, 1846; resided in Frankfort in 1897; was postmaster four years, and was state representative; he was a mariner and farmer; went round the world twice.

3011   Frank Leslie Tyler, born Aug. 3, 1848; married Martha Hutchinson; was a mariner; no children; administrator of mother's estate.

3012   John Louis Tyler, born May 5, 1853; died in Frankfort May 1, 1875, unmarried.

1214   SALLY[6] TYLER (Andrew[5]), born in Frankfort, Maine, April 15, 1798; died in Searsport, Maine, October 10,

1839; married, January 6, 1828, Captain Charles Gordon, born in Exeter, N. H., December 2, 1794; died January 12, 1873; son of Joseph Gordon and grandson of James Gordon, of Exeter, both soldiers of the Revolution, and descended from Alexander Gordon, who came from Scotland to Exeter in 1660. (Captain Charles married [2], October 17, 1841, Mrs. Eliza W. Perkins, born Jones, in Castine, Maine, October 27, 1808. By his second marriage he had a son, Charles F. Gordon). Captain Gordon moved to Belfast in 1798; he was a bank cashier; he took part in the War of 1812; became a leading citizen of Searsport when it was set off from Belfast. He represented Belfast in 1835-1836, and later represented Searsport in the state legislature. The children were born in Belfast.

CHILDREN:

3013 (Captain) John Gordon, killed while in command of gunboat *Reno*, near Newburn, N. C., Oct. 7, 1864.

3014 Charles Gordon, lost at sea Oct. 1, 1841.

3015 Andrew Gordon, a mariner; died unmarried in Havana, Dec 28, 1855; in the West India trade.

3016 Anne Gordon, died in Boston, May 13, 1898; married, Oct. 12, 1867, Edward B. Sheldon, who lost his right arm in the Battle of Gettysburg; he was postmaster of Searsport 1869-1885; patent officer in Washington under Harrison; has a son (Charles G.), who is an optician in Exeter, N. H.

CHILD, by second wife:

3017 Charles Frederick Gordon, born May 7, 1813. He was treasurer of the Searsport Savings Bank and cashier of the National Bank there; also treasurer of the Board of Trade; and has been selectman; unmarried.

1216 JOHN⁶ TYLER (Dominicus⁵), born probably about 1797; married Hannah Coburn; resided in Winterport, Maine. Children:

3018 Daughter.

3019 Edgar Tyler, a mariner, died, unmarried, at sea.

3020 Anna Tyler.

3021 Daughter.

1218 CAPTAIN ALLISON[6] TYLER (Dominicus[5]),
born in Scarboro, Maine, 1800; died in California intestate,
1850; married, January 20, 1824, Jane Nichols, of Searsport,
Maine; daughter of James and Nancy (Fowler) Nichols.   He
was a captain of militia.   He moved to Frankfort, thence to
Prospect, Maine, and in the time of the gold excitement he
went to California.   His estate was probated in Belfast, Maine,
July 11, 1851, the widow being appointed administratrix.   The
children were born in Prospect.   Children:
3022   Alice J. Tyler, born Nov. 12, 1825; married Josiah
        Black, of Searsport, Maine, she resided there a
        widow, s. p.
3023   Caroline Tyler, born Sept. 30, 1827; married George
        Gould; resided a widow, s. p., in Dixmont, Maine.
3024   Nancy Tyler, born Dec. 19, 1829; died young.
3025   Abbie Tyler, born March 7, 1832; married Oliver
        Clark; resided a widow in Searsport with one daugh-
        ter (Sarah J.), who was unmarried.
3026   Andrew Tyler, born May 18, 1835; died young.
3027   Woodburn Tyler, born July 4, 1836; married Nov. 11,
        1860, Hannah B. Cunningham, of Searsport, daugh-
        ter of William and Mary (McNelly) Cunningham.
        He was a farmer and stonecutter and resided in
        Swanville, Maine; they had one child, who died in
        infancy.
3028+   Andrew Tyler, born Aug. 11, 1838.
3029   Nancy A. Tyler, born Sept. 30, 1843; died unmarried
        aged about 19.
3030   Angeline B. Tyler, born Aug. 20, 1845; married Henry
        Nichols, a mariner, of Searsport, Maine, who died;
        four children (Levi, Oliver, Oscar, Andrew).
3031   Josephine E. Tyler, born Oct. 2, 1847; married Henry
        Wilson, of Grinnell, Iowa, where they lived; two
        children (Henry, Fanny).

1219 SALLY[6] TYLER (Dominicus[5]), born in Frankfort or Scarboro, Maine; married Thomas Seavey, a farmer of
Frankfort.   Children:
3032   Harris Seavey.
3033   Nathaniel Seavey; died unmarried in Frankfort.
3034   Obed Seavey, went to California.

3035 John Seavey.

3036 Esther Seavey, died unmarried.

3037 Sarah Seavey, married (1), Hiram Holmes; married (2), James Lord.

3038 Abby Seavey, died young, unmarried.

1220 MEHITABLE[6] TYLER (Dominicus[5]), born in Frankfort, Maine; married Daniel Waldron, a farmer, of Frankfort. Children:

3039 Nathaniel Waldron.

3040 Charles Waldron.

3041 William Waldron; resided in Rockland, Maine.

3042 George Waldron.

3043 Russell Waldron.

3044 Sidney Waldron.

3045 James Waldron.

3046 Jane Waldron.

3047 Mary Waldron.

1221 ABIGAIL[6] TYLER (Dominicus[5]), born in Frankfort, Maine; married Joseph Blethen, a farmer, of Frankfort. Children:

3048 John Blenthen, resided in South Thomaston, Maine.

3049 Joseph Blenthen, resided in Frankfort.

3050 Washington Blenthen.

1222 ELSIE[6] TYLER (Dominicus[5]), born in Scarboro or Frankfort, Maine; married, November, 1830, Captain John Philbrooks, Jr., born September 26, 1803. He was of Winterport, Maine, and followed the sea for 40 years; he was living in 1892. Children:

3051 John Philbrooks, born in Isleboro, Maine, Sept. 21, 1831; died unmarried.

3052 Betsey Philbrooks, born May 5, 1833; died in 1842.

3053 Martin Varnum Philbrooks, born June 21, 1836; a mariner, of Frankfort; married and had a family.

3054 Isaac Philbrooks, born April 16, 1838; a mariner, of Frankfort, unmarried.

3055 Rinaldo Philbrooks, born Nov. 14, 1841; a sea-captain, of Chelsea, Mass.

3056   Lorenzo Philbrooks, resided, s. p., in Newburyport, Mass.

3057   Darius Philbrooks, a mariner and stonecutter, of Frankfort.

3058   Martha Philbrooks, married Jackson Curtis, of Monroe, Maine; no children.

1240   BENJAMIN[6] TYLER (Abraham[5]), born in Scarboro, Maine. He was in the War of 1812 (*Pension Book*, p. 65, No. 11). He married, but his wife's name is unknown. He had eight boys and three girls; the names of four only are known. Children:

3059+   Albion P. Tyler.

3060   Benjamin S. Tyler, lived in Fiddletown, Cal.

3061   John A. Tyler, lived in Guilford, Maine; had a son (Frank A.).

3062   Nancy B. Tyler, married —— Brown.

1244   WILLIAM[6] TYLER (John Smith[5]), born in Cape Elizabeth, Maine, January 9, 1791; died in Auburn, Maine, January 27, 1872; married, in Pownal, Maine, October 1, 1813, Judith B. Currier, born in Durham, Maine, May 31, 1789; died in Auburn, Maine, November 17, 1869. He was a farmer. He had a land grant in Pownal from Zebulon Trickey, September 14, 1821. He resided in Pownal and his children were born there. Children:

3063+   Joseph Currier Tyler, born July 9, 1814.

3064+   Mary Ann Tyler, born May 29, 1816.

3065   Elinor Johnson Tyler, born July 16, 1818; married (1), Henry Toby, of Cape Elizabeth, Maine; married (2), Isaac Allen; had two children (George and Lizzie) who died.

3066   Rebecca Trickey Tyler, born Sept. 21, 1820; died unmarried in Pownal, June 1, 1842.

3067   Sarah Folansbee Tyler, born March 23, 1823; died unmarried in Pownal, Jan. 19, 1846.

3068+   Irene Graves Tyler, born Aug. 10, 1825.

3069   Abbie Goodwin Tyler, born July 29, 1827; died in Durham, Maine, Aug. 8, 1881; married in Haverhill, Elbridge Palmer; had one child (Austin Avery), who lives in Haverhill.

3070+   Emeline Elizabeth Tyler, born Sept. 20, 1829.

1245 REBECCA[6] TYLER (John Smith[5]), born in Scarboro, Maine, July 30, 1792; died October 5, 1832; married Cyrus Jones, who died June 18, 1846. Children:

3071   Edward Jones, born Nov. 21, 1817; died Nov. 30, 1817.

3072   Martha Jones, born Dec. 11, 1819; died Feb. 29, 1847; married Lowell Clapp and had three sons and a daughter.

3073   Lucy Ann Jones, born Nov. 25, 1822; married, Aug. 11, 1842, Captain Peter W. Brown; they had two daughters and a son.

3074   Louisa Jones, born Nov. 8, 1824; died Sept. 16, 1839.

3075   Emery Jones, born Sept. 16, 1827; married, May 1, 1851, Eunice C. Merrill, resided South Freeport, Maine; he was a ship carver; they had five sons and a daughter.

3076   Wesley Jones, born June 1, 1830; died Aug. 30, 1894; married Sophia P. Jones; resided in Portland, Maine; one daughter.

1246 ZEBULON[6] TYLER (John Smith[5]), born (probably) in Hiram, Maine, March 12, 1794; died in Durham, Maine, July 12, 1824; married, April 3, 1821, Betsey Ferguson, who died in Northport, Wis., May 10, 1881. The children were born in Durham. Children:

3077   George Ferguson Tyler, born Sept. 3, 1822; died April 19, 1824.

3078+   Zebulon Tyler, Jr., born March 6. 1824.

1248 EVELINE[6] TYLER (John Smith[5]), born in Scarboro, Maine, October 2, 1798; died in Portland, Maine, May 17, 1893; married, September 30, 1821, Johnson Libby, of Scarboro, born February 4, 1797; died February 5, 1845; son of Captain Joshua and Ruth (Libby) Libby. He was lame and kept a store. In her girlhood, she lived west with her uncle Trickey. The children were born in Scarboro. (For Libby Family see *Collections of Maine Historical Society*, Vol. IV, p. 68.) Children:

3079   Eliza Ann Libby, born Feb. 15, 1822; died Sept. 30, 1874; married Thomas Skillings, of Gray, Maine, and had nine children.

3080+ Lucy Tyler Libby, born May 30, 1823.

3081+ Zebulon Tyler Libby, born Jan. 23, 1825.

3082   Horace B. Libby, born Oct. 19, 1827; died Feb., 1901;
       married (1), Mary Townsend; married (2), Lizzie
       Stevens; married (3), Mary Stetson; by second mar-
       riage he had a son (Frank); resided in Randolph,
       Mass.

3083   Addison Libby, born Aug. 8, 1830; married (1), Lizzie
       Kilburn; married (2), Marcia Lawrence; had three
       daughters.

3084+ John Tyler Libby, born April 29, 1832.

3085   Granville Libby, born March 21, 1834; married (1),
       Amanda Richards; married (2), Nettie Cortland;
       by first marriage four children; resided in Pleasant-
       dale, Maine.

3086   Charles S. Libby, born July 17, 1836; married Georgia
       Hasty; three children; resides in Pleasantdale, Me.

3087   Phebe H. Libby, born Aug. 23, 1838; died March 25,
       1853.

   1250   JOHN[6] TYLER (John Smith[5]), born in Pownal,
Maine, October 2, 1803; died in Pownal March 27, 1874; mar-
ried, October 27, 1833, Zilpha Pond, of Paris, Maine, born
May 16, 1806; in 1897 resided with son John in Pownal.
John was a ship carpenter and farmer. The children were
born in Pownal. Children:

3088   Flora Tyler, born Feb. 20, 1836; unmarried.

3089   Amanda Tyler, born May 13, 1838; died July 25,
       1862; unmarried.

3090+ Morseen G. Tyler, born Feb. 1, 1841.

3091   Elbridge O. Tyler, born Jan. 29, 1843; resided, unmar-
       ried, in Pownal, a house-joiner and farmer.

3092   Joseph E. Tyler, born Oct. 25, 1845; died unmarried
       Sept. 11, 1867.

   1252   LUCY[6] TYLER (John Smith[5]), born after 1806
in Scarboro, Maine; married —— Roberts, of Durham, Maine,
where the children were born. Children:

3093   Nehemiah Roberts.

3094   John Roberts, living in Freeport, Maine, in 1897.

3095 Harriet Roberts, married —— Brown; lived in Yarmouth, Maine.
3096 Sarah Roberts, married —— Libby; lived in Yarmouth, Maine.
3097 Henry Roberts.
3098 Mary Roberts.
3099 Frank Roberts, died in the Civil War.
3100 Helen Roberts, married —— Stetson; lived in Iowa.

1253 SOPHIA ANN⁶ TYLER (John Smith⁵), born after 1806; married Samuel Newell; in 1897 resided a widow in Lisbon, Maine. Children:
3101 Harriet Newell.
3102 Elizabeth Newell.
3103 Rosco Newell.
3104 Zebulon Newell.
3105 Edwin Newell.
3106 Frank Newell.
3107 Everett Newell.
3108 Alfreda Newell.

1260 EUNICE⁶ TYLER (David⁵), born in Freedom or Bowdeinham, Maine; died November 5, 1831; married, August 11, 1811, Abraham Libby, born July 1, 1785; in Scarboro, Maine; son of Josiah and Sarah (Libby) Libby; lived in Pownal, Maine. Children:
3109 Zebulon Libby, born Dec. 1, 1813; was unmarried; burned to death in a logging camp.
3110 David Tyler Libby, born Oct. 31, 1815; married Hannah L. True.
3111 Phineas Libby, born May 1, 1817; married (1), Mary A. Waldron; married (2), Nancy A. Noyes.
3112 (Captain) Alfred Cotton Libby, born Dec. 22, 1818; married Elizabeth Libby.
3113 Cyrus Libby, born Oct. 23, 1821; married Julia P. Goddard.
3114 Charles Libby, born Feb. 19, 1823; married Lucy Ann Doan.

....1261 ORVILLE⁶ TYLER (David⁵), born in Freeport, Maine, 1806; died December 23, 1852, intestate, in Troy,

Maine; married Abigail Leonard, born in Albion, Maine, March, 1800; died 1884. His estate was probated in Belfast, Maine, and the inventory was $2253.50; the widow was appointed administratrix. The two elder children were born in Freedom, N. H.; the two younger in Troy, Maine. Children:

3115   Delia M. Tyler; died in infancy.

3116   Ann Mariah Tyler, born 1834; died unmarried 1862.

3117+   George M. Tyler, born in Unity, Maine, Jan. 27, 1837.

3118   Sarah J. Tyler, born 1842; married N. W. Barker, of Troy, Maine.

3119   Thomas S. Tyler, born 1848; married Louise Barker; lived in Troy, where a farmer and selectman.

1263   MAJOR[6] TYLER (David[5]), born probably in Freedom, Maine; died there intestate in 1840, having been drowned; estate was probated in Belfast, Maine; inventory, $1066.74; wife Rebecca was administratrix. He was a farmer. Children:

3120   Charles Tyler, resided in Albion, Maine; has a son (Frank).

3121   Major Tyler, Jr., resided in Albion, Maine, s. p.

1266   LENDELL[6] TYLER (Daniel[5]), born in Gorham, Maine, August 28, 1805; married Sally Whitney. Children:

3122   Robert B. Tyler, resided in Calais, Maine (Milltown); married ——— s. p.

3123   Harrison Tyler, resided Federalsburg, Md.; married ——— s. p.

3124   Lendell Tyler, Jr., died unmarried in Calais, Maine, 1888.

3125   Emma Tyler, living unmarried in Calais (Milltown).

1267   MARY E.[6] TYLER (Daniel[5]), born in Gorham, Maine, July 2, 1807; died ———; married Daniel R. Mattocks, of Belfast, Maine. Children:

3126   Martha Mattocks, married Jonas Ferguerson, a mariner, of Belfast.

3127   Sarah Mattocks, married Samuel Gilbreth, mariner, of Belfast.

3128   Mary Ann Mattocks, married Slathy Otis; her daughter (Abbie) married Dr. Augustus Kilgore.
3129   Samuel Mattocks.

1269   SALLY[6] TYLER (Daniel[5]), born in Gorham, Maine, August 16, 1811; married David L. Hosmer, a blacksmith, in Bangor, Maine.   Children:
3130   Helen Hosmer; married Daniel Fernald, a mason, of Bangor, Maine.
3131   Thomas Hosmer.
3132   Martha Hosmer.
3133   Mary Augusta Hosmer.
3134   Sarah Frances Hosmer.

1271   EMILY[6] TYLER (Daniel[5]), born in Gorham, Maine, August 27, 1818; married John Shales, a machinist, of Boston, Mass., who died in Belfast, Maine.   Children:
3135   William Henry Shales; died unmarried in Libby Prison, in the Civil War.
3136   Lendell Tyler Shales, married Emma Woods; had a son and daughter.
3137   Arthur Shales; died young.

1273   MARTHA[6] TYLER (Daniel[5]), born in Gorham, Maine; married (1), Elijah Hunt, a blacksmith, of Belfast, Maine; married (2), Jeremiah Evans, a farmer, of Waldo, Maine.

CHILDREN, by first marriage:
3138   Emily Hunt, married Captain John Richardson, Portland, Maine.
3139   John Hunt, resided unmarried in Waldo, Maine.

CHILD, by second marriage:
3140   Edward Evans, resided in Waldo, Maine.

1274   JOHN[6] TYLER (Samuel[5]), born in Saco, Maine, March 27, 1800; died in Hartford, Maine, May 21, 1855; married Abigail E. Parsons, of Hartford, who died September 8, 1894.   He moved with his widowed mother to Hartford in 1820, where his children were born.   Children:
3141   William J. Tyler, born Feb. 12, 1838; died May 17,

1889; he was unmarried; enlisted in 1861 in Company C, 23d Maine Infantry, and served one year; was totally disabled and drew a pension.

3142+ Mary C. Tyler, born April 27, 1839.

3143+ Dorcas L. Tyler, born April 26, 1840.

3144+ John F. Tyler, born July 31, 1842.

3145 Edmond S. Tyler, born July 4, 1844.

3146 Hannah L. Tyler, born March 4, 1846; died Sept. 28, 1876; married, 1868, Clifton Jones, of Canton, Maine; had one son (Fred T.) who died.

3147 Lucy B. Tyler, born Jan. 12, 1848; married, April 13, 1883, Walter Farrar, of Paris, Maine; no children.

1275 GRACE[6] TYLER (Samuel[5]), born in Saco, Maine, September 9, 1802; married, February 17, 1828, Daniel Cluff, of Saco, where their children were born. Children:

3148 Samuel Cluff.

3149 Daniel Cluff.

3150 Nancy Cluff.

1276 JAMES JOSSE[6] TYLER (Samuel[5]), born in Saco, Maine, April 20, 1805; died in North Buckfield, Maine, July 17, 1890; married, April, 1831, Harriet Bisbee, of Sumner, Maine. He was a farmer, and moved about 1820 to Hartford, Maine, with his mother, after the death of his father; his three elder children were born there. Children:

3151+ Gilbert Tyler, born Feb. 5, 1832.

3152 Desire Drake Tyler, born July 14, 1833; died, s. p., Oct., 1856; married, Feb. 6, 1856, Simon A. Abbott, of Andover, Maine; no children.

3153+ Mary Emery Tyler, born Jan. 27, 1842.

3154 Harriet Bisbee Tyler, born in Turner, Maine, April 4, 1844; married (1), 1868, Loring Hunter, of Readfield, Maine, who died Feb., 1870; married (2), William C. Mooney, of West Paris, Maine, where she was living in 1899; had one son (Frank Herbert, born 1860; died 1870).

3155 Annette Rice Tyler, born June 13, 1847; died May 5, 1858.

1277 DORCAS[6] TYLER (Samuel[5]), born in Saco,

Maine, August 2, 1807; married Abram Parsons, of Lyndon, Maine. They had several children. Child:

3156 John Parsons, born in Lyndon, lived there in 1899.

1278 MARY STEPHENS[6] TYLER (Joseph[5]), born in Scarboro, Maine, October 13, 1785; died in Sebago, Maine; married, March 12, 1816, Reuben Cook, of Limington, Maine, who moved to Sebago where he died. Children:

3157 Ann Cook.
3158 Jane Cook.
3159 Jason Cook.
3160 Mary Ann Cook.
3161 Zilpha Cook.
3162 Albaronia Cook.

1279 BENJAMIN[6] TYLER (Joseph[5]), born in Limington, Maine, June 19, 1787; baptised in Scarboro, Maine, October 4, 1787; died May 24, 1852; married, December 13, 1813, Eunice Libby, born in Limington, July 4, 1795; daughter of Philemon and Martha (Small) Libby, an innkeeper. He was licenced as an innholder in East Baldwin, Maine, September 13, 1824; in 1825 he was chosen fence viewer and field driver; in 1826 highway surveyor. The children were born in Limington. Children:

3163 Martha Jane Tyler, born Oct. 16, 1814; died Aug. 30, 1875; married Sewell L. Murch (published in Baldwin, Maine, Nov. 1, 1846). They had one daughter (Mary Elizabeth).

3164 Mary B. Tyler, born Sept. 16, 1816; died Oct. 16, 1816.

3165+ Abraham Tyler, born Oct. 4, 1817.

3166+ James Edwin Tyler, born Dec. 3, 1819.

3167 Elizabeth N. Tyler, born Aug. 25, 1822; died July 17, 1825.

3168 Elizabeth N. Tyler, born Sept. 25, 1825; married (1), March, 1849, Charles Barker; married (2), James Smith; living in 1896 in Leeds, Maine; had four children (William, Mary E., Alphonso T., Charles) by first marriage and one daughter by second marriage (Elizabeth).

3169 Mary Libby Tyler, born July 4, 1829; died Aug. 14,

1879; married Walter Berry, of Baldwin, Maine (published July 20, 1850); had five children (Melville, Charles, Frank, Leonard W., Emily).

3170   Benjamin Francis Tyler, born June 19, 1831; died Nov. 30, 1832.

3171+   Benjamin Francis Tyler, born Jan. 19, 1834.

1280 ANNA[6] TYLER (Joseph[5]), born in Limington, Maine, November 2, 1788; died February 13, 1861; married (1), February 29, 1806, David Richardson, born in Limington, September 13, 1785; perished in his burning house, with his six-year-old son Isaac, 1822; son of David and Sarah (Wiley) Richardson. He first lived in Limington; from about 1811-1814 he lived in Standish, Maine. His widow was granted administration papers on his estate. (*York Probate Records*, Vols. 30 and 32.) She married (2), previous to June 13, 1826, Theophilus Waterhouse, who died November 14, 1847, aged 75. Her children were all by the first marriage and all were born in Limington except the second and third.

CHILDREN:

3172   David Richardson, born July 3, 1806; married Susan Libby.

3173   James M. Richardson, born in Standish, Jan. 4, 1811; married Maria L. B. Strout.

3174   Benjamin Richardson, born Aug 15, 1812; robbed and murdered in Texas in 1836; he was unmarried.

3175   Nathaniel Marshall Richardson, born June 10, 1814; married Mary McDonald.

3176   Isaac Richardson, born in 1816; burned March 22, 1822, with his father.

3177   Charlotte Richardson, born April 28, 1817; married Cyrus Fogg, of Limerick, Maine.

3178   John Colby Richardson, born 1818; died unmarried aged 18.

3179   Almira B. Richardson, born May 14, 1821; married, Jan. 17, 1841, Gilman Lougee, of Parsonfield, Me.

3180   Ann Maria Richardson, born Sept. 13, 1822; married, Sept. 29, 1841, Moses Strout, of Buxton, Maine, born in Limington, Jan. 20, 1818. They had three sons and three daughters, who all married. The eldest son (James) was mayor of Biddeford, Maine.

1281   ELIZABETH⁶ TYLER (Joseph⁵), born in Limington, Maine, April 10, 1791; married, January 4, 1816, John Bickford, of Buxton, Maine; born December 17, 1793; died in Sebago, Maine, 1874.   The children were born in Sebago. Children:

3181   William Bickford, born 1816; married Lucy Chadbourne.
3182   Joseph Bickford, born in 1818; married Sarah Davis.
3183   Elizabeth Bickford, born 1820; married Royal Tyler, No. 3188.
3184   Lydia Bickford, born 1822; died young.
3185   James Bickford, born 1824; married Sophronia Davis.
3186   Samuel Bickford, born 1826; married Ellen Hopkinson.

1282   JOSEPH⁶ TYLER (Joseph⁵), born in Scarboro, Maine, October 10, 1792; married November 20, 1814, Margaret Libby, of Limington, born June 3, 1796, daughter of Henry and Margaret (Meserve) Libby.   They settled in Baldwin, Maine, (after living in Limington for a time) where, in 1827, was licensed as an auctioneer; in 1828 licensed as a "retailer," and was chosen Tythingman.   He died in Pleasant Hill, Mo.   The two elder children were born in Limington. Children:

3187+   Freedom Tyler.
3188+   Royal Tyler, born in 1817.
3189+   Henry L. Tyler, born in Sebago, Maine.
3190   Lot Tyler, went west; married and had three children, all daughters; died and was buried in the Indian Territory.
3191+   Sylvester Tyler, born in Baldwin March 14, 1827.
3192+   William R. Tyler, born probably in Baldwin.
3193   Eliza Ann Tyler, born probably in Baldwin; died in Waverly, N. S.; married Charles Hayward, hotelkeeper; they had one son (Alonzo), who lives in Waverly.
3194   Margaret Jane Tyler, died unmarried in Baldwin, Maine, aged about 16.
3195   Jane Maria Tyler, married C. Calwell; lives in Ayer Junction, Mass.; no children.
3196   Mary Susan Tyler, married Perry Leland, of Ayer Junction; one daughter.

3197   Caroline Avilda Tyler, born probably in Baldwin; married Langdon Merrill, of Hopkinton, Mass., who died; had a son (William) who lives in Framingham, Mass.

1283   MARTHA[6] TYLER (Joseph[5]), born in Scarboro, Maine, December 30, 1794; died December 2, 1867; married Joshua Strout, of Raymond, Maine, who died August 26, 1831. The children were born in Raymond. Children:
3198   Mary A. Strout, born in Raymond, Dec. 18, 1816; died June 28, 1869.
3199   Syrena Strout, born Feb. 17, 1818; died Aug. 1, 1861.
3200   Jane Strout, born Aug. 15, 1819; died Sept. 25, 1870.
3201   Alonzo Strout, born Jan. 3, 1821.
3202   Albert Strout, born May 17, 1822.
3203   Edwin Strout, born March 25, 1824.
3204   Freeman Strout, born Sept. 17, 1825.
3205   Elizabeth Strout, born Oct. 25, 1827.
3206   Alberona Strout, born March 27, 1829; married Henry L. Tyler, No. 3189.
3207   James Strout, born July 20, 1830.
3208   Margaret Strout, born Jan. 26, 1832.

1284   ABRAHAM[6] TYLER (Joseph[5]), born in Limington, Maine, March 7, 1798; will dated January 23, 1834; probated in Saco, Maine, June 2, 1834; married (1), April 14, 1825, Dorothy Libby; born Aug. 20, 1805; daughter of Harvey and Sarah (Small) Libby, of Limington; married (2), Eliza Small (sister of his brother Daniel's wife), who married (2), sea-captain Wedgewood and moved to Farmington, Ill., where died. Abraham was a seaman and had a residence in East Baldwin, Maine, where in 1841 and 1842 he was highway surveyor. The children were born in Limington.

CHILDREN, by first marriage:
3209+   James Libby Tyler, born Aug. 14, 1825.
3210   Daniel W. Tyler, born 1828; died in Limington, Maine, s. p., 1890; married Abbie Howe, of Southboro, Mass.

CHILD, by second marriage:
3211+   Charles Abraham Tyler, born Jan. 22, 1834.

1285 REV. SAMUEL[6] TYLER (Joseph[5]), born in Limington, Maine, March 7, 1800; married, May 10, 1831, Emily Settler, of Cape Elizabeth, Maine, who lived in Sebago and died there, October 13, 1867. He was an " old-fashioned Baptist preacher "; was selectman and town clerk of Sebago. Children:

3212   Mary Frances Tyler, born in Watertown, Maine, March 30, 1832; died in Portland, Maine, May 4, 1894.

3213   Miriam L. Tyler, born in Lyman, Maine, July 10, 1834; married, Dec. 24, 1879, John C. Porter, who resides in Portland, Maine.

3214   Elizabeth J. Tyler, born in Woolwich, Maine, March 11, 1838; resides in Portland, Maine.

1286 CAPTAIN JAMES[6] TYLER (Joseph[5]), born in Scarboro or Limington, Maine, February 28, 1801; died at sea of fever; married ——. He sailed his own ship to South America for 20 years. He was buried in Baltimore, Md. Children:

3215   Moses Tyler.

3216   Samuel Tyler.

3217   Virginia Tyler; married —— Booth.

3218   Charles Tyler.

1287 JANE[6] TYLER (Joseph[5]), born in Scarboro, Maine, May 12, 1802; died in Braintree, Mass.; married Asa Coolbroth, who died in Braintree. Children:

3219   Wilson Coolbroth.

3220   Greenleaf Coolbroth.

1288 HON. DANIEL[6] TYLER (Joseph[5]), born in Limington, Maine, May 4, 1806; died in Washington, D. C., June 22, 1875; married, 1830, Lavinia Small, born July 25, 1807, in Limington, Maine; died in Brooklyn, N. Y., January 11, 1891. She was descended from Frances Small, of Falmouth (now Portland), Maine, 1630; her mother was descended from Colonel March, who commanded a brigade of Continental troops and was a descendant of the Earl of March of William Wallace times. He studied law and in 1833 was appointed postmaster for West Newfield, Maine; justice of the peace, 1835; represented York County in the state legislature, 1835-1839; identified politically with his life-long friend,

Hannibal Hamlin.   About 1840 removed to Limington, Maine,
where was postmaster, 1842.   He was sergeant and captain in
the militia, deputy-sheriff York County 1844.   About 1847
removed to Calais, Maine, where he practiced law.   Removed to
Wisconsin, Winnebago County, in 1856.   He and all his sons
were in the Civil War, in the Union Army, and he was a paymaster with General McClellan; about 1865 he removed to
Washington, D. C., and he was a district justice in the District of Columbia, 1870-1873.   The two elder children were
born in Limington; the next three in Newfield, and the youngest in Calais.

CHILDREN:

3221+   Charles Mellen Tyler, born 1831.

3222   Henry Dunreath Tyler, born June 2, 1834; married
        (1), Dec. 9, 1865, Mary Frances Clark, born Dec.
        7, 1843; died, s. p., Sept. 23, 1871; married (2),
        June 1, 1891, Lucy Hamilton Warner, niece of
        Senator Harris, of Albany, N. Y.; a writer of chil-
        dren's story-books.   He enlisted for the war in 1861
        and raised a company of sharpshooters.   Was cap-
        tain and major on General Hooker's staff.   He is
        a writer and public speaker; has written several
        poems: "Apostrophe to the Flag (1875); "Forty
        Years Ago" (Limington, Maine, Celebration);
        "Honored Kinsmen" (1891), and others.   He is a
        lawyer in New York City and a brilliant speaker.

3223   Daniel James Tyler, born in 1836; died in Liming-
        ton, from effects of wounds received in Texas, Oct.
        3, 1879; was unmarried.   He enlisted in Company
        F, 8th Maine Volunteers.

3224   John March Tyler, born 1838; twice married; no chil-
        dren.   Was in the Civil War, First sergeant, 18th
        Maine regiment.

3225   Harriet Newell Small Tyler, born 1840; died in Wash-
        ington, D. C., unmarried, April 13, 1865.

3226   Charlotte Lavinia Tyler, born May 3, 1851; married
        Solomon Rice Kilby, of Brooklyn, N. Y.   She is a
        writer on art, a newspaper correspondent, and a
        painter of merit.   Her husband was present at the
        performance in Ford's Theater the night Lincoln
        was shot.

1289 CAPTAIN JAMES[6] TYLER (Samuel[5]), born in Edgecombe, Maine, June 6, 1785; died there about 1862; married (1), —— Tripp, of Swansville, Maine, who left him; married (2), published 1835, Sally Rines, of Edgecombe. He lived in Westport Island, Maine, and Edgecombe. He was in the fishing business, and owned his boat. The first wife's children all went with her to Swansville, when the separation occurred, and they were all born in Edgecombe.

CHILDREN, by first marriage:

3227 Martha Tyler.
3228 Matilda Tyler.
3229 Nancy Tyler.
3230 Jane Tyler.
3231 Elvira Tyler.
3232 William Tyler.
3233 James Tyler.
3234 Jonathan Tyler.

CHILDREN, by second marriage:

3235 Betsey Tyler.
3236 Amy Ann Tyler; married, as his second wife, George Whitten, of Westport, Maine, and died.
3237 Alice Tyler, married George Whitten, of Westport, and died young, s. p.
3238 James Winthrop Tyler, said to have been lost on a monitor ·during the Civil War.
3239 Ezra Tyler.

1297 EZRA[6] TYLER (Samuel[5]), born in Edgecombe, Maine, May 27, 1804; died January 4, 1882; was knocked overboard and lost at sea; married Amy Davis, of New Sharon, Maine, born March 11, 1805. He resided in Westport, Maine. Apparently he left two children, Mrs. Phebe M. Fowler and Mrs. Mary Jane Whitten, of Westport, Maine, who are mentioned in his will, probated in Bath. Other beneficiaries under the will are John F. and Sarah A. Dow, of Bath, and Willie Tyler Flint, son of Charles N. Flint, of Bath, who is one of the executors; the other one is George W. Flint, of Collinsville, Conn. His children were born in Westport.

CHILDREN:

3240   Phebe Royal Tyler, born May 26, 1826; married ——
        Fowler, of Westport.
3241   William Henry Tyler, born Dec. 13, 1827; died young.
3242   Mary Jane Tyler, born Nov. 12, 1828; married ——
        Whitten.
3243   Bethiah Tyler, born July 27, 1830; died Jan. 6, 1833.
3244   Alice Ann Tyler, born Jan. 9, 1835.

1299 MARTHA⁶ TYLER (James⁵), born in Gorham,
Maine; married in Portland, Maine, Ephraim Bowers. The
children were born in Portland. Children:
3245   Caroline Bowers.
3246   Lucy Ellen Bowers, married, Nov. 18, 1855, George
        Gallison, of Portland, Maine; had six children, three
        daughters surviving (Clara E., Etta A., Ada C.).
3247   Henry F. Bowers, a railway engineer in Pennsylvania.

1300 MELINDA⁶ TYLER (James⁵), born in Portland,
Maine; married John B. White, of Portland, where the children
were born. Children:
3248   Mary Greenough White, married Cyrus Gallison, of
        Portland; had two daughters (Alice and Grace) and
        a son (Frank).
3249   Charles White, resided in California.

1306 SIMON HOUSTON⁶ TYLER (James⁵), born in
Gorham, Maine, 1820; died in San Francisco, Cal., 1878; married in Boston, Elizabeth Hildreth. He ran away from home,
and fought in the Black Hawk war three years. They had
three sons and a daughter, but we have records of only two
children. Children:

3250   Frank Tyler, born in San Francisco, July, 1854;
        married, in 1880, Ella Hall Morrison, daughter of
        John H. Morrison; had one daughter (Elizabeth,
        born 1883).
3251   Lizzie Tyler, was killed accidentally by a pistol shot,
        about 1880; she was unmarried.

1308 RUTH⁶ TYLER (Jacob⁵), born in Methuen, Mass., August 9, 1785; died March 5, 1860, in Nashua, N. H.; married, November 21, 1811, John Pettengill, born in Methuen, May 3, 1789; died in Nashua, N. H., August 19, 1867; son of John and Hannah (Burbank) Pettengill. The three younger children were born in Salem, N. H. Children:

3252   Ruth Tyler Pettengill, born Nov. 24, 1812; died Feb. 5, 1866, in Methuen, Mass.; married, Nov. 30, 1831, Elbridge M. Clark.

3253   Hannah Worcester Pettengill, born July 6, 1814; died Dec. 12, 1895, in Winfield, Kas.; married (1), Oct. 26, 1833, John C. Smith; married (2), April 2, 1839, Albert Hastings, of Methuen.

3254   John Edwin Pettengill, born May 4, 1816; died May 13, 1851, in Chelsea, Mass.; married, Dec. 22, 1842, Hannah M. Hoyt, of Nashua, N. H.

3255   Lydia Tyler Pettengill, born April 7, 1818; died Sept. 4, 1850, in Methuen, Mass.; married, Oct. 3, 1836, Alfred Clark, of Methuen, Mass.

3256   Phiomela Pettengill, born Feb. 26, 1820; died July 21, 1843, in Nashua, unmarried.

3257   Sarah Frances Pettengill, born in Salem, N. H., Dec. 11, 1822; died Jan. 16, 1895, in Chelsea, Mass.; married, Oct. 23, 1842, Eliphalet N. Badger, of Nashua.

3258   Mary Tyler Pettengill, born Sept. 14, 1824; married, April 17, 1845, John Cluff, of Methuen.

3259   Jane Pettengill, born July 13, 1827; married, Sept. 7, 1858, Lewis Kimball, of Nashua.

1309 LYDIA⁶ TYLER (Jacob⁵), born in Dracut, Mass., June 25, 1787; died September, 1816; married, 1808, Deacon Jesse Clark, of Tewksbury, Mass., who was born October 21, 1783; died December 20, 1866. Children:

3260   Abigail B. Clark, born March 4, 1810; died Oct. 30, 1838; married Thaddeus Osgood; lived in Methuen and had one daughter.

3261   John Clark, born Sept. 28, 1811; died Dec. 13, 1890; married Elizabeth R. Trull; lived in Tewksbury, and had two sons and two daughters.

3262   Jacob Clark, born Jan. 20, 1814; died Jan. 19, 1867;

married Jane Colcord; moved to Greenville, Ill.; no children.

3263 Jonathan Clark, twin to Jacob, died June 2, 1894; married Persis Whittier; lived in Winchester, Mass.; had three daughters.

1310 JOHN[6] TYLER (Jacob[5]), born in Methuen, Mass., September 12, 1790; died in Pelham, N. H., where he went early, August 8, 1855; married, February 24, 1814, Jemima Howe, born in Methuen, February 24, 1788; died in Cambridge, Mass., at home of her son, John M. Tyler, February 19, 1866. He was a farmer. The children were born in Pelham. Children:

3264+ John Milton Tyler, born July 20, 1816.
3265 Eliza Tyler, born July 30, 1819; died, unmarried, Nov. 14, 1869; moved to Cambridge in 1855.
3266+ Joseph Howe Tyler, born Feb. 11, 1825.

1313 SALLY[6] TYLER (Jacob[5]), born April 4, 1796; died April 15, 1822; married, May 12, 1821, Rev. Marcus Smith, A. M.; born June 15, 1790; died in Dunkirk, N. Y., July 1, 1871. He was a graduate of Middlebury, Vt. College, in 1818, and of Andover Theological School. Author of work on Systematic Theology, in 1837; he preached forty years. After his wife's death he married again, and was survived by a widow. Child:

3267+ Henry Martyn Tyler Smith, born in Winchester, Vt., Feb., 1822.

1315 VARNUM[6] TYLER (Jacob[5]), born June 11, 1797; died in Methuen, Mass., May 17, 1867; married, November 3, 1825 (published October, 1825), Charlotte Currier, who died September 29, 1868, aged 68. He was a farmer. Children:

3268 Jacob Tyler, born March 10, 1828; died Jan. 16, 1848; unmarried.
3269+ Sarah Elizabeth Tyler, born Sept. 23, 1835.
3270 Infant, died young.
3271 Infant, died young.
3272 Infant, died young.

1316 JEREMIAH⁶ TYLER (Jacob⁵), born in Methuen, Mass., January 11, 1799; his will was probated in Salem, Mass., August 26, 1859, case 55932; married, June 12, 1828, Thankful Church, of Pelham, N. H., who died there; her will was probated in Salem, in 1878, case 55944. He was a successful country merchant in Pelham, N. H., where he went early in life, but on account of ill health he retired about twenty years prior to his death and went to Newburyport, where he died. The inventory of his estate was as follows: real estate, $1,500; personal, $8,709.36. His wife had the most of the estate and left all of it to her daughter Hannah.

CHILDREN:

3273   John Hubbard Church Tyler, born Nov. 9, 1834; died unmarried, aged about 20.

3274   Hannah Farnum Tyler, born July 3, 1837; died April 10, 1895; *en route* to Jerusalem, and was buried at sea; had $600 left her in her father's will.

1321 WILLIAM⁶ TYLER (Jeremiah⁵), born in Woburn, Mass., October 1, 1789; died in Amesbury, Mass., March 6, 1868; married (1), April 20, 1819, Elizabeth Pillsbury, of Newburyport, Mass., who died September 28, 1833; married (2), May 26, 1841, Abiah Marshall of Tewksbury, Mass. He was a carpenter and resided in Georgetown, D. C. and Newburyport, Mass. His estate was administered upon in Salem, Mass., January 1, 1869.

CHILDREN, by first marriage:

3275+   Aphia Ann Russell Tyler, born in Georgetown, Nov. 22, 1820.

3276   William Pillsbury Tyler, born in Newburyport, June 6, 1824; died unmarried, July 19, 1848.

3277   Frances Elizabeth Tyler, born in Amesbury, Dec. 15, 1828.

3278   Ann Monroe Tyler, born in Salisbury, Mass., Jan. 6, 1832; died Dec. 13, 1834.

1322 BENJAMIN⁶ TYLER (Jeremiah⁵), born in Woburn, Mass.; died in Newburyport, Mass., 1877; married (1), Eliza H. Hubbard, of Sullivan, N. H., who died in Lancaster, Mass., May 15, 1835, aged 40; daughter of Roswell H. Hub-

bard; married (2), in Lancaster, January 1, 1838, Mrs. Mary
Phelps, who died there March 19, 1839, aged 36; married (3),
———, who resided, his widow, in Newburyport, Mass. He was
a shoemaker. His estate was administered upon in Salem, June
11, 1877.

CHILDREN, by first marriage:

3279   Eliza Ann Tyler, born in New Ipswich, N. H., March
        10, 1820; died in New Market, N. J., about 1856;
        married, in 1853, Jubal Harrington, of New Mar-
        ket; their daughter (Mrs. T. J. Connelly, of Galva,
        Ill.), resided in 1901, in Zavier, Montana, and had
        two sons and two daughters.

3280   Ellen Grace Tyler, born in Lancaster, Mass., Sept.
        9, 1827; married ——— Barlow, of North Brookfield,
        Mass., and died soon after, leaving an infant.

1324 FANNY⁶ TYLER (Jeremiah⁵), born in Woburn,
Mass., April 3, 1785; died in St. Johnsbury, Vt., December
6, 1867; married (1), March 5, 1809, John Locke, born May
6, 1788; died in Lowell, Mass., June 30, 1832; son of David
and Betsey (Kibbe) Locke; married (2), Deacon Jonas Rugg,
of Lowell, Mass. She resided in Ashby, Mass., with her first
husband until about 1830, when they removed to Lowell; about
1852 she removed with her second husband to St. Johnsbury.
(See *Locke Genealogy*.) The children were born in Ashby.

CHILDREN, by first marriage:

3281   George Locke, born April 4, 1809; died in Brattle-
        boro, Vt., Oct. 10, 1851; married Jane Parks, of
        New Market, N. H.; he was a painter in Boston.

3282   Almira Locke, born April 8, 1811; died in Lowell
        about 1830.

3283   Mary Munroe Locke, born Nov. 12, 1813; married
        Henry Nye, of Gilsum, N. H.; a woolen manufac-
        turer of Bristol, N. H.

3284   Samuel Locke, born Nov. 20, 1851; married Mary
        Nichols, of Nashua, N. H.; resided in Lawrence,
        Mass.; removed to Rochester, N. H.

3285   Harriet Newell Locke, born Aug. 1, 1818; married
        Jubal Harrington, of St. Johnsbury, Vt.; had a
        family.

3286   Elizabeth Burnett Locke, born Jan. 27, 1821; married (1), Dec. 28, 1847, Calhoun Mathews, of St. Johnsbury, who died in 1880; married (2), Minot F. Winch, who died in 1889.

3287   Charles W. Locke, born June, 1825; he had a daughter Catherine, who married H. C. Kinney, of Grant's Pass, Oregon.

3288+ Catherine B. Locke, born Dec., 1827.

1325   MARY[6] TYLER (Moses[5]), born in Boston, Mass., February 2, 1797; married, in Lancaster, Mass., May 16, 1822, Deacon Charles Chase, Jr., of Lancaster. Children:

3289   Louisa Maria Chase.

3290   Eleanor Bridges Chase.

3291   Sarah Chase.

3292   Mary Chase.

3293   Elizabeth Walker Chase.

3294   George Henry Chase.

1327   JONATHAN[6] TYLER, JR. (Jonathan[5]), born in Woburn, Mass., September 17, 1781 or 1782; died in Bradford, Mass., July 14, 1858-9; married, January 12, 1809, Mary Osgood, of Amesbury, Mass., who died June 10, 1863. He lived in Newburyport, Mass., where the children were all born. Children:

3295   Nathaniel Bayley Tyler, born Dec. 23, 1809; died Oct. 15, 1846, unmarried.

3296   Jonathan Tyler, born July 7, 1811; died May 5, 1852, in Boston; married, Feb. 27, 1847, Eliza Jaquith; no children.

3297+ George Washington Tyler, born Nov. 4, 1812.

3298+ Charles Tyler, born Oct. 29, 1814.

3299   Mary Tyler, born Aug. 8, 1816; died in Boston, Dec. 6, 1897; married, Jan. 21, 1841, Anthony Gardner, of Swansea, Mass.; he died Jan. 6, 1883, s. p.

3300+ Albert Moses Tyler, born Nov. 18, 1818.

3301   Harriet Tyler, born April 2, 1820; died April 11, 1869; married, Nov. 21, 1847, Stephen Pike; she is buried in Bradford, Mass.; no children.

3302+ Osgood Tyler, born May 6, 1822.

3303+ Hannah Tyler, born Aug. 14, 1824.

3304   Eliza Ann Tyler, born Oct. 26, 1828; died in Dorchester, Mass., April 12, 1902; married, Dec. 18, 1851, A. Judson Day, of Bradford, Mass., who died Aug., 1883; one child (Elvena May, born May 1, 1857).

1333   MARY⁶ TYLER (Jonathan⁵), born in Woburn, Mass.; married Lewis Shaw, of Roxbury, Mass.; probably moved to Woburn. Children:

3305   Lewis Shaw, a tanner; had two children living in 1897 (Charles and Warner).
3306   Mary Shaw, married Benjamin Millett, of Woburn, Mass., who was a deacon in a Baptist church; they lived in Salem; no children.

1335   HANNAH⁶ TYLER (Jonathan⁵), born in Woburn, Mass., September 25, 1793; died March 13, 1870; married, September 25, 1819, Joseph Shedd, born in Woburn, July 20, 1792; died December 6, 1822. The children were born in Woburn. Children:

3307   Mary Ann M. Shedd, born July 15, 1820; died Sept. 26, 1888; married William S. Adlington, a shoemaker, born April 23, 1818; died March 24, 1892; had two sons and one daughter; all are deceased.
3308   Sarah S. Shedd, born Aug. 17, 1822; married, Aug. 23, 1848, Cyrus Cummings, of Woburn, born Sept. 19, 1817; son of Deacon John Cummings, of Woburn; he was a patent leather manufacturer. She was living in 1897 in Cummingsville, Mass. They had six children, four of whom died in infancy (the survivors are John and Cyrus).

1338   JOSEPH⁶ TYLER (Jonathan⁵), born in Woburn, Mass., 1798; died in Wilmington, Mass., of old age, February 17, 1876; married (1), April 13, 1826, Betsey Butters, of Wilmington, who died December 22, 1831, aged 34; married (2), Emeline M. Davis, who died in Andover, Mass., March 12, 1893. He lived in Wilmington, near Cumming's Hill. The four elder children were born in Woburn; the others in Wilmington.

CHILDREN, by first marriage:

3309   Joseph H. Tyler, born 1827; died in Wilmington, May
       9, 1832.
3310   Frank Tyler, born 1829; married Hannah Tasker;
       lives in North Woburn; has a daughter (Mary L.),
       unmarried.
3311   Elizabeth Tyler, married Augustus Jacqueth, of New
       Hampshire; had a son and a daughter who died
       young.
3312   Lucy Tyler, born Dec. 22, 1831; died in Wilmington,
       Sept. 8, 1832.

CHILDREN, by second marriage:

3313   John N. Tyler, born 1847; died Sept. 5, 1865, of
       typhoid fever.
3314   Phebe Annie Tyler, born June 30, 1849; living, unmar-
       ried, in 1896 in Worcester, Mass.

1341   RHODA BRUCE⁶ TYLER (Jonathan⁵), born in
Woburn, Mass., December 14, 1802; died July 24, 1866; married, June 15, 1832, George May, of Boston, who died April
17, 1866.   Total deafness prevented his engaging in business
but he inherited a fortune from his father Perrin May, a
wealthy Boston merchant of the old time.   Perrin was a son
of Moses May, who was a grandson of John May, the immigrant, who came from Mayfield, England, on his own ship,
The James, in 1730.   He was a member of the "Boston Tea
Party."   Children:
3315   George Perrin May, born April 15, 1833; died Sept.
       15, 1894; married, May 11, 1853, Henrietta Jones,
       of Boston; one son and one daughter (George and
       Jennie).
3316   Josephine May, born May 17, 1834; died, unmarried,
       1898, in Weston, Mass.
3317   Edwin May, born Jan. 17, 1836; died Sept. 14, 1867,
       unmarried.
3318   Ernestine May, born June 23, 1837; married, Aug.
       5, 1875, Lorenzo N. Kettle, born in London, Eng.;
       no children.

1352 BENJAMIN FRANKLIN[6] TYLER (Jonas[5]), born in Charlestown, Mass., April 4, 1821; died there February 10, 1895; married (1), January 27, 1845, Joanna Fellows; born in Ipswich, Mass., July 7, 1820; died February 1, 1890; married (2), May 1, 1893, Annie Frances Simonds; daughter of William H. and Anna E. Simonds; she survives, him with no children. Mr. Tyler was an accountant, and for ten years reporter for a mercantile agency. He took toll on the old Warren bridge for some years, served in the Common Council of Charlestown for one term and was actively interested in the affairs of the city. He was a man of commanding presence, and numbered his friends by the score. Retired in 1891. The children were born in Charlestown.

CHILDREN, by first marriage:

3319   Marie Louise Tyler, born Nov. 7, 1845; unmarried.
3320+   Emeline Bridge Tyler, born Nov. 7, 1847.
3321   Franklin Tyler, born July 15, 1853; died unmarried, Dec. 26, 1885.
3322   Rebecca Tyler, born June 29, 1856; died unmarried, Dec. 23, 1871.
3323+   John H. Tyler, born April 12, 1860.

1355 HANNAH[6] TYLER (Moses[5]), born in Warren, R. I., April 4, 1764; died October 30, 1836; married Captain Samuel Martin, of Barrington, R. I., who died September 18, 1826; buried in " Tyler's Point." He was in the Revolutionary War. Children:

3324   Moses Tyler Martin, born about 1792; died " 1 November, 1806, aged 14 years, 6 months and 19 days."
3325   Samuel Martin, born 1796; died April 4, 1820, in Cuba, W.: I., aged 26; married Hannah Luther Tyler, No. 1376.

1357 MARY[6] TYLER (Moses[5]), born in Warren, R. I., February 18, 1768; died August 16, 1802; married, October 16, 1791, Captain Haile Bowen, of Warren, where he died September 7, 1799, in his 37th year. She is buried in the " North " cemetery of Warren. The children were born in Warren. Children:

3326 Jonathan Bowen, born Aug. 7, 1792; died unmarried, in Mantanzas, Cuba, Aug. 1, 1817.

3327 Haile Bowen, born April 7, 1794; married, Dec. 2, 1817, Elizabeth Johonnot, daughter of Daniel Johonnot, descended from David, the Huguenot immigrant of 1686. David's wife Susan, was the daughter of Andræ Sigourine. Mr. Bowen had six sons and three daughters. He received his grandfather's gun, captured from the Hessian soldier as told under his record.

3328 Polly Tyler Bowen, born Oct. 25, 1795; died aged 14 years.

3329 Pardon Bowen, born Oct. 10, 1797; died in second year.

3330 Moses Tyler Bowen, born 1799.

1358 JOHN[6] TYLER (Moses[5]), born in Warren, R. I., November 26, 1769; died November 3, 1813; buried at "Tyler's Point"; married Eliza Martin, born 1768; the widow of John died February 12, 1853, aged 85. He was town clerk of Barrington, R. I., 1827-1838 (where he was a tanner), and deputy to the General Assembly, 1832-1833. Child:
3331+ John Tyler, born in Warren, March 26, 1802.

1376 HANNAH LUTHER[6] TYLER (Elisha[5]), born in Boston, Mass.; married (1), Samuel Martin, Jr., No. 3325, of Barrington, R. I., who died in Cuba, April 4, 1820; she married (2), —— Wilbour; married (3), —— Hogan. Her uncle Edward Tyler, No. 445, left her $5,000 in his will.

CHILDREN, by first marriage:
3332 Elizabeth Maria Martin, born 1816; married, 1836, Elisha Tyler Coburn, son of Mary (Bass) Coburn, No. 1372, and grandson of Hannah (Tyler) Bass, No. 448. They had a child who died young in Cuba.

3333 Hannah Tyler Martin, married Samuel Hanscomb, and had four sons and one daughter.

1378 CAPTAIN EDWARD[6] TYLER (Ellis[5]), born in Boston, Mass., November 10, 1776; died suddenly, in Harvard, Mass., December 26, 1823; married (1), by Rev. John Eliot,

in Boston, January 17, 1799, Mary G. Thomas, of Boston;
born there 1774; died there; daughter of Gershom and Susannah (Glover) Thomas; married (2), in Boston, June 15,
1808, Susanna Thomas, born 1774, in Boston; died there July
21, 1811; sister of his first wife; married (3), in Harvard,
March 2, 1814, Alma E. Holden, of Shirley, Mass. Went to
sea at 14; traded mostly to the north and placed the United
States flag for the first time on the shore of Iceland, and
brought the first cargo of eider-down to the United States.
On the way to Ireland in the War of 1812 was taken prisoner
and carried into some British province, where Captain Mellen
proved a friend to him. He then left the sea, moved to Harvard, Mass., and bought a farm. He was a large man, a good
talker and interested in the affairs of state and church. Took
the *Boston Recorder* from its inception. When he went to sea
he carried a folio edition of John Flavel's works and named a
son after the author. The two elder children born in Boston;
the others in Harvard.

CHILDREN, by first marriage:

3334   Mary Tyler, born April 16, 1805; died Oct. 18, 1873;
married (1), Henry Farley, of Concord, N. H., who
died Nov. 20, 1838, aged 48; married (2), 1843,
James Coburn of Franklin, N. H.; she had a daughter by the first marriage.

3335+   Edward Luther Tyler, born Aug. 5, 1806.

CHILDREN, by third marriage:

3336+   Alma Ellery Tyler, born Jan. 5, 1815.
3337+   Susannah Tyler, born July 30, 1816.
3338   John Flavel Tyler, born June 30, 1818; died of consumption, Feb. 8, 1844; began to study medicine.
3339+   Harriet Newell Tyler, born May 29, 1820.
3340   James Richards Tyler, twin to Harriet, was living in
Harvard, Mass., in 1897, unmarried.
3341+   Elizabeth Tyler, born June 21, 1823.

1382   SARAH[6] TYLER (Ellis[5]), born in Boston, Mass.;
married, 1808, Sylvester Richmond, son of Nathaniel Richmond, born in Dartmouth (Westport), Mass., April 13, 1771;
died there 1833. He was a merchant; also captain and super-

cargo of his own boat several years. Was impressed into English service while in Liverpool; was with Lord Nelson at the battle of Trafalgar; obtained release after two years. Once, when navigating a brig to the West Indies was taken by a British ship of war and a prize master and small crew were put aboard to run her to Halifax. But on the way, he with a man and boy left on board of his own crew, re-took the brig and brought her to an American port. After leaving the sea he spent most of his time in Elizabeth City, N. C. His daughters were born in Boston.

CHILDREN:

3342   Eliza Richmond, born 1809; married, 1837, Darius P. Chase, and resided in Somerset, Mass., where she died April 6, 1856; they had several sons, three of whom survived (William R., Mark P., George F.).
3343   Abby Anna Richmond, born 1815; died Aug. 25, 1824.

1400 ALCEMON[6] TYLER (Asa[5]), born probably in Canterbury, Conn., October 16, 1784; married Hannah ——, of Pomfret, Conn. He went to Brooklyn, Conn., from Canterbury. Children:
3344   Gardiner Tyler, born in Pomfret, May 20, 1804.
3345   Lyman Tyler, born in Brooklyn, May 18, 1805.
3346   Frederic Tyler, born June 22, 1806.

1415 DOCTOR JAMES[6] TYLER (James[5]), born September 16, 1774; his estate was administered April 6, 1802, and John Williams was administrator; the settlement mentions only the widow; married, December 21, 1796, Eliza Williams. He practiced with Dr. Baker, of Brooklyn, for a time, whose daughter married Dr. James' cousin, Pascal P. Tyler. He acted as administrator for the estate of his sister Anna Tyler, in 1797. Probably the children died young, as they are not mentioned in the settlement of Dr. James' estate. Children:
3347   Eliza Tyler, born April 25, 1798.
3348   James Tyler, born Sept. 28, 1800.

1422 MOLLY[6] TYLER (Daniel[5]), born in Pomfret, Conn., August 1, 1772; died June 12, 1832; married, January 23, 1793, Samuel Sumner, of Pomfret, born November 1, 1766;

died December 31, 1821; son of Samuel and Dorothy (Williams) Sumner. The children were born in Pomfret. Children:

3349+ George Sumner, born Dec. 13, 1793.

3350   Sarah May Sumner, born July 25, 1796; died Oct., 1873; married John C. Howard.

3351   Mary Sumner, born June 3, 1799.

3352   Elizabeth Tyler Sumner, born Aug. 15, 1801; died March 30, 1841.

3353+ Samuel Putnam Sumner, born Feb. 8, 1807.

1423 PASCAL PAOLI[6] TYLER (Daniel[5]), born in Pomfret, Conn., May 15, 1774; died August 31, 1847; married, September 17, 1797, Elizabeth Baker, born February 19, 1780; died October 9, 1862; daughter of Dr. Joseph Baker, of Brooklyn, Conn., whose genealogy is given in Weaver's *Ancient Windham, Conn.* Pascal was in business with his father and he also kept a noted tavern. Children:

3354   Daniel Putnam Tyler, born July 17, 1798; died Nov. 6, 1875; married, June 9, 1834, Emily Cecelia Tyler, No. 3359; they had no children. He was a lawyer and at one time Secretary of State for Connecticut and a great political stump speaker. He was proprietor of the Brooklyn, Conn., Academy. In general, he was a very prominent man in his day and was well known throughout the state.

3355+ Caroline Elizabeth Tyler, born April 24, 1802.

3356+ Mary Baker Tyler, born Aug. 17, 1812.

1426 WILLIAM P.[6] TYLER (Daniel[5]), born in Pomfret, Conn., October 7, 1782; died in Brooklyn, Conn., December 2, 1859; married in Brooklyn, January 1, 1809, Waty Williams, born in Canterbury, Conn., 1788; died January 29, 1858; daughter of Nathan and Hannah (Putnam) Williams. The *History of Windham County*, Vol. ii, by Larned, says: "August 18, 1826, William Tyler appointed Keeper of jail in Brooklyn." The twins were born in Warren, Vt.; the other children in Brooklyn. Children:

3357   Elizabeth Tyler, born Oct. 19, 1809; died unmarried, April 29, 1839.

3358+ Maria Cordelia Tyler, born Sept. 3, 1811.

3359   Emily Cecelia Tyler, twin to Maria, died Feb. 13,
        1869; married Daniel P. Tyler, No. 3354.
3360+   Waty Williams Tyler, born Aug. 27, 1814.
3361   William P. Tyler, born July 7, 1815; died Sept. 10,
        1816, in Brooklyn.
3362   William Williams Tyler, born July 30, 1818; died
        Jan. 18, 1865; married, Jan. 22, 1855, Joanna Far-
        rington, of Elizabeth, N. J.
3363   Hannah Putnam Tyler, born March 15, 1819; died
        Jan. 30, 1892; married, July 14, 1840, David Gill-
        mur.

    1427 BETSEY[6] TYLER (Daniel[5]), born in Pomfret,
Conn., June 18, 1784; married there, January 30, 1804, Joseph
Warren Eldredge, of Warren, Vt. She rode horseback from
Connecticut to Vermont. The children were born in Warren.
Children:
3364   Betsey Tyler Eldredge, born Dec. 1, 1806; died s. p.,
        July 10, 1856.
3365   James Frederic Eldredge, born Oct. 3, 1808; married
        Caroline Spaulding; had a daughter (Ellen), who
        died in Warren, Feb. 13, 1835.
3366   Daniel Tyler Eldredge, born Nov. 14, 1813; went to
        California; had two sons (Charles T. and George
        W.).
3367   Mary L. Eldredge, born Sept. 16, 1815; died Dec.
        15, 1815.
3368   Mary Lucretia Eldredge, born Nov. 15, 1816; married
        Albert Mosher; two sons.
3369   Edward Augustus Eldredge, born June 5, 1819; mar-
        ried Elutheria Nichols; several children.
3370   Lucy P. Eldredge, born Oct. 17, 1825; died Sept. 8,
        1841.

    1429 SARAH (SALLY) PIERPOINT[6] TYLER*

* The Porter Family Genealogy, on page 380 has this erroneous lineage:
"William Tyler, Milford, Conn., had John Tyler, of Wallingford, Conn.,
who had William Tyler, who married Jerusha Sedgwick, who had Daniel
Tyler, who married Sarah Edwards, who had Sarah Pierpoint Tyler."
Readers of this work will learn that the "Milford" line (except for
certain intermarriages), is entirely distinct from this, the "Andover"
line, from which Sarah Pierpoint Tyler sprung. "John Tyler" had no
such son, "William Tyler"; Jerusha Sedgwick married Samuel Tyler, son
of William Tyler, son of William Tyler, son of William Tyler of Milford.

(Daniel[5]), born in Brooklyn, Conn., April 25, 1791; died there
November 7, 1857; married, November 21, 1817, Rev. Samuel
Porter Williams, of Newburyport, Mass., who died December
23, 1846; son of Rev. Ezekiel Williams. He was graduated
from Yale College in 1796; was ordained in Mansfield, Conn.,
in 1801; his first wife was Mary Webb. Children:

3371   Septimus Tyler Williams, born Dec. 22, 1818.
3372   Edwards S. Williams, born March 20, 1820.
3373   Josiah D. Williams, born April 22, 1821.
3374   William Pierpoint Williams, born Nov. 22, 1822.
3375   Mary F. Williams, born Feb. 22, 1826.

1430   CAPTAIN EDWIN[6] TYLER (Daniel[5]), born in
Brooklyn, Conn., November 24, 1793; died in Philadelphia,
Pa., August 4, 1838; married (1), September 29, 1821, Alla
Mary Edwards; she died September 22, 1833, aged 34; married (2), Charlotte Musgrove Wharts, a widow, who had no
children. He was graduated from West Point United States
Military Academy, appointed from Connecticut. He was first
lieutenant and deputy commissary of ordnance, March 12,
1813; promoted to captain and deputy commissary of ord-
nance, August 5, 1813, in the fifth district of Maryland and
Virginia. Retained as captain of ordnance, February 8, 1815.
Dismissed August 13, 1819. (From *Register of the Officers of
the United States Army*, 1813). The children were born in
Brooklyn, Conn.

CHILDREN, by first marriage:

3376   Sally Edwards Tyler, born Sept. 18, 1822; died in
        Oakland, Cal., Aug., 1894; married —— Henshaw;
        had four children (Edwards, Tyler, Frederick, Wil-
        liam).
3377   Edwin Tyler, born Dec. 6, 1827; died unmarried, in
        Oakland, Cal., June 21, 1868; was graduated from
        Yale University in 1848; was an engineer in mining
        and assaying, etc.

1431   FREDERICK[6] TYLER (Daniel[5]), born in Brooklyn, Conn., May 7, 1795; died in Hartford, Conn., August 3,
1880; married in Abington, Conn., February 6, 1816, Sophia
Sharp, born in Abington, Conn., March 18, 1793; died in

Hartford, Conn., June 19, 1861. He lived in Brooklyn where the three elder children were born; but during a period extending from about 1825 (or a little later) to and including 1834 (and possibly longer), he lived in Hunter, N. Y., where the three younger children were born. Children:

3378   Edwin Tyler, born Nov. 1, 1816; died Feb. 10, 1818, in Brooklyn.

3379+   Sarah Sophia Tyler, born June 29, 1820.

3380+   George Frederick Tyler, born Aug. 4, 1822.

3381   Jane Grey Tyler, born in Griswold, Conn., July 28, 1825; died in Hunter, N. Y., July 31, 1828.

3382   Helen Edwards Tyler, born June 23, 1829; died in Philadelphia, Pa., July 13, 1860; married, in Hartford, April 28, 1852, Ciprian Nichols Beach, of Hartford; born there Sept. 9, 1828; died in London, Eng., Feb. 9, 1887, s. p.

3383   Robert Ogden Tyler, born Dec. 22, 1831; died in Boston, Mass., Dec. 1, 1874, unmarried. He was appointed to the United States Military Academy at West Point from the State of Connecticut, from which he was graduated in 1853; assigned to the Third artillery and served on the frontier, being in the Spokane expedition of 1858. In April, 1861, he went to relieve Fort Sumter and witnessed its bombardment; was made assistant quartermaster with rank of captain and served on the defences of Washington. At the special request of the Connecticut authorities he was allowed by the war department to undertake the reorganization of the Fourth Connecticut regiment and he became its colonel. The regiment became one of the very best in the service under him, and in January, 1862, it was made the Second Connecticut Heavy Artillery. With it he took part in the Peninsular campaign and on November 29, 1862, he was made brigadier-general of volunteers. At Fredericksburg he had charge of the artillery of the center grand division and was brevetted for gallantry; May, 1863, was given command of the artillery reserve of the Army of the Potomac. After this he was in the battle of Chancellorsville, and of Gettysburg, where he had

two horses shot under him; was in the Rapidan
campaign, and subsequently became a division commander in the 22d Corps; assigned a division of
heavy artillery that acted as infantry; after Spottsylvania was publicly thanked with his men by General Meade. Wounded at Cold Harbor, he thus
became permanently lamed. He saw no more active
service. He received several brevets for gallantry
at Spottsylvania, Cold Harbor and Gettysburg,
and for general services throughout the war; he was
retired in 1865 with the brevet rank of brigadier-
general. He was thanked by the Connecticut Legislature in a resolution and the citizens of Hartford
presented him with a sword. After the war General
Tyler served as chief in the quartermaster-general's
department, being stationed successively in Charleston, Louisville, San Francisco, New York City and
Boston, with the rank of lieutenant-colonel.

3384+ Edwin S. Tyler, born Oct. 10, 1834.

1432 GENERAL DANIEL[6] TYLER (Daniel[5]), born
in Brooklyn, Conn., January 7, 1799; died in New York City,
November 28, 1882; married in Norwich, Conn., May 28, 1832,
Emily Lee, born March 17, 1813, in Cambridge, Mass.; died
in New York City, March 9, 1864. He was a cadet in the
United States Military Academy at West Point, appointed from
Connecticut in 1816; graduating as second lieutenant of light
artillery in 1819. He served in garrisons in New England and
Fort Monroe, Va., from 1819 to 1824, and gained the rank of
first lieutenant; on duty until the close of 1827, when he was
commander of Pikesville arsenal, near Baltimore, Md. While
there he translated from the French *Manoeuvres of Artillery*,
which led to his being sent abroad on professional duty. From
January, 1828, to the spring of 1834, he was on duty in
Europe and America, and resigned May 21, 1834. He became
a civil engineer. Was president of the Norwich, Conn. and
Worcester, Mass. Railway Company, 1840-1844; of the Morris Canal & Banking Company, N. J., 1844-1846; of the Macon
& Western Railway Company, Ga., 1846-1848. In 1849 was
a member of the Board of Visitors of the Military Academy
at West Point. From 1849-1851 was superintendent of engi-

neers of the Cumberland Valley Railway, Pa., from Harrisburg to Chambersburg; general superintendent of the Dauphin & Susquehanna Railway and Coal Company, Pa., 1852-1860; also superintendent of engineers of the Auburn & Allerton Railway Company, Pa., 1855-1857, and its president, 1859-1861. He was also president of the Schuylkill & Susquehanna Railway Company, 1858-1861. He served in the Civil War from 1861-1864. Was on duty in the defence of Washington, beginning with March, 1861, and appointed colonel of the First Connecticut Volunteers, April 23, 1861; brigadier-general of Connecticut State Volunteers, May 10, 1861; re-appointed as brigadier-general of United States Volunteers, March 13, 1862. He was in the battle of Bull Run, and at the advance upon and siege of Corinth until early in June, 1862; he was on sick leave for about six weeks in that summer. Returning to duty in August, he organized the Connecticut Volunteer regiments. Appointed commander of Camp Douglass, Ill, he served from the middle of September until the end of November and then was on a military commission investigating General Buell's camp in Kentucky and Tennessee, until early in May, 1863. He guarded the Upper Potomac during a part of June, 1863, being commander in Harper's Ferry and Maryland Heights, at the time the Confederates invaded Pennsylvania. Later, was commander of the troops in Baltimore. Then commander of the District of Delaware until April, 1864. He had charge of the artillery which, at " Bloody Angle," is said to have saved the battle of Gettysburg. In a mass-meeting of his fellow citizens in Connecticut it was said of him: " No man rendered such service in organizing Connecticut's forces as the Colonel of the First regiment of Connecticut, Daniel Tyler, of Norwich, a worthy representative of the father and grandfather bearing the same name, so long honored in Brooklyn and Windham County. Educated at West Point and experienced in military discipline, to him was assigned the most arduous task of making an army out of entirely raw material . . ." When through with the Civil War he built the town of Anniston, Ala., and was president of the Mobile & Montgomery Railway, 1873-1879. He invested in Texas lands, and " Capote Farm," of 20,000 acres, was his winter residence. The eldest child and the two younger children were born in Norwich; the others in Farrandsville, Pa.

CHILDREN:

3385+   Alfred Lee Tyler, born May 19, 1834.

3386+   Gertrude Elizabeth Tyler, born Feb. 14, 1836.

3387+   Edmund Leighton Tyler, born May 2, 1838.

3388+   Mary Low Tyler, born March 2, 1841.

3389+   Augustus Cleveland Tyler, born May 2, 1851.

1437   ASAHEL⁶ TYLER (Phineas⁵), born in Canterbury, Conn., July 6, 1768; married in Brookfield, Vt., 1791,
Drusilla Carley.   He moved to Brookfield with his father,
where, October 12, 1792, he had 100 acres from Moses D. Collins.   His father and mother, February 5, 1800, took a "life
lease" from him.   The children were born in Brookfield.   Children:

3390+   Carley Tyler, born Feb. 7, 1792.

3391+   Asahel Tyler, born July 31, 1794.

3392+   Royal Tyler, born Dec. 6, 1796; probably moved to
         Mantua, O.

3393   Polly Tyler, born July 16, 1799.

1438   JOHN⁶ TYLER (Phineas⁵), born in Canterbury,
Conn., July 15, 1770; married, in Brookfield, Vt., March 20,
1793, Ruby Bennett.   He moved with his father to Brookfield and Randolph, Vt.   Children:

3394+   John Hazen Tyler, born in Randolph, Nov. 30, 1793.

3395   Henry Tyler, born in Brookfield; married Ann Henion,
         of Yates, N. Y.; moved to Michigan in 1854; one
         son (Professor John Henry Tyler, of Gaylord,
         Mich).

3396   Levinia Tyler, married Joseph Cady; she had a son
         who is a dentist in Chicago, Ill.

3397   Diademia Tyler, married Jesse Hall; had a son (Rich-
         ard), who resided in Millers, N. Y.

1444   ZERVIAH⁶ TYLER (Oliver⁵), born in Canterbury, Conn., March 16, 1776; died in Morrisville, Vt., June
10, 1853; married, March 11, 1805, Elisha Herrick, of Morrisville and Bethel, Vt., who died in Minneapolis, Minn.   Children:

3398   Sophia Herrick, born March 10, 1806; died unmarried,
         1862.

3399   Nathan Herrick, born April 28, 1807; died in Minneapolis; his daughter married —— Hale, Minneapolis.

3400   Abigail Herrick, born Sept. 3, 1808, of So. Woodstock, Vt.

3401   Mary L. Herrick, born June 16, 1810; died 1831.

3402   Elisha Herrick, born March 18, 1812; died 1878.

3403   Caroline Herrick, born Feb. 29, 1815, Wolcott, Vt.

3404   Warren T. Herrick, born July 27, 1817.

1446 PERLEY[6] TYLER (Oliver[5]), born in Canterbury, Conn., December 6, 1778; died in Northfield, Vt., 1855; married, October 27, 1803, Betsey Rood, of Brookfield, Vt., born September 15, 1787; died 1849. He went to E. Randolph, Vt., with father, and bought 100 acres on " Tyler's Hill " (north of Judge Paine's). Children:

3405   Martin Perley Tyler, born Nov. 15, 1804.

3406   Matilda Tyler, born Sept. 3, 1806.

3407   Juliet Tyler, born March 7, 1809.

3408   Squire Tyler, born June 4, 1811.

3409+   Daniel Tyler, born Aug. 2, 1812.

3410+   Royall Tyler, born Nov. 30, 1815.

3411   Edward Tyler, born Feb. 2, 1817.

3412   Jason Tyler, born June 11, 1819; died in infancy.

3413   Louisa Tyler, born Oct. 19, 1822.

3414   Jason Cook Tyler, born May 4, 1825; resided Aztalan, Wis.; married Elizabeth Rose; has two sons (Edward and James).

3415+   John Alfred Tyler, born July 25, 1827.

1449 ORRIS[6] TYLER (Oliver[5]), born in East Randolph, Vt., December 26, 1783; died September 28, 1859; married Susan Town, born December 20, 1787; died in East Randolph, March 12, 1860. The children were born in East Randolph. Children:

3416   Satyra Tyler, born Aug. 9, 1808; died unmarried, Oct. 9, 1887.

3417+   Clarissa Tyler, born Jan. 30, 1813.

3418   Abigail Tyler, born Aug. 28, 1816; died July 3, 1886; married Jonathan Smith, of East Randolph;

she had a son (Eugene), and a daughter (who married —— Bagley).

3419+   Susan Tyler, born Dec. 29, 1819.

3420+   Sophia Tyler, born Oct. 29, 1821.

3421   Orris Tyler, born June 12, 1824; died June 5, 1869;
widow resides in East Randolph, Vt.

3422+   Hazen Tyler, born July 13, 1826.

3423+   Melissa Tyler, born March 12, 1828.

3424   Semantha Tyler, born July 22, 1831; died September,
1881; married (1), Dr. Dodge of Michigan; married
(2), ——.

1462   COLONEL MOSES[6] TYLER (Elisha[5]), born in
Preston, Conn., August 16, 1761; died April 15, 1829; married,
May 29, 1793, Olive Coit, No. 1506, born February 22, 1772;
died in Sutherland, in 1840, at which time she was the wife
of Rev. John Dorrance of that place; daughter of John and
Mehitable (Tyler) Coit, No. 516. Colonel Tyler was a private
in the " 3d Militia Company in the Town of Preston " in the
war of the Revolution. Afterward he became a student in the
famous academy in Plainfield, Conn. He received the following
certificate:

April 16, 1785.

" We hereby recommend Mr. Moses Tyler, the Bearer, as
a Young Gentleman of amiable and unblemished morals and
well accomplished to teach and give instruction in reading,
writing, English Grammar and Mathematiks, we doubt not to
good exceptance."

By the year 1793 he was settled in the " mansion house "
on the Tyler " homestead farm " in Preston (afterward Griswold). His letters still extant, show him to have been a man of
cultivated mind, devout and affectionate; he was dignified, with
a rather stately bearing; his title of Colonel testifies to his high
position in the militia. Long after his death his townspeople
used to speak of his lofty courtesy, his military bearing, and
especially of the nobility of his look as he rode horseback over
his farm, directing his men. The children were born in Griswold.

CHILDREN:

3425+   Elisha Tyler, born Nov. 2, 1794.

3426   Lucretia Tyler, born Jan. 11, 1797; died June 3,

1822; married, May 14, 1821, Colonel Charles Coit,
born Feb. 19, 1793; son of Nathaniel and Betsey
(Morgan) Coit, and cousin to Lucretia; he married (2), Lydia Tyler, No. 3429 (his first wife's
sister), born Dec. 1, 1803; died Oct., 1834; he married (3), Sarah P. Grosvenor, and died Oct. 26,
1855; two children died young.

3427 Mary Ann Tyler, born June 14, 1798; died unmarried, Oct. 21, 1824.

3428 Olive Coit Tyler, born June 6, 1801; died unmarried,
Dec. 25, 1824.

3429 Lydia Tyler, born Dec. 1, 1803; married Colonel
Charles Coit, her cousin, and widower of her sister
Lucretia; she died Oct., 1834.

3430 Rebecca Coit Tyler, born March 8, 1810; died unmarried, in Sunderland, Mass., May 30, 1836.

1463 HANNAH[6] TYLER (Elisha[5]), born in Preston,
Conn., July 23, 1764; died in Hartland, Vt., November 22,
1817; married Colonel Edward Swan, of Stonington, Conn.,
who removed to Hartland, Vt. Children:

3431 Mehitable Swan, married William Miner, of Hartland.

3432 Moses Tyler Swan, married —— Miner, of Hartland.

3433 Hannah Swan, married Ahima Sherwin, of Hartland,
who removed to Cleveland, O., where he died.

1477 LIEUTENANT JAMES[6] TYLER (Samuel[5]),
born in Preston, Conn., August 3, 1763; died February 5,
1843; married, November 1, 1789, Sarah Cushman, who died
August 23, 1851, in Bethel, Vt. He was in the Revolution.
(See *Pension Book*, page 56, No. 8.) James was a corporal in
the " 3d Militia Company in the town of Preston." He moved
to Tunbridge, Vt., in 1810, where he built the first frame
house. The children were born in Preston. Children:

3434 Samuel Tyler, born July 10, 1790; died in Bethel, Vt.,
s. p., Aug., 1853.

3435+ William Belcher Tyler, born Jan. 3, 1792.

3436+ Sarah Tyler, born Jan. 16, 1794.

3437 Eunice Tyler, born Jan. 30, 1796; died young.

3438+ John B. Tyler, born May 21, 1798.

3439   Lavinia Tyler, born Oct. 13, 1800; married James
        Bryant, of Weston, Vt.; had four sons.
3440   Irene Tyler, born Aug. 5, 1802; married James Heren-
        deen, of Herkimer, N. Y.; had sons and a daughter
        (Sarah.)
3441+   Benjamin Tyler, born March 3, 1805.
3442   James Tyler, born Aug. 17, 1807; was drowned in
        Ohio before 1840; unmarried.

    1478 DOCTOR BISHOP[6] TYLER (Samuel[5]), born in
Preston, Conn., January 27, 1767; died April 12, 1844; married, November 29, 1797, Alice Morgan, of Plainfield, Conn.,
born August 13, 1770; died September 9, 1843. He was a
private in Captain E. Prentice's company, Colonel McClallen's
regiment, from September 24 to November 22, 1782. He was
a pensioner in 1832, residing in New London, Conn., and in
1840, a pensioner, residing in Griswold, Conn. (*Conn. Men of
the Revolution.*) In 1834, he is noted on the *Rev. Pension
Rolls*, as private and corporal. In the War of 1812 he was a
Surgeon, and his place of service was New London, June 8-17,
1813, Commander Lieut.-Colonel William Belcher.

CHILDREN:

3443   Eliza Cotton Tyler, born in Griswold, Feb. 26, 1802;
        married Dwight Ripley Tyler, No. 1519.
3444+   Alice Augusta Tyler, born in Preston, Sept. 12, 1804.
3445   Samuel B. Tyler, born 1808; died March 16, 1826.
3446   Joseph M. Tyler, died Feb. 7, 1814, aged one year
        and two months.

    1479 ESTHER[6] TYLER (Samuel[5]), born in Preston,
Conn., July 17, 1769; died in Attleboro, Mass., January 19,
1811; married, January 1, 1790, Rev. John Wilder; born in
Templeton, Conn., March 22, 1758; died in Attleboro, February 12, 1836; son of Jonas and Elizabeth Wilder, who moved
to Lancaster, Mass., in 1776 (See *Wilder Genealogy*.) He was
graduated from Dartmouth College in 1784; studied theology
with Dr. Hart of Preston, Conn., and was ordained in Attleboro, January 27, 1790, where he was settled as minister of the
parish over thirty-two years. (He married [2], Mrs. Eliza-

beth [Griffin] Austin, of New Hartford, Conn., a sister to Dr.
E. D. Griffin; she died March, 1847, aged 72.)

CHILDREN:

3447   Esther Wilder, born 1790; died 1858.
3448   Eliza Wilder, born 1792; died 1831; married Hon.
       Lemuel May, of Attleboro.
3449   Julia Wilder, born 1794.
3450   (Rev.) John Wilder, Jr., born 1796; married Mary W.
       James; died 1844.
3451   Jonas Wilder, born 1798; married Parthenia Hyde;
       died 1838.
3452   Samuel T. Wilder, born 1800; a lawyer, Rochester,
       N. Y.; died 1837.
3453   Charles Baker Wilder, born 1802; resided Jackson-
       ville, Fla.
3454   Betsey Brown Wilder, born 1804.
3455   Amy Ann Wilder, born 1809; married Rev. J. W.
       Smith; died 1843.
3456   Joseph A. Wilder, born 1811; resided Louisville, Ky.;
       died 1854.

1480 JOHN BROWN[6] TYLER (Samuel[5]), born in
Preston, Conn., November 9, 1773; died in Griswold, Conn.,
November 22, 1848; married, January 3, 1804, Mary Stewart,
of Griswold, of direct Scotch extraction; born April 18, 1783;
died October 6, 1872. He was a farmer, residing in Preston,
where his children were born. Children:
3457+ Mary Amy Tyler, born Oct. 15, 1804.
3458+ Samuel Alexander Tyler, born Nov. 13, 1809.

1481 AMY B.[6] TYLER (Samuel[5]), born in Preston,
Conn., November 9, 1773; married John Wylie. Child:
3459   Lucy Wylie, probably born in Preston, Conn.; married,
       Jan. 16, 1816, Amos Prentice; had two sons (Samuel
       and Amos Wylie).

1482 DANIEL[6] TYLER (Joseph[5]), born in 1773; died,
probably in Scotland, Conn., October 13, 1849; married, April
13, 1806, Olivia Cady, who died April 12, 1866, aged 87. He
is buried in the cemetery in Scotland, Conn. His will is dated

April 7, 1846; probated in Windham, Conn., November 5, 1849; the inventory amounted to $6,675.89. Child:

3460   Mary Ann Tyler, born in Scotland, May 19, 1808; married Dr. Calvin B. Brumley, who was executor of Daniel Tyler's will.

1484   JOSEPH[6] TYLER, JR. (Joseph[5]), born in Brooklyn, Conn., 1777; died there (probably) September 15, 1857; buried there; married Lois ——, who died July 25, 1819, aged 38. Child:

3461   Mary Tyler, born in Brooklyn, 1804; died there Nov. 24, 1805, aged one year and five months.

1486   STEAVENS (or STEVENS)[6] TYLER (Joseph[5]), born in Brooklyn, Conn. (probably) in 1782; died December 20, 1809, in his 28th year; married Betsey ——. His estate was probated February 6, 1810, in Pomfret, Conn., and his wife is there named, and infant child; Daniel Tyler, 2d administrator. Inventory, $607.58. Child:

3462   Elizabeth Tyler, born in Brooklyn, 1809; died there March 18, 1819, in her tenth year; buried in Brooklyn.

1494   HARRIET[6] TYLER (James[5]), born in Preston, Conn., January 15, 1800; died in Jewett City, Conn.; married Rev. Paul Couch, who died in Mystic, Conn., at home of son, about 1885. He came, originally, from Bridgewater, Mass., and was a Congregationalist. Children:

3463   Joseph James Couch, married Mary ——; lives in Brooklyn, N. Y.; in the Collector's Office in the Custom House, N. Y. (1896); no children.

3464   John P. Couch, is married and lives in San Francisco (1896), where he is a bookkeeper in the Custom House; has two daughters.

3465   Harriet Elizabeth Couch, married, May, 1862, Alfred A. Young, of Jewett City, where she died in 1875; he is living (1896) there.

3466   Thomas Tremlet Couch, died in New York, unmarried.

3467   Ebenezer Punderson Couch, was residing, single, in Mystic, Conn., about 1896.

1514 JOSEPH COIT[6] TYLER (John,[5] Jr.), born in North Preston (now Griswold), Conn., February 5, 1781; died January 8, 1826; married, April 10, 1810, Hannah Woodward, of Plainfield, Conn., died February 22, 1833, aged 48. He was in the War of 1812. The children were born in Preston. Children:

3468+ Frances Mary Tyler, born July 8, 1811.

3469+ Elizabeth Tyler, born Dec. 31, 1815.

3470+ Frederick William Tyler, born April 17, 1817.

3471 Jane Tyler, born Oct. 8, 1818; died in Norwich, Conn., Oct. 13, 1864, unmarried.

1515 MARY[6] TYLER (John,[5] Jr.), born in Griswold, Conn., October 26, 1782; died in Southampton, Mass., November, 1817; married Gamaliel Pomeroy, of Southampton. He was a hotel-keeper. The children were born in Southampton. Children:

3472 Eunice Pomeroy, married ——.

3473 Betsey Pomeroy, married Daniel Kingsley.

3474 Mary Pomeroy, married ——.

3475 Jonathan Pomeroy, went west and married.

1516 OLIVE[6] TYLER (John,[5] Jr.), born in Griswold, Conn., November 29, 1784; died December 13, 1843; married, March 20, 1806, Christopher Avery. He was.a storekeeper in Jewett City, Conn. The children were born either in Jewett City or Plainfield. Children:

3476 Albert Avery, born Jan. 23, 1807; was a cripple and never married.

3477 Mary Avery, born Aug. 4, 1810; married —— Hoxie, of Plainfield, Conn.

3478 George Avery, born March 31, 1814; married —— Wills, of Lebanon, Conn.

3479 Elbridge Avery, born July 22, 1816; married and lived in Jewett City.

3480 Abby Avery, born Feb. 11, 1819; married Henry Bennett and moved to Oshkosh, Wis.

3481 Wolcott Avery, born Aug. 9, 1822; moved to Wisconsin and married.

3482 Lucius G. Avery, born Nov. 23, 1825; moved to Wisconsin, and married.

3483 Infant, died young.

1517   JOHN[6] TYLER (John,[5] Jr.), born in Griswold, Conn., September 17, 1789; died there June 3, 1830; married Abby B. Coggswell, of Griswold, who died there February 4, 1850, aged 56. He was a farmer, in Griswold, where his children were born. He was in the War of 1812. Children:

3484   Mehitable Coit Tyler, born 1813; died Jan. 30, 1851; married, 1843, Edwin Ames, born July 29, 1810; died Jan. 30, 1891; three children (Ann Tyler, Edward Tyler, William).

3485+ Ann Mercy Tyler, born Dec. 22, 1819.

3486   John Tyler, born 1820; died Dec. 6, 1820, aged 10 months.

3487+ Mary Esther Tyler, born Feb. 5 ,1824.

1518   HENRY COIT[6] TYLER (John,[5] Jr.), born August 9, 1791; died February 18, 1875; married (1), March 12, 1823, Harriet Hyde, born July 9, 1797; died November 24, 1827; married (2), Tirzah Moss; born March 16, 1802; died September 10, 1864. He was a farmer and lived in Griswold, where his children were born. He was in the War of 1812, as a private under Commander Asa Copeland, September 14, 1813, to November 1, 1813. (*Conn. Militia, War 1812.*)

CHILDREN, by first marriage:

3488+ Lucy Belcher Tyler, born Feb. 5, 1824.

3489+ John Spaulding Tyler, born Nov. 23, 1826.

CHILDREN, by second marriage:

3490   Son, died Aug. 25, 1829.

3491   Son, born June 27, 1830.

3492   Mary Boardman Tyler, born Sept. 15, 1831; lived in Griswold, unmarried; a nurse.

3493   Son, born Nov. 28, 1832.

3494+ Harriet Tyler, born June 2, 1834.

3495   Olive Tyler, born Nov. 9, 1839; married Alba Stevens, and lived in New Canaan, Conn.

3496   Henry Tyler, born July 19, 1841; married, Feb. 26, 1878, Elisa M. Wheeler, of Stonington, Conn.; no children; lives in Great Bend, Kan.

1519   DWIGHT RIPLEY[6] TYLER (John,[5] Jr.), born

in North Preston, Conn. (now Griswold), June 30, 1795; died there August 14, 1879; married (1), December 23, 1823, Eliza Cotton[7] Tyler, No. 3443, born in North Preston, February 26, 1802; died s. p. October 12, 1845; daughter of Dr. Bishop and Alice (Morgan) Tyler; married (2), February 23, 1846, Mary Kinne Johnson, born in Griswold, January 17, 1810; died in Greenfield, Mass., June 10, 1900; daughter of Deacon Stephen and Lydia (Larned) Johnson, of Griswold. At an early age Mr. Tyler was a student in the Plainfield Academy in Plainfield, Conn. He taught school a number of years. At the age of 19 he served as corporal in Captain John Avery's company in Groton, Conn., in the War of 1812. The larger part of his life was spent on the farm where he died. Mr. Tyler was a member and valued supporter of the First Congregational Church in Griswold for many years. He had a deep interest in the affairs of his state and of the nation, and was a staunch Republican in politics.

CHILD, by second marriage:

3497+ Mary Eliza Tyler, born in Griswold, April 23, 1847.

1520 THOMAS SPAULDING[6] TYLER (John,[5] Jr.), born in Griswold, Conn., January 7, 1798; died there October 19, 1880; married, December 1, 1824, Dolly Cogswell, born December 15, 1802; died in Griswold, March 22, 1878. He was a farmer, residing in Griswold, where his children were born. Children:

3498+ Joseph Cogswell Tyler, born Feb. 9, 1827.

3499   Charles Wheeler Tyler, born Oct. 10, 1828; married (1), Jan. 28, 1863, Mrs. Hannah (Bennett) Sutleff, who died August 24, 1886; married (2), Oct. 3, 1888, Abbie L. Carpenter, of Akron, Ohio; he is living in Warren, Ohio; no children.

3500+ Dwight Ripley Tyler, born Dec. 25, 1831.

3501   Edward Spaulding Tyler, born Sept. 13, 1834; is living, unmarried, in San Francisco.

3502+ George Tyler, born Feb. 22, 1841.

1521 ABBY[6] TYLER (John,[5] Jr.), born in Griswold, Conn., July 31, 1800; died there September, 1862; married Frederick Brewster, of Griswold, son of Elias and Margery

(Morgan) Brewster. The children were born in Griswold.
Children:

3503 George Brewster, died Oct. 3, 1830, at an early age.

3504 Edward Brewster, lives in California, probably unmarried.

3505 John Tyler Brewster, died June 25, 1836, when young.

3506 Frederick Brewster, married Mary Frances Edmond,
daughter of Mary E. (Tyler) and Andrew Edmond, No. 3487; they had a son who died young;
she married (2), George Loring, of Plainfield, Conn.

3507 Dwight Tyler Brewster, married in 1871, Emily F.
Read; lives in Boston.

3508 Mary Tyler Brewster, married Henry Lathrop, of
Griswold; she was living, a widow, in 1896; no
children.

3509 Jane Brewster, married, in 1873, William B. Robertson,
of Preston, Conn.; no children.

3510 Emily Huntington Brewster, married, in 1869, Andrew
Jackson Willoughby, of Canterbury, Conn.

1543 ASA KIMBALL⁶ TYLER (Joseph⁵), born in
Preston, Conn., March 29, 1790; died April 11, 1878; married
Ada Brown, of Preston, who died January 31, 1878, aged 82.
He lived in Canajoharie, N. Y. He was a man of leisure and
something of a rover. Children:

3511 Stephen D. Tyler, born 1821; died Sept. 4, 1824.

3512 Lucy Tyler, died, s. p., Nov. 6, 1870; married ——
McClure.

3513 Avis Lucinda Tyler, born 1825; died, Oct. 20, 1842.

3514 Walter Tyler, born 1837; died Sept. 7, 1838.

1544 JOSEPH⁶ TYLER, JR. (Joseph⁵), born in Preston, Conn., June 22, 1792; died November 26, 1868; married
(1), February 1, 1816, Huldah Pride, who died June 3, 1825,
aged 28; married (2), May 29, 1827, Damaris Kimball, who
died May 24, 1855, aged 55.

CHILDREN, by first marriage:

3515 Joseph Pride Tyler, born Sept. 26, 1817; died Oct.
26, 1821; scalded to death in Poquetannock, Conn.

3516 Infant daughter, died Jan. 10, 1819, aged 1 day.

3517   Infant daughter, died Feb. 19, 1821, aged 7 days.

3518   Huldah Tyler, born Sept. 26, 1822; died July 20, 1895, in Brooklyn, N. Y., unmarried.

3519   Mary Tyler, died July 22, 1825, aged 2 months.

CHILDREN, by second marriage:

3520+ Elizabeth Tyler, born Jan. 13, 1828.

3521   John Tyler, born Aug. 22, 1830; married Ellen ——; resided, s. p., in Chicago.

3522   Frank Tyler, born Oct. 1, 1832; died Sept. 12, 1833.

3523   Josephine Tyler, born June 28, 1838; died Oct. 11, 1895, in Brooklyn, N. Y., unmarried.

1545 POLLY[6] TYLER (Joseph[5]), born in Preston, Conn., September 16, 1794; died December 29, 1884; married, April 18, 1818, Mundator Tracy Richards, of Norwich, Conn.; born June 30, 1794; died December 5, 1880. A merchant in Preston and prominent there. (See *Richards Genealogy.*) The children were born in Preston. Children:

3524   Charles Tyler Richards, married Lucy Ann Coates and moved to Albion, N. Y. He was a barrel manufacturer; had two boys.

3525   Mary Prentiss Richards, married John C. Utley, a merchant, of Norwich, Conn., and had a large family.

3526   Martha Elizabeth Richards, married Deacon John W. Gallup, of Preston, Conn., a farmer, who lived on the old Hopestill Tyler homestead; had four children.

3527   Huldah Jane Richards, married Rev. William Wilbur, Saxton's River, Vt.; she died Sept. 29, 1867, aged 41 (they had a son, named for his father, who was a doctor); he married (2), Harriet Richards, sister of his first wife.

3528   Lydia Tyler Richards, married Obadiah Touson, of Virginia, and had two sons and a daughter.

3529   John Richards, lived in Baltimore, Md., a grocer; married (1), Mary Chalker, of Saybrook, Conn., and had one child; married (2), a widow, ——.

8530   Daniel Tyler Richards, lives in Preston, Conn.; succeeded to father's business; married (1), Lydia

Maria Fuller, of Suffield, Conn.; had two children; married (2), Mary Barnes; no children.

3531   Harriet Richards, married Rev. William Wilbur, whose first wife was Huldah J. Richards, his second wife's sister; Harriet had a daughter (Mary).

1546   DANIEL MEECH[6] TYLER (Joseph[5]), born in Preston, Conn., March 31, 1797; died in Baltimore, Md., February 5, 1847; married there, October 29, 1829, Ann Bancroft, born October 29, 1805; died in Baltimore, December 9, 1875; daughter of John and Lucy (Davis) Bancroft. The children were born in Baltimore. Children:

3532   Mary Richards Tyler, born Aug. 8, 1830; died, unmarried, Feb. 9, 1856.

3533   William Stephen Tyler, born July 29, 1833; died Jan. 4, 1877.

3534+   Joseph Edwin Tyler, born June 25, 1835.

3535+   John Alpha Tyler, born Sept. 11, 1837.

3536   George Daniel Tyler, born Sept. 13, 1839; died Dec. 30, 1840.

3537   Emma Ann Tyler, born Oct. 28, 1841; died April 19, 1894.

3538+   Martha Elizabeth Tyler, born June 20, 1844.

3539   Daniel Meech Tyler, Jr., born April 26, 1847; died July 15, 1848.

1547   CHARLES[6] TYLER (Joseph[5]), born in Preston, Conn., November 21, 1799; died in Baltimore July 15, 1881; married Mary H. Bill, of Canajoharie, N. Y., who died September 20, 1887. He was a lumber dealer early and then retired. Children:

3540   Caroline Tyler, born Aug. 5, 1832; died Dec. 18, 1879, unmarried.

3541   Susan Tyler, born 1836; died young, unmarried.

1548   LYDIA[6] TYLER (Joseph[5]), born in Preston, Conn., May 26, 1802; died December 24, 1892; married, April 5, 1818, Elder Levi Meech, of Preston; born February 14, 1795; died June 4, 1873, in North Stonington, Conn. The children were born in North Stonington. Children:

3542   Lydia Tyler Meech, born Feb. 27, 1819; married, Oct.

16, 1861, Robert S. Avery, who died s. p., Washington, D. C., Nov. 18, 1890.

3543 Levi Witter Meech, born June 24, 1821; married, Sept. 25, 1857, Susan Maria Hayward, of Monson, Mass.; they had three children, all of whom died young. A famous mathematician; author of life tables for insurance companies, and a book of calculation tables; a student of Bible chronology.

3544 Stephen Tyler Meech, born March 6, 1823; a bachelor, living in 1896 in Preston.

3545 (Rev.) William Witter Meech, born June 23, 1825; married, June 4, 1861, Jeanette Dubois, Frankfort, Pa.; they had two daughters, the elder of whom married and had two daughters (Anne D. and Lydia J.). He was a chaplain in the Civil War and in later years a fruit grower.

3546 Lucy Maria Meech, born June 9, 1838; married, Jan. 16, 1862, Joseph Leander Lord, of Lyme, Conn.; born in Suffield, Conn., and son of Rev. Levi Lord. He is in the hardware business in Northampton, Mass. Mrs. Lord had the advantage of a college training; have one son and five daughters (Edward A., married Jennie A. Thorne; Clara G., an organist; Helen A., a physician, died 1900; Grace, a violinist; Susan L., a violincellist; married R. B. Brandagee; Lucy E.).

1549 OLIVER SPICER[6] TYLER (Joseph[5]), born in Preston, Conn., August 3, 1804; died in Norwich, Conn., January 7, 1858; married, January 3, 1831, Anna Lester, of Groton, Conn., born June 20, 1801; died April 23, 1882; daughter of Amos and Sarah (Avery) Lester. He was a wool broker and had a general store in Poquetannock, with his brother Joseph. He was long a sufferer from asthma. The three elder children were born in Poquetannock and the three younger in Norwich, Conn. Children:

3547+ Lucy Ann Tyler, born Nov. 15, 1831.

3548 Gilbert Tyler, born July 13, 1833; died in Norwich, July 17, 1841.

3549 Daniel Webster Tyler, born Oct. 11, 1834; died in Norwich, July 10, 1841.

3550   Mary Elizabeth Tyler, born Sept. 27, 1837; died in
        Norwich July 9, 1841.
3551   Ellen Tyler, born June 11, 1839; died in Norwich
        July 16, 1841.
3552   Sarah Lester Tyler, born Nov. 16, 1842; was living,
        unmarried, in 1896.

    1550 DOCTOR GUERDON KIMBALL[6] TYLER (Joseph[5]), born in Preston, Conn., October 1, 1806; died in Baltimore, Md., March 23, 1891; married, September 2, 1835, Susan Bancroft, born December 15, 1807; died August 6, 1887; daughter of John and Lucy (Davis) Bancroft. The children were born in Baltimore. Children:

3553+   Charles Tyler, born July 4, 1836.
3554+   Lucy Bancroft Tyler, born Aug. 15, 1838.
3555+   George Guerdon Tyler, born Nov. 23, 1840.
3556   Sarah Stephens Tyler, born Nov. 14, 1842.
3557+   James Edward Tyler, born March 21, 1845.
3558+   Susan Tyler, born Dec. 30, 1847.
3559   Hopestill Tyler, born Jan. 29, 1850; died April 20,
        1850.
3560+   Frank Kimball Tyler, born June 12, 1851.
3561+   Joseph Henry Tyler, born June 8, 1855.

    1589 MARY WELLES[6] TYLER (Nathan[5]), born in Uxbridge, Mass., April 2, 1792; died in Boston, Mass., September 16, 1886; married, in 1810, Enoch Brown, born April 17, 1789, in Wrentham; died in Beverly, 1867; a merchant of Boston, of the firm of Brown and Waldo, importers. Retired from business to live in Wrentham, in 1859, thence to Beverly. She was educated in Wrentham in Day's Academy until the age of 15, when she was sent to Mrs. Rawson's Female Seminary in Boston, where she received medals for writing and embroidery. A descendant writes: " She was a Tyler through and through. She inherited her father's qualities, even to his delicate constitution. Was beautiful in mind and manners and in person. The embodiment of intelligence, delicacy and refinement, spirituality and every virtue. Never one more gentle." The children were probably all born in Boston.

3562 Mary Tyler Brown, born April 8, 1813; died June 2,
1896; married William Fox Richardson, of Boston,
born there Sept. 12, 1816. He was in the iron and
steel business; vice-president of the North Avenue
Savings Bank in Cambridge; founder of the Boston
Penny Savings Bank and its president for many
years; member of the Cambridge school committee.
His widow was living in Boston as late as 1897.

3563 Caroline Francour Brown, born Oct. 16, 1815; died.

3564 Anna Mann Brown, born Aug. 25, 1817; married,
Dec. 22, 1841, Hon. Aaron Hobart, of Abington,
Mass., born there Oct. 8, 1803; died in Boston May
8, 1880; a descendant of Edmund Hobart, an early
settler of Hingham, Mass. Went early from Boston to Charleston, S. C., where he remained 16 years;
returned to Boston and entered the dry goods business; served on the governor's council and was a
candidate for mayor. They resided at one time in
Glen Ridge, N. J. There were six children (one,
Arthur, the only one whose name is known).

3565 Adelaide Brown, born May 12, 1820; died young.

3566 Adelaide Brown, born March 19, 1822; died.

3567 William Henry Brown, born Nov. 20, 1825; died.

3568 Cornelia Brown, born May 8, 1828; died.

3569 Isabel Graham Brown, born Oct. 17, 1831; married
John L. Morse, a leading merchant of Beverly,
Mass., who was living in 1897.

3570 Oliver Selwyn Brown, born May 11, 1835; was living
in 1897, but had been an invalid many years.

3571 Ellen Salisbury Brown, born June 15, 1837; married
Hon. (Col.) William Raymond Driver, son of a sea-
captain of Beverly; was treasurer of the Bell Tele-
phone Company from its earliest organization. At
the time of the Civil War he enlisted in the Salem
Light Infantry, later entering the 19th Mass. regiment. He rose from the ranks to be a major, and
at the close of the war was made brevet-colonel of
volunteers for gallant service. He resided winters
in Boston and summers in Beverly.

1595 ROYAL WELLS[6] TYLER (Royal S.[5]), born in
South Coventry, Conn., July 25, 1796; married, in Salem,
Conn., Fanny Holmes. In 1850 he moved to Ohio City, Ohio.
Children:

3572   Infant, died young.
3573   Infant, died young.
3574   Infant, died young, on journey to Ohio.
3575   William S. Tyler, resided in Cleveland, Ohio.

1596 DOCTOR GEORGE WASHINGTON[6] TYLER
(Royal S.[5]), born in South Coventry, Conn., June 27, 1798;
died in Providence, R. I., October, 1853; married, in Cranston,
R. I., October 3, 1822, Mary Elizabeth Aborn. The children
were born in Cranston. Children:

3576+   Mary Theresa Tyler, born Oct. 30, 1823.
3577   Abby Watson Tyler, born Jan. 8, 1825; died in child-
        hood.
3578   Royal Samuel Tyler, born March 27, 1827; died Aug.,
        1850.
3579   Jonathan Aborn Tyler, died in childhood.
3580+   Abby Watson Tyler, born June 16, 1834.
3581   George Washington Tyler, Jr., born in 1840; died in
        1842.

1597 ABIGAIL WATSON[6] TYLER (Royal S.[5]), born
in Andover, Conn., November 25, 1801; died in Palmyra, N. Y.,
August 26, 1882; married, October 13, 1828, Dr. Alfred Riggs,
of Balston, N. Y.; born there June 20, 1800; died in Plainfield, N. J., November 24, 1871; son of Miles Riggs, descendant
of Edward the immigrant of 1633. He lived in Groton and
Lyons, N. Y., as a merchant and musician until 1836; moved
to New York City and began the study and practice of dental
surgery in which he became eminently conspicuous. Was the
original patentee of the application of atmospheric pressure
to artificial plates, substituting those then in use with clumsy
springs. This was a revolutionary step in dentistry. The
children were born in Groton, N. Y., except the youngest, who
was born in New York City.

CHILDREN:

3582   Adeline Emilia Riggs, born Aug. 19, 1830; resided
        unmarried in Rutherford, N. J.

3583   (Rev.) Herman Camp Riggs, born Oct. 2, 1832; married (1), March 28, 1863, Clara Loraine Wheeler, of Williamstown, Mass., who died in Potsdam, N. Y., May 27, 1865; married (2), April 17, 1872, Agnes Elizabeth Bates, of Malone, N. Y. He was graduated from the University of New York in 1852; from Union Theological Seminary, 1856; ordained in 1857. Was called to several churches and in 1897 was engaged in his second pastorate at St. Peters Church, in Rochester, N. Y. Has one son by first marriage (Dr. Herman Clarence, who practices medicine in Brooklyn, N. Y.).

3584   Henry Scott Riggs, born Aug. 5, 1836; married, Oct. 18, 1864, Fannie Fairman Goodrich, of Stockbridge, Mass. He was in business in New York City, but lost his health and moved to Palmyra, N. Y.; has one son and three daughters (Walter, Louise, Grace and Clara).

3585   Alfred Tyler Riggs, born Sept. 18, 1839; married, Nov. 15, 1877, Georgia Wells Hine, of Milford, Conn. He was a merchant in New York many years; was out with the emergency men in the Civil War to repel the invasion of the Confederates into Pennsylvania; he lost his health and moved to San Jose, Cal.; no children.

1599   DOCTOR BENJAMIN S.[6] TYLER (Royal S.[5]), born in Andover, Conn., about 1805; died August, 1881; married (1), in Connecticut, ——; married (2), in Connecticut, ——; married (3), in Ohio, Helen Marr Young, born in Canada about 1823; died December 7, 1897. He went to Royalton, Ohio, where the children by his third marriage were born. He then moved to South Brooklyn, Ohio, thence to Brooklyn, now a part of Cleveland, Ohio. The children by his first marriage were born in Connecticut.

Children, by first marriage:

3586   Mary Tyler, died young.
3587   Benjamin Tyler, lived in the west; died unmarried, in Cleveland, aged about 60.

CHILDREN, by third marriage:

3588   Royal Tyler, born about 1849; married, near Toledo, Ohio, Abbie Morris. He is a farmer and lives in Yondota, Ohio; has a son (Ambrose; born 1885).

3589   Willis Tyler, born about 1851; died, s. p., in Brooklyn, Ohio, about a year after his marriage; married Maria Bush, daughter of Rev. Mr. Bush, of Brooklyn; he was a business man.

3590   George Tyler, died young.

3591   George Tyler, died young.

3592+   Clayton Tyler, born 1855.

3593   Abby Tyler, born 1858; died unmarried, Feb., 1879.

3594+   Helen Maria Tyler, born Jan. 25, 1860.

1601   GIDEON WELLS[6] TYLER (Royal S.[5]), born in Andover, Conn., August 15, 1810; died in Oberlin, Ohio, March 31, 1878; married (1), in Granger, Ohio, April 15, 1841, Diana M. Hickox, who died January 21, 1851, aged 30; married (2), September 6, 1852, Mrs. Charlotte Jennett (Ames) Munson, of Milford, Conn.; born July 26, 1821; died in Oberlin, February 2, 1892. In 1826 he moved to Cleveland, Ohio; about 1840 moved to Granger, Ohio; about 1854 he moved to Medina, Ohio, where he owned the leading store and where he was county auditor two terms; in 1873 he moved to Oberlin. He was a successful business man, owning stock farms and mills, and active in church and public affairs; an enthusiastic abolitionist. His estate was probated in Elyria, Ohio, April 8, 1878. The elder children were born in Granger; the youngest in Medina.

CHILDREN, by first marriage:

3595   Richard Henry Tyler, born June 18, 1842; died May 12, 1843.

3596+   Mary Adelia Tyler, born April 1, 1844.

3597   Nathan Elmore Tyler, born Feb. 18, 1846; died unmarried, Aug. 9, 1873, in Chicago, Ill.; studied in Oberlin and was in business in St. Louis and Chicago.

3598   Lydia Matilda Tyler, born Aug. 9, 1847; died unmarried, Nov. 9, 1900; residence was Greenwich, Conn.

3599   Richard Henry Tyler, born Jan. 14, 1851; a world's
        traveler.

CHILD, by second marriage:
3600+   George Wells Tyler, born Aug. 1, 1859.

1607 HANNAH PARKMAN[6] TYLER (John Eu-
gene[5]), born in Westboro, Mass., September 25, 1803; died in
1857; married Onslow Peters.   Through her mother, who was a
daughter of Breck and Susanna (Brigham) Parkman, of Westboro, Mrs. Peters was descended from the Parkmans of Westboro and the Brighams of Northboro.   (See *The History of the
Brigham Family*.)   Children:
3601   Susan Tyler Peters, born June 21, 1831; died May 9,
        1852; married George Blakely.
3602   Mary Lovett Peters, born April 7, 1833; married, Oct.
        26, 1856, Henry G. Weston, D. D., who died s. p.
        in Upland, Pa.; president of Crozer Theological
        Seminary.
3603   Onslow Edward Peters.
3604   Hannah Breck Peters, married, Oct. 26, 1856, John
        Rollins, of Fort George, Fla.
3605   Hugh Peters.
3606   Eugene Parkman Peters.

1609 ANNA SOPHIA[6] TYLER (John Eugene[5]), born
in Westboro, Mass., January 25, 1809; died January 20, 1889;
married, February 11, 1845, Hon. Christopher Columbus
Denny, of Keene, N. H. (whose first wife was Susan Brigham
Rockwood); born January 10, 1813; died July 8, 1895; son
of Joseph Denny, of Leicester, Mass.   He was a merchant in
Keene, N. H., afterwards removing to Leicester, Mass., where
he was a card clothing manufacturer for over 20 years.   Was
in the state legislature, one term, and was, at various times,
selectman, town clerk, and assessor, and for many years was a
deacon in the Congregational church and superintendent of
the Sunday-school.   On her mother's side, Mrs. Denny was
descended from Breck and Susanna (Brigham) Parkham, of
Westboro.   (See *The History of the Brigham Family*).

CHILDREN:

3607   Theodore Addison Denny, born Aug. 21, 1846; died
         Sept. 13, 1846.
3608   Herbert Eugene Denny, born May 21, 1849; died May
         30, 1863.
3609+   Parkman Tyler Denny, born Dec. 20, 1851.

1610   SARAH AUGUSTA[6] TYLER (John Eugene[5]),
born in Westboro, Mass., June 11, 1811; died April 15, 1875;
married John A. Fayerweather, of Westboro. For her ancestry on her mother's side, see *The History of the Brigham
Family.* Her children were born in Westboro. Children:
3610   John Tyler Fayerweather, born Oct. 17, 1833; died
         Oct. 24, 1833.
3611   Sarah Wheelock Fayerweather, born May 29, 1835;
         married, Feb. 7, 1866, William R. Gould, who died.
         He was a merchant and resided, s. p., in Westboro,
         where his widow lives.

1614   DOCTOR JOHN EUGENE[6] TYLER (John Eu-
gene[5]), born in Westboro, Mass., December 9, 1819; died March
9, 1878; married (1), Caroline Amelia Denny, born November
12, 1825; died September 27, 1848; married (2), November 8,
1852, Augusta Maria Denny, born February 28, 1825; died
December 15, 1899; daughter of George and Charlotte S.
(Parkman) Denny, of Boston. He was graduated from Dartmouth College in 1842; he attended a course of medical lectures
at the Dartmouth Medical School and then completed this
course at the University of Pennsylvania, graduating in 1846;
he also received a diploma from Dartmouth. After six years
of successful practice in Salmon Falls, N. H., he was elected
superintendent of the New Hampshire Insane Asylum. In
1858 he was chosen superintendent of the McLean Asylum,
Somerville, Mass. He resigned this position on account of
his health in 1871 and was in practice in Boston as a distinguished consulting physician and expert until his decease.
(For his genealogy on his mother's side, see *The History of
the Brigham Family.*) Child:
3612   Charlotte Amelia Tyler, born June, 1848; died July,
         1848.

1617 ELIZABETH ANN⁶ TYLER (Joseph⁵), born in Boston, Mass., September 12, 1810; died in Charleston, S. C., September 10, 1850; married, September 11, 1832, James Henry Taylor, of Charleston, where the children were born. Children:

3613   Julia Caroline Taylor, born Oct. 31, 1833; married, April 28, 1863, Benjamin Curtis Hard, of Williamston, S. C.; had five children.

3614   Henry Clarence Taylor, born Oct. 26, 1835; killed at the Battle of Seven Pines, May 31, 1862; was in the Hampton Legion, C. S. A.; married, Sept., 1855, Louisa C. Doerrer, of Cincinnati, Ohio; had one child.

3615   Constantia Whitridge Taylor, born Feb. 15, 1837; married, May 18, 1855, Joseph Righton Robertson, of Charleston; had three children.

3616   Elizabeth Cornelia Taylor, born Dec. 3, 1838; died s. p., Nov. 1, 1894.

3617   John Edward Taylor, born Oct. 28, 1840; died in infancy.

3618   Alfred Taylor, born Feb. 16, 1842; died in infancy.

3619   George Edwyn Taylor, born Feb. 14, 1844; married, May 15, 1866, Emma Catherine Hard, of Pendleton, S. C.; had seven children.

3620   Frank Eugene Taylor, born March 22, 1846; married, Oct. 14, 1868, Clara Wilson; lives in Charleston; has nine children.

3621   Mary Everlyn Taylor, born June 14, 1848; died Oct. 24, 1863.

3622   Charles Herbert Taylor, born Oct. 28, 1850; died Feb. 8, 1851.

1623 COLONEL FISHER AMES⁶ TYLER (Nathan⁵), born in Mendon, Mass., March 15, 1812; died in Holly Springs, Miss., January 31, 1902; married (1), May, 1840, Virginia Ann Townes, who died March, 1879; daughter of Armstead Townes, "Gentleman," of Amelia Court House, Va., and Grenada, Miss.; married (2), June, 1880, Mrs. Rosa (Barton) Goodloe, of Holly Springs; daughter of Roger Barton, a leading lawyer of Mississippi. She was a teacher; once assistant principal of Franklin Female College; then of a private school for young ladies. Colonel Tyler studied law, finishing his course in Cincinnati, Ohio, in 1834-1835, in which latter year he moved to Vicksburg, Miss. He bought half an interest in the *Daily Register* in 1836 and was editor four years. Forming a law partnership with E. S. Fisher, later of the Mississippi Supreme bench, he moved to Granada, Miss.; also practiced at Panola, Memphis, Tenn., and Holly Springs, Miss. In 1847 he felt impelled to the ministry and attended the Cincinnati Presbyterian Theological Seminary, after which he had a church for ten years; he then moved to Memphis to edit a church paper. Lost all in the Civil War; was on the staff of General Price, C. S. A., with rank of colonel. After the war he bought an interest in the *Daily Appeal* of Memphis, and later started an evening daily *Register*. He then bought *The South* at Holly Springs, which he edited until 1891. He was a man of high ideals, strict integrity and great ability.

CHILDREN, by first marriage:

3623   Townes Tyler, died in childhood.
3624   Macon Tyler, died in childhood.
3625   Lelia Tyler, died aged 18.
3626+   Fisher Ames Tyler, born in Cincinnati, Dec. 3, 1847.
3627   Eliza Tyler, died in childhood.
3628   Arthur Tyler, died in childhood.

CHILD, by second marriage:

3629   Roger Barton Tyler, born March, 1881; resided in Gainesville, Texas, unmarried.

1630 CATHERINE BARNARD CLAPP[6] TYLER (Nathan[5]), born in Mendon, Mass., September 7, 1829; married, May 17, 1848, in Providence, R. I., George Capron, son of Collins Capron, of Blackstone, Mass.; he was graduated from Brown University in 1848, and at time of death was general agent of the State Mutual Life Assurance Company, of Worcester, Mass. She resided in Newton Center, Mass., in 1898. Children:

3630   Mary Tyler Capron, born Aug. 17, 1852; died July 12, 1857.
3631   George Collins Capron, born April 22, 1857; married (1), June 15, 1882, L. M. Whitten; two sons; married (2), June 10, 1896, L. N. White.

3632   Arthur Granger Capron, born Nov. 16, 1859; died Aug. 12, 1861.

3633   Caroline Silsby Capron, born July 1, 1862; married, June 17, 1896, Edward Duble; one daughter.

3634   Susan Tyler Capron, born Sept. 17, 1864; died Feb. 26, 1867.

3635   Fanny Isabel Capron, born Aug. 31, 1866; married, Feb. 14, 1895, Harry A. Tomlinson.

3636   Philip Ward Capron, born Jan. 31, 1869.

3637   Catherine Capron, born March 19, 1870; died Dec. 19, 1870.

3638   John Farill Capron, born Dec. 12, 1873.

1632   THOMAS STEPHEN[6] TYLER (Aaron[5]), born in Mendon, Mass., August 27, 1810; married Mercy Chandler, of Bath, Maine. He early moved to California. The entire list of his children is not known. Children:

3639   Elizabeth Tyler, married George Sperry, of Oxford, Conn.; she died.

3640   Jane Tyler, died young.

3641   Justin Tyler.

1637   HON. AARON[6] TYLER, JR. (Aaron[5]), born either in Mendon, Mass., or Bath, Maine; murdered at the Courthouse (Chicago) in 1871; married Elizabeth Boswell, of Peacham, Vt. He was a lawyer in Chicago, Ill., and judge of the 10th Illinois Judicial Circuit Commission, August 20, 1860. Children:

3642   William Wirt Tyler, a farmer, and resides in Malcom, Iowa.

3643   Mary Boswell Tyler, unmarried, residing in St. Louis; an artist.

3644   Grace Tyler.

1639   DOCTOR JOSEPH ALONZO[6] TYLER (Aaron[5]), born in Bath, Maine, 1834; died in Albany, Ore., July 17, 1887; married Margaret ———, who, in 1897, resided in San Francisco. He was a physician in Portland, Eugene and Albany, Ore. Children:

3645   Aaron Alonzo Tyler.

3646   Mamie Editha Tyler.

1644   ELIJAH[6] TYLER (Nathan Web[5]), born in Westhampton, Mass.; married Louisa Hewitt, of Castleton, Vt. He resided in Chesterfield, Mass., where his children were born. Children:

3647   Alsina Tyler.

3648   Almira Tyler, drowned, while trying to save the life of a friend in Northampton, Mass.

3649   Harriet Tyler.

3650   Louisa Tyler.

3651+   Nathan Tyler, born 1812.

3652   Lidia Tyler, married (1), ——; married (2), Asa Tubbs; living in 1897.

3653+   Elijah Tyler, born Feb., 1816.

3654+   Nancy A. Tyler.

3655+   Henry P. Tyler, born in 1820; married Frances Edwards.

3656   Sarah Tyler.

3657   Julia Tyler.

3658   Almira Tyler, married John Alrien; in 1897 was a widow living in Cohoes, N. Y.

1645   BENJAMIN OWEN[6] TYLER (Stephen[5]), born in Buckland, Mass., September 24, 1789. His wife's name is not known. He made a fac-simile of the Declaration of Independence. Children:

3659   Howard Tyler, resided and died in New York City.

3660   Henry C. Tyler, moved west.

1646   EPHRAIM[6] TYLER (Stephen[5]), born in Buckland, Mass., April 19, 1791; died in Guilford, Vt., August 24, 1878; married, December 1, 1819, Mary Bissell, who died in 1861 eldest daughter of Asahel and Polly Bissell. He was a citizen of Wilmington, Vt., for forty years, where his children were born. He owned a fine farm and was closely identified with early town history; he was postmaster under President Adams and state representative in 1828. He moved to Guilford in 1840, where he held many town offices. His mind was clear to the last. Children:

3661+   Benjamin O. Tyler, born Sept. 7, 1820.

3662+   Ansel L. Tyler, born Oct. 11, 1822.

3663+   D. Clinton Tyler, born Oct. 10, 1825.

3664   Minerva Tyler, born March 20, 1828; died, s. p., Jan. 31, 1858; married, July 10, 1854, Dr. D. W. Jones, of Medfield, Mass.; now of Boston.

3665   Sarah M. Tyler, born Feb. 12, 1831; lives with her brother on the homestead in Guilford.

3666+   James M. Tyler, born April 27, 1835.

3667   William H. Tyler, born Nov. 27, 1839; married, Jan. 11, 1881, Belle Newcomb, of Leyden, Mass. He is a farmer and lives on the old homestead in Guilford. He was educated at the Brattleboro Academy. Was in the 16th Vt. Volunteers in the Civil War, at Gettysburg and in other battles. He has held town offices and was state representative in 1890.

1647   ELI^6 TYLER (Stephen^5), born in Buckland, Mass., May 20, 1793; died in Newfane, Vt.; name of wife unknown. Children:

3668   Stephen Tyler, died ——.

3669   Lewis Tyler, died ——.

3670   Charles Tyler, resided in Newport, Vt.

1649   CHESTER GRINNELL^6 TYLER (Stephen^5), born in Westhampton, Mass., November 19, 1797; died in Richmond, N. H., October 11, 1856; buried in West Boylston, Mass.; married Roxanna Harris, of Whitingham, Vt. He resided in Whitingham and Bennington, Vt., and moved in 1855 to Richmond, N. H. All but the eldest child were born in Bennington. Children:

3671   Anna Maria Tyler, born in Whitingham, Vt., Aug. 20, 1824; married (1), —— Sturtevant; married (2), Joseph Derrigan, of Fitchburg, Mass.; married (3), —— Wight; she had one child, which died young; resided in East Princeton, Mass.

3672+   Oscar Stephen Tyler, born Jan. 20, 1828.

3673   Jane Caroline Tyler, born Jan. 20, 1830; married (1), Amos Burleigh, who died in Ashuelot, N. H.; married (2), —— Ward, who died; resides in Fitchburg, Mass.; has one son and two daughters.

3674   Elizabeth Celia Tyler, married George Munyon, who

died aged 30 years; she resides in Shirley, Mass.; has two sons and two daughters.

3675+ Henry Clay Tyler, born 1835.

3676   Chester Warren Tyler, born about 1838; died in Libby Prison, aged 26, unmarried; was lieutenant of the 26th N. Y. Cavalry.

3677   Susan Sophia Tyler, born 1854; she died s. p. about 1894; married —— Fairbanks; she was an insurance agent in Boston, Mass.

3678   Roxanna Tyler, born 1856; died 1860.

3679   Frances Tyler, born 1857; married —— Taylor; resided in Richmond, N. H.

1654 HANNAH⁶ TYLER (Moses⁵), born in Hadley, Mass., February 24, 1795; married, February 9, 1814, Eldad Brewster, of Bridgewater, Pa., where the children were born. Children:

3680   Tyler Brewster, born March 24, 1815; died in Harford, Pa., Jan., 1885.

3681   Lucania Brewster, born Nov. 20, 1816.

3682   Horace Brewster, born Oct. 10, 1818; had a daughter (who married E. C. Smith); had a son who was a doctor in Scranton, Pa.; another son was an attorney in Montrose, Pa.

3683   Daniel Brewster, born Nov. 22, 1820; died Oct., 1895; was a blacksmith in Montrose, Pa.

3684   Warren Brewster, born Dec. 11, 1822; died 1874.

3685   Andrew Brewster, born March 23, 1827; a blacksmith in Montrose, Pa.

3686   Sally Brewster, twin to Andrew, married S. A. Hempstead, of Binghamton, N. Y.

3687   Moses Coleman Brewster, died 1859.

3688   Ann Mariah Brewster, born July 18, 1831; married Ansel Stearns, of Harford, Pa.

1655 MOSES COLEMAN⁶ TYLER (Moses⁵), born in Wilmington, Vt., April 7, 1802; died January 26, 1885; married (1), December, 1825, Mary French, born June 24, 1806; died March 1, 1840; she was of Binghamton, N. Y.; married (2), October 18, 1841, Cornelia G. Read, born in Montrose, Pa., September 8, 1820; died May 4, 1845; married (3), May

15, 1847, Harriet Harris, of North Sea, L. I., born May 18, 1807; died 1897. He moved to Montrose, Pa., where he was a judge. Was in business in New York City for a time. The children of the second and third marriage were born in Montrose. This line is extinct.

CHILDREN, by first marriage:

3689   Owen Benjamin Tyler, born in Montrose Aug. 16, 1826; died unmarried in Downersville, Cal., June 12, 1860; an attorney.

3690   Clark Kellogg Tyler, born in New Jersey, Sept. 13, 1828; died unmarried in St. Louis, July 3, 1857; a clerk.

3691   Coleman Merriam Tyler, born Elizabethtown, N. J., Aug. 22, 1831; died Aug. 26, 1837.

3692   Henry Cass Tyler, born in Montrose, June 18, 1836; died June 10, 1891; married June 15, 1864, Frances E. Wilcox; resided s. p., in Montrose.

CHILDREN, by second marriage:

3693   George Kearl Tyler, born Oct. 7, 1842; died Aug. 31, 1843.

3694   Ella Cornelia Tyler, born Jan. 27, 1845; died Jan. 21, 1852.

CHILD, by third marriage:

3695   William Cooper Tyler, born Aug. 4, 1851; died Jan. 21, 1852.

1657 EMMA[6] TYLER (Moses[5]), born in 1806, one record says " in Montrose, Pa. "; but another record says that her father did not remove to Montrose from Wilmington, Vt., until 1807; died in Willet, N. Y., August 10, 1863; married, January 1, 1826, Samuel E. Newcomb, born in Bridgewater, Pa., December 1, 1806 (see *Newcomb Genealogy*). Children:

3696   Therese E. Newcomb, born Oct. 11, 1829; married Gilbert Greene.

3697   Elizabeth E. Newcomb, born March 5, 1831; married J. Cook.

3698   Adaline Newcomb, born Oct. 15, 1832; married Orlando Avery.

3699   Sarah O. Newcomb, born Aug. 23, 1834; married
Stephen J. Adams.

3700   Louise Newcomb, born July 25, 1836; married Angelos
M. Clark.

3701   Gilbert L. Newcomb, born April 19, 1840; married
Lizzie Sunderland; he was graduated from the University of New York City Medical College in 1861;
assistant surgeon U. S. A., and practiced in New
York City.

3702   Franklin Newcomb, born July 19, 1842; married Lib-
bie Thurston.

3703   Curtis S. Newcomb, born March 5, 1843; married
Pluma Mathews.

3704   Willis Newcomb, born Nov. 3, 1845; a druggist in
New York City.

3705   Ella Newcomb, born March 3, 1847; married ——
Delavan.

3706   Marion Newcomb, born Aug., 1849; died 1860.

3707   Cornelia Newcomb, born Nov. 7, 1851; died 1852.

1658   EMILY⁶ TYLER (Moses⁵), born in Montrose,
Pa., 1807; died October 6, 1863; married, October 4, 1826,
Uri Newcomb, born in Montrose, August 2, 1806 (see *New-
comb Genealogy*). The children were born in Montrose.
Children:

3708   Marvin Alonzo Newcomb, born Sept. 14, 1827; first
mayor of Tama City, Iowa; had a family.

3709   Emma Ann Newcomb, born Dec. 20, 1828; married
James W. Wright, of Tama City, Iowa; had a
family.

3710   Uri Clark Newcomb, born Oct. 12, 1830; married
Caroline Munson, of Tama City, Iowa; had a family.

3711   Alburn R. Newcomb, born Aug. 1, 1832; married Lura
Morgan, and resides in Glencoe, Minn.

3712   Martin Van Buren Newcomb, born Sept. 10, 1834;
married Roseltha Taylor; resided Earlville, Iowa;
had a family.

3713   Frances Adelia Newcomb, born Feb. 1, 1837; married
Ezra B. Gord; resided Dunlap, Iowa; had a family.

3714   Sarah Amanda Newcomb, born June 26, 1839; married
Thomas Smith, of Montrose.

3715   Eugene S. Newcomb, born Aug. 21, 1844; married
        Jennie Trinter; resided Manchester, Iowa.
3716   Frederick Peter Newcomb, born June 22, 1847; mar-
        ried Julia Munson; resided Tama City, Iowa; had
        a family.
3717   Emily Eudora Newcomb, born Sept. 27, 1850; died
        Feb. 6, 1864.

    1669 SIMEON⁶ TYLER, JR. (Simeon⁵), born in West-
hampton, Mass., December 6, 1797; died in Brooklyn, Pa., in
1857; married, Oct. 30, 1822, Wealthy Warner, who died
March, 1838. He lived in Montrose, Pa., and also in Dimmock, Pa., where his children were born. Children:
3718+   Amanda R. Tyler, born Feb. 10, 1823.
3719+   Eliza O. Tyler, born July 9, 1825.
3720+   Caspar William Tyler, born March 6, 1837.

    1670 BETSEY⁶ TYLER (Simeon⁵), born in West-
hampton, Mass., December 6, 1799; died 1868; married (1),
October 10, 1822, Harry Clark; married (2), George W.
Lewis, a hotel-keeper in Dimmock, Pa.

            CHILDREN, by first marriage:
3721   Ruby E. Clark, married James Bullard, of Brooklyn,
        Pa.; had a son who died, and a daughter (Stella, who
        married Lester Tewksbury, of Brooklyn).
3722   Anna Clark, died unmarried in 1863.

    1671 ANSEL⁶ TYLER (Simeon⁵), born in Wilmington,
Vt., February 14, 1803; died in East Bridgewater, Pa., March
10, 1848; married, January, 1835, Isabella Young, of Yardley-
ville, Pa., born in 1805; died in 1895; daughter of Andrew
Young, of Montrose, Pa. He resided in Dimmock and Bridgewater, Pa. The four elder children were born in Dimmock,
and the others in Bridgewater. Children:
3723+   Leander Ansel Tyler, born Feb. 23, 1836.
3724+   Duane Legrange Tyler, born in 1837.
3725+   Ellen Lucenia Tyler, born Sept. 8, 1839.
3726   Andrew Osias Tyler, born Dec. 4, 1840; no record of
        marriage received; was with the 151st Pa. Volun-

teers and wounded at Gettysburg; resided in Tiffany, Pa.

3727+   Clark Lewis Tyler, born Feb. 20, 1842.

3728+   Martha Tyler, born March 5, 1844.

1672 HARVEY[6] TYLER (Simeon[5]), born in Wilmington, Vt., April 1, 1804; lived and died in Montrose, Susquehanna County, Pa., about 1889; married (1), September 27, 1827, Sarah Coyle, of Philadelphia, Pa.; married (2), June 26, 1849, Amanda Bullard, who resided in 1900 in Montrose, where all the children were born.

CHILDREN, by first marriage:

3729   William Larned Tyler, born May 8, 1833; died in California, leaving two sons; he moved to Belle Plain, Minn., and then to California, and from thence to New Orleans, La., about 1861. He was a printer.

3730   Charles B. Tyler, born Sept. 21, 1834; a printer; lived in Marshall, Minn., and had four children, two of whom died. The town of Tyler, Lincoln County, Minn., was named for Mr. Tyler, who, at that time was register of the U. S. Land Office in the district. He went to Minnesota in 1858.

3731   Logan Osceola Tyler, born June 22, 1836; killed at Chancellorsville, May 3, 1863, in the Civil War; was first lieutenant of Company H of the 141st Pa. Infantry in Aug., 1862.

3732   Sarah Adelaide Tyler, born Nov. 24, 1840; married, Oct. 2, 1865, Thomas Williams, of Franklin, Pa., who died; they had two sons (Charles T. and Mark).

CHILDREN, by second marriage:

3733+   George W. Tyler, born Nov. 16, 1850.

3734   Harvey J. Tyler, born March 15, 1859; died Sept. 8, 1863.

1673 ABIGAIL[6] TYLER (Simeon[5]), born in Wilmington, Vt., August 19, 1806; married, December 6, 1827, Levi B. Guernsey, a farmer, of Bridgewater, Pa.   Children:

3735   George Mortimer Guernsey, born in Tioga, Pa., Oct. 4, 1828; died in Platteville, Wis., Oct. 4, 1885; married, Dec. 15, 1856, Martha Roach, of Bridgewater, Pa. He was graduated from Amherst College in 1856; taught from 1857-1867; in the insurance business 1867-1875; superintendent of the Platteville schools from 1875-1885; had two daughters (Fanny, married Rev. Reuben B. Whipple, of Conn., and Maud E.).

3736 Sarah O. Guernsey, born Nov. 2, 1830; married —— Sweet, who was killed in the Civil War; one child.

3737 Peter C. Guernsey, born May 30, 1833; married twice; had a son and daughter, each of whom died unmarried; she lives in Amherst, Mass.

3738 Ophelia Guernsey, died young, unmarried.

1692 MOSES W.[6] TYLER (Joseph[5]), born in Townshend, Vt.; died in Erie, Pa., in 1893, aged 86; married Sarah Potter. He lived in Townshend, Brattleboro, Vt., and Erie, Pa. Children:

3739 Ellen Tyler.
3740 Frances Tyler.

1694 FERDINAND[6] TYLER (Joseph[5]), born in Townshend, Vt., 1808; died in Brattleboro, Vt., June 19, 1876; married, August 16, 1837, Sophronia Miller. He was in the hardware business in Brattleboro, of the firm of " Williston and Tyler." Child:

3741 John Tyler, died unmarried in Brattleboro, Jan. 11, 1880, aged 41; was graduated from college and served in the Civil War.

1697 DEACON JOSEPH CURTIS[6] TYLER (Joseph[5]), born in Townshend, Vt., October 8, 1814; died in Boston, Mass., October 16, 1889; married Mary A. ——. For many years he was deacon and prominent supporter of the Mt. Vernon church in Boston. He was an importer of foreign fruits, under the firm name of J. C. Tyler & Co.; was president of the Boston Seaman's Friend Society, and president of the Penitent Females' Refuge and Bethesda Society. Children:

3742 Joseph Curtis Tyler, Jr., died in Manila, Philippine Islands, aged 40.

3743 Columbus Tyler, resides in Seattle, Wash.

1702   HIRAM WARD[6] TYLER (Timothy[5]), born in Townshend, Vt., March 3, 1802; died 1882; married, February 22, 1841, Susan S. Baile.   Child:
3744+   Frank M. Tyler, born April 25, 1843.

1704   MARY ALMIRA[6] TYLER (Joseph[5]), born in Charlton, Mass., January 30, 1811; married, April 2, 1833, Samuel Scott Seagrave, of Uxbridge, Mass.; moved to Wellesley, Mass.   Children:
3745   Gilbert Henry Seagrave, born April 23, 1834; married Mrs. L. A. Townsend.
3746   Mary Lucinda Seagrave, born April 11, 1836; died March 30, 1849.
3747   Helen Ross Seagrave, born Oct. 4, 1838; married, Dec. 7, 1865, John Simpson.
3748   Elvira Adeline Seagrave, born March 16, 1841; married, Feb. 13, 1860, John Simpson; had two children (Jessie and Helen).
3749   John Newton Seagrave, born Oct. 14, 1843; married Margaret Mannel.
3750   Edward Payson Seagrave, born July 5, 1846; married Carrie A. Barrows.
3751   Frederic Scott Seagrave, born June 16, 1849; married Adelaide G. Ruttledge.
3752   Caroline Augusta Seagrave, born Sept. 8, 1851; married, July 22, 1869, Elmer E. Snell; had one child (Ellis G.).
3753   Ida Laurie Seagrave, born March 1, 1854; married, Nov. 5, 1872, Charles E. Colby; had three children (Grace, Gertrude and Mary).
3754   George Edwin Seagrave, born Nov. 14, 1858.

1706   HIRAM[6] TYLER (Joseph[5]); married Martha W. Grant, of Worcester, Mass.   He was a great mechanic; went west and had a boat on the Ohio River.   He lived in Portsmouth or Cincinnati, Ohio, and was an inventor in steam engineering.   Children:
3755   Hiram Tyler, married Ella ——; she died before her husband.   He was an engineer of repute, and went to South America to set up engineering in large government boats; he returned to Ohio and died

soon after of fever. He had two sons; both were adopted young by the mother's family, who lived in "Quaker Bottom City" (?).

3756 Amanda Tyler.
3757 Florence Tyler.
3758 Lawrence E. Tyler, born in Worcester, Jan. 20, 1849.

1707 SOPHIA[6] TYLER (Joseph[5]). She ran away to New York City and married Dr. Brown. Left her husband and resumed her maiden name, which her child afterwards bore. She later married —— Weed, who died in Worcester, Mass.

CHILD, by first marriage, name changed to Tyler:
3759+ Albert Winslow Tyler.

CHILD, by second marriage:
3760 Joseph Weed, died aged 21.

1722 SYLVANUS[6] TYLER (Royal[5]), born in Uxbridge, Mass., October 19, 1811; died February 19, 1889; married (1), October 8, 1835, Mary E. Quick, born September 15, 1810; died February 2, 1841; married (2), April 14, 1842, Nancy Quick, born April 8, 1822; died November 12, 1881. He moved in 1820 to Dimmock, Pa., with his father. The children were born there.

CHILDREN, by first marriage:
3761+ William P. Tyler, born July 14, 1836.
3762 Samuel S. Tyler, born Nov. 5, 1837; died March 9, 1880; married Sarah Blakeslee of Dimmock.
3763 Frances E. Tyler, born Feb. 23, 1839; died Oct. 9, 1886, s. p.; married Asa Mecham.
3764 Jefferson C. Tyler, born Jan. 4, 1841; married Louisa Carlin; resides in Auburn, Pa.; has four children, two of them sons.

CHILDREN, by second marriage:
3765+ Henry H. Tyler, born Jan. 18, 1843.
3766 Mary Tyler, born Aug. 4, 1848; married Alonzo Blakeslee, of Watertown, N. Y.; three children.
3767 John M. Tyler, born Aug. 13, 1850; married Dora

(or Dara) Young, of Wilkesbarre, Pa.; has three
children, one of them a son.

3768   George B. Tyler, born April 26, 1857; died July 10,
1859.

1723   MOSES S.[6] TYLER (Royal[5]), born in Uxbridge,
Mass., October 18, 1814; died in Bridgewater, Susquehanna
County, Pa., November 16, 1884; married, March 11, 1840,
Cordelia Ackley, of Bridgewater, where he moved. Children:
3769   C. Edgar Tyler; resides Montrose, Pa.
3770   Ackley Tyler.

1724   MARY[6] TYLER (Royal[5]), born in Rhode Island
February 13, 1819; married, May 25, 1843, Sterling Ackley, a
farmer and lumberman, born in Wyalusing, Bradford County,
Pa., December 20, 1817; died February 23, 1894. Children:
3771   Cordelia Ackley, born Feb. 28, 1847; unmarried.
3772   Newell Sylvanus Ackley, born July 17, 1849; married, Oct. 22, 1872, ——; lived in Merryall, Pa.;
had three children (Lena, Royal Tyler, Bertha).

1725   LOUISA SOUTHWICK[6] TYLER (Royal[5]), born
in Dimmock, Pa., December 16, 1820; died in Sycamore, Ill.,
July 1, 1892; married, October 5, 1841, Marshall Stark, born
in Lucerne County, Pa., August 12, 1813; died December 26,
1882; son of Oliver Stark. Went to Sycamore, DeKalb
County, Ill.; was sheriff there in 1852 and county supervisor.
Children:
3773   Harmon Marshall Stark, born July 5, 1842; married
(1), Mary J. Patten; married (2), Susan Clark;
had seven children (James, Louisa, Herbert, Emma,
Grace, Henry, Ray).
3774   Martha Samanthe Stark, born Dec. 26, 1843; married Hosea M. Atwood; had six children (Richard,
John, Henry, Stark, Kate, Morris).
3775   Mary Elizabeth Stark, born June 1, 1845; married L.
Curtis Harris; had one child (Jefferson S.).
3776   Jefferson Oliver Stark, born April 4, 1847; s. p., 1901;
married Lydia J. Carver; was a stock dealer in
Sycamore.

3777   Henry Jerome Stark, born June 8, 1849; s. p., 1901; married Carolyn Anderson; dealer in stock and hay.

3778   Theron Monroe Stark, born Nov. 3, 1851; married Sylvia W. Galder; dealer in stock in Sycamore; had four children (Maud, Frank, Arthur, Dorothy).

3779   Adah Louise Stark, born April 27, 1856; married James Maitland, a farmer, of Sycamore; had two children (Everett, Howard, who died).

3780   Ella Amanda Stark, born Feb. 10, 1858; married Adolphus W. Brower, a hardware dealer in Sycamore; had two children (Anna L. and Floyd E.).

3781   Emma Jane Stark, born Nov. 15, 1859; married Charles F. Wiggins, a farmer in Colorado, later of Iowa; had four children (Elmer, Theron, Howard, Ella).

3782   Hattie Marinda Stark, born Dec. 13, 1863; married Burton W. Lee, a farmer in Sycamore; had three children (Marshal, Charles, Frank).

1727 ROYAL[6] TYLER, JR. (Royal[5]), born in Dimmock, Pa., January 16, 1825; died in Oak Valley, Kan., March 20, 1894; married Mary A. Miller, who resided in 1901, in Independence, Kan. The children were born in Oak Valley. Children:

3783+   Emma L. Tyler.

3784   Priscilla Tyler, married Scott Marden, a farmer, of Oklahoma. They had two sons and two daughters (Frank, Francis, Grace, Ellie.)

3785+   James Tyler.

3786   Ida J. Tyler, was unmarried and resided with mother.

3787   Martha Tyler, married Alford E. Thomas, a farmer, in Kansas; they had three daughters (Lettie B., Elsie A., Eda O.)

3788+   Edgar Tyler.

3789+   Oratus Tyler.

3790   Olive Tyler.

1728 JAMES[6] TYLER (Royal[5]), born in Dimmock, Pa., June 11, 1827; married Mary Haverly. He went to Los Angeles, Cal. Children:

3791   Louisa Tyler, married —— Daily, of San Ventura, Cal.
3792   Lena Tyler, died Sept., 1895.
3793   Julia Tyler, died July, 1893.
3794   Sterling Tyler, died in 1894.

1731 WILLIAM H.[6] TYLER (Parker[5]), born in Copley, Ohio, January 22, 1825; died in Attica, Ind., March 12, 1886; married (1), 1847, Cyntha Brier, of Warren County, Ind., who died in Uniontown, Kan., March 18, 1877; she came of a leading Indiana family; married (2), 1875, Mrs. Moore. He was a farmer and a Justice of the Peace. He went to Indiana with his father about 1840 with whom he remained several years after coming of age, helping him to develop his farm. He made the round trip on foot to Copley and back again to collect for his father deferred payments on his farm there sold. After his marriage he bought 80 acres near the Tyler homestead and kept adding until he had 320 acres. He sold out in 1868 and moved to Fort Scott, Coffee County, Kan., and thence to Uniontown, Kan. He returned to Indiana where he died and was given a Masonic burial. He was a Republican and member of the M. E. church. His children were born in Williamsport, Ind.

CHILDREN, by first marriage:
3795+   Byron Tyler, born April 24, 1849.
3796+   George Brier Tyler, born March 10, 1851.
3797   James A. Tyler, born Jan. 7, 1853.
3798+   Samuel Tyler, born Feb. 24, 1855.
3799   Lucretia Ellen Tyler, born May 12, 1858; married, 1879, Charles Beever, of Winthrop, Ind.; they had two daughters.
3800   Benjamin F. Tyler, born Nov. 14, 1860; married, May 24, 1899, Allie Mack, of Omaha, Neb. He was a school-teacher, a carpenter, and later became a grain commission merchant, and a member of the Kansas City Board of Trade, in which place he has his residence. He is a Knight Templar and a Knight of Pythias.
3801   Bruce Tyler, born Oct. 16, 1863; he is a telegraph operator and a conductor on the Mexican National

Railway; speaks and writes Spanish; a Mason of a
high degree; lives in Acambaria, Mexico.

1732 MARTHA[6] TYLER (Parker[5]), probably born in
Copley, Ohio; married William Jones, of Yates Center, Kansas.
Children:
3802 Wilbur Jones, merchant in Vernon, Kansas.
3803 Albert Jones, lawyer, Yates City, Woodson County,
Kansas.
3804 Anna Jones, married —— Mix; has a family.
3805 Eva Jones, married —— Harned, Girard, Kansas;
has a family.

1733 GEORGE CLINTON[6] TYLER (Parker[5]), born
in Copley, O., November 1, 1828; died in Marshfield, Ind., July
7, 1896; married, 1851, Harriet Swank. He was a large
farmer; a member of the board of County Commissioners. The
children were born in Marshfield. Children:
3806 Jennie Tyler, born Feb. 1, 1853; married, Feb. 14,
1870, T. J. Graves, of Toledo, O. They had three
sons and one daughter (Arthur, Bert, Lou, Earl.)
3807 Flora Tyler, born April 5, 1855; married, April 30,
1879, D. Clinton Andrews, of Hendrick, Ind.; they
had one son (Arnet, born March 2, 1880.)
3808+ Ella Tyler, born March 21, 1857.
3809+ Julia Tyler, born March 22, 1859.
3810 Emma Tyler, born Dec. 18, 1861; married Dec. 24,
1883, W. D. Rosebraugh; resided, s. p., Tampico,
Ill.
3811 Laura Tyler, born March 31, 1866.
3812 George Clinton Tyler, Jr., born Jan. 6, 1870; resided
in 1897 at home with mother.

1734 JAMES[6] TYLER (Parker[5]), born probably in
Copley, O.; resided in West Lebanon, Ind. The name of his
wife is not known. Children:
3813 Mabel Tyler, unmarried, night telegraph operator in
West Lebanon.
3814 Laura Tyler, married —— Jones, cashier of the bank
in West Lebanon.
3815 Emma Tyler, telegraph operator in Fort Wayne, Ind.

3816   Ollie Tyler, married —— Swain; resides in Danville,
        Ill.; a commercial traveler; two children.
3817   Nettie Tyler, married Professor Erickson, of Danville,
        Ill.; one son.

    1735 HIRAM[6] TYLER (Parker[5]), born probably in
Copley, O.; resided in West Lebanon, Ind. The name of his
wife is not known. Children:
3818   Son, killed about 1880.
3819   Lora Tyler, died about 1895.
3820   Anna Tyler, married, Sept. 30, 1896, Art Anderson,
        of Elston, Ind.; no children.
3821   Brenda Tyler, a teacher; lives at home.
3822   Della Tyler, married John Whitten, of West Lebanon,
        Ind.; no children.

    1736 HARRIET[6] TYLER (Parker[5]), born presumably
in Copley, O.; married Hudson Wood. Children:
3823   Frank Wood, had three children (Park, Levurn, De-
        light.)
3824   Sallie Wood, married —— Morgan; had three chil-
        dren.
3825   Emma Wood, married —— Lash, Butler, Mo.; had
        two children.

    1739 BENJAMIN[6] TYLER, JR. (Benjamin[5]), born in
Copley, O., March 22, 1821; died in Greenleaf, Wis., March
30, 1874; married (1), March 3, 1842, Mary Ann Krotzer,
born in Wadsworth, O., September 12, 1819; died July 3,
1862, in Wrightstown, Wis.; married (2), August 22, 1862,
Mrs. Nancy E. (Le Grant) Clarke, born October 8, 1836;
daughter of Abraham and Margaret (Brands) Le Grant (by
her first marriage she had a son); in 1897 she lived in Mitaca,
Minn. Benjamin was a farmer and in the Civil War. The
children of the first marriage were born in Wadsworth. Children, by first marriage:
3826+   Ann Mariah Tyler, born Nov. 4, 1843.
3827+   William Henry Tyler, born Jan. 8, 1845.
3828   Olive Rosina Tyler, born Nov. 2, 1853; died Jan. 10,
        1891; married, Dec. 25, 1869, Willard Beaulieu,
        of Neillsville, Wis.

Children, by second marriage:

3829   Arthur E. Tyler, born Sept. 26, 1863; married, Sept.
        28, 1893, Viola Hatch, born Aug. 8, 1868; she was
        of Princeton, Minn.; he lives in Milaca, Minn., s. p.

3830+   Ella Bertha Tyler, born Dec. 22, 1867.

1740 JOSEPH[6] TYLER (Benjamin[5]), born in Copley,
O., August 14, 1822; in 1896 was living in Wadsworth, O.;
married (1), December 22, 1846, Eliza Ann Williams, who died
in Wadsworth, June 5, 1893; married (2), October 30, 1895,
Mrs. Lucia L. Cunningham, of Wadsworth, daughter of William and Aurilla Phelps (she had a son by her first marriage).
Joseph Tyler was in the Secret Service of the United States
during the Civil War, attached to the receiving ship *Clary
Dobson,* and was most efficient and faithful. The children
were born in Wadsworth.

Children, by first marriage:

3831   Augusta T. Tyler, born Oct. 16, 1847; in 1896 was
        living with her father.

3832+   Rush S. (or H.) Tyler, born Oct. 15, 1851.

3833+   Jessie R. Tyler, born Sept. 17, 1856.

1743 ROSINA[6] TYLER (Benjamin[5]), born in Wads-
worth, Ohio, October 5, 1827; living in 1897 in Greenleaf,
Wis.; married in 1846, in Wisconsin, Amos S. Hart, a farmer.
Moved to Wrightstown, then to Greenleaf. Children:

3834   Harriet A. Hart, born in 1852; married, 1870, James
        Ellis; had nine children.

3835   Orvilla Hart, born 1859; married, 1879, Samuel
        Smith; had four children.

3836   Hall Hart, twin to Orvilla; married, 1895, Matilda
        Cross.

3837   Ida Hart, born in 1869; married, 1890, Frank Mc-
        Clure; had two children.

1745 REV. ALBERT[6] TYLER (Timothy[5]), born in
Smithfield, R. I., November 16, 1823; married (1), May 31,
1845, Wealthy H. Drury, of Auburn, Mass., born 1826; daughter of Alvah and Mary Drury, who died in Worcester, Mass.,

January 24, 1868; married (2), December 31, 1868, Eliza A.
D. Josephs, of Quincy, Mass., born 1843. In 1838, the last
month of the year, he went into the printing office of the Worcester *Spy*, and remained until 1844; from there he went to
Barre, Mass., as printer of the *Patriot*, till 1849, when he
bought an interest in the *Worcester Palladium* printing office.
In August, 1851, he was ordained a Universalist minister, and
in 1852 he took a charge at Oxford, Mass. In 1854 he removed to Granby, Conn., and in 1860 to Quincy, Mass. In
1861 he returned to Worcester, where he bought in the job
printing office of the *Spy*, which he held until 1882. In 1873
he went to Oxford as a minister, and in October, 1885 he established there its first paper, the *Mid-Weekly*. He was representative to the Legislature in 1883 and on the school committee several years, and was chairman of the board at one
time. The fourth child was born in Oxford, as were the three
younger. The fifth, sixth and seventh were born in Granby.

CHILDREN:

3838   Jessie Eudora Tyler, born in Barre, Mass., Dec. 18,
        1845; assistant librarian in the Public Library of
        Worcester, Mass.

3839   Phebe Amelia Tyler, born in Worcester, June 5, 1848;
        died Sept. 1, 1849.

3840   William Tyler, born in Worcester, May 30, 1850;
        died Aug. 15, 1881.

3841+   Martha Tyler, born May 5, 1853.

3842   Harry Bates Tyler, born March 18, 1855; a civil engi-
        neer in New Granada, South America (Santa Mar-
        ta, U. S. C.).

3843   Albert Hawes Tyler, born Jan. 21, 1858; died Dec.
        11, 1882, unmarried, in Honda, U. S. C.

3844+   Walter Drury Tyler, born April 6, 1860.

CHILDREN, by second marriage:

3845   Mary Eliza Tyler, born March 7, 1874; died March
        10, 1874.

3846   Josie Alberta Tyler, born April 12, 1875; resides in
        Oxford, Mass.

3847   Royall Tyler, born June 21, 1877.

1746 CHARLES E.⁶ TYLER (Timothy⁵), born in

Smithfield, R. I., February 8, 1835; married (1), 1855, Lucinda Drumond, Palmer, Mass.; married (2), Mrs. Martha Brigham, of Palmer, Mass.; married (3), Mary Paul, of Oxford, Mass. Child, by first marriage:

3848+ Sarah Frances Tyler, born in Oxford, Oct. 20, 1856.

CHILD, by second marriage:

3849 Freddie Tyler, born July 19, 1867; died Feb. 17, 1881.

1747 CYNTHIA⁶ TYLER (Solomon⁵), born June 14, 1829; died in 1890; married —— Hodge, of Wadsworth, O., where her children were born. Children:

3850 Tyler Hodge, married and resided in Akron, O.; works in the pottery.

3851 Francis Hodge, a railway engineer; resides in Fort Wayne, Ind.

1750 LEMUEL⁶ TYLER (Solomon⁵), born August 13, 1835; died 1881; married, 1861, in Copley, O., Annie Hammond, born in England, 1839. He was a farmer and dealt in sheep and cattle in Rensselaer, Ind. Children:

3852 James Newell Tyler, born Jan. 29, 1862; married, in 1894, ——; resides in Rensselaer, Ind., and had a son born in 1898.

3853 Frank Hubbard Tyler, born Oct. 18, 1864; married in 1886, ——. He resides in Waverly, Ill., and has a son and daughter (Ray and Susie).

3854 Marilla May Tyler, born May 17, 1868; died Sept. 10, 1873; married, 1892, ——.

3855+ Alice Augusta Tyler, born Aug. 7, 1871.

3856 Solomon Frederick Tyler, born Sept. 23, 1874; teacher; unmarried in 1898 and resided at home.

3857 Charles Lewis Tyler, born Aug. 26, 1877; unmarried in 1898.

1759 MINERVA⁶ TYLER (Newell⁵), born in Uxbridge, Mass., July 9, 1847; died in Worcester, Mass., August 20, 1894; married in Worcester, September 14, 1871, William C. Young, born in Leominster, Mass., in 1848. He was a manufacturer there. Children:

3858 Mabel Minerva Young, born July 18, 1872; was in Wellesley College, class of 1898.

3859   Alice Marion Young, born Jan. 15, 1874; died March
        27, 1875.

3860   Edith Caroline Young, born Oct. 29, 1877; was in
        Wellesley College, class of 1900.

3861   Infant daughter, born and died, Nov. 11, 1884.

3862   Ethel Sawyer Young, born July 12, 1888; died Aug.,
        1888.

    1760 MERCY[6] TYLER (John[5]), born in Attleboro,
Mass., November 5, 1769; died Sept. 9, 1840; married, Dec. 9,
1790, Obadiah Carpenter, born August 2, 1767; died May 14,
1833.   Moved to Harford where the children were born.   Children:

3863   Lois Carpenter, born Feb. 8, 1792; died Sept. 26, 1843;
        married (1), Lee Richardson, born June 7, 1792;
        died June 24, 1833; married (2), William Hendrick;
        had ten children by first marriage.

3864   Mercy Carpenter, born Sept. 22, 1793; died March 10,
        1866; married Nov. 22, 1814, Stephen Richardson
        Thacher, born July 11, 1787; died Sept. 11, 1823;
        had two children.

3865   Asa Carpenter, born Oct. 27, 1795; died Dec. 18, 1845;
        married (1), Betsey Ellsworth, born Feb. 3, 1792;
        died Nov. 26, 1862; married (2), Catherine Ranny;
        had several children.

3866   Achsah Tyler Carpenter, born March 9, 1798; died
        July 9, 1868; married, Jan. 1, 1818, Tingley Tiffany, born Oct. 28, 1798; had six children, three
        died young.

3867   Amherst Carpenter, born March 5, 1799; died 1877;
        married, July 12, 1821, Fanny Sweet, born Sept. 3,
        1801; had four children.

3868   Adah Carpenter, born Jan. 22, 1801; died Jan. 14,
        1803.

3869   Remember Carpenter, born Aug. 25, 1802; died Aug.
        26, 1802.

3870   Infant, born June 6, 1803; died June 7, 1803.

3871   Cynthia Carpenter, born May 10, 1804; died Jan. 4,
        1874; married, March 9, 1824, Jacob Clark, born
        Feb. 17, 1797; had two children.

3872   Hannah Carpenter, born Feb. 3, 1806; married (1),

Austin Ellsworth, who died Dec. 27, 1828; married
(2), Joseph Blodgett; had one son by first marriage
and six children by second marriage.

3873 Obadiah Lee Carpenter, born March 2, 1808; died
Dec. 18, 1867; married Eliza Tingley; had four
children.

3874 Pennel Carpenter, born Aug. 26, 1810; married, March
31, 1836, Caroline Greene, born Aug. 2, 1814; had
five children.

3875 Silence Carpenter, born Sept. 20, 1813; died Sept.
20, 1813.

1761 MARY⁶ TYLER (John⁵), born in Attleboro,
Mass., November 5, 1769; died July 13, 1834; married, April
15, 1790, Cyril Carpenter, born in Attleboro, Mass., Sept. 14,
1766; died November 23, 1811; he was a farmer in Harford,
Pa., where the children were born. Children:

3876 Lucinda Carpenter, born Dec. 19, 1790; died March
6, 1840; married David Avery, born March, 1795;
died Feb. 6, 1872; had two daughters.

3877 Mary Tyler Carpenter, born March 20, 1793; died
Sept. 11, 1857; married Edmund Worth; had five
children.

3878 Achsah Carpenter, born May 20, 1794; died Aug. 9,
1794.

3879 Tyler Carpenter, born July 9, 1797; died Dec. 13,
1798.

3880 Tilghman Carpenter, born June 15, 1798; married
(1), Oct. 10, 1816, Juliana F. Buchanan, born Aug.
9, 1798; died Dec. 3, 1865; married (2), June 22,
1867, Maria Isaac Carpenter, born Nov. 24, 1811;
had six children.

3881 Lucy Carpenter, born July 11, 1800; died Sept. 25,
1800.

3882 Tyler Carpenter, born Oct. 27, 1802; married, Oct.
27, 1823, Mary Graham, born Dec. 2, 1803; died
April 6, 1873; had nine children.

3883 Cyril Carpenter, born Feb. 12, 1806; married, Feb.
14, 1825, Thirza Hobbs, born Jan. 10, 1808; had
ten children.

3884 Dan Carpenter, born March 27, 1807; married, Oct.

5, 1831, Lydia Cobb, born June 18, 1812; had seven
children.

3885   Electa Carpenter, born Aug. 27, 1809; married Nov.
4, 1833, Joseph H. Robinson, born Feb. 12, 1813;
had seven children.

1762 POLLY[6] TYLER (John[5]), born in Attleboro,
Mass., September 15, 1771; died May 28, 1811; married, February 21, 1793, her cousin, John Carpenter, No. 1769, September 1, 1776; died March 2, 1838 (he married [2], 1813,
Lydia Potter).   He was a farmer and one of the " Nine Partners " who moved to Harford, Pa.   Children:

3886   John Carpenter, born Dec. 30, 1793; married Phebe
Brigham; resided in Harford; he was a merchant
and teacher; lost on Lake Erie.

3887   Asahel Carpenter, born June 7, 1796; died Dec. 8,
1842; married, June 10, ——, Amanda Thayer,
born Oct. 6, 1806.

3888   Polly Carpenter, born Aug. 14, 1798; died March 19,
1870; married, Sept. 30, 1824, Austin Jones, born
Feb. 24, 1788; died April 2, 1861; had five children.

3889   Jesse Carpenter, born Feb. 24, 1801; married 1827,
Hannah Coleman.   He was a farmer and manufacturer in Pawtucket, R. I.

3890   Betsey Carpenter, born March 1, 1803; died June 4,
1886; married Clark S. Tanner, born March 12,
1798; died April 12, 1869.   He was a farmer; had
six children.

3891   Nancy Carpenter, born May 13, 1804; married Mil-
bourne Oakley, a farmer; had seven children.

3892   Son, born May 28, 1811; died same day.

3893   Daughter, twin to the son; died same day.

1763 NANNY[6] TYLER (John[5]), born in Attleboro,
Mass., August 31, 1773; married, 1791, Thomas Sweet, born
1768; died November 12, 1849; she died April 25, 1837.   The
children were born in Harford, Pa., where their mother had
moved with her father in early life.   Children:

3894   Charlotte Sweet, born Aug. 27, 1792; died April 24,
1837; married, March 19, 1812, Rev. Lyman Richardson, born March 20, 1793; died Oct. 1, 1867.

He was one of a famous family of educators in north-eastern Pennsylvania; and was the first teacher in Latin of Prof. William Seymour Tyler; had three children.

3895 (Doctor) Thomas Sweet, born June 13, 1796; died Oct. 8, 1872; married (1), 1824, Elizabeth Myer, born 1804; died 1826; married (2), April 24, 1828, Charlotte Forbes (or Fobes), born April 4, 1808.

3896 Nancy Sweet, born Jan. 9, 1799; died unmarried Feb. 21, 1857.

1764 JOHN⁶ TYLER, JR. (John⁵), born in Attleboro, Mass., February 22, 1777; died May 26, 1857; married, February 28, 1806, Mary Wadsworth, born May 31, 1781; died October 9, 1819. Mrs. Tyler was descended from Captain Joseph Wadsworth, who hid the Connecticut charter in the Charter Oak in 1687, and also from Captain Eli Catlin, of the Colonial army, and from Rev. Peter Thacher, of Salisbury, Eng., and his son, Rev. Thomas Thacher, first pastor of the Old South church in Boston. Mr. Tyler was one of the early pioneers of "Nine Partners," later of Harford, Pa., and by reference to his father's biography it will be seen that he participated in the stern struggles and duties of that new region in which he and so many Attleboro Tylers acquitted themselves with faithfulness and distinction. The male line is extinct.

CHILDREN:

3897 (Professor) John Wadsworth Tyler, born Nov. 28, 1806; died unmarried June 11, 1833. He was a graduate of Union College and a distinguished professor in Cazenovia Seminary, and several years its principal. His early death was a great loss to the cause of education, which has been so largely advanced by the descendants of the Harford pioneers.

3898+ Clara Catlin Tyler, born April 9, 1810.

3899+ Harriet Ann Tyler, born April 27, 1817.

1765 JOB⁶ TYLER (John⁵), born in Attleboro, Mass., August 22, 1779; died in Harford, Pa., July 7, 1857; married, May 5, 1803, Sally Thacher, born June 23, 1781; died May

29, 1860. He went to Harford, Pa., with his father, when he
was not far from 18 years of age, where his father was a leading man, and where he and his brothers and sisters took active
part in the development of the new country and the advance-
ment of the best things of civilization. The children were born
in Harford. Children:

3900+ Nancy Tyler, born April 12, 1804.

3901+ Jared Tyler, born April 21, 1806.

3902   Polly Wadsworth Tyler, born Nov. 20, 1820; married,
       May 15, 1850 (As second wife), Silas Brewster
       Guile, a tanner of Harford, Pa., born Jan. 1, 1809;
       died March 16, 1887; no children.

1766 ACHSAH⁶ TYLER (John⁵), born in Attleboro,
Mass., April 20, 1782; died August 11, 1830; married (1),
January, 1806, Rev. Whiting Griswold, who died January 13,
1815, aged 35; married (2), August 4, 1816, Major Jason
Torry, born June 3, 1772; died November 21, 1848. Lived
in Harford and Bethany, Pa.

CHILDREN, by first marriage:

3903   Joab Whiting Griswold, born in Harford, Pa., Sept.
       14, 1807; died Oct. 3, 1873; married, 1831, Sarah
       Smith; had seven children.

3904   Achsah Milissa Griswold, born Sept. 19, 1812; married
       Jeremiah C. Gunn, born July 21, 1804; died April
       19, 1889.

CHILDREN, by second marriage:

3905   James Torry, born in Bethany, Pa., Sept. 9, 1817;
       died July 30, 1833.

3906   (Rev.) David Torry, D. D., born Nov. 13, 1818; mar-
       ried (1), Oct. 3, 1848, Mary E. Humphrey, born
       Sept. 26, 1827; died April 8, 1867; married (2),
       Aug. 28, 1872, Georgiana Worth Mitchel Mosely,
       Dec. 9, 1832; had two children by first marriage.

1767 DEACON JOAB⁶ TYLER (John⁵), born in Attleboro, Mass., July 23, 1784; died in Amherst, Mass., January
11, 1869; married (1), November 16, 1809, Nabby Seymour,
born in Berlin, Conn., January 31, 1788; died in Amherst,

Mass., at the home of her son, Prof. W. S. Tyler, August 28, 1844; daughter of Deacon Jonathan and Abigail (Hart) Seymour, of Oswego, New York, and descended from Thomas Wells, Governor of Connecticut, Anthony Hawkins and Richard Treat, all original patentees of the royal charter of that colony; married (2), Sophronia D. Johnson, who died in 1890.

Prof. W. S. Tyler says: " My mother was practical and sensible. But she was also intellectual, reflective, imaginative, emotional, spiritual, fond of reading and intent on the intellectual and spiritual improvement of her children far beyond the average of women and much above the level of those by whom she was surrounded. She was a beautiful woman, with a broad high forehead, large liquid dark blue, almost black, eyes, and a figure at once winning and commanding. . . . Her voice was musical, and fitted her to be the leading female singer in the choir. . . . A cultivated mind and a loving heart were the sceptre of her power. My father, naturally stern and firm almost to obstinacy, was softened and swayed by her influence. . . . And though she overworked body and mind and heart, and died when she was only fifty-six, she lived to see all her sons, not only converted and educated, but actively and successfully engaged in the work of educating others."

A biography of Deacon Joab Tyler would include much of the early history of the town of Harford, to which he came when ten years of age and began to undergo the hardships of the pioneer. He was twenty-six when his father turned over to him his Harford home and left him to take a leading part, throughout his long life, in the history of the town. He was his father's favorite son and partner. He was soon made deacon in his father's place and he and his partners ran the village store. He was justice of the peace. Prof. W. S. Tyler says in an obituary notice: " In all the several lines of material, educational and religious progress, Deacon Joab Tyler was truly pioneer, building miles of turnpike and plank road with his own limited means; contributing to the extent of his ability, and even beyond his ability to the erection of improved schoolhouses and attractive churches; taking the lead in support of capable and faithful teachers and preachers; struggling against nature and untoward circumstances with efforts and expenditures that might have created a city under more favorable auspices, to build up a flourishing town in the backwoods

and among the Alleghany Mountains, but in all his toils, laboring and praying chiefly that it might be a city of the living
God.

"In those days when distilling and rum selling were universally deemed lawful and proper occupations, he was a distilling and rum selling deacon; and inasmuch as his house
(being near to the church) was always the hotel for ministers
from out of town, it often occurred, on the arrival of some
clergyman, especially at some 'Ministers' meeting,' that the
writer, in his boyhood, was sent off to the store with his hands
full of 'decanters,' for a fresh supply of whiskey, rum and
brandy, for their refreshment. But no sooner had Doctor
Beecher with his coadjutors blown their blasts, and announced
the temperance reformation, than Deacon Tyler bought out
his partners, and at a great pecuniary sacrifice, closed the dis-
tillery and stopped the sale of rum in the store." The children were born in Harford.

CHILDREN:

3907+   William Seymour Tyler, born Sept. 2, 1810.
3908+   Wellington Hart Tyler, born Oct. 14, 1812.
3909+   Edward Griswold Tyler, born July 23, 1816.

1768 JABEZ[6] TYLER (John[5]), born in Attleboro,
Mass., March 13, 1787; died ——; married (1), Nov. 7, 1811,
Harriet Wadsworth, born July 30, 1787; died December 31,
1820; married (2), November 3, 1823, Mary R. Kingsbury,
born December 29, 1797. He went with his father from Attleboro to Harford, and shared with the others of his family all
the hardships of opening up a new region to civilization. He
moved to Ararat, Pa., where his children were born. The male
line is extinct.

CHILDREN, by first marriage:

3910   Royal Tyler, born July 27, 1813; died s. p. March 20,
       1888; married, Oct. 29, 1857, Mary Jane Evans,
       born Aug. 13, 1837.
3911   Edward Catlin Tyler, born Nov. 11, 1816; died March
       30, 1817.
3912   Daughter, born and died May 26, 1818.
3913   Son, born July 27, 1819; died the same day.
3914+ Harriet Wadsworth Tyler, born Dec. 19, 1820.

CHILDREN, by second marriage:

3915 Williston Kingsbury Tyler, born Oct. 11, 1825; died, s. p., Oct. 15, 1864; married, Oct. 18, 1854, Jane Harris, born June 14, 1833.

3916+ Ebenezer Denison Tyler, born Feb. 6, 1828.

3917 Julius Tyler, born Oct. 23, 1832; married, May 17, 1865, Ellen C. Fletcher, born April 18, 1843; he was living, s. p., in 1899; he was a poet.

1786 LUCINDA⁶ TYLER (Ebenezer⁵), born November 6, 1785; died August 15, 1820; married Edward Richardson. Children:

3918 Edward Tyler Richardson; married —— Stanley.

3919 Elial Falkner Richardson; died in infancy.

3920 Horatio Nelson Richardson; married —— Dean.

3921 Charles Stewart Richardson.

3922 Mary Lucinda Richardson; married —— Henry Starkey.

1787 REV. WILLIAM⁶ TYLER (Ebenezer⁵), born in Attleboro, Mass., January 7, 1789; died in Auburndale, Mass., Sept. 27, 1875; married (1), July 1, 1813, Betsey Balcom, who died in Weymouth, Mass., June 9, 1822; aged 32; married (2), Nancy N. Newell, who died in Auburndale February 14, 1876, aged 75. He was graduated from Brown University in 1809. He went into the manufacture of cotton goods with his father in Pawtucket, and after a time determined upon the ministry as a profession. His style was epigrammatic and he was fearless in uttering his thought. He was settled as the colleague of Rev. Simeon Williams over the Congregational church of South Weymouth and remained as sole pastor thirteen years. In 1832 he was installed pastor of the church in South Hadley, Mass., and remained seven years. In 1839 he removed to Amherst, Mass., where he remained for some time under a commission from the Mass. Home Missionary Society. In 1847 he became proprietor and editor of the Northampton *Courier*, and remained two years. In 1852 he removed to Pawtucket, Mass., which he represented in the Massachusetts Constitutional Convention in 1853. In 1863 he went to live in Auburndale. He was much interested in Mt. Holyoke Seminary, one of its first trustees, and a valued friend and advisor of its

founder, Miss Mary Lyon. For many years Mr. Tyler was
an untiring pioneer in the cause of the Tyler family biography.
November 13, 1866, in addressing a kinsman, he said: "I
have spent time and money for years; and now, lacking less
than 2 months of 78 years, I wish to finish the business and
leave it in good shape for my survivors." Alas, his dream, to
"finish" and publish a Tyler family history, was never real-
ized! Among many generous thoughts, one very dear to him
and long entertained, was some day to bring together members
of the whole clan Tyler into a genuine family reunion; the mate-
rialization of this happy vision was never in his lifetime seen!
After long, long years of waiting, the Tyler reunion occurred
in 1896, in North Andover, Mass., but Mr. Tyler had passed
beyond.

CHILD, by first marriage:

3923+   William Ebenezer Tyler, born in Attleboro, April 20,
1822.

CHILDREN, by second marriage:

3925   Elizabeth Balcom Tyler, born in Weymouth, Mass.,
Sept. 8, 1826; resided, unmarried, in Auburndale,
Mass.
3926+   Anna Newell Tyler, born in Weymouth Feb. 1, 1828.
3927   Henry Erastus Tyler, born Nov. 29, 1829; a broker in
Maiden Lane, N. Y.
3928+   Evarts Cornelius Tyler, born Feb. 10, 1832.
3929   Edmund Whiting Tyler, born in South Hadley, May
28, 1834; resides in Auburndale; a music dealer.
3930   John Augustus Tyler, born April 21, 1837; died Sept.
22, 1837.
3931   Arthur Frederick Tyler, born Nov. 3, 1838; died Sept.
15, 1846.
3932+   Francis Maurice Tyler, born in Amherst, May 27,
1843.

1789 ANN[6] TYLER (Ebenezer[5]), born in Pawtucket,
R. I., July 19, 1794; died December 31, 1841; married, April
8, 1812, Daniel Greene, born April 16, 1793; son of Timothy
and Lucy (Wilkinson) Greene, an early tanner and manufacturer of Rhode Island. The children were born in Pawtucket.
Children:

3933 Joseph Greene, born Jan. 15, 1814.

3934 William Greene, born Dec. 31, 1816; died Sept. 16, 1860; unmarried.

3935 Mary Greene, born April 2, 1818; died Jan. 2, 1870; unmarried.

3936 Samuel Dean Greene, born Dec. 18, 1821; died Nov. 15, 1835.

3937 James Greene, born April 24, 1823.

3938 Ruth Ann Greene, born May 16, 1825; died Feb. 4, 1833.

3939 Sarah Hall Greene, born March 10, 1828; married Quincy Roberts.

3940 Elizabeth Tyler Greene, born May 1, 1831.

3941 Ruth Ann Greene, born Aug. 17, 1833; died Nov. 1, 1845.

3942 Samuel Wilkinson Greene, born Dec. 15, 1835.

1792 GEORGE[6] TYLER (Othniel[5]), born probably in Sudbury, Mass.; died about 1860; married (1), ——; who died in Galena; married (2), Mrs. Mary (Feehan) Reilly, widow of John Reilly, who moved soon after Mr. Tyler's death, to California, where she married Mr. Weatherwax, and died about 1897.

Children, by second marriage:

3943 Elinor Tyler, born in Galena; died there about the age of six.

3944 George Tyler, born in Galena and died in California, unmarried.

1794 SAMUEL[6] TYLER, JR. (Samuel[5]), born in Ashford, Conn., April 2, 1785; died in "Tyler Hollow," Marcellus, N. Y., September 23, 1844; married, 1810, Tabitha Whiting, born in Connecticut July 17, 1784: her family settled in Split Rock, N. Y.; she died in Perry, Ohio, January 6, 1864. He remained on his father's farm until his death, having gone to Marcellus when nine years old. His children were born in "Tyler Hollow." Children:

3945+ Ralph Tyler, born Sept. 25, 1810.

3946+ John Tyler, born April 22, 1813.

3947+ Jared Whiting Tyler, born April 8, 1816.

3948+ George Tyler, born April 23, 1818.

3949   Giles Wilson Tyler, born Nov. 28, 1819; died Sept. 18, 1821.

1797   DOCTOR DAVID[6] TYLER (Samuel[5]), born in "Tyler Hollow," Marcellus, N. Y., in 1792; died in Ann Arbor, Mich.; married Hannah Burtess, who died in Chicago March 22, 1877, aged 84; daughter of John Burtess, of Deckerstown, N. J. He was graduated from Onondaga Academy and received degree of M. D. He lost his property through signing a note for a friend. In 1830 he moved to Ann Arbor. The children were born in Marcellus. Children:

3950+   James Meakle Tyler, born March 15, 1817.
3951+   Charles Rollin Tyler, born Oct. 6, 1820.
3952+   Cornelia Maria Tyler.
3953+   Catherine Elizabeth Tyler.

1798   REV. JOB[6] TYLER (Samuel[5]), born in "Tyler Hollow," Marcellus, N. Y.; died at sea and buried in San Diego, Cal.; married Sally Ann Piper, of New York. About 1836 he moved to Colon, Mich. Children:

3954   De Witt C. Tyler.
3955   Liza Tyler.
3956   Matthew Tyler.
3957+   Mary Ann Tyler.
3958   John Tyler.
3959   James Tyler.

1799   HON. COMFORT[6] TYLER (Samuel[5]), born in Marcellus, N. Y. ("Tyler Hollow"), March 7, 1801; died in Colon, Mich., January 16, 1873; married Desire Belote. He received a common school education and assisted his father in farming, milling, wool-carding and dressing cloth until he was 24 years old. In 1834 he removed to Colon, and bought a large farm, where he lived the rest of his life. He was 25 years a supervisor; in 1841 state representative; in 1859 state senator, and in 1867 a member of the Constitutional Convention. He was first a Whig and then a Republican in politics. Children:

3960   Julia Tyler.
3961   Samuel Tyler.
3962   Ancel Tyler.

3963 Laura Tyler.

3964 Mary Tyler, married George Williams; lived in Burr Oak, Mich.

3965 Asher Tyler, educated in Ann Arbor; moved to California to the town of Martinez.

1800 JAMES[6] TYLER (Samuel[5]), born in Marcellus ("Tyler Hollow"), N. Y.; died there 1828, and was buried on his father's farm; married Mary Baker. The children were born in Marcellus. Children:

3966 Hiram Tyler, resided in Grand Rapids, Mich.

3967 James Tyler.

3968 Annie (?) Tyler.

1801 DEBORAH WEMPLE[6] TYLER (Comfort[5]), born in Onondaga, N. Y., March, 1787; died September 24, 1826; married, September 4, 1804, Cornelius Longstreet, of Onondaga Valley, N. Y., born 1777; died December 17, 1814; went to New York from New Jersey about 1802. The children were born in Onondaga. Children:

3969 James Longstreet, born May 24, 1806; died May 22, 1873; married, Dec. 31, 1829, Laura Breed, born Jan., 1806; died Sept. 17, 1876. He had six children (Cornelius, James O., Joseph B., Ellen E., Louisa A., and Laura B.).

3970 Elizabeth Longstreet, born March 9, 1808; died June 8, 1827; married, Jan. 1, 1826, Oren Tyler, No. 1804.

3971 Helen Longstreet, born July 15, 1810; died Sept., 1816.

3972 Jane Longstreet, born June 6, 1812; died July 10, 1880; married, April 28, 1835, Charles Lord Skinner, born 1794; died Sept. 5, 1863; three children (Charles H., James L., Sarah L.).

3973+ Cornelius Tyler Longstreet, born April 19, 1814.

1802 MARY[6] TYLER (Comfort[5]), born in Onondaga, N. Y., 1788; died 1870; married, 1802, George W. Olmstead, of Cohoes Falls, N. Y., born 1784; died 1884. Children:

3974 George Tyler Olmstead.

3975   Elizabeth Tyler Olmstead, died Troy, N. Y.; un-
        married.
3976   Mary Olmstead, married Lansing Tracy.
3977   Charles Augustus Olmstead, married Delia ——.

1803   LORA⁶ TYLER (Job⁵), born in Onondaga, N.
Y., January 4, 1792; died December 13, 1827; married, January 13, 1808, Ansell Kellogg, of Marcellus, N. Y., born October 21, 1787; died October 6, 1831.   The children were born
in Marcellus.   Children:
3978   Augustine Kellogg, Oct. 9, 1810; died Sept. 3, 1854;
        married (1), March 6, 1840, Chloe B. Tafft, who
        died April 25, 1842; married (2), Emeline Hatch.
3979   Charlotte Kellogg, born Aug. 9, 1813; died Aug. 8,
        1876; married, Nov. 9, 1841, Philander K. Wil-
        liams, born Oct. 5, 1803; died June 29, 1886.
3980   Susanna Kellogg, born Feb. 4, 1817; died June 16,
        1884; married, April 6, 1840, Benoni Lee, born June
        7, 1812; died Dec. 7, 1886.
3981   James Kellogg, born April 1, 1819; married Mary F.
        Stoner, of San Francisco, Cal.
3982   Mortimer Kellogg, born Oct. 3, 1821; died Nov. 16,
        1870.
3983   Hulda Kellogg, born Sept. 28, 1824; died Sept. 10,
        1825.
3984   Tyler Kellogg, born April 22, 1827; died Feb. 29,
        1828.

1804   OREN⁶ TYLER (Job⁵), born in Onondaga, N. Y.,
August 21, 1795; died in 1874; married (1), January 2, 1820,
Huldah W. Marsh, born May 9, 1800; died Aug. 4, 1823;
married (2), January 1, 1826, Elizabeth Longstreet, No. 3970,
born March 9, 1808; died June 8, 1827; married (3), January
11, 1829, Nancy Bliss, born December 25, 1798; died March
25, 1862.   The children were born in Onondaga.

CHILDREN, by first marriage:
3984a   Captain Edwin Job Tyler, born April 21, 1821; died
        Oct. 18, 1870; married Mary Elizabeth Cole, who
        died, s. p., Jan. 24, 1889.   For 18 years he was in
        the mercantile business, and in 1849 he sailed for

California, returning in 1851. In April, 1861, he
assisted in raising troops for the Civil War and was
made first lieutenant, his company becoming Company A, 33d N. Y. Volunteers, and was in Smith's
Division of the Army of the Potomac. He was
promoted to captain, and acting adjutant during
the Peninsular campaign. He was present at the
battles of Williamsburg, Garrett's Farm, Golding's
Farm, Savage Station, White Oak, Malvern Hill,
Second Bull Run, Antietam, Fredericksburg, Salem
Heights and Chancellorsville, besides minor fights.
In storming Maryland Heights his clothing was
pierced with bullets. After the battle of Golding's
Farm, he was officially commended by his colonel.
He was mustered out of service June, 1863. (See
History of the 33d N. Y. Vols., by David W. Judd.)

3985+   Ellen Tyler, born July 21, 1823.

CHILD, by second marriage:

3986+   Celia Deborah Tyler, born Oct. 12, 1826.

CHILDREN, by third marriage:

3987+   Darwin Tyler, born Sept. 15, 1831.

3988   Caroline Bliss Tyler, born Nov. 25, 1833; died Feb.
      21, 1881, s. p.; married James Bryant, who died
      Dec., 1883.

3989   Charlotte Tyler, born April 19, 1834; resided in
      Hartford, Conn., unmarried in 1897.

3990+   Mary Elizabeth Tyler, born Dec. 2, 1835.

3991   Seneca Tyler, born July 31, 1837; married Hannah
      Griffin; resided s. p. in Council Grove, Kan.

3992   Welthea Butler Tyler, born Dec. 6, 1837; married,
      Aug. 4, 1886, Robert E. Day, of Hartford, Conn.;
      she was a teacher; has no children.

1805 HON. ASHER[6] TYLER (Job[5]), born in Onondaga, N. Y., May 10, 1798; died in Elmira, N. Y., August
1, 1875; married, October 18, 1828, Matilda Youle, born May
27, 1802; she survived her husband; daughter of John Youle,
of New York. He was educated at Hamilton College, and was
graduated in the class of 1817; he was admitted to the bar, and

became the agent of the Devereaux Land Company, attending
to their legal work, but not otherwise engaging in the profession of law.   He resided for a number of years in Ellicottville,
Cattaraugus County, N. Y., and represented the county in the
Twenty-eighth Congress.   He became land agent of the Erie
Railroad Company, and served the company with ability and
distinction.   In 1848 he moved to Elmira, and was a charter
member of the Elmira Rolling Mill Company.   He spent the
later years of his life retired from business cares in the company
of his books.   Probably there was no one living in his day who
was more learned in Indian character, habits and origin than
Mr. Tyler.   He was generous and charitable; as a conversationalist, he was most extraordinary.

CHILDREN:

3993   John Alexis Tyler, born Nov. 14, 1829; died in Minneapolis June 22, 1865, unmarried.
3994   Amelia Charlotte Tyler, born June 6, 1831; unmarried.
3995   Mary Olmstead Tyler, born March 31, 1833; died unmarried.
3996   Jane Anne Tyler, born Nov. 3, 1834; unmarried.
3997   Josepha Tyler, born Oct. 9, 1836; unmarried.

1806   CHAUNCEY[6] TYLER (Job[5]), born in " Tyler
Hollow," Marcellus, N. Y., December 27, 1800; died May 12,
1871, in Graham, Mo.; married, April 23, 1825, Hannah Clodie.
He was early a contractor on the B. & O. Canal, and lived in
Georgetown, Md.   He emigrated from New York to Wisconsin
Territory in 1846, via the canal to Buffalo, thence by steamer
to Sheboygan, Wis., and then by teams to Waupun.   About
1870 he moved to northwestern Missouri, where some of his
children had settled after the war.   He was educated for a
doctor, but preferred farming.   His children were born in
New York State, except the youngest.

CHILDREN:

3998   Job Tyler, born July 19, 1828; died in Fillmore, Mo.,
        s. p. Nov. 6, 1878; married, Aug. 11, 1871, Martha
        Wardlow, of Fillmore; she died.   He enlisted with
        his brother Asher in the Civil War and was the
        bugler of his company until Feb. 1, 1862; did not
        re-enlist because of poor health.   He was a farmer.

3999+   Asher Tyler, born Aug. 6, 1831.

4000+   Helen Mary Tyler, born Dec. 14, 1833.

4001+   Lora Elizabeth Tyler, born April 5, 1837.

4002+   William Henry Harrison Tyler, born March 26, 1840.

4003   Isaac Clodie Tyler, born April 26, 1842; died unmarried Nov. 26, 1860.

4004   Nancy Roselia Tyler, born Nov. 8, 1845; died s. p. May 6, 1872, in Missouri, where she moved; married William Ayshford.

4005+   Herbert Milton Tyler, born in Waupun, Wis., Aug. 25, 1848.

1809   JOHN⁶ TYLER (John⁵), born in Ashford, Conn., October 3, 1805; died October, 1870; married, January 10, 1838, Roxanna Holman, who was living in 1896, aged 84. His farm was in Tolland, Conn., where the children were born. Children:

4006+   Mary Jane Tyler, born Nov. 11, 1838.

4007   John Emman Tyler, born Sept. 6, 1843; died in 1860.

4008   Andrew H. Tyler, born Nov. 7, 1846; died in 1850.

4009   Son; died young.

1810   GEORGE⁶ TYLER (John⁵), born in Ashford, Conn., March 19, 1810; died February 5, 1882, in Union City, Mich.; married, Sept. 18, 1839, Esther Robbins, born in Ashford, Conn., May 20, 1820. The two elder children were born in Munson, Mass.; the others in Union City, Mich. Children:

4010+   George De Witt Tyler, born May 2, 1841.

4011   Mary Ellen Tyler, born Sept. 24, 1842; died in Lynn, Mass., Oct. 23, 1885; was unmarried; interred in Union City.

4012   Emma Esther Tyler, born Jan. 21, 1849; resided in Union City.

4013+   Giles Merrill Tyler, born April 18, 1851.

4014+   Clara Zeruiah Tyler, born July 18, 1854.

4015+   John E. Tyler, born Nov. 2, 1856.

1416   William Tyler, born July 6, 1866; is unmarried; a teacher of music in Union City.

1814   AUGUSTUS⁶ TYLER (William⁵), born in Marcellus, N. Y., September 8, 1808; died in Platteville, Wis., No-

vember 11, 1875; married in Middlebury (now a part of Akron),
Ohio, December 31, 1833, Elizabeth Hanchett, born in Salisbury, N. Y., March 9, 1816; daughter of Dr. Elijah and Elizabeth (Durkee) Hanchett; her father was a surgeon in the
War of 1812; her grandfather Durkee was a Revolutionary
soldier. Mr. Tyler kept a hotel in Galena, Ill., in the days
before the war, when General U. S. Grant was " teaming," and
he used to stay at the hotel. Between 1836 and 1847 he lived
in Notawa Prairie, Mich., where the children from the second
to the sixth were born; the three youngest were born in Hazel
Green, Wis.

CHILDREN:

4017+   Mary Elizabeth Tyler, born in Middlebury, Ohio,
Dec. 4, 1834.

4018   William Elijah Tyler, born Dec. 16, 1836; died April
17, 1840, in Notawa Prairie.

4019+   Flora A. Tyler, born Nov. 20, 1839.

4020+   Adaline M. Tyler, born Sept. 20, 1841.

4021   Helen Tyler, born Nov. 12, 1843; died Aug. 3, 1844,
in Notawa Prairie.

4022+   Kate Tyler, born June 4, 1845.

4023   Ellen Tyler, born May 27, 1847; died in Platteville,
June 15, 1865.

4024+   George Hiram Tyler, born June 14, 1849.

4025   Martha I. Tyler, born Aug. 24, 1853; married, Sept.
23, 1881, Joel Garretson, of Massachusetts; her
home was in Scott River, Cal., but she is in the State
Hospital for the Insane, with no hope of recovery.

1821 GEORGE[6] TYLER (William[5]), born in Marcellus, N. Y., July 11, 1817; died in Ossawattamie, Kan., August
20, 1882; married, May 15, 1855, Eliza Chapman, born in
New Bridge, Onondaga County, N. Y., April 20, 1837. She
lives (1907) in Heyburn, Idaho, with her sons. When Mr.
Tyler was about nine years old his father died, and he became
the ward of his uncle, John Tyler, who was one of the projectors of the Erie Canal with De Witt Clinton and others,
and lived in Syracuse. George Tyler started the clothing business in Syracuse and increased gradually until he was one
of the leading merchants of the city. He bought the first sew-

ing machine in that part of the state, and at one time con-
trolled a large part of the salt industry in northern New York.
His widowed mother and the younger children lived with him in
Syracuse and he educated his brothers, and Hiram and Laurens
became associated with him in business. About 1853 he opened
a large business house in Burr Oak, Mich., his brothers looking
after the Syracuse house, and later going also to Burr Oak.
There he built up a store not unlike the great department stores
of the present day, and kept everything that the people in the
surrounding country would need; great corn cribs were built
and all kinds of grain were taken from the farmers in exchange
for other goods. His business averaged over a hundred thousand dollars a year for a number of years. There was no larger
business of the kind between Buffalo and St. Louis than his, at
one time. In one brief hour, however, a fire swept it all away;
but from the ashes Mr. Tyler started anew, paying off all his
indebtedness. Mr. Tyler had vast energy and great business
capacity and was very social and genial. In 1879 he retired on
account of failing eyesight. He had made the town of Burr
Oak and his death was mourned by many, far and near. His
generosity and helpfulness, together with his social gifts and
power of repartee gave him an honored place in the life of the
people. The children were born in Burr Oak.

CHILDREN:

4026+ Genevieve Tyler, born Aug. 8, 1856.

4027 William Augustus Tyler, born Jan. 19, 1859; a lumber dealer in Hope, Idaho, since 1897; married, 1904,
Bertha Wise; no children.

4028 Mary S. Tyler, born Aug. 16, 1862; died about 1899;
married, about 1895, William Loyid, who served in
the Civil War; she left a daughter.

4029 Grove Laurens Tyler, born April 7, 1867; lives in
Heyburn, Idaho; unmarried; carries on the largest
nursery of trees and shrubbery in the state, with
his brother George, on the new irrigated land.

4030 George Chapman Tyler, born Sept. 19, 1877; was
graduated from Blackburn University, in Carlins-
ville, Ill., in 1902; is unmarried, and lives in Heyburn, Idaho, where he is in business with his brother,
Grove L., and where he teaches; he has been super-

intendent of the Clarkston, Idaho, schools for several years.

1845   JOHN⁶ TYLER, JR. (John⁵), born in Providence, R. I., April 26, 1813; died there December 1, 1891; married (1), Maria Bowen, of Warren, R. I., who died May 4, 1843; married (2), Mary P. Brightman, born October 14, 1827; died in Providence, October 21, 1867. The children were born in Providence. Three (one named William, the others unnamed) of the first marriage died when less than a year old.

Children, by first marriage:
4031   Emily Tyler, born July 20, 1838; died Nov. 12, 1842.
4032   Anna Maria Tyler, born July 21, 1840; died Oct. 20, 1862.

Child, by second marriage:
4033+   Alonzo Tyler, born Jan. 4, 1846.

1848   JAMES R.⁶ TYLER (John⁵), born in Providence, R. I., February 28, 1820; died there June 19, 1891; married, March 24, 1844, Amelia Brown, of Providence, born January 13, 1828; died August 17, 1888.   Children:
4034   Rebecca C. Tyler, born Feb. 28, 1845; died March 9, 1847.
4035+   James R. Tyler, Jr., born Aug. 27, 1847.
4036   Amelia A. Tyler, born Nov. 27, 1849; died Nov. 28, 1869.
4037   Thomas D. Tyler, born Jan. 14, 1853; married Frances R. Haynes, who died March 24, 1900.
4038   William N. Tyler, born May 26, 1856.

1850   EBENEZER C.⁶ TYLER (John⁵), born in Pawtucket, R. I., May 19, 1823; died in Providence, R. I., November 5, 1887; married, February 1, 1842, Abby Reynolds, of Smithfield, R. I., who died in Providence, February 9, 1896. The children were born in Providence.   Children:
4039+   Ebenezer C. Tyler, Jr., born May 19, 1843.
4040+   John H. Tyler, born Dec. 23, 1844.
4041   Abby Ann Tyler, born March 27, 1850; died young.
4042+   Oliver C. Tyler, born April 22, 1853.

4043   Samuel M. Tyler, born March 20, 1855; married ——.
4044   Emily Elizabeth Tyler, born Nov. 28, 1857; died
        young.

1851   ALBERT D.[6] TYLER (John[5]), born in Providence, R. I., February 21, 1826; married, May 16, 1847, Dolly
L. Gorton, of Jewett City, Conn., who died January 27, 1859.
The children were born in Providence. Children:
4045+   Albert D. Tyler, Jr., born April 27, 1848.
4046   William F. Tyler, born June 15, 1850; died Aug. 19,
        1851.
4047+   Edwin F. Tyler, born Nov. 20, 1854.
4048   Frances E. Tyler, born June 12, 1858; died Aug. 7,
        1858.
4049   Phila Ann Tyler, born 1828; died 1832.

1856   ELIZABETH TYLER MERRY[6] (Phila. B.[5]),
born October 17, 1815; died June 10, 1848; married, October
24, 1839, Jesse S. Thornton, born July 29, 1812; died April
27, 1856. Children:
4050   Charles Thornton.
4051   Almira Thornton, born Dec. 7, 1842; married, Dec.
        14, 1864, Lyman B. Goff, a manufacturer in Paw-
        tucket, R. I.

1876   CHLOE[6] TYLER (Moses[5]), born in Richmond,
N. H., July 1, 1778; died 1846; married, April 2, 1798, as
third wife, Rev. David Ballou (brother of Rev. Hosea Ballou,
of Boston), born September 15, 1758, in Pawtucket, R. I.;
was a devout Baptist in his father's church (Rev. Maturin
Ballou), but changed to Universalism, and became a minister
in Rowe, Mass., where he farmed and preached without pay.
Children:
4052   Chloe Ballou, born July 28, 1799; died aged two years.
4053   Mercy Harris Ballou, born Nov. 27, 1800; married
        Charles Walcott, Monroe, Mass.
4054   (Rev.) Moses Ballou, born March 24, 1811; married
        1837 Almena Damaris Giddings.
4055   John Ballou, born March 16, 1813; married, 1835,
        Hannah Maria Hicks.
4056   Chloe Tyler Ballou, born June 1, 1815; married, 1833,

Rev. Joseph Barber, a famous M. D., but later became a Universalist minister.

1880   MOSES[6] TYLER, JR. (Moses[5]), born in Richmond, N. H., August 29, 1786; died there October 8, 1847; married Abigail Gale, born June 27, 1789; died October 13, 1876; daughter of Jonathan Gale, of Royalston, Mass. His will was filed December 5, 1876. He was drafted in the War of 1812 and was on the defense of Portsmouth, N. H. He was a farmer and prominent in town affairs. He lived in the west part of Royalston, but after his father died he returned to the homestead in Richmond. He made two bass viols and he and his children were all musical. His daughters taught school. The children were born in Richmond, except David and Jonathan, who were born in Royalston.

CHILDREN:

4057+   Danford Tyler, born Oct. 2, 1812.

4058+   David Tyler, born Jan. 24, 1815.

4059   Jonathan Gale Tyler, born Nov. 12, 1817; died in Keene, N. H., Jan. 5, 1899; he was in the woolen mills in South Royalston; was frail in body, but a very popular and well-read man.

4060+   Patience A. Tyler, born June 11, 1820.

4061   Loren Francis Tyler, born Feb. 27, 1822; died in Boston, May 8, 1894; married, Nov. 11, 1856, Anna N. Hitchcock, of Strong, Maine. He went to California in 1849; returned to Boston in 1852; was a merchant tailor until 1862, when he retired; his widow lived at 101 Beacon St., Boston; no children. By his mother's will he had the old family clock.

4062+   Laura J. Tyler, born Dec. 23, 1823.

4063+   Rhoda Gale Tyler, born April 1, 1827.

4064+   Juda Ann Tyler, born July 8, 1829.

1882   JOHN[6] TYLER (Moses[5]), born in Richmond, N. H., May 31, 1791; died in Wharton, Texas, August 8, 1846; married, August 1, 1821, in Columbia, Ky., Sarah R. ———; born July 1, 1806, in Danville, Ky. He moved early to Columbia, Ky., and thence to Liberty, Ky., thence to Danville, Lebanon and Spring, Ky., and finally to Austin, Texas. The

two elder children were born in Columbia; the three youngest in
Austin, Texas. Children:

4065   Mary Ann Tyler, born Feb. 13, 1822; married, April
         1, 1841, in Grimes, Texas, ———.
4066   Malinda Tyler, born March 3, 1823; married, Aug.
         20, 1840, in Grimes, Texas, ———.
4067+ Oscar Tyler, born in Liberty, April 26, 1825; married
         Harriet A. ———.
4068   Luella Tyler, born in Danville, Oct. 8, 1826; married
         in Houston, Texas, ———.
4069   Amanda Tyler, born in Liberty Feb. 2, 1828.
4070   Charles M. Tyler, born in Lebanon Sept. 23, 1829; a
         farmer; married, June 29, 1854, in Washington,
         Texas, ———; moved to Arizona.
4071   Julia F. Tyler, born in Spring April 11, 1831.
4072   Eliza D. Tyler, born Jan. 30, 1833; died July 27,
         1835.
4073   William L. Tyler, born Feb. 11, 1837; a farmer.
4074   Albert C. Tyler, born Nov. 13, 1840; a farmer.
4075   John Tyler, born July 12, 1843; a farmer.

1889   SIMEON STILLMAN[6] TYLER (Zelotes[5]), born
in Attleboro, Mass., October 22, 1803; moved to Jacksonville,
Fla., where he died May 13, 1859; married Margaret C. White.
Went South for his health and settled first in Charleston, S. C.,
where he built the first flat car on the South Carolina Railway,
which was at first propelled by a sail. Children:

4076+ Mary White Tyler.
4077+ William Leigh Richmond Tyler, born in Coliton Dis-
         trict, S. C., 1838.
4078   Agnes Sophia Tyler, died unmarried in 1857.
4079   Richard Robert Tyler, unmarried.
4080+ John Fletcher Tyler.
4081+ Edmond Marshall Tyler.
4082+ Orville Zelotes Tyler.
4083   Franklin Stewart Tyler; married Catherine Rogers.
         He was an undertaker in Jacksonville, Fla.; one
         daughter (Beatrix Catherine).

1891   ORVILLE[6] TYLER (Zelotes[5]), born in Attleboro,
Mass., July 22, 1808; died in West Newton, Mass., January 1,

1889; married (1), March 24, 1824, Mary Ann Page, of
Bedford, Mass., who died September, 1849; married (2), October 9, 1857, Mary Ann Kendall, of Nashua, N. H.

CHILDREN, by first marriage:
4084+   Mary Josephine Tyler, born Feb. 6, 1835.
4085   Louise Maria Tyler, born April 21, 1837; married
        R. L. Cook; died s. p.
4086+   George Le Van Tyler, born Oct. 23, 1841.

1893   DANIEL⁶ TYLER (Zuriel⁵), born in Essex, Vt.,
November 26, 1795; died August 2, 1875; buried in Essex
Center; married in Colchester, Vt., March 25, 1821, Permelia
Ferrand, born October 22, 1803; died in Essex, January 31,
1890.   He was in the War of 1812 (see *Pension Book*, p. 66,
No. 4), and had bounty lands; was a Free Mason for 60
years.   The children were born in Essex.   Children:
4087   William Dexter Tyler, born March 17, 1824; married,
        Sept. 1, 1855, Mary E. Haynes, Plattsburgh, N. Y.
        He was admitted to the Franklin County bar in
        1864; appointed registrar at Irasburgh, 1865-1866;
        opened an office there; town clerk in 1868 and in
        the legislature in 1874-1875.
4088+   Chloe Irene Tyler, born in 1827.
4089   Erasmus H. Tyler, born Feb. 19, 1833; died June 28,
        1888, s. p.; married April 23, 1867, Jane Harriet
        Farrand; No. 4108.   She resides in Fon du Lac,
        Wis.   He was a corporal in Company D, 13th Vt.
        regiment from Oct. 10, 1862, to July 21, 1863;
        was a Free Mason; held town office.
4090   Milton R. Tyler, born March 18, 1835; was graduated
        from University of Vermont 1859; was principal of
        " Essex Academy " two years; was admitted to
        Franklin County bar, 1860; opened an office in
        Irasburgh; was judge of probate in the Orleans
        district 1863-1865.   Moved to Bakersfield, Vt., and
        lived there 13 years; then moved to Burlington,
        where he was judge of the city court several years;
        in 1899 he was a lawyer in Fergus Falls, Minn.

1894   RODNEY⁶ TYLER (Zuriel⁵), born in Essex, Vt.,

September 30, 1797; died in Dickenson, N. Y., October 4, 1874; was buried in Essex Center; married, 1824, Sabra (called Sabrina) Austin, born in Essex, September 7, 1805; died February 16, 1883, at home of daughter Mary; daughter of Gardner and Nancy (Crandall) Austin. The children, except the youngest, were born in Essex. Children:

4091+ Charlotte Eliza Tyler, born Oct. 23, 1825.
4092+ Mary Electa Tyler, born March 7, 1827.
4093+ Julia Pierce Tyler, born May 1, 1830.
4094 Harmon David Tyler, born June 13, 1833; died March 28, 1864.
4095+ Sarah Jane Tyler, born March 26, 1835.
4096+ Hannah Maria Tyler, born March 2, 1837.
4097+ John Harvey Tyler, born Feb. 26, 1839.
4098+ Betsey E. Tyler, born May 13, 1841.
4099+ Harriet Sabrina Tyler, born in Colchester, June 27, 1843.

1895 ROXEY[6] TYLER (Zuriel[5]), born in Essex, Vt., February 12, 1800; died in Colchester, January 30, 1865; married, December 21, 1820, Cyrus Farrand, son of David and Sarah (Hine) Farrand, of Colchester, born in Burlington, Vt., December 30, 1793; died in Essex June 25, 1883. The children were probably born in Colchester. Children:

4100 Achsah Melissa Farrand, born Oct. 22, 1821; died in Essex Jan. 14, 1853; married, March 2, 1851, Holman Bates, son of Moses Bates.
4101 Frances Emily Farrand, born May 17, 1824; died in Colchester, Jan. 9, 1866; married (1), Jan. 26, 1846, Elijah Bates, son of Jacob and Lois Bates; married (2), March 30, 1854, Holman Bates.
4102 Mary Farrand, born March 3, 1826; died Oct. 20, 1884.
4103 Caroline Farrand, born April 6, 1828; died in Fon du Lac, Wis., Jan. 23, 1880; married (1), Aug. 20, 1849, Samuel Thrasher; married (2), —— Stone, at Essex.
4004 Fanny Roxanna Farrand, born April 15, 1830; died Aug. 1, 1898, in Manhattan, Kan.; married, Dec. 7, 1853, John C. Neal, son of Henry Neal, of Berlin, Ohio.

4105   Joseph Franklin Farrand, born March 3, 1832; resided at Belle Prairie, Minn.; married, Oct. 16, 1856,
Mary Hamilton.   He was a farmer and mechanic.

4106   Julia Ann Farrand, born April 13, 1834; resided in
Fon du Lac; married, May 11, 1874, Harmon
Bryan, son of Nathan Bryan.

4107   Henrietta Ellen Farrand, born Jan. 24, 1836; married,
Aug. 10, 1858, George H. Perry, of Rhode Island;
he resided in Manhattan, Kan.

4108   Jane Harriet Farrand, born May 3, 1839; married,
April 23, 1867, Erasmus H. Tyler, No. 4089.   She
lived in Fon du Lac, Wis.

1897   ORLIN[6] TYLER (Zuriel[5]), born in Essex, Vt.,
October 11, 1804; died March 6, 1890, aged 85 years; married (1), 1828, Mary Austin, daughter of Gardner and Nancy
Crandall, born in Essex, June 3, 1809; died there January 3,
1835; married (2), January 11, 1836, Lucretia Hoar, born
January 29, 1805; died May 24, 1890.   The children were
born in Essex.

CHILDREN, by first marriage:
4109+   Lewis Orlin Tyler, born Sept. 19, 1829.
4110+   Allen Zuriel Tyler, born June 6, 1832, in Joliet, Ill.

CHILDREN, by second marriage:
4111+   Edward Judson Tyler, born Feb. 2, 1837.
4112+   Willard Aden Tyler, born Jan. 4, 1839.

1898   RUBY[6] TYLER (Zuriel[5]), born in Colchester, Vt.,
January 23, 1809; died there March 4, 1895; married, July
9, 1829, Garry B. Munger, born in Hinesburgh, Vt., November
4, 1807; died in Colchester, May 9, 1893.   The children were
probably born in Colchester.   Children:

4113   Dexter C. Munger, born June 10, 1830; died 1832.

4114   (Rev.) Henry Newton Munger, born March 14, 1834;
married (1), Mary D. Dutton; married (2), Cornelia B. Rinefield.

4115   Charlotte E. Munger, born Feb. 24, 1836; died in St.
Albans, Vt., Sept. 21, 1892; married Henry D.
Sabin, of Milton, Vt.

4116   Frances Ora Munger, born Nov. 23, 1840; married, 1899. Alanson W. Farnsworth, of Milton.

1900 DOLLY⁶ TYLER (Rufus⁵), married Benjamin Goddard, of Webster, Mass. The children were born in Webster. Children:

4117   Dolly Goddard, married Jesse Heath; had two sons and two daughters (Henry, Charles, Sarah, Alice).
4118   Lydia Goddard, married James Bixby.
4119   Amy Goddard, married James Curtis, Oxford, Mass.; died s. p.
4120   Ann Goddard, married Charles Chapman.
4121   Relief Goddard.
4122   Lucy Goddard, married Lewis Whitney; had two daughters (Augusta, Ellen).
4123   Rufus Goddard.
4124   Benjamin Goddard.
4125   Major Goddard, born Aug. 8, 1822; married Matilda Briggs; had one child (Susan).
4126   Samuel Goddard.
4127   Candice Goddard, married ―― Woodward.

1901 SALLY⁶ TYLER (Rufus⁵), married George Town, of Thompson, Conn. The children were born in Thompson. Children:

4128   Marcus Town; had three sons (Vernon, George, Adford) and one daughter (Lucy).
4129   Rufus Town.
4130   Noahdia Town.
4131   Lucy Town; married Joseph Perry; died s. p.

1902 ESTHER⁶ TYLER (Rufus⁵), born Måy 9, 1801; died in Thompson, Conn., October 12, 1848; married Deacon Halcy Bixby, born February 14, 1801; died September 26, 1880. The children were born in Thompson. Children:

4132   (Deacon) Allen Tyler Bixby, lived in Thompson.
4133   Moses Bixby.
4134   (Deacon) George Bixby, lived in East Woodstock, Conn.
4135   Henry Hudson Bixby, born April 18, 1834; died April 2, 1882; married Julietta H. Rhodes; had three sons

(William H., Joseph H., Charles N.) and one daughter (Mary E.)

4136   Albert R. Bixby, died June 8, 1832, aged three years.

4137   Loring Bixby, died April 18, 1832, aged eight months.

4138   Franklin Bixby, in the Custom House in Boston.

4139   Esther Bixby, died June 10, 1848, aged six years.

1903   NANCY[6] TYLER (Rufus[5]), married Elisha Allen and resided in Van Etten, N. Y. The children were born in Van Etten. Children:

4140   Julany Allen, born May 25, 1823.

4141   Nancy M. Allen, born April 11, 1825.

4142   Isaiah Allen, born April 5, 1827.

4143   Joanna Allen, born Oct. 12, 1828.

4144   Rufus Allen, born Sept. 13, 1830.

4145   Sylvester Allen, born June 31, 1835.

4146   Almira R. Allen, born July 11, 1838; married Richard Tilbury, of Edith, Mo.; had one child (Allen L.).

4147   Mary E. Allen, born June 11, 1842.

1907   DAVID[6] TYLER (David[5]), born in Essex, Vt., January 6, 1797; moved to St. Charles, Ill., about 1865, then to Chicago; was twice married. The children were probably born in Essex.

CHILDREN, by first marriage:

4148   Fidelia Tyler, married Hiram Brown; had one daughter (Louise), who resided in Joliet, Ill.

4149   Roswell Tyler, went west; was a paper manufacturer and when last heard from was in Quincy, Ill.; had two sons (John and Davis).

4150   Amelia Tyler; married George D. Woodworth, a bookkeeper in Chicago; resided in Glen Ellyn, Ill.; had one son (George) and one daughter (Ruth).

CHILDREN, by second marriage:

4151   Edwin P. Tyler; married —— Wells; a widower and resides in Stephens Point, Wis.

4152   Warren O. Tyler; a paper dealer in Chicago; unmarried.

4153+   Frederick C. Tyler, born July 3, 1848.

4154   William H. Tyler; married Adelia Clark; has two

daughters who reside in Chicago (Clara Belle and Venevia).

4155   Frank P. Tyler; a paper dealer in Chicago; died about 1898; unmarried.

4156   Mattie A. Tyler; unmarried; resides in Chicago.

4157   Julius Tyler, born 1855; died Jan. 11, 1857.

1913 SAMUEL⁶ TYLER (David⁵), born in Essex, Vt., April 8, 1815; died there; the children were born there. The name of his wife is not known. Children:

4158   Adelaide Tyler, married Grayton Brand.

4159   (Rev.) Amory Tyler, left a family.

4160   Horace Tyler.

4161   Franklin Tyler.

1916 ERASTUS⁶ TYLER (George⁵), born in Essex, Vt., November 14, 1802; died in Alexandria, Ohio, August 29, 1874; married, June 5, 1834, Mary Griffin, daughter of John and Mary Griffin, born June 2, 1811; died in Alexandria October 23, 1875. Was a farmer; he drove overland to Ohio, Delaware County, about 1835; thence in a few years to Alexandria. The second, third and fourth children were born in Lima, Ohio. Children:

4162   Truman Jackson Tyler, born in Granville, Ohio, April 30, 1837; died in Alexandria, May 9, 1848.

4163+ George W. Tyler, born May 31, 1839.

4164   Malinda Tyler, born Aug. 29, 1843; died in Alexandria, May 10, 1848.

4165   Mary Jane Tyler, born Jan. 11, 1846; died in Alexandria, May 12, 1848.

4166   De Witt Clinton Tyler, born in Alexandria, Oct. 29, 1849; died there Aug. 2, 1851.

4167+ Andrew Jackson Tyler, born in St. Albans, Ohio, Sept. 12, 1852.

1917 LORIN⁶ TYLER (George⁵), born in Essex, Vt., Sept. 27, 1804; died in Ohio April 3, 1850; buried in Essex; married, April 18, 1827, Emeline J. Bliss, daughter of Elias Bliss, of Essex, born September 13, 1807; died March 13, 1871. He was a merchant in Essex, but moved to Ohio. The children were born in Essex. Children:

4168   Son, died in infancy, May 5, 1829.
4169   Daughter, died March 3, 1839.
4170   George Edward Tyler, born June 27, 1831; died in
        Essex, April 3, 1850; unmarried.
4171+   Beulah Elizabeth Tyler, born Aug. 5, 1833.
4172   Daughter, died in infancy, Oct. 21, 1846.
4173   James Lorin Tyler, born May 5, 1839; died Jan. 1,
        1894, in San Francisco, aged 54 years. Was three
        years in the Civil War, first lieutenant of Company
        I, 32d Ohio Infantry; with Sherman " to the Sea ";
        unmarried.
4174   Wilbur Tyler; died in infancy, July 21, 1849.

    1919   GEORGE RISING⁶ TYLER (George⁵), born in
Essex, Vt., March 20, 1810; died in Alexandria, O., February
25, 1857; married in Essex, March 4, 1846, Rhoda A. Emery,
born in Reading, Vt., October 8, 1826; daughter of Dr. J. W.
Emery. He was a merchant in Burlington, Vt. Children:
4175   George W. Tyler, born in Burlington, Feb. 24, 1847;
        moved from Ohio to Michigan, June, 1857; was a
        merchant in Paw Paw, Mich.; unmarried.
4176   Loren E. Tyler, born in Essex, April 13, 1853; died
        in Paw Paw, Dec. 31, 1869.

    1920   LYMAN EARLY⁶ TYLER (George⁵), born in
Essex, Vt., June 18, 1812; died in Columbus, O., March 15,
1898; married in Granville, O., about 1835, Almira Hobart,
who died in Columbus, October 29, 1886. He moved to Granville, when 21 and soon after to Harlem, O., where he resided
many years; a farmer and a fine citizen. The children were
born in Harlem. Children:
4177+   Frances Esther Tyler, born June 17, 1837.
4178+   Louisa Emeline Tyler, born June 9, 1839.
4179   Loren Butler Tyler, born Sept. 1, 1843; died Nov. 27,
        1846.
4180+   Josephine Amelia Tyler, born Jan. 11, 1846.
4181+   Jane Adelaide Tyler, born Aug. 6, 1849.
4182+   George Edgar Tyler, born June 13, 1852.

    1921   CASSIUS⁶ TYLER (George⁵), born in Essex,
Vt., August 2, 1815; died October 30, 1900, aged 85 years;

married, December 17, 1845, Malinda Case, born in Randolph, N. Y., February 24, 1823; daughter of Esau Case. At 21 Cassius moved with his father to Jersey, Licking Co., O., and bought the homestead of 200 acres in 1840. He was a very active man and could cut and cord five cords of wood in a day. He was a farmer and stock-raiser. The children were born in Jersey. Children:

4183+   Henry Tyler, born Oct. 3, 1846.

4184   Albert M. Tyler, born May 26, 1849; married Linnie Dispennett; they had no children in 1900; lives in Alexandria, O.

4185   Lorin C. Tyler, born Jan. 1, 1854; resides in Alexandria; unmarried.

4186+   Wilbur Tyler, born Dec. 16, 1856.

4187+   Douglas S. Tyler, born Aug. 1, 1860.

    1922   EMMELINE[6] TYLER (George[5]), born in Essex, Vt., February 22, 1818; married, November 11, 1840, Guy C. Hobart, of Granville and Jersey, O. The three elder children were born in Granville; the others in Jersey. Children:

4188   Josephine Hobart, born Oct. 6, 1841; married, May 12, 1855, J. J. Miller, of Alexandria, O.; has three children and resides in Fostoria, O.

4189   Mary E. Hobart, born Feb. 25, 1844; resides in Pendleton, Kan., unmarried.

4190   Edward Hobart, born June 18, 1847; married, Jan. 25, 1872, Helen Case, of Columbus, O.; has three children; resides in Granville.

4191   George Hobart, born Dec. 30, 1849; married, May 10, 1884, Annie Green, of Granville; has four children; resides in Paoli, Kan.

4192   Annette Hobart, born Sept. 19, 1851; married, Feb. 5, 1880, E. E. Pendleton; has one child; resides in Pendleton, Kan.

    1923   FOSTER[6] TYLER (George[5]), born in Essex, Vt., July 5, 1820; died February 9, 1892; married, November 17, 1852, Martha A. Alward, born January 20, 1826; died in Alexandria, O., November 21, 1897. He went to Alexandria, in 1836, and the children were born there. Children:

4193+   Emma Edna Tyler, born June 13, 1854.

4194   Lyman B. Tyler, born Oct. 20, 1856; died April, 1857.
4195+   Reuben Foster Tyler, born Sept. 15, 1858.
4196   Ella Tyler, born Sept. 21, 1862; married, Aug. 23 1898, Dr. George L. Garner, of Lansing, Mich.

1924   JOEL LAFAYETTE[6] TYLER (George[5]), born in Essex, Vt., September 17, 1823; died in Columbus, O., September 8, 1891; married, January 21, 1851, Laurinda Waterman, of Alexandria, O., who died in 1863. He moved with his father to Alexandria, Licking County in 1836; had 140 acres of land in St. Albans township, on Raccoon Creek; took premium in 1870 and 1874 for the best improved farm in the county. In 1860 he was appointed United States Marshal; took census of the county and was state representative in 1877 and 1879; he was fond of fine horses. The children were probably born in Alexandria. Children:
4197   Cora E. Tyler, born Feb. 22, 1852; married, Feb. 15, 1876, Wellington M. Evans, who died Feb., 1899, s. p. In 1900 she was residing in Columbus; was graduated from Wesleyan Female College, O.
4198   Edward W. Tyler, born April 29, 1854; married Nov., 1887, Nina Ruggles; s. p. in 1900. He was of the firm of Tyler & Carlisle, wholesale hardware dealers, Cleveland, O.
4199+   Fide L. Tyler, born Aug. 21, 1857.

1926   RUFUS A.[6] TYLER (Judson[5]), born in Essex, Vt., April 18, 1818; died in Kalamazoo, Mich., May 6, 1886; married in Keesville, N. Y., June 1, 1852, Sarah Potter; he was a school teacher at Granville, O. The children were born in New York. Children:
4200   Jessie P. Tyler, born in Au Sable Forks, N. Y., March 8, 1855; lives Knoxville, Tenn.
4201   Son, died in infancy.
4202+   Joel Claverly Tyler, born Aug. 26, 1857.

1928   SARAH ABIGAIL[6] TYLER (Judson[5]), born in Essex, Vt., April 16, 1827; married, March 20, 1862, Uri Colgrove, of Alexandria, O., who died in Ashtemo, Mich., September 29, 1887; he moved to Ashtemo in 1865. Children:

4203   Judson Uri Colgrove, born in Alexandria, May 17,
        1864; died June 4, 1865.
4204   Charlotte R. Colgrove, born in Ashtemo, Dec. 16, 1867.

1935   LOVINA[6] TYLER (William[5]), born in Cheshire,
Mass., February 22, 1789; died April 20, 1844; married Joseph
Bradford, born March 30, 1788; died January 23, 1879 in
Newport, N. Y.; he was a farmer.   Child:
4205   Hopestill Bradford, born in Newport, N. Y., Nov. 19,
        1812; married, Jan. 24, 1843, Rebecca M. Luther,
        born May 27, 1822; had one son (George L., in a
        bank in Utica, N. Y.), and two daughters (Alice
        E., Lovina C.).

1938   SAMUEL[6] TYLER (William[5]), born in Newport,
N. Y., January 17, 1794; died in Mansfield, O., February 17,
1879; married, 1820, Betsey (Elizabeth) Pool, born in Stephen-
town, N. Y., 1800; died in Mansfield, February 21, 1863;
daughter of Elisha Pool, of Little Hoosac, N. Y.   The child
was born in Newport.   Child:
4206+ William F. Tyler, born June 7, 1824.

1939   WILLIAM[6] TYLER (William[5]), born in Newport, N. Y.; died in Illinois during the Civil War; resided in
Geneseo, N. Y.   He had two sons and four daughters.   His
wife's name is unknown.   Children, whose names are known:
4207   W. D. Tyler, resided in Clinton, Mo.
4208   Nellie Tyler, married —— Custer; resided in Clinton.
4209   Mary Tyler, married —— Weller; resided in Geneseo.

1943   THOMAS[6] TYLER (William[5]), born in Newport, N. Y.; moved to Kalamazoo, Mich.   Wife's name not
known.   Children:
4210   Almeron Tyler.
4211   Frances Tyler.
4212   Hetty Tyler.

1944   BENJAMIN BROWN[6] TYLER (William[5]), born
in Newport, N. Y., September 10, 1810; died in London, Madison County, O., April 13, 1879; married Katherine Kelly, of
Herkimer County, N. Y., who died October 4, 1879.   He was a

farmer and moved to Geneseo, N. Y., about 1840 and in 1856 to London. The children were born in Newport. Children:

4213+ Benjamin Franklin Tyler, born July 12, 1835.
4214+ William Henry Tyler.

1947 HENRY[6] TYLER (Thomas[5]), born in Adams, Mass., July 26, 1795; died there, July 26, 1871; married, December 2, 1824, Electa Hodge, born June 8, 1800; died March 3, 1867, daughter of Irena Ives of North Adams. The children were born in Adams. Children:

4215+ Mary Amelia Tyler, born March 15, 1826.
4216   Celestia Ann Tyler, born May 18, 1828; died Oct. 9, 1888; unmarried.
4217   William Henry Tyler, born Sept. 8, 1831; died July 20, 1864; was a quartermaster in Civil War; unmarried.
4218   Daniel Dennison Tyler, born June 23, 1833; died May 4, 1835.
4219   Abraham Alphonso Tyler, born April 26, 1836; died March 30, 1872; in business in Adams, Mass.

1948 LUCY[6] TYLER (Thomas[5]), born in Adams, Mass., April 27, 1797; died February 25, 1864; married, March 18, 1827, Amasa Arnold, born June 26, 1791; died October 8, 1853; son of Nathaniel and Mary Arnold, of Rhode Island. The children were born in Adams. Children:

4220   Mary Phillips Arnold, born Feb. 16, 1828; married, March 28, 1852, Alanson Jones; had five children; resided in Adams in 1897.
4221   Julia Arnold, born Dec. 29, 1831; died Aug. 16, 1836.
4222   Amy Arnold, born Oct. 8, 1833; resided in Adams.

1949 DUTY SAYLES[6] TYLER (Thomas[5]), born in South Adams, Mass., March 23, 1799; died in North Adams, August 26, 1857; married, December 25, 1825, Amy Arnold Brown. From 1826 to 1840 was in the milling business in North Adams, then retired to a large farm. In 1836 he became joint owner in Union Mill; was president of Adams National Bank from 1842 to 1857, when he resigned; was deacon of a Baptist church from 1834 to 1857. (From *Hist. North Adams*,

Spear, 1885). The children were born in North Adams. Children:

4223+ John Brown Tyler, born Oct. 3, 1826.
4224 Cornelia Tyler, born June 10, 1828; died June 5, 1832.
4225+ Marie Louise Tyler, born Feb. 21, 1834.

1955 LUCINDA[6] TYLER (Ebenezer[5]), born in Brewer, Maine, June 4, 1800; died in Orono, Maine, July 20, 1871; married, 1818, Elijah Webster, of Bangor and Orono; born in Orono, 1790; died June 28, 1863, son and eighth child of Andrew, Jr., and Martha (Crane) Webster, from Salisbury, Mass. to Bangor and Orono, 1770. He was a lumberman; selectman, 1827; county commissioner, 1838-1841. The children were born in Orono. Children:

4226 James Webster, died April 11, 1888, aged 62 years; married, Dec. 30, 1850, Anna B. Baker, of Augusta, Maine; had children. Was a representative and a lumber manufacturer.
4227 Lavina T. H. Webster, married, Feb. 1, 1842, Rev. A. T. Loring, of Bangor; moved to Omaha, Neb.
4228 Ellen M. Webster, died in 1890; married (1) (published July 22, 1842), Benjamin Silsby; married (2), Rev. Horatio Illsley, of South Freeport, Maine, who died in 1889.
4229 Richard P. Webster, married Mary S. Thaxter, of Bangor; (published Aug. 25, 1838).
4230 John B. Webster.
4231 Bradshaw H. Webster.

1960 HARRIET AUGUSTA[6] TYLER (Rowland[5]), born in Dixmont, Maine, November 24, 1806; died December 24, 1841; married John Philips, M. D. The children were probably born in Dixmont. Children:

4232 Louisa Philips.
4233 Harriet Philips.
4234 (Capt.) John W. Philips; was master of a vessel in the Mexican War; lives in Beverly, Mass., and is the only child now living.
4235 Rowland Philips.

4236   Augustus Philips.
4238   Walter Philips.
4237   George Philips.

1964   LUCINDA[6] TYLER (Rowland or Roland[5]), born
in Dixmont, Maine, August 25, 1814; died March 13, 1846;
married Steward S. Mitchell, of Unity, Maine, youngest child
of Isaac Mitchell, who was one of 14 children of John Mitchell,
a Scotchman, and the second man to settle in Unity after the
Revolution. He was a member of the Presbyterian church and
so strict that he would not allow food to be cooked in the
house on Sunday. Isaac owned a farm of over a thousand
acres and built and carried on " Mitchell's Mills," in Unity,
sawing lumber and grinding grain; he was an extensive land
owner. Steward had a large farm, also, and took charge of the
grinding mills and he also carried on a lumber mill; he died
May 20, 1848. Mrs. Mitchell died when her youngest child
was a baby. Children:

4239   Wilford S. Mitchell, educated himself; he went across
         the plains to California when he was 18; returned
         to Maine and married, and entered into trade. The
         war came and broke into his life, and he went into
         the army, falling in the engagement at Port Hud-
         son; his burial place is unknown.

4240   Roland Tyler Mitchell, married Miss Stevens, of
         Unity; went to California in 1859, as a boy. He
         enlisted in the First California regiment and served
         in the Indian country for three years. He carried
         on after the war, a large vegetable and milk farm,
         carrying both commodities into Sacramento; failing
         health obliged him to sell his business, and since then
         he has been a superintendent at the Capitol Park
         at the State House, and the only man at the Capitol
         to receive a re-appointment from a Democratic
         governor.

4241   (General) Henry Lyman Mitchell, born Feb. 6, 1845;
         married, Sept. 22, 1879, Emma L. Ryder, born in
         Washington, Maine, July 22, 1856; daughter of
         Dr. Robert E. and Emily (Rust) Ryder. She met
         with a severe accident in 1878, which destroyed her
         health and deprived her of many opportunities of

enjoying life, still she maintained an amiable, lovable and generous disposition. General Mitchell lived among strangers until he was past 12 years old. He attended Corinna Academy and other graded schools, and was a private student under Prof. J. H. Sawyer, four years, and hoped to be a physician and surgeon, but was induced when very young to enter the cavalry service of the United States army, under a promise of speedy promotion; he was assigned to Company B. 1st Maine Cavalry Volunteers; he was injured by the fall of a horse upon him and also badly wounded. He was admitted to the bar in 1866, and practises in Bangor, Maine; city solicitor of Bangor, ten years; Commander H. Hamlin Post, G. A. R.; Past Chancellor of Lodge No. 5, K. of P.; Past Master Workman, A. O. U. W.; Colonel of the Second Volunteer Militia, five years; brigadier-general commanding First Brigade Volunteer Militia, five years; was chairman of the standing committee of the Independent Congregational church of Bangor for ten years. He resides in Bangor; no children.

1966 CAROLINE HERRICK⁶ TYLER (Rowland⁵), born in Dixmont, Maine, April 3, 1818; married, December 17, 1837, Greenleaf Smith, born in Parsonsfield, Maine, April 23, 1818; died October 7, 1891. She lived with her son Llewellyn. Mr. Smith bought the old Tyler place in Dixmont, where the four younger children were born. Children:

4242   Charles Frederick Smith, born in Glenburn, May 4, 1839; killed at Hilton Head, S. C., March 3, 1862; was in 9th Maine Volunteer regiment; enlisted Sept., 1861; unmarried.

4243   Llewellyn D. Smith, born Feb. 8, 1841; was in 9th Maine Volunteer regiment, and served three years; married, Feb. 11, 1866, Susan Jane York, born Feb. 12, 1848; a prosperous farmer; lives on the home place.

4244   Walter Greenleaf Smith, born Feb. 17, 1843; married, Dec. 25, 1868, Anna M. Powlesland, born Oct. 25, 1852; was in 9th Maine Volunteer regiment and served 14 months; resides, a farmer, in Dixmont; has eight children.

4245   Laura Louise Smith, born Feb. 5, 1848; died May 30, 1866.

4246   Irwin F. Smith, born Jan. 27, 1852; died Feb. 5, 1852.

     1967   LOUISA ELVIRA[6] TYLER (Rowland[5]), born in Dixmont, Maine, September 11, 1820; married, March 7, 1844, Lorraine Judkins Drew, born in Wayne, Maine, July 8, 1818. He was an architect and carried on an extensive business in building in Boston and vicinity; he made his home on Parker Hill in Roxbury, where he died. She lived in Brookline after his death. The children were born in Roxbury. Children:

4247   Albert William Drew, born June 4, 1845; died Jan. 1, 1850.

4248   Charles Lorraine Drew, born April 12, 1847; married in Omaha, Neb., Cordelia C. Page; has three sons and five daughters; lives in San Francisco, Cal.

4249   Emma Caroline Drew, born June 20, 1849.

4250   Arthur Francis Drew, born July 25, 1852; died same day.

4251   George Irving Drew, born Jan. 12, 1857; married in San Francisco, Cal., June, 1876, Louise E. Salzer; has two sons and three daughters.

4252   Annie Mabel Drew, born April 12, 1860; married, Oct. 20, 1883, Odin Fritz; has one child.

     1972   LOUISA R.[6] TYLER (Abijah Weld[5]), born in Attleboro, Mass., 1804; died March 14, 1853; married Deacon Atherton Wales, of Attleboro, born probably in Portsmouth, R. I., May 24, 1806; died August 2, 1888. He married four times, twice in the Tyler family; his second wife was Elizabeth S. Tyler, No. 1986, who died s. p. He learned the blacksmith trade in Newport, R. I. The children were born in Attleboro. Children:

4253   Elizabeth Frances Wales, born 1831; died Dec. 28, 1836.

4254   (Rev.) Henry Atherton Wales, died in 1898.

4255   Abijah Tyler Wales; residing in Attleboro in 1898.

4256   Louis Wales.

4257   Charles Wales.

1981 HUMPHREY M.[6] TYLER (Crawford[5]), born in
New Ipswich, N. H., December 8, 1825; died in Soldier's Home,
Togus, Maine, May 26, 1887; buried in Milford, N. H.; married, January 3, 1849, Mary E. Wing, born November 1, 1827,
daughter of Philip and Betsey (Smith) Wing, of Grafton,
Mass. He enlisted as a private in Company F, 18th N. H. Volunteer Infantry for one year; mustered in as sergeant. He was
long a prominent citizen of Milford, N. H.; was for a time
deputy sheriff and collector of internal revenue. Child:
4258+ Hattie E. Tyler, born in Grafton, Mass., Oct. 28,
    1849.

1985 EUNICE DOGGETT[6] TYLER (Samuel[5]), born
in Attleboro, Mass., April 3, 1813; married Henry C. Read,
of Attleboro, where the children were born. Children:
4259 (Major) Samuel Tyler Read, born May 11, 1836;
    died in New Orleans, La.; had two children (Martha
    and Kathryn).
4260 Eunice Tyler Read, born 1845; married —— Craw-
    ford; had two children (William A. and Lincoln).

1990 SAMUEL WILLARD[6] TYLER (Samuel[5]), born
in Attleboro, Mass., May 14, 1838; died in Clinton, Mass.,
February 19, 1886; married, May 21, 1865, Eldora Persis
Bemis, born May 22, 1845; daughter of Hiram P. and Mary
E. (Sergeant) Bemis, of Paxton, Mass. When he was twelve
his father died; he remained on the farm until he was twenty-
one and his district school advantages were supplemented by
a brief academic course. He was musical, became an organist
and was a musician in the Civil War; was selectman four years,
assessor ten years and water commissioner two years. The
children were born in Clinton, Mass. Children:
4261+ Samuel Willard Tyler, born Feb. 11, 1866.
4262 Harriet Frances Tyler, born April 1, 1882; resided in
    1898 at home; unmarried.